THE PICK OF THE SEASON

THE PICK OF THE SEASON

The best of British football writing 1995–96

Edited by

STEPHEN F. KELLY

MAINSTREAM
PUBLISHING

EDINBURGH AND LONDON

To Judith, Nicholas and Emma

First published in 1996 by
MAINSTREAM PUBLISHING COMPANY (EDINBURGH) LTD
7 Albany Street
Edinburgh EH1 3 UG

ISBN 1 85158 891 4

A catalogue record for this book is available from the British Library

Typeset in Bembo

Printed and bound in Great Britain by Butler & Tanner Ltd

CONTENTS

Acknowledgements   9

Introduction   11

1   THE PEOPLE'S GAME

Hugh McIlvanney   *The Flavour of '96*   16

Garry Nelson   *Down Among the Deadwood*   20

Robert Philip   *The Hancock Man*   23

Ken Jones   *An Impossible Job*   28

Martin Johnson   *World Cup Kick-off*   30

Amy Lawrence   *The Medicine Men*   34

Henry Winter   *Training with Liverpool*   37

Robert Banks   *It's All Over Now*   40

David Bennie   *The Kids' Cup*   44

Kevin Borras   *Alternative Ulster*   48

Jim Gardiner   *To a Far, Foreign Land*   55

Ivor Baddiel   *The Club Mascot*   61

Dave Cottrell   *Raising Dumps*   65

Shelley Webb   *Players' Wives*   70

Tom Watt   *The Everton Cook*   73

Andrew Walpole   *London Pride*   76

Bill Borrows   *After-Dinner Mint*   80

Vincent Hanna   *Fading Away*   84
David Meek   *No Place in Sport*   86
David Bull   *The Politics of Sport*   88

2   THE PLAYERS

David Stubbs   *The Lost Emperor*   94
Ian Stafford   *Ruud Gullit*   100
Martin Thorpe   *Steve McManaman*   104
Amy Lawrence   *David Ginola*   107
Richard Williams   *The Boy from Brazil*   113
Richard Williams   *Fergie's Fledglings*   117
Ian Ridley   *Les Ferdinand*   120
Karen Buchanan   *Stan Collymore*   122
Richard Forest   *From the City Ground*   128
Sue Mott   *Ally McCoist*   130
Michael Heatley   *Jeff Astle*   134
Bob Holmes   *Wilf Mannion*   137
Robert Philip   *Jim Baxter*   140
Chris Lightbown   *Dennis Bergkamp*   145
Olivia Blair   *Teddy Sheringham*   148
Gary Lineker   *The England Team*   155

3   THE MANAGERS

Glenn Moore   *Glenn Hoddle*   160
Hugh McIlvanney   *Alex Ferguson*   163
John D. Taylor   *Roy Hodgson*   167
Joe Lovejoy   *Kevin Keegan*   170
Eamon Dunphy   *Big Jack Beaten by Fear*   173
Stephen F. Kelly   *Bill Shankly*   176
Paul Rowan   *Jack Charlton*   180
Mark Staniforth   *Frank Clark*   183
Jeremy Novick   *Ron Atkinson*   187
Ian Stafford   *Tommy Burns*   190
Robert Fisk   *Terry Yorath: a Welshman in Beirut*   194
Ron Scalpello   *Graeme Souness*   198

Shaun Campbell   *The Vote of Confidence*   206
Stephen F. Kelly   *Bob Paisley*   211

4   THE TEAMS

David Lacey   *The Ajax Way*   214
Keith Dewhurst   *Manchester United*   216
Robert Philip   *Cowdenbeath*   219
Sue Wallace   *Manchester City*   223
Lord Howell   *Aston Villa*   225
Frank Keating   *Hereford and Brazil*   227
John Duncan   *Brighton*   229
Paul Hayward   *Glory, Glory, Canvey Island*   231
John Ley   *Torquay Diary*   234

5   THE GAMES OF THE SEASON

Michael Parkinson   *Liverpool 4, Newcastle 3*   240
Richard Williams   *Juninho's Début*   242
Ian Ridley   *Cantona's Return*   244
David Lacey   *Manchester United 5, Nottingham Forest 0*   246
Martin Thorpe   *FA Cup Semi-final: Liverpool 3, Aston Villa 0*   248
David Lacey   *FA Cup final: Manchester United 1, Liverpool 0*   250

6   THE BUSINESS OF FOOTBALL

Cynthia Bateman   *The Man Who Really Signed Juninho*   254
Derick Allsop   *Nice Little Earner: Eric Hall, Agent*   256
Colin Cameron   *Down the Bookie's*   262
Tom Watt   *Rescuing Gillingham*   266
Pete Davies   *Architectural Awards*   273
Patrick Barclay   *McCann of the Celtic*   279
Chris Fewtrell   *The Boxing Man*   283
Mark Robison   *Transfer Deadline*   287
Jeff King   *Where Drugs Rule Football*   290

7 THE MEDIA

Ken Jones   *Journalists in Charge*   298
Stan Hey   *Motson is Back*   300
Derick Allsop   *The Radio Man*   302
Paul Simpson   *Match of the Day*   308
Frank Keating   *Another Booking from Sportspages*   315
Tom Watt   *Programme Editor*   317

8 EURO '96

David Lacey   *Patrick's Night*   322
Paul Hayward   *A Slow Start*   324
Nick Harris   *The Spirit of Culloden*   327
Richard Williams   *Unexpected and Unforgettable*   329
Ken Jones   *A Slice of Luck*   332
Matthew Engel   *A Place of Honour*   334
Matt Tench   *The Fans' Games*   336
Richard Williams   *I Have Seen the Future*   340
Ian Ridley   *Football's Coming Home*   343
Hugh McIlvanney   *Getting High on Decent Stuff*   347
Ken Jones   *Vogts' Triumph Over Adversity*   351

ACKNOWLEDGEMENTS

As ever, I am indebted to all those journalists and writers whose contributions are in this edition, and I would like to thank especially the various newspapers, magazines and publishers for permission to reproduce their work. This volume represents very much their efforts rather than mine.

My thanks are also due to Samantha Clarke who once more helped whenever she could, fitting in bouts of photocopying and so forth, in between sitting her finals. Her endeavours and suggestions helped ease the burden of work considerably. I am grateful also to all those colleagues and friends who delivered articles and bundles of back copies of various newspapers at regular intervals. In particular I would like to mention Anthony Rowe Jones and Hugh Cairns. My thanks also to David Bull for supplying me with cuttings from various fanzines.

I am again indebted to my agent John Pawsey for his continuing support and especially to my publishers, Mainstream, who took on this project at such late notice and with such enthusiasm. In particular, I must single out Bill Campbell and Judy Diamond who have worked so hard in putting together this nightmare of an administrative production.

Finally, I am, as ever, grateful to my family who for months have, yet again, been forced to circumnavigate ever mounting piles of newspapers. My thanks to Judith, my wife, for her encouragement and help, and to Nicholas and Emma for their laughter.

Acknowledgements and thanks are due to the following authors and publishers for the use of copyright material:

MAGAZINES
Football Italia and John D. Taylor; *Forever Forest* fanzine for the article by Richard Forest; *FourFourTwo* magazine and its editor Paul Simpson for the articles in *FourFourTwo* by Olivia Blair, Karen Buchanan, Colin Cameron, Shaun Campbell, Pete Davies, Stephen F. Kelly, Amy Lawrence, Paul Simpson and Tom Watt; the editor of *The Game* for the article by Mark Staniforth; *Goal* magazine and editor Paul Hawksbee for the articles in *Goal* by Kevin Borras, Bill Borrows, Dave Cottrell, Mark Robison, Ron Scalpello, David Stubbs and Andrew Walpole; the editor of *Matchday* for the articles by Michael Heatley and Chris Fewtrell; *New Statesman and Society* for the article by David Bull; Southampton Football Club and David Bull for extracts from their match programme by Keith Dewhurst, Lord Howell and Sue Wallace; the editor of *Through the Wind and Rain* and Jim Gardiner for his article; the editor of *Total Football* for the article by Ivor Baddiel; *Total Sport* magazine and Jeff King.

NEWSPAPERS
The Daily Telegraph Limited for the articles in the *Daily Telegraph* and the *Sunday Telegraph* by Patrick Barclay, Paul Hayward, Martin Johnson, John Ley, Sue Mott, Michael Parkinson, Robert Philip and Henry Winter; Times Newspapers Limited for the articles in the *Sunday Times* by Chris Lightbown, Joe Lovejoy, Hugh McIlvanney and Shelley Webb; Hugh McIlvanney for his articles; Newspaper Publishing PLC for the articles in *The Independent* and the *Independent on Sunday* by Eamon Dunphy, Robert Fisk, Nick Harris, Stan Hey, Ken Jones, Glenn Moore, Ian Ridley, Ian Stafford and Matt Tench; Eamon Dunphy for his article in the *Independent on Sunday*; Guardian Newspapers Ltd for the articles in *The Guardian* and *The Observer* by Cynthia Bateman, John Duncan, Matthew Engel, Vincent Hanna, Frank Keating, David Lacey, Gary Lineker, Martin Thorpe and Richard Williams; Frank Keating for his article in *The Guardian*; David Meek and the *Manchester Evening News* for his article.

BOOKS
Robert Banks and Independent UK Sports Publications for an extract from *An Irrational Hatred of Luton*; Virgin Publishing for an extract from Stephen F. Kelly's *Shankly*; Headline Book Publishing for an extract from Garry Nelson's *Left Foot Forward*; Mainstream Publishing
and Derick Allsop for two extracts from *The Game of Their Lives*;
and David Bennie for an extract from *Not Playing for Celtic*;
and Bob Holmes for an extract from *My Greatest Game*;
and Jeremy Novick for an extract from *In a League of Their Own*;
and Paul Rowan for an extract from *The Team That Jack Built*;
and Tom Watt for an extract from *A Passion for the Game*.

Finally, the publishers wish to point out that every effort has been made to trace all copyright holders for permission to include their pieces in this anthology. They apologise for any errors that may have occurred in the form of acknowledgement.

INTRODUCTION

This is my second successive collection of seasonal football writings to be published. Once again my thanks must primarily go to all those writers, newspapers and magazines who have given their permission for the reproduction of the various articles in these pages. Without their help and goodwill, this anthology could never have been possible.

On the footballing front, 1995–96 was another memorable season. A neck-and-neck race for the Premiership, which at one stage had looked bound for Newcastle, finally went to the wire with victory for Manchester United. And, as if that was not enough, United then went on to lift their second Double, unnerving arch-rivals Liverpool in the Wembley final. The game itself may have been distinctly forgettable, but the sight of United's joy at their achievement was worthy of the occasion. And all because of Cantona. It was bubblegum football.

Elsewhere, the once mighty Sunderland returned to the top flight, Manchester City slipped out of the Premiership, while Liverpool, Aston Villa and Spurs were resurgent. It was also the year of youth when United and Liverpool gave full reign to their youngsters, offering more than a glimmer of hope for the future of English football.

There was plenty happening off the field too. Terry Venables quit as England manager to be replaced by the hallowed Hoddle. Others also departed their managerial chairs. There was the usual flush of multi-million-pound signings and the import of South American and European stars helped bring a dash of flair and excitement to the Premiership. The South Americans went north to Middlesbrough and Newcastle while Arsenal and Chelsea were equally innovative with big-name signings Bergkamp and Gullit. Suddenly the Premiership discovered that, when it came to money, it could compete with the best in Italy, and could easily outbid Spanish, French, German and Dutch clubs.

And what a turnaround for Eric Cantona. Just a year after his famous kung-fu kick he was named Footballer of the Year. Days later he was leading his side up the steps at Wembley. It was all richly deserved.

The tabloids, as ever, continued to entertain us all with their diet of speculation and sensation. Mostly it was harmless stuff but on occasion the stories could be hurtful. Typical was their reaction to Robbie Fowler's full début against Croatia. Entering the match dubbed 'the next Jimmy Greaves', he was pilloried just days later as 'Fowler Howler'. Fowler had missed an opportunity to win the game for England and that was it; his future as an international striker was suddenly in question. It weighed heavily on his young shoulders as he failed to score for his club again all season. There was worse to come during the European Championships as the tabloids stooped to new depths, the *Daily Mirror* going so far as to declare football war on Germany. It was all so unnecessary. Gazza, likewise, was subjected to some of the more nonsensical reporting of the year, though at times his behaviour hardly helped his cause.

Another example, cleverly pieced together by *FourFourTwo* magazine, was the transfer stories with their usual speculative nonsense. Ince was going to Arsenal, or was it back to Old Trafford; Klinsmann was heading for Chelsea, Asprilla was going to Leeds, Giggs was going to Barcelona, as was Steve McManaman. And Manchester United were linked with just about every big name under the sun, from Shearer to Stoichkov. But it was all speculation, designed to bring a splash of excitement to some poor supporter's life, and to increase flagging circulation figures.

But there were pluses. The broadsheets extended their catalogue of quality writing while even more glossy football magazines rolled off the presses and onto the shelves. *FourFourTwo* was joined by *Goal*, *Total Football* and *Total Sport*, all welcome additions to what is now becoming a saturated market, though admittedly each title targets a different audience. *Goal*, in particular, has provided many a new angle on the game, while *Total Football* has injected a fanzine-like humour. The 'male glossies' have also upped their sporting content, particularly *Loaded*, although its brand of laddish humour, though undeniably popular with many, did not always contribute to the sum of our knowledge and experience.

And then there were the supplements. How did we ever survive Sunday and Monday mornings without those sports supplements to devour? And soon we're promised a daily sports paper to add to the forest of sporting newsprint that appears on the shelves each week. Not before time. Maybe in the future someone will take a leaf out of the French sporting daily, *L'Equipe*, by producing a Saturday colour supplement devoted to sport.

Finally, there were the European Championships, the biggest sporting event held in this country since the 1966 World Cup. It turned out to be every bit as glorious. England may not have won, but they gave a heroic performance in the reaching the semi-finals and, with more luck, could have gone all the way. Scotland, too, played with determination and honour.

As with last year's edition, *The Pick of the Season* is not an attempt to summarise or accurately reflect the season which has just passed. Rather, it is simply a taster of the football year. The defining principle has been the quality of the writing rather than the event it describes. For that reason, there are articles about some of the more obscure aspects of the game, and the more unfashionable clubs. Football, after all, is not just about what happens in the Premiership.

This year there is also less emphasis on extracts from the daily newspapers. The broadsheets are still there, of course, still providing some of the finest writing around, but there are now new sources of material. The sudden glut of monthly glossy magazines has, I hope, been more accurately reflected by the articles chosen for this collection. The fanzines, too, are represented, though not as much as hoped. Many of their articles are still either too crude or too incestuous for the casual reader, requiring an inner knowledge of a particular club. The aim of this book is to provide a good read for all, and not solely for the supporters of any one club. Hopefully, there will be something for everyone in its pages.

Stephen F. Kelly,
Manchester,
August 1996

The People's Game

THE FLAVOUR OF '96

Hugh McIlvanney

Other sports can dream as much as they like about how increasing professionalism and more frequent exposure on television will bring them a growing share of public interest. But 1996 has already supplied a strong, if unnecessary, reminder that for the British, football is still far and away the biggest game in town.

The title race is perhaps a week short of an inevitably dramatic conclusion and we have a potentially enthralling Cup final and the European Championship to come. Yet the current Premier League season has done enough on its own to demonstrate that football continues to stir the nation's emotions and imagination as no other jockstrap theatre can.

In fact, if we have a worry it is surely not that there is declining enthusiasm for the national sport but that too many of our people are obliged to lead lives in which the contrived dramas of a ball game assume a pervasive and exaggerated importance. When the cameras have panned across the faces of Newcastle supporters after each of the recent blows to their team's challenge for their first league championship in nearly 70 years, it has taken an effort to remember that the images of distraught foreboding relate to nothing more serious than the outcome of a football competition. Of course, photo-finishes always create tension but a betting shop full of embezzlers could not match the gloom-ridden anxiety of those fans.

If such a depth of commitment can be alarming, it clearly has its positive aspects too. Where else in our fragmenting society can we find the sense of communal involvement engendered by football in places like the North-east?

It has been the good fortune of three of the great blue-collar cities of Britain – Manchester, Newcastle and Liverpool – to be centre-stage as the game they have supported for generations provided the most entertaining season it has given us in years. Claims made on behalf of the top league in this country, stretching back to the days when it was called the First Division, have traditionally included the assertion that it was the best in the world. As far as technique is concerned, this boast has long been been baseless. Even the period of concentrated success for English clubs in the European Cup could be regarded as reward for tactical organisation and determined athleticism rather than brilliance. Anybody who doubts that assessment should consider how many of the climaxes our teams created would make it on to a list of the five or six best European Cup finals. Sensible sellers of our domestic football have always emphasised its capacity to generate excitement and even in this season that may be its paramount virtue. But, as they have competed for the title, the two Uniteds and Liverpool, with some admirable help from others further down the table (most conspicuously Aston Villa), have leavened the thrills with much attacking play of wonderful quality. Obviously, it would be prudent to avoid getting carried away, since the European competitions of next season may yet bring the kind of painful collision with reality endured in the past years or two. But what we have been seeing lately undoubtedly justifies celebration, especially as it confirms the presence in seats of huge influence of managers whose approach is consistently positive, unblemished by the slightest contamination from the helter-skelter tendency.

Liverpool's failure to remain embroiled in the struggle at the top has done nothing to blur the achievements of Roy Evans since inheriting the confusion and uncertainties left at Anfield by the brief reign of Graeme Souness. To many good judges, Liverpool seemed for a long time to be the most comprehensively equipped of the title challengers, and the most rabid of Manchester United devotees will hesitate about betting on their team in the Cup final, aware as they are that the job of keeping Robbie Fowler off the score-sheet constitutes a nightmare for defenders.

Fowler is the most exciting young player in England, a forward whose very slightness appears to reinforce his genius for infiltration. Both the cleanness of his first touch and his mercilessness in front of goal deserted him during his England début last Wednesday night but even such an insouciant prodigy must be expected to suffer occasional traces of edginess and it is impossible to believe that Terry Venables would be wise to head into the European Championship without him.

The cascade of goals Fowler has produced for Liverpool testifies to a standard of positional play, ball-striking, composure and nerve associated with only the most natural predators. He is a key component of the youthful element in Evans's playing strength which gives Liverpool the right to believe that over the next few seasons they will once again be an intimidating power in English football. But, in that respect, no club is more entitled to optimism than Manchester United. When all the triumphs of Alex Ferguson's stewardship are tabulated, none – not the ending of the 26-year championship drought, nor the winning of the European Cup-Winners' Cup and the completion of the League and FA Cup double – will rank higher than the re-creation of a youth policy that had fallen into hopeless disrepair. Ryan Giggs, Phil and Gary Neville, Nicky Butt, David Beckham and Paul Scholes have all skipped off the conveyor belt Ferguson put in place to bolster his squad so impressively that the departure of such major figures as Paul Ince, Mark Hughes and Andrei Kanchelskis has not prevented them reaching the point where they will take the field against Nottingham Forest at Old Trafford today as favourites to win their third title in four years.

Another towering success for Ferguson (and no doubt the one most crucial to his current prospects of a second double) is, of course, the rehabilitation of Eric Cantona following his leap into infamy at Selhurst Park 15 months ago. The Frenchman's performances since his suspension ended in October have represented a small miracle of psychological adjustment and by deploying his rich talents with remarkable self-control he has made himself quite simply the most influential and productive footballer in our game. Those who question the decision of the Football Writers' Association to make him their Player of the Year are applying criteria which fly in the face of all logic and fairness.

Cantona's refusal, thus far at least, to let frustration explode in out-rageous behaviour cannot have been made any easier by the obligation to play alongside Andy Cole, who has had the sort of season that encourages objective witnesses to wonder whether he would have been selected as regularly had he cost £700,000 rather than the £7 million paid to Newcastle for his transfer. Quick feet, and the confidence to pounce on every proffered chance as if he had a divine right to score goals by the bagful, made Cole deadly with Newcastle. But at Old Trafford the assurance has evaporated, exposing a technical clumsiness exemplified by some of the worst-timed jumping to be seen in top-class football. The heart goes out to Cole as he battles with his demons. However, if Manchester United do not win the championship, his misses will haunt him, and tens of thousands who have suffered with him.

His team's ability to compensate for Cole's shortcomings has been spectacular and might have been more so had Ferguson succeeded in filling satisfactorily the role of right-wing attacker once filled by Kanchelskis. It was no surprise to learn that the manager recently inquired about bringing back Keith Gillespie, the 21-year-old Irish winger who went to St James' Park as part of the Cole deal.

Improbable as it may seem, when the dust settles Gillespie could be recognised as having had substantial significance in the contest for the title. His pace and skills have plainly been missed at Old Trafford and a majority of Newcastle supporters are convinced that his absence from their side has contributed materially to the cruel slump from the status of swaggering, 12-point leaders of the League to that of breathless pursuers.

They view the Colombian Faustino Asprilla, for all his bursts of dazzling ball-control, as a dubious blessing. Although they know Gillespie's fitness has been sporadic, they suspect that Kevin Keegan was unduly swayed by the Irishman's bout of betting madness. Les Ferdinand, they recall, was scoring far more freely when Gillespie was rampaging along a flank.

Should Newcastle fall short, no fan will be more tortured than their most distinguished player, Peter Beardsley. The little man is a magnificent embodiment of everything that is to be cherished about a great game. He is a blend of virtuosity, honesty and spirit. Seeing him denied would almost be sufficient to make a Mancunian of the red persuasion weep. Almost, but not quite.

Sunday Times, 28 April 1996

DOWN AMONG THE DEADWOOD

Garry Nelson

The ecstatic crowd rise from their seats in adulation. A thumping 4–0 victory has just secured three vital points towards promotion. The excited fans make their hurried exit to the pub. Thirty minutes later, a totally disregarded group makes its way from the still-buzzing dressing-rooms onto the hallowed turf. Its task is not to replace the so recently created divots, but to justify their presence on the playing staff by performing extra-curricular training. A heavy duty running session is going to be their only reward for not being involved today. These not so merry men are of course, the 'stiffs'.

What we're looking at is the cruel contrast between life in the first team and life in the reserves. At first glance a prolonged spell among the deadwood appears to hold as much attraction as an end-of-season trip to Iraq. Its downsides are all too easy to identify.

Ageing pros can find themselves in the reserves for a number of reasons: a sudden and unexpected loss of form; a niggling injury; the emergence of a young star who – Sod's Law just happens to have it – plays in your position. Most disconcerting of all has to be the manager's big money purchase of a direct replacement for you. This time your downgrading could be permanent.

And that's just for starters. You also have to compete with, and against, other equally pissed-off stars, also struggling to come to terms with the fickle ways of the game. On the pitch, such frustrations can easily translate themselves into a constant tirade of criticism aimed at the younger lads in the team just when they are most looking to the old hands for a little bit of encouragement.

But the kids are not the only handy target for getting it out of your system. They're merely the safer option. 'You're crap, ref. You've no fucking chance of making the list.' Bad mistake, as the comments reverberate around the empty stadium. The refs (quite rightly, many would say) are having none of it. Forget the fact that you're having a bad time, your contract expires in July and you might be out of a job. They have only just received their new FA directive and the assessor is, quite possibly, at the game – referees are assessed in 50 per cent of games and only those being considered for the Football League list are monitored. Name, son?

Bookings for dissent cost 10 per cent of your weekly salary, a sending-off as much as a week's wages. With reserve-team win bonuses still at the £10 mark for many clubs, showing frustration at your unhappy lot can leave you well short at the end of the week. And disciplinary points racked up here count in a player's individual tally, so enough of them can mean suspension.

And there's more. Mix in a distinct lack of numbers in the crowd, a proliferation of clubs allowed to use the unmanicured grounds of non-League neighbours, constant alterations to the fixture schedule and very few rest days, and you have a recipe that appears to make life in the reserves a pretty miserable affair.

But reserve-team football has many positive aspects. For any young player it is a proving ground where he can show he has the attitude and ability to make that giant leap forward from school and youth-team starlet into tomorrow's star. The budget of a good many clubs will determine that there is no room for maybes.

And scouting networks cover this green and pleasant land. All in search of that bargain of the century.

On a more day-to-day level, reserve-team football serves many useful purposes. Players certainly prefer a game to training. They positively need the competition and improved fitness borne from active combat. Training week in, week out without the prospect of some form of match can be really demoralising. Man cannot live by foreplay alone. Hence the extreme frustrations experienced by the long-term injured. But, here again, reserve-team football comes to the psychological rescue. The healing process is deemed to be over the moment you stroll out for your first recuperative game. It may only be the second string, there may only be a few witnesses, but, boy! are you glad to be back.

The player who has the professional pride not to let his standards slide will often be a man well worth having. For the ageing pro total commitment at this humble level can be the difference between earning a new contract or being out of a job.

Happily, the disturbing trend of several years ago, when many of the clubs in the lower leagues discarded their reserve sides, seems to have been reversed. The footballing disadvantages far outweighed the fiscal savings and reserve football is thriving again.

Organisations such as Avon Insurance have bravely backed reserve football with sponsorship deals and award schemes. A few far-sighted clubs, such as Leicester and Norwich City, have gone so far as to make reserve games attractive nights out for all the family. Attendances regularly run into several thousands and youngsters are introduced to the thrill of watching football without the intimidation of the really big crowd or a crippling burden on the wallets of their parents.

What the fledgling fans will see will be high-quality football that may just be the game where a new Ryan Giggs launches his career on the road to superstardom. As for us players, you can never quite be sure just who you will be up against in that empty stadium. Now, there's this young lad by the name of Collymore . . .

Left Foot Forward (Headline, 1995)

THE HANCOCK MAN

Robert Philip

Christmas morning 1946 and 17-year-old Dulwich Hamlet Juniors goalkeeper Alan Simpson is feeling dead miserable. Ten seconds played and he is picking the ball out of the net while the Chelsea scout on the touchline at Champion Hill playing fields in South London scribbles away furiously in his notebook.

'But we won 8-3 in the end and I eventually got a letter from Chelsea inviting me for a trial,' recalls Simpson these 49 Yuletides on. 'I was flashing it around as though I'd been picked for England.

'The truth of the matter was that just after the war, even First Division clubs were giving trials to anyone who knew a ball was round. As it happens, I was due to go to Stamford Bridge in the June of '47 and contracted TB in the May. At the time, I thought it was the end of my life. Well, you do tend to think along those lines when you're given the last rites. I was in bed for three years and never kicked a ball again but it was the best thing that ever happened.'

For, by a simple twist of fate, lying in the next bed was Ray Galton, who had just been given six weeks to live but who was equally determined to succumb to neither tuberculosis nor boredom; by the time the two teenagers were released from the sanatorium in 1950, they had already embarked on the script-writing career which would unleash Anthony Aloysius St John Hancock upon 30 million unsuspecting radio listeners. *Steptoe & Son* would follow but no comic character before or since has so held the nation in thrall as 'the lad himself'.

Christmas 1995: Tony Hancock has been dead 27 years but Galton and Simpson, now 12 months past official retirement age, are busily at work adapting five of the original Hancock scripts for Paul Merton, the panellist on *Have I Got News For You?*, to be broadcast on ITV in February. The genius for making us laugh has survived, as has Alan Simpson's early love of football.

Comedy has taken him from East Cheam to Beverly Hills where he traded chit-chat with Frank Sinatra and Marlon Brando at Hollywood parties; football has taken him from Dulwich Hamlet to Sunbury-on-Thames where he has served as president of ICIS League Division Two worthies Hampton FC since 1968.

'I would have given anything to be a professional footballer – that was my ambition at 17 when I became ill. But I know deep down I'd never have made it. I was the original cowardly goalkeeper.

'As after-dinner speaker Bob Bevan says: "I was known as The Cat because I stayed out all night and gave my defence kittens." I perfected the knack of avoiding getting hurt while giving the impression I deserved a VC for courage.

'The trick in any 50-50 ball situation – which I must say had to be 90-10 in my favour – was to dive at the centre-forward's feet too soon so he had time to go round me, or too late, long after he'd already gone round me.

'Unfortunately, I was playing in the days when goalkeepers still hung their heads in shame whenever they conceded a goal. You automatically took the blame. I think it was Peter Shilton who invented "the glare". Now the minute the ball goes into the net, the goalie races out of his goal berating everyone else in sight, even if he's just let the ball through his legs. Bloody marvellous that.'

If the stack of Hancock scripts, books and videos crammed into Simpson's Thames-side cottage are the treasures of his endeavours – on the day of our wine and cheese-sandwich lunch he had just completed filming of *The Missing Page* (with Merton's wife, Caroline Quentin, in Sid James's old role) – the porcelain goalkeeper defending the trap-door leading down to the wine cellar is evidence of an abiding love of football, not to mention claret.

'I was born in Brixton but brought up in Streatham and my whole family were mad-keen Chelsea fans. All my uncles worked on the turnstiles or sold programmes – one was on the ground staff – so, being naturally perverse, I hated Chelsea. I had a stack of colour photographs of the First Division teams and put all the ones with a red strip, my favourite colour, in a hat and pulled one out. And that's how I came to support Brentford. When you think about it, I was bloody lucky they were in London. In those days you had Manchester United, Sheffield United, Middlesbrough, or, horrors of horrors, Arsenal.'

Simpson attended his first match at Brentford as an eight-year-old on Easter Monday 1938 and watched his adopted heroes pummel the Arsenal 3-0. The next three decades of Saturday afternoons (save for his years in the sanatorium) were spent at Griffin Park or Craven Cottage if Brentford, where he remains a shareholder, happened to be out of reach.

'Fulham were always the showbiz team. Walking into Craven Cottage was often like walking on to the set of *Coronation Street*. But I went because of Johnny Haynes, who gave me more pleasure than any footballer I have ever seen.'

Though Tony Hancock was a passionate Birmingham City supporter and avid cricket follower, his alter-ego on television cared little about sport.

'Ray was never particularly sports oriented and when you're writing about a subject, you've really got to "feel" it. But we did write a couple of episodes involving cricket; I remember Sid flogged Lord's to Tony once as a metropolitan farm. When Hancock went down to survey his new pastureland, he met what he took to be three farmers, all dressed in white. And that's how Colin Cowdrey, Frank Tyson and Godfrey Evans came to be on the show.'

By 1961, Brentford were in decline and Hancock was reaching the fateful decision to break with Galton and Simpson following one final, classic series best remembered for *The Blood Donor*, which, surprisingly, will not feature in the new Paul Merton run.

'Paul desperately wants to do *The Blood Donor* and it's been decided that if we do a second series, then it'll be number one. Ray and I have already started updating the script. So it won't be "A pint!?! Have you gone raving mad?", it'll be "Half a litre? That's very nearly an armful!" '

Thirty-four years may have passed since Hancock heaped insults upon the very large woman in the blood bank waiting-room but most lines remain timeless. 'Best of luck. Just think, Cliff Richard might get yours,' he said to her departing broad beam in '61, before muttering quietly, 'That'd slow him down a bit.'

With *Steptoe & Son* proving only marginally less popular than *Hancock's Half Hour*, Galton and Simpson were flown to Hollywood to 'inject a few gags' into a proposed 1700s Caribbean pirate adventure yarn entitled *Pieces of Eight*, starring Michael Caine and Diana Rigg. 'We were also supposed to get the budget down from $15 to $12 million but by the time we were finished it was up to $20 million.'

Universal decided to scrap the venture in favour of the Julie Andrews musical *Thoroughly Modern Millie* and the two scriptwriters bade farewell to Tinseltown at a party thrown by Vanessa Redgrave, who had just finished shooting *Camelot* with Richard Harris, Franco Nero and David Hemmings.

'It was great. A real Hollywood bash. Everyone was there, Sinatra . . . Brando . . . the lot. But my abiding memory is of Ray – who'd had a few drinks, I have to admit – laying into Robert Mitchum for America's involvement in Vietnam. Pure Hancock it was. Ray kept jabbing his finger in Mitchum's chest and hurling abuse. Eventually Mitchum got a word in

– and ever so polite he was. "Well, I wouldn't necessarily agree I'm a stupid f*****, exactly".'

Simpson returned to Sunbury from Hollywood to find an invitation from the chairman of Hampton FC awaiting him. Having been generous enough to donate £5 towards the club's floodlight fund, would he now care to become president? 'Until then I didn't even know there was a football ground round the corner. Actually, most people in Sunbury still don't. You could stop a local right outside Beveree Park in Station Road and ask directions on a match night – when the floodlights are on full and crowds of people are going past in red-and-blue scarves – and they'll say "A football ground? Around here? Blimey, search me mate."

'Anyway, I went along to a game and enjoyed it. Then I went into this little corrugated shed they had for a bar to have a drink. It was lovely. Everyone was really friendly and they had this gas stove behind the bar frying sausages.

'In my naïvety I thought it was so charming and romantic I agreed to become president. I was flattered to be asked and thought all I'd have to do was go along once a season, allow someone to pour me a vast drink and hand over the Player of the Year award at the annual dinner. That was 27 years ago and I've followed them home and away ever since. I doubt if I've seen more than ten professional games in all that time. I couldn't be more involved. I know all the players, I've lent the club a bit of money. It's more than a hobby, it's my *raison d'être* in many ways.'

With Simpson's financial help and boyish enthusiasm, a new covered terrace has been built, a boardroom created out of the old gents' lavatory ('we usually don't tell guests they're eating a pork pie on the site of what was urinal No 2') and Hampton have designs on a place in the ICIS Premier Division under the peerless guidance of Chick Botley.

'It's a little-known footballing fact that Albion Rovers have given this country two of our greatest football managers – Jock Stein and Chick Botley.'

But for the moment, Hampton must share Simpson's time and affections with Hancock. 'We know the scripts stand the test of time. The BBC asked us to rewrite *The Economy Drive* back in the 1970s for Arthur Lowe and Jimmy Beck [the spiv in *Dad's Army*]. They were brilliant. Then Jimmy died and, on top of Hancock's death, Arthur got a bit superstitious so that original pilot episode was the first and last.'

Knowing Simpson's love of football (plus Hancock's propensity for getting names wrong), do not be surprised if Adam Faith is substituted by a certain midfielder cometh *The Blood Donor*, when he aggravates the increasingly harassed nurse by pontificating volubly on the different monetary values we place on society.

'Now just take modelling. You get some skinny bird up the West End dragging a piece of fur along a platform – 5,000 quid a week. And there's you lot, dedicated, three years' training, humping great trolley loads of mince about all day. It's not right! Now is that right? There's Bamber Gascoigne at Rangers earning ten times as much as the Prime Minister. Is that right? IS THAT RIGHT? . . .'

Daily Telegraph, 18 December 1995

AN IMPOSSIBLE JOB

Ken Jones

Doubtless Glenn Hoddle will bear in mind that managing England is not a job, it is a responsibility. It means less of a private life, ringing telephones, arrogant assumptions and coming under the pontifical scrutiny of amateur strategists.

It means attempting to restore a reputation that exists only in the minds of blinkered patriots; 30 years since England won the World Cup, nothing either side of that achievement. And never mind the technical flaws, the British cultural divisions evident in great club teams, who has been held to blame? The managers.

Constrained by autocratic selectors who were not above applying quite ludicrous regional bias, England's first manager, Walter Winterbottom, resigned in 1962, unable to get beyond the quarter-final stage in four World Cups. Alf Ramsey, the fêted hero of 1966, was fired after failing to qualify for the 1974 finals in West Germany.

Less than a year into his term of office, Don Revie, who had built Leeds into one of Europe's most feared teams, was conceding privately that he had taken on an impossible task. 'I got carried away, simply didn't pay enough attention to the fact of how many important players in the First Division wouldn't be available to me as manager of the England team,' Revie admitted. 'I'm scraping the barrel and it will be a miracle if we qualify [for the 1978 finals].'

Soon after it became obvious that England would not get through, and suspecting that it was only a matter of time before he was sacked, Revie took off scandalously for the Middle East without bothering to inform his employers.

Ron Greenwood restored respectability to a role he should have been considered for earlier, and got England to the last eight in the 1982 finals before handing over to Bobby Robson. It was during Robson's tenure that the task of managing England became one nobody should consider without first demanding a heat shield. Forced to withstand probes into his personal life and a mounting flood of criticism, Robson had aged perceptibly by the time Argentina put England out of the 1986 finals in Mexico. He hung on, and despite tactical blunders in the early rounds, he came within a penalty shoot-out of the final in Italy four years later.

Of all the appointments in sport, few carry such an overwhelming sense of national responsibility as being manager of England and it proved too much for Robson's successor, Graham Taylor. In attempting to refine the direct method he favoured as a club manager, Taylor got lost, his teams neither one thing nor another, the subsequent vilification brutal.

Particularly as he was a member of Robson's squad, Hoddle is acquainted with the weight of expectation borne by managers of the national team. To my mind anybody who even considers the job is a suitable case for treatment but in fact this may be the right time in Hoddle's career to succeed Terry Venables.

History emphasises that football clubs are notoriously fickle. There are no guarantees: a hero one season, a victim the next. Plenty of praise has come Hoddle's way for the Ruud Gullit-inspired football Chelsea have played this season but it only got them as far as the FA Cup semi-finals and a mid-table place in the Premiership. There is the matter of dissent in the boardroom, too. How deeply does Ken Bates resent the fact that Hoddle appeared to side with his rival Matthew Harding?

Thinking practically, it would be unlikely to affect Hoddle's career a great deal if things did not work out for him with England – less, I think, than if they went wrong for him at Chelsea.

If, as seems probable, Hoddle takes over the national team, one of the things for him to guard against will be the usual glut of mindless presumptions. 'Tel wants England to play like Brazil,' bellowed one of our popular prints when Venables, who remains unquestionably the best man for the job, was appointed.

Another is the suggestion that it would be an advantage to have Gullit at his side. A great player, an intelligent man, a wise head, but too big a personality.

The Independent, 2 May 1996

WORLD CUP KICK-OFF

Martin Johnson

It ends in Paris in a blaze of global publicity, 28 months from now, and gets under way tomorrow afternoon, on a small, impecunious Caribbean island, with such an absence of fanfare that only those thumbing through the small print with a magnifying glass in search of the greyhound results or overseas subscribers to the *Dominican Weekly Chronicle* are likely to stumble on the outcome.

Game number one of the 635 qualifying matches to be played for football's 1998 World Cup is Dominica versus Antigua, and while it would come as no great surprise if it has bypassed the rest of the universe, it is, of course, driving the islanders here into a frenzy of anticipation. Er, not quite. During the past few days the question, 'Are you going to the match on Sunday?' has been met with an unwavering response. 'Match? What match?'

Driving around Dominica offers plenty of time to take in the sights, mainly because there are large potholes to be negotiated every ten yards, or else one of the locals has pulled up in the middle of the road to offload some bananas, or simply have a chinwag with a bloke on the pavement. And as you sit tapping the steering-wheel, your eyes are drawn to posters and billboards advertising Coca-Cola, sand and gravel supplies, parish prayer meetings . . . just about everything bar the forthcoming match.

A telephone call to the Dominican Football Association was scarcely more informative. The number listed in the FIFA handbook rings out unobtainable, but there are two more in the island telephone directory. The first one gives the following message: 'I'm sorry, the number you have dialled is out of service. This is a recording.' The second clicks you onto another recording, offering advice about what to do in the event of a hurricane.

It is nowhere near such a frustrating exercise trying to get through to the Antiguan Football Association office, because there is no point in trying. They don't have one. Their secretary, Chad Green, works for a shipping company, and when he has the odd spare minute he handles his soccer business from there. On Thursday afternoon he said that he was still trying to find out where they were supposed to be staying, and while he was 'pretty sure' the game was taking place on Sunday, he had yet to be informed as to the time of the kick-off.

Mr Green added that the president of FIFA, Joao Havelange, had originally been scheduled to attend the game, but it was now thought he wasn't coming after all. This is hardly surprising, if Havelange has spent most of the week on the telephone being appraised about what to do in the event of a hurricane striking. Incidentally, for those who might be interested, the two main pieces of advice are to keep some rags and cloth handy to prevent water gushing into the house, and to stay sober. They ought to have a recorded message for people trying to get through to the Football Association. Get drunk.

Eventually, the vice-president of the Dominican FA, Ferdinand Frampton, was tracked down to an office at the Dominican Broadcasting Corporation, where he announced his surprise that the Antiguans were unaware of either their hotel accommodation or the kick-off time. However, he did confirm that it did not surprise him at all that the islanders themselves had yet to cotton on to the fact that there was a World Cup soccer match taking place, but that the publicity machine was about to spring into action. This, apparently, will consist of a van with a loudspeaker driving around the streets of the capital, Roseau, 24 hours before the match. The theory behind it is that most people in Dominica will be in town doing their shopping on Saturday, and that it is cheaper and more effective than advertising on TV. Furthermore, despite this rather eccentric marketing technique, Mr Frampton expects around 4,000 people to attend the game, some of whom will pay to get in.

In theory, they all should, but while the ground – Windsor Park – has a certain rustic charm and a scenic backcloth of lush mountain vegetation, Old Trafford it is not. Mr Frampton said: 'The walls are not very high, and you must realise that with a large percentage of our population not earning much money, most people will try to storm the ground. We have to spend a lot of money on police and security.'

So how many of the 4,000 does he expect to muscle in for nothing? He laughed. 'About half.'

It is not only the spectators who barely earn enough money to afford the Eastern Caribbean $10 admission price (about £2.50, half for children), but the players themselves are not likely to be arriving by air-conditioned team bus, or wearing silk suits and designer bracelets. The Dominican team is made up of a few civil servants and one or two casual labourers, but most are unemployed. If everyone was unemployed, said Mr Frampton, it would be easier to arrange training sessions; as it is they squeeze them in, in late afternoon.

It is all a far cry from the last match to be played in the World Cup, the 1994 final in Pasadena, when the players' combined salaries would have swamped Dominica's GNP, and the attendance was substantially higher than Dominica's official population of 71,000.

If you dropped the directory of Dominican sporting superstars on your foot, it wouldn't leave much of a bruise, and the two main stands at the football stadium (which doubles as the cricket ground) are named after two fairly obscure West Indian cricketers, Irving Shillingford, and the former Essex all-rounder, Norbert Philip. As for the stands themselves, they are a bit like the sort of structures you might find at a Fourth Division rugby union ground, with a seating capacity of around a hundred each, and air-conditioned corrugated roofing (i.e., more holes than a colander). If they build another stand, it will probably be named after the Dominican-born Phillip DeFreitas, whose own chances of a World Cup-winner's medal with England's cricketers are probably about the same as Dominica's football team.

As for the ground itself, it is the equivalent of the village green with two sets of goalposts, though the playing surface is certainly less bumpy than the road outside. Just to the side of the centre circle is the cricket pitch, which is set on a raised plateau, a good two feet higher than the rest of the playing area. The diagonal slope from corner flag to corner flag makes Yeovil's old pitch look like the home of the Flat Earth Society. The groundsman does his best with what equipment is available – so hi-tech that the local goats are called off the substitutes' bench when his lawnmower is not working.

On Thursday he was sitting watching a dozen or so schoolchildren having an impromptu game in one of the goalmouths, without looking unduly concerned. 'They won't do any damage,' he said, 'and anyway, there aren't many places here where kids can play safely away from the traffic.' This may be a World Cup game, but in a family-orientated island like this they have a substantially more balanced view of priorities than most societies.

There shouldn't be any trouble in the game either, assuming that the band strikes up the right anthem for Antigua. In a recent Pan-American Cup game between Honduras and Brazil, there was a 15-minute hold-up when the Hondurans returned to the dressing-room in protest at standing proudly to attention for what turned out to be the national anthem of Panama.

The Antiguans are slight favourites to win over the two legs, and go on to play Barbados in the next round, though Dominica's vice-president claims that his team are 'on the up' and confident. And if the Dominican footballers are as creative as the artist who designs some of the hotel's brochures here (which bear as much resemblance to the real thing as Batley Town Hall does to the Taj Mahal) then they are definitely in with a shout.

Daily Telegraph, 9 March 1996

THE MEDICINE MEN

Amy Lawrence

Sitting on the England team bus travelling down Wembley's Olympic Way, Dave Butler turns to Alan Smith with a mock yawn: 'Bloody 'ell, here we are again at the Twin Towers.' The pair roar with laughter. They couldn't be more proud of their association with England if their faces replaced the Queen's on the nation's stamps. Smith confesses he had tears in his eyes when he was given the job. Butler admits it was a dream come true. Both cite being appointed England physiotherapists as their greatest moment in football. It's not a job you can apply for, it's by invitation only, and as both are at pains to point out, it's 'the ultimate honour'.

For Terry Venables, knowing that the medical side of any England get-together is well organised and will run smoothly is as important as training with Alan Shearer, consulting Don Howe or studying a report of the opposition.

'The England backroom staff is very close-knit,' says Smith. 'Terry's got people around him he can trust,' adds Butler. 'Not "yes men". People who will tell him something if it needs saying. It's a very comfortable situation.' Venables knows he has two men who, as well as being qualified to deal with everything from bruises to broken bones, will do absolutely anything for the cause. Smith and Butler are on call 24 hours a day during an England gathering. They're always the first to arrive and the last to leave. Dead keen, like.

It's the Thursday before England's friendly against Switzerland and, true to form, Smith and Butler are at the team hotel hours before anyone else. Already changed into their 'England Green Flag' embossed tracksuits, they are busy setting up the medical room, waiting for the kit to arrive and taking messages from any club physios who need to pass on information about their players: Smith has just had a call from Newcastle physio Derek

Wright, with news of Les Ferdinand's groin strain.

The players report to the hotel for 9 p.m. and Smith and Butler, together with Doctor Crane, examine all of the squad that night. Anyone carrying an injury is immediately assessed, and the gaffer is informed of any potential problems. Venables doesn't need to be bothered with the details, he leaves that to the medical staff. He just wants to know who'll be at peak fitness and who might not make it. 'Can we heal injuries in the four days before the boss names his team? That is the key,' says Smith.

The next morning they're on the phone to the players' rooms by 8.15 a.m. to see if anyone needs any treatment or wants any strappings or rubs prior to training. Then it's off to Bisham Abbey. They sort out high-energy drinks for the lads and bananas for the coach journey back.

The players wouldn't dare to underestimate the importance of carbohydrates. Butler stays with the team, watching, being ballboy, dealing with any niggles on the field, while Smith is in the gym with the injured Ferdinand. The two men split their responsibilities down the middle. Tomorrow it will be Butler with Ferdy while Smith chases footballs. During the 90 minutes of a match they will take it in turns to treat players who go down. The 'spare' one of the two will sprint on behind his pal to observe and, if needed, help out. Butler nudges Smith: 'It's my turn Wednesday, Alan.'

The last time they saw any 'action' was in the closing minutes of England's Umbro Cup game against Brazil when they raced to the rescue of John Scales. 'He had a depressed fracture of the zygomatic arch,' tuts Smith. Roughly translated that's a busted cheekbone. Smith looked after Scales in the dressing-room while Butler stayed on the bench. What a partnership.

On match days they arrive at Wembley four hours before kick-off to prepare the dressing-room. 'We like to have everything done an hour before the players arrive. Then we sit down and have a cup of tea,' smiles Smith. 'When the players walk in, everything is immaculate. Nobody wants for anything. That hour before kick-off is vital.'

Smith and Butler love it. There are plenty of qualified physios but they don't all breathe football. That understanding of the game is crucial at international level. 'It's important to fit into the environment, to be on the same wavelength as the players,' says Butler.

Smith and Butler are encouraging, willing and slot into the spirit of the occasion. They are part of the family. Win or lose they share the emotions of Venables and the lads. If they read criticism in the newspapers they are sensitive about it. 'I tend not to read it because I get upset,' says Smith. Butler does read it: 'You feel it because you know what the people around you are trying to achieve.'

There's no room for prima donnas or jobsworths in the England set-up and Smith and 'Butts' have no complaints about mucking in. Anything from putting studs on boots, taking the kit to the washing machines, collecting training balls. 'We polish the lads' boots,' says Butler. 'We don't have to. We just say, "Give us your boots," and if they're not polished we'll do it so that they [the players] aren't rushed.' That's the England way. After a game Bryan Robson always picks up all the spare kit. If there's a ball missing Robbo will be the first to look for it. Bit keen for the next England manager elect . . .

Smith and Butler had similar apprenticeships: professional physios through all four divisions for over 20 years (Smith reached his club pinnacle with Sheffield Wednesday, Butler with Spurs); simultaneously climbing the English ladder; playing hopes dashed by serious injury. They were even born a mere two miles apart, in the north-east. Yet there's no real competition between them. Just a healthy dose of gentle ribbing.

As I leave they're recounting an early meeting with Venables. A waitress brought over some tea and asked the England manager if he cared for sugar. 'Sugar! Are you sure?' howled Butler. Smith, remembering the scene, is beside himself with hysterics.

FourFourTwo, January 1996

TRAINING WITH LIVERPOOL

Henry Winter

Some of Britain's most functional buildings possess the most evocative auras. Even when emptied of human presence, footballing arenas stimulate memory after memory, images of great sportsmen, of redoubtable managers, of loyal congregations who root a club in the community. The aesthetic nature of such settings is irrelevant. It is the people, the actors on these utilitarian stages, who stir the soul and quicken the pulse.

Nowhere is this more true than at Melwood, Liverpool's training ground, a place low on pretence yet so redolent a rehearsal venue for many of the game's finer practitioners. Driving through its forbidding metal gates, past a gaggle of autograph-hunters, for a training session organised by Liverpool's sponsors, Adidas, the attention turns to the practice fields, where the club's constant dreams have so often been coaxed into reality.

This small collection of pitches is as unassuming as the location, the turf even patchy in parts. A private school would demand more. But this misses the point. It is the people who work here who matter.

People like Roy Evans and Sammy Lee, humorous men of Merseyside who quietly maintain the Liverpool tradition of excellence without excess. People like Jamie Redknapp and Robbie Fowler, too young to remember properly the seemingly annual red-shirted crusades across Europe but both capable yet of reviving former glories.

Fowler is outside, lurking with intent on a practice pitch, drilling ball after ball at that colossus of England's past, Joe Corrigan, the former Manchester City goalkeeper. The blur of objects passing at ridiculous speeds is akin to standing by the fast lane of a motorway. Corrigan saves and misses and cajoles, exhorting Fowler to beat him. The challenge is accepted.

Inside the brick clubhouse is Redknapp, resembling a model who cannot remember whether he is on assignment for Timberland or Calvin Klein. He wanders through the kitchen, picking at food, staring without emotion at a video of his free-kick that so scared Blackburn Rovers last May.

His thoughts are doubtless distracted by an unwelcome first acquaintance with hamstring trouble, which remains sore after another failed fitness test, so removing him from contention for this weekend's glamour game: tomorrow's visit of Manchester United to Anfield.

The last meeting between England's two most famous clubs was overshadowed by Eric Cantona's liberation from his sporting Elba, the tickertape and tricolours hiding Fowler's impudent brace. Reminiscences of that momentous October Sunday are curtailed as Lee marches over, a compact, wise-cracking figure eager for the session to run properly. Off we go on a warm-up run, a small group of semi-fit media men, waiting on little Lee's every instruction. Studs clatter across a paved path. 'They go over the Melling Road for the first time,' comes the cry from the puffing pack.

Lee smiles. He's heard it all before. This will quieten them. Long dormant muscles receive a rude awakening as the stretching exercises begin. Stretch and hold, shake out, and repeat. The warm-up does not last long but the glow does. Time for one final tuning of the hamstrings. 'Make it good,' Lee barks. 'The housewives could be watching.' Hopeful glances are stolen over the wall towards grey suburbia. A pigeon stares back.

Time for action. Evans, Fowler, Neil Ruddock and Steve Harkness stroll over to lend their expertise. Dribbling first, teasing a ball through cones placed cruelly close together. So this is how Steve McManaman does it. No wonder he is so willowy; Kate Moss would struggle to glide through this slalom run.

Then ball juggling. Lee shouts a number that the man in possession must keep the ball up for. The figure rises. 'Five', '10', then '70' when one of Fleet Street's less fleet members receives the ball. Failure brings press-ups, gleefully counted out by Ruddock in that age-old routine of 1, 2, 3, 4, 3, 4, 5, 4, 5, 6.

Then shooting, partly to examine the swerving tendencies of the Adidas Predator range, sophisticated boots which have more rubber fins than Cynthia Payne's nightie. Harkness and Fowler peel away to work with the left-footers. Ruddock marshals the righties, his reservoir of quips constantly refreshed by the wayward shooting. When a representative of a Sunday tabloid retrieves a ball from behind Ruddock, Razor bemoans: 'Oh no, I've got the *News of the World* following me again.'

One wannabee is nicknamed Stan, due to his likeness to Collymore. When he misses the target, Ruddock chimes, 'What a waste of money.' The crack remains vibrant at Liverpool, fostered by the likes of Evans and Lee, inheritors and perpetuators of club traditions. Evans, the popular gaffer with a hint of steel, ambles around, making suggestions, dropping in words of encouragement. Ruddock also proves a sympathetic teacher, making the usual suggestions of 'keep your head down' and 'try not to put the ball over the wall'. But do professionals have to go round to neighbours' houses and ask for their ball back please, mister, like the rest of us?

On observing this participator's umpteenth miss, Lee mutters kindly: 'You must be a centre-half.' Thanks. He has one final demand: warming-down. Certain hands reach for cigarettes but Lee has more modern ideas: another spell of stretching and loosening.

The work-out has gone well (no one collapsed), so maybe Liverpool, given their recent poor form, could use some reinforcements. Terms are not on offer, but tea is. The pot poured, Evans expands on Melwood training and the process of pass-and-move, which he has helped oversee for 21 years. 'Our training is based around small-sided games, like five-a-side,' he says. 'But you've got to run as well. Not the long stuff – more short, sharp stuff.'

Sounds like Ajax and Holland. 'We watched the Dutch train here the other day [before the Euro '96 play-off] and their training was very similar to ours: small-sided games, a lot of possession. That shows in their play, doesn't it?'

Indeed, as Evans's match-day home witnessed later that Wednesday. Yet Liverpool's manager plays down the suggestion that foreigners train harder on individual skills: 'The weather conditions are different. We couldn't be standing around too much on winter days, working on different systems and different parts of the game.'

With the domestic calendar so crowded, and games so intense, working on individuals and specifics had become 'quite difficult' in a world of play-recover-play. Managers can address problems on blackboards but can rarely devote training-ground time to working with players on solutions.

But it is the same for Manchester United and Newcastle, the leaders whom Liverpool trail by 11 points. Is Evans worried about the gap? 'Yes. I'm not saying we are not title contenders now, but we've made it a lot more difficult for ourselves.'

Their position would improve if Collymore, a forward who prefers the ball dispatched early, could be incorporated more fully in a team geared to more measured build-ups.

'Stan is quite capable of joining in with the short stuff. It's a bit of give and take,' says Evans. 'We've always been a passing team. I don't see much reason to change that, even on the back of probably our worst period for many years. That doesn't mean the style is wrong.'

And with the right people in charge, footballing fortunes have a habit of changing quickly.

Daily Telegraph, 16 December 1995

IT'S ALL OVER NOW

Robert Banks

West Ham scored 80 league goals in 1989–90. That was pretty good going and a good sign for things to come. In all competitions, the total was 99. Defensive frailties had proved to be the undoing and were the biggest concern about a return to the top flight.

The weekend before the start of the season saw two testimonial games take place. An unusual fact in itself, made even more strange by the fact that they were both for goalkeepers. On Friday, West Ham played Spurs at White Hart Lane in a benefit match for Ray Clemence. On the Sunday, Ipswich Town visited Upton Park in a testimonial game for Phil Parkes. I travelled to the Tottenham game alone, straight from the office, meeting a fellow lone traveller on the tube and we watched the game together. Nothing unusual about the game – Spurs had a good side with Gascoigne and Lineker at their peak after the World Cup. One would have expected them to win, especially as it was a benefit game for a Tottenham player.

On the Saturday night I had been due to go to a party – on my own. Karen had finished her year at work. Unable to stand her a minute longer than was absolutely necessary they had released her dead on twelve months. I, on the other hand, being sweet and lovable (and the author of this book, therefore able to create whatever impression I like) was allowed to stay on until I went back to college. I got on well with everyone at Farrars and was grateful for the chance to keep working. What pissed me off was coming home at seven in the evening and finding Karen had been lounging around watching TV all day, while the flat looked like a small nuclear weapon had gone off in the lounge. I encouraged her to get a part-time job, and she got one behind the bar of a local pub, which meant working unsociable hours. It did, at least, give me the chance to do a bit of socialising alone. I had fully intended to go to the party, but after taking

Karen to work on the Saturday night I looked at my surroundings; the pile of ironing in the corner and the dirty dishes in the sink, and decided to blitz the flat instead. With the flat spick and span, I finally retired to bed. Exciting, this little story, isn't it? I awoke at six o'clock on Sunday morning to find the other side of the bed empty. I took a quick look around the flat to see if Karen had crashed out on the sofa so as not to disturb me, but knew she was not that considerate. She was nowhere to be seen. It was a measure of my resignation that I ignored her absence and went straight back to sleep. I woke again at eight and phoned the pub. I spoke to an extremely irate manager, who said she had slept over at the pub because she had finished very late and was very tired. I demanded to speak to her. She trudged from her bed, blissfully unaware of the fact that I didn't really give a toss, but I was going to make the bitch stew for this.

'Where the hell have you been?' I demanded.

'Oh, I was so tired.'

'Too tired to call me to let me know you weren't coming home?'

'I'm sorry.'

'I should fucking well think so.' I slammed the phone down very convincingly. I decided to leave the flat immediately in case she had any ideas about coming straight over to explain. I went over to Anne-Marie's house, which took an hour and a half, during which time Karen had already rung her.

'Karen just phoned,' Anne-Marie said. 'She wanted to know if you were here and if you were angry.'

'What did you tell her?'

'I told her I'd be bloody angry if I was Rob.'

'Nice one, A-M. Put the kettle on!'

I told A-M all about what had been going on, and despite being her best friend, she advised me to walk away. I wasn't sure. In a perfect world, Karen would walk away from me. I didn't want to have to go back to my parents with my tail between my legs. But then, this isn't a perfect world. In a perfect world, West Ham would do better than a 1–1 draw against Ipswich in a testimonial game.

The match was like a West Ham old boys' reunion. Billy played for our side, and the visiting team included Alan Devonshire, who had moved on to Watford, Geoff Pike who was at Notts County, Bobby Barnes from Northampton Town and Paul Goddard who was trying to resurrect his career at Milwall. Jimmy Quinn inevitably scored for us, and I went home to face Karen. She was hiding under a quilt on the sofa. I ripped it off and asked for an explanation.

'Do you want to try again?' she asked.

'No.' I said, staring out of the window. 'I've had enough.'

Karen had nowhere to go. Her brother only had a tiny flat and she couldn't go back to her parents because she needed to be in the area to go back to college. The flat at Lennard Road was a contractual obligation: we had to keep it until November, so I agreed she could stay at the flat, while I packed a few things and went back to mum and dad. A very difficult and, in hindsight, brave thing to do.

My first phone call on Monday morning was to a good pal of mine, Kevin. Kevin had been going out with one of Karen's friends and we had become close mates. He had just graduated from Southampton University and was working as a solicitor in Bromley. He was an idealist; and a confirmed right-winger. He was a Young Conservative and proud of it. He had ambition, too. He still has. Watch this space. This guy wants to be Prime Minister and he seriously believes he will make it. Both myself and Michael Heseltine have our doubts, however. Kevin invited me to a reception held by the President of the Board of Trade. Kevin's MP introduced us to Heseltine, saying that Kevin had a burning desire to be a politician.

'Is that right?' Heseltine asked. 'You'd like to be Prime Minister?'

Kev put on his best *Yes Minister* voice and replied mockingly, 'Well, if my country saw fit to call upon my talents, I would seriously consider it.'

Heseltine just looked at him and said: 'You might as well not bother, then.' I laughed. Heseltine has his own reasons for doubting that Kevin will be Prime Minister, I have my own – who ever heard of a Prime Minister called Kevin? He had a sympathetic ear in those days. He had listened when we had been to the theatre as a foursome with his girlfriend a few weeks earlier and was half expecting the news. He was upset when I told him we had finished. He said he liked Karen. I said I would like Karen if I didn't have to live with her. He just laughed and bought me another pint.

It was during these troubled times that I realised how many good friends I had. I was very lucky. My parents supported me through thick and thin. I still haven't found anything to blame them for. My bed was waiting for me when I turned up that Sunday evening, and both mum and dad revealed that they didn't like Karen in the first place. I had thought as much, but it's not the sort of thing you tell your son, is it? My sisters were both delighted that I had got shot of her. They were always suspicious of her motives. I was just blinded by her body. On several occasions I went back to the flat to pick up clothes and possessions and on two occasions we ended up back in bed. In the end it made me hate her for being a tart, but if the truth be known I was the biggest slag of them all. Since I met Karen, I've never had a pure thought in my head, and I doubt I ever will again.

At work things continued to rumble along. They all knew Karen quite well because she used to come into the office to meet me after work, and to check I wasn't feeling Jackie up behind the filing cabinet. They were all shocked, too. 'We thought you were perfect for one another,' they all said. Just goes to show how wrong you can be.

On the opening day of the season I was still up to my neck in books, records, tapes, football programmes and financial settlements. The fact we had drawn 0–0 at Middlesbrough was incidental. Close used to work around the corner from me, and he came around to the office to meet me before the game against Portsmouth. My colleague, Rod MacLeod, a professional Scotsman and brilliant wit, remarked the next morning that he didn't think much of my new girlfriend. The first home game of the season was a disappointing 1–1 draw with Portsmouth. We needed to win every home game – a draw was not acceptable. At least Frank McAvennie showed that he might be back on form and scored his first goal in his second spell at the club. The following Saturday, we played Watford at Upton Park. It was an action replay of the previous season's game, winning 1–0 through a Julian Dicks penalty, but the performance was far from convincing. Close and I were going to more and more games together. Most of the others had dropped out: Bean Head came along occasionally, and Stain Tooth was still a regular, but the original gang was depleted. Close couldn't be bothered to go to Leicester. After the performance we had witnessed against Watford, we felt the only logical result was a defeat. Instead, we watched the video highlights of season 1989–90 at his flat, and wondered if we would make it this season. We flipped over channels for the football results. We had won 2–1. Maybe we would.

An Irrational Hatred of Luton (Independent UK Sports Publications, 1995)

THE KIDS' CUP

David Bennie

The final year of primary education was a glorious orgy of kick-about football, from dawn to dusk, played on makeshift pitches in school playgrounds, public parks, back gardens, back streets and church halls. Those of us lucky enough to be in 7A even had the girls' empty playground to ourselves every school day between 3 and 4 p.m., when the much-loved Mr Strachan permitted the boys out to play seven-a-sides on a marvellously uncongested concrete playing area (the girls did knitting, embroidery, basket-weaving, flower-arranging and spelling bees, depending on the day of the week, while the male pupils of Miss Cratchet's 7B spent the final hour doing maths, when not nipping out on toilet passes to press their envious faces against the corridor windows overlooking the girls' playground). None of us knew how the 60-odd intake was divided up each year into two classes, A and B – it wasn't based on alphabetical order or intelligence quotients – but we were eternally grateful that six years earlier we'd been selected for Miss Birrel's 1A; otherwise we'd have ended up enduring 7B's football-free curriculum. And although we revelled in our good fortune, its arbitrary nature genuinely unsettled us when we thought about it, because we couldn't imagine school life without our daily fix of free-flowing football (as compared to break-time matches, when moves had to be constructed through an obstruction course of younger pupils playing tig, kick-the-can, hide-'n'-seek, conkers, marbles and other juvenile irrelevances).

These were definitely the happiest hours of my life, and my grown-up classmates of today probably share this sentiment because there was never any aggro or argy-bargy, just good-natured and unbridled enthusiasm. The picking of players went like clockwork, too, with 12 of us just pleased to be picked by one of the unofficial captains (the two best – or most aggressive — players), while our 15th man, Georgie Esslemont, stayed indoors with the girlies, by choice, weaving his baskets and knitting his scarves into, respectively, surrealistic sloping cones and never-ending woollen worms.

The games flowed up and down with rarely more than two goals separating the sides, and with Strachan refereeing them we tended to play to our positions, instead of crowding round the ball *en masse* like iron filings chasing a magnet or flies congregating over dog shit. And no one was bullied into being goalkeeper every day, since Strachan made us take equal turns.

Strangely, Strachan wasn't a football fan himself, and he refereed from a standing position beside the water fountain, dressed as always in a dark three-piece suit and heavy black tortoise-shell spectacles. Like Mr Chipps, I think he just liked to see us happy. But he was no mug or easy touch, since our truancy rate was zero, while Miss Cratchet's charges absconded so often that she eventually married a Corporation truancy inspector.

7B did of course get to play football in break-times — morning, lunch and afternoon — and their opponents were invariably Strachan's Superstars. If our seven-a-side were training bounce games, with the emphasis on entertainment, the 15-a-side encounters were win-at-all-costs battles, waged from Monday through Friday for a plastic domino trophy (awarded weekly at the end of the Friday dinner hour to the team with the highest cumulative score).

On a typical Friday, when the dinner bell rang, I grabbed my satchel and sprinted the mile home, where I wolfed down a jelly piece and glass of milk, while trying not to choke on regurgitated strawberry jam as the *Watch With Mother* brigade of *Andy Pandy* and *The Woodentops* dangled and jerked their way across our black-and-white TV screen. Neither *Playschool* ('Oh, the square window but who cares?'), *Trumpton* ('Hugh, Pugh, Barney McGrew, Cuthbert, Dibble and GRUBB!') or *Bill and Ben* ('Weeeeed . . .') held my attention for long, and I was soon 'Flobalobbing' goodbye to my mother and dashing back up the hill like Muffin the Mule with his testicles tied together with a set of clackers. I would find out the score and join the deprived diehards from 7A who ate school dinners, as they played down the slope of the boys' playground (for some reason we *always* played down the slope). As time passed more home-lunchers would reappear to join the fray — from both sides — while the playground became more and more congested with little kids (some of whom played parallel games, while others attempted to play against the cross-flow, but needless to say we 11- and 12-year-olds had right of way).

When the bell rang that was the final whistle. Normally we were two or three ahead for the week in what resembled a basketball or cricket scoreline — although different cumulative scores could run in tandem for days, because of arithmetic discrepancies and disputed goals.

In the picking-of-teams pecking order for our extra-curricular seven-a-side games, I was normally chosen before any embarrassment could have me shuffling awkward feet, but I was rarely the boy-of-the-match or the player who enjoyed most possession. In the 7A–7B stramashes I liked to think of myself as a useful attacking full-back, but the glory of goal-scoring I normally left to others – bigger if not better players. One lunch-time, however, I became a fully fledged star, scoring 16 goals and relishing the unaccustomed space in midfield (a strange form of religious mania had infected the boys and girls of our year, and each Monday lunch-time ever-growing numbers of converts attended the bible-study group held in the gymnasium, until both teams were depleted in terms of numbers and ability). With all the ball-hoggers on their knees, I took the opportunity to run up something approaching a record score. Sitting in class, mentally wallowing in my achievement, I decided to commemorate my staggering tally in hard statistical form.

An A4 piece of white cardboard was procured from the art supplies cupboard, and I drew up a bar graph, each class member having a cross-hatched bar to the level of the number of goals scored. Rather than title the graph I left it ambiguously blank, refusing to tell those who asked what it represented. For the rest of the week, I memorised all our goalscorers and updated the graph each day. By Friday morning I was still in the lead, just, but no one had yet tumbled to the graph's significance (not even with my 16–2–0–0 results for the four days that week). Interest was nevertheless intense and I eventually had to divulge what the graph was measuring.

When they knew what it was, it had to be passed around class, so that everyone could stare for minutes at a time at their statistically analysed performance and think: 'I've scored a goal, therefore I exist.' It was a thing of beauty, outlined painstakingly in pencil and coloured in using felt-tip pens. Statistics have a magical fascination for sports fans, and when I got the graph back I was delighted to see that there wasn't so much as a dirty thumb print to spoil its look, and someone usefully suggested that I cover it with tracing paper to protect it, which I did by sticking plasticine dots to the top edge, so that the tracing paper could be lifted back to show an unknowing guinea pig his results in this experiment of empirical analysis.

But during that dinner hour's final competitive game of the week, a funny thing started to happen – the experiment became subject to deliberate fraud and interference on the part of the subjects. Needless to say, everyone stopped being generous with goal-creating passes, individuals became obsessed with scoring all by themselves, and all collective effort by a team of supposedly co-operating individuals ceased. Our tactics were limited to long-range shots from impossible distances and selfish dribbling when surrounded by opposing defenders.

Predictably, 7B – who couldn't understand why our players kept stopping to count on their fingers – came from a dozen or so goals behind and won the Plastic Domino Cup for the first time that term. But none of my class-mates cared – they just queued in front of my desk, bad-temperedly, waiting to submit their tallies. This continued for almost a week, until occasional fraud on the part of the disgusted investigator became a factor, when I started to fiddle my goal tally upwards (at home at night, by just one or two goals a day). When I eventually pulled level with the leading goalscorers, a lynch mob was formed, and I was interrogated with my head down a urinal, with a flushed cistern for every goal I couldn't justify and that no one else could recall. After that, people played with pencils and bits of paper, on which they noted *all* goal-scorers. 7B retained the Plastic Domino Cup three times in a row.

Not Playing for Celtic (Mainstream, 1995)

ALTERNATIVE ULSTER

Kevin Borras

Gillingham striker Darren Freeman, 22, is on loan at Glenavon who play in the town of Lurgan in the heart of County Armagh. Two of the largest bombs ever to go off in Northern Ireland exploded here. 'I must be honest. I expected to see tanks and things all over the place when I got over here,' he says. 'I knew there was peace, but I was surprised it had happened so quickly. It's a lovely place, actually. I'm really surprised by it.'

In many ways, more than 25 years of sectarian violence have left the game in Ulster largely unharmed, except for one important factor. In 1968, when the British Army was sent to the province, attendances at the top Irish League clubs, like Glentoran and Linfield, frequently reached 20,000 – often topping 30,000 when the two clubs played each other. Now, a meeting between the Glens and the Blues is unlikely to generate a third of that.

Don't be misled – Northern Ireland is football-crazy. The problem is, it's crazy about English football now. Glentoran manager Tommy Cassidy, the former Newcastle and Northern Ireland midfielder, blames the Troubles. 'In the late '60s we were getting crowds of 30,000. Now our average gate is perhaps ten times less. Even though there was never any sectarian violence at the games, there often had been in the surrounding areas and people just stopped coming.

'It was at the same time that English football was being shown regularly on TV and parents preferred to have their kids stay in and watch that. Now they've grown up not going to matches and their children have got too much football to watch on the box.'

This is the first season that the Irish League has consisted of two divisions of eight clubs (Premier and First) rather than a single division of 16. Glentoran are one of four Premier Division clubs in Belfast, the others are Crusaders (the current league champions), Linfield and Cliftonville. The city is also home to First Division club Distillery, who sold Martin O'Neill to Nottingham Forest back in the early '70s.

The split was designed to create season-long excitement with the prospect of promotion and relegation for the first time in the league's 106-year history. But it hasn't worked out that way. Clubs now play each other four times, and with six cup competitions, it's quite feasible that Premier Division Portadown, for example, will meet their close neighbours Glenavon up to eight times this season.

Geographically, the Premier Division is a cost-cutter's dream. The four Belfast clubs all lie within four miles of each other; Glenavon and Portadown are six miles apart and only 25 miles south-west of the capital; Bangor and Ards are five miles from each other and 13 miles from Belfast.

In contrast, the First Division clubs are spread out all over the province. Ballymena United, for one, feel more than a little aggrieved. 'The split has had a great effect on us – we don't get the revenue generated by playing Linfield and Glentoran anymore,' grumbles Ballymena boss Alan Fraser. 'It's a real case of the rich getting richer and the poor getting poorer.

'There wasn't enough thought put into the dividing up of the league. It was decided one evening without a great deal of consultation. They knew the smaller clubs like ourselves wouldn't like it much, but the bigger clubs weren't going to complain and that's who they care about.'

Cliftonville secretary John Duffy is in accordance with the Ballymena boss, even though his club is in the Premier League. 'The idea was that the top clubs would do well out of it, but it's certainly not the case with us. The costs have gone up, the players' wage demands have increased but the crowds are down, if anything.'

Cliftonville are still perceived as the only Catholic club in the Irish League, and Linfield as the staunchest upholders of Loyalist doctrine. Yet the playing staff of both clubs are made up of both Catholics and Protestants, and, although the supporters are not quite as integrated as they might be, religion barely plays a part.

This was not always the case, however. Cliftonville have been barred from playing their home games with Linfield at their rather inappropriately named Solitude ground since 1970 because of the potential for sectarian violence. Instead, the game is played at the latter's Windsor Park – home of the national team.

'It's an obvious advantage for us, but we as a club didn't create the situation,' protests Derek Brooks, secretary at Linfield. 'Politically, we're on the road to normality now, although I don't know how far down it we've gone, yet.'

Perhaps the most notable example of the Troubles affecting football was in 1972, when the RUC claimed they could no longer guarantee the safety of spectators or players who came to Derry City.

Derry, who had already been playing their home games in Coleraine for two seasons, 'left' the Irish League and, rather bizarrely, joined the League of Ireland in the Republic. They've been marooned there ever since, the most northerly club in Ireland playing in the South.

'The Irish League needs Derry and Derry needs the Irish League,' argues Glenavon defender Stuart Gauld, who signed from Derry in November 1995. 'When Derry play Cork City, it's a 16-hour round-trip there and back. It's ridiculous to have to take the best part of a day to get to and from a league game, and obviously, it's a strain financially.'

Most of the grounds in the Irish League are – like the quality of football – of English Third Division standard, although some, such as Portadown's Shamrock Park (Shambles Park, as it's known outside the town) would struggle to be accepted.

Portadown's Lewis Singleton makes no attempt to hide the fact. 'Our board was caught between two stools, really: do we build a new ground to attract good players, or do we buy good players and hope the extra revenue they bring will enable us to build a new ground? I'm not sure we did the right thing by doing the latter.'

There are several ways for clubs to raise necessary funds. One is from the affiliated social clubs. League champions Crusaders, who survive on gates of around 1,000, insist that up to 50 per cent of their takings come from their social club. But however much Guinness your fans drink, it's not going to pay for a 1,500-seater, £500,000 cantilever stand.

Another way is for them to sell their best players to English and Scottish clubs, although this is something which is becoming increasingly difficult. Not because Northern Ireland isn't producing the players, but because the best ones, like Keith Gillespie, Jim Magilton and Phil Gray, never even reach the Irish League in the first place. Thanks to improved scouting Gillespie, for example, joined Manchester United at the age of 12.

By general consent, this is the biggest problem afflicting the game in Northern Ireland. It stems from the fact that the Irish clubs aren't allowed to sign schoolboys. Harry Davidson, secretary of Crusaders, explains: 'We don't get to see them in the Irish League at all. Scouts get them straight from school and tempt them with money. It would benefit us if we could keep them at least until they were 16.'

Bangor's Fred Anderson concurs with his Belfast counterpart. 'Even when the good players do stay, there's a tendency for English or Scottish clubs to come here and sign them for £50,000 and then sell them on again for about £250,000, like Celtic did with our Paul Byrne, who's at Southend now.'

Tommy Cassidy cites Glentoran as a case in point. He's seen at first hand boys who have gone 'over the water' and then come back again wanting the earth. 'They play a couple of hundred games in the youth team over there and then they get told they aren't good enough and come back here at 19, either disillusioned with the game or thinking they're stars. They walk in here and I say, "How many first-team games did you play?" "None." "Reserves?" "Two." "Youth team?" "195." And their father wants £10,000 for them to sign for us, plus £300 a week.'

Glenavon's administration and marketing director, George Ruddell, goes one further: 'Young players here, the good ones, see us as stepping stones to the Premiership. We sold Gerard McMahon to Tottenham in 1992 for £120,000. If we'd demanded £500,000 for him and Spurs had said no, then the next good junior that we tried to sign would inevitably say to himself, "I'm not going there – they stopped McMahon going to Spurs."

'In 1988 we produced Gerry Taggart and Neil Lennon in the same season. But they were non-contract players and at the end of their 12-month amateur contracts with us, Manchester City just took them. They didn't pay a penny for them. We wrote to them, but they didn't even reply.

'There are so many English and Scottish scouts over here that the good youngsters get snapped up at a very early age. We're hoping to start up a school of excellence here in Lurgan to try to get the youngsters to stay. We don't mind if they view us as a stepping stone because they want to impress the scouts. Then, when we do sell them on, we can use the money to buy good experienced players from other Irish clubs, or use it to improve our grounds.

'We know that Middlesbrough are trying to sign one of the best young players in Lurgan at the moment. He's only just turned 12. We're trying to persuade him, and his parents, that it would be better for him to play for our junior club first and work his way up. I don't know if we'll succeed, but we have to try.'

Scout Robbie Walker was employed by Tottenham for more than ten years and recommended a steady stream of players. In his decade-long tenure as Tottenham's lone spotter, he gave them Michael Hughes, Jim Magilton, Phil Gray, Keith Rowland, Steve Morrow and Gerard McMahon. The fact that only two have ever been seen in a Spurs shirt is neither here nor there. They've all gone on to play for Northern Ireland. Walker is now employed by West Ham and one of his recommendations, Graeme Philson, has just signed for the Hammers from Coleraine.

'The natural ability of kids over here is very high, but they get homesick,' says Walker. 'They also have to be much better than the local boys. The English clubs would rather sign a boy who lives just round the corner than a lad who comes from Northern Ireland and is away from his family and friends, possibly for the first time.'

Although some Irish League players are professional footballers, the majority have other jobs. Glentoran striker Trevor Smith runs a clothes shop in Belfast. Crusaders keeper (and PFA Player of the Year) Kevin McKeown is an advertising executive. Linfield's Alan Ewing is a plasterer and Glenavon's Northern Ireland international winger, Raymond McCoy, is a progress manager at Lurgan Fibre, a company that manufactures egg boxes.

McCoy had trials with Tottenham, Brighton, St Mirren and Dundee United, but it wasn't to be. He can quite understand how some players turn down the chance of going to England or Scotland when they have the relative security of a job and a well-known face in Northern Ireland.

'The younger lads are attracted by the glamour and it's hard to resist the chance to go over and have a trial with a club in England, but the older ones can't really afford to give up their jobs and just leave. There's not going to be a job waiting for them when they come back disappointed.'

Ards boss Roy Coyle, a former Northern Ireland international, believes there's another side to the argument: 'Because many of the players who are good enough to play in England can't afford to, they lose their ambition. It's ironic that, although most clubs in Northern Ireland are struggling financially, it's the fact that they pay their players too much that is holding the game back.'

You'd think the best way of making money and ploughing it back into your stadium would be by getting into Europe and being lucky in the draw. Try telling that to the clubs who have been drawn against teams from Iceland for three successive years, or a club like Bangor, whose first experience of European football didn't leave them with a particularly good impression. 'We drew Sigma Olomouc of what was then Czechoslovakia, and we didn't get as big a gate here as we thought,' recalls Bangor's Fred Anderson. 'We didn't make a huge amount of money from the away leg and the flights and arrangements cost us more than we made. We claimed back what we lost from UEFA. You get 80,000 Swiss francs for qualifying but you don't get it until June or July of the following year. You have to have a patient bank manager.'

A good draw is one in which the club has almost no chance of winning over the two legs but can make enough money from the away leg and TV rights to stay afloat for the next couple of seasons. Like the one Glenavon were given in this season's UEFA Cup. They beat Hafnarfjordur of Iceland in the qualifying round and were paired with Werder Bremen in the first round proper.

Before the draw was made, the club had the foresight to sign a lucrative deal with a German TV company which offered attractive benefits from live TV coverage of the Irish leg of any tie against a German side. Glenavon lost 7–0 over the two legs but made over £200,000 from it. The extra revenue will be put to good use. For a start, their plush new stand needs paying for.

'It cost £400,000 to build and we only got a £30,000 grant from the Football Trust,' reveals director George Ruddell. 'Unlike English and Scottish clubs, we're not allowed to go to the Trust directly. We have to accept an equal share of the grant that the League receives on the clubs' behalf.'

Michael Mailey, president of the Premier Blues Association, one of three Glenavon supporters' clubs, adds: 'Glenavon has done more to canvas new support than any other club. They go to schools to involve and interest the children in the game. Football in Northern Ireland is becoming more and more like a business. You have to go out and find customers. If you don't, you'll go to the wall.'

Many clubs look enviously at Linfield, the most successful team in the Irish League's history, with 42 championships behind them (Glentoran are a distant second with 19). Much of the envy, however, is caused by the ground that the club call home. Derek Brooks opens the case for the defence.

'It's our ground. The national team have played here since the 1930s and they're contracted to play here until 2086, so it's a bit premature for people to start planning a new national stadium.

'We attract a certain amount of jealousy because, although it's our ground, the IFA pay for improvements, and we get a cut of the gate receipts for internationals and merchandising. They're resentful of that, as you can imagine, but what they don't seem to remember is that we get a lesser grant for our own improvements and also we have to contribute to improvements that we wouldn't need to comply with ourselves for international regulations.'

It's impossible to judge whether the national team's imminent resurgence will have any effect on the club game but for Richard Whittle, a Linfield fan living and working in Rome, a strong Northern Ireland side can only be good for the game in general.

'We're very proud people, and after all that's gone on in the last 25 years, it would mean so much if the national team could qualify for tournaments again. But we have to do it with Irish players. If success was achieved by using Scots and Englishmen, like the Republic have done, it wouldn't mean anywhere near as much.'

The resignation of Jack Charlton and the possibility that the Republic's cycle of success is coming to an end has further boosted the North's voracious appetite for football. The two Irelands finished on the same number of points in their European Championship qualifying group. Popular opinion here suggests that the Republic team have grown old together and that the North has unearthed a crop of good youngsters for the first time since 1982.

'You need four or five quality players to be a successful international side, and it looks like we might have them now,' says Bangor's Fred Anderson. 'In the last ten years, we've only had two or three at the same time. When the last crop of good players went, they all went more or less together – Pat Jennings, Martin O'Neill, Gerry Armstrong, Sammy

53

McIlroy. It's only now that we are beginning to get back on a par with the Republic.'

The future looks brighter for Northern Irish football. As long as it rests in the hands of people like former international and QPR and Newcastle winger Ian Stewart, it can only get brighter still.

Stewart is currently Sports Development Officer at the Irish Football Association and in charge of the evolution of Mini-Football, part of the Making Belfast Work scheme. The aim is to get Mini-Football introduced into the school curriculum. Stewart, famed in Northern Ireland for his winner against West Germany in Hamburg in 1983, explains.

'It's not just football matches, but football-based games. It's primarily fun for the kids, but it's teaching them co-ordination, how to run properly, participation and team skills. We're 20 years behind here, but with this type of programme we're hoping to catch up years at a time. What we want to produce is enthusiastic kids. We've missed a generation and a half.'

Despite what people tell you, it's obvious that Northern Ireland's socio-political history has damaged its football but the game has still provided Ulster with some of its greatest sporting moments, produced several national heroes and given the world arguably its greatest-ever player. If the game can reap the dividends that the last 18 months of peace have brought, things, as they say, can only get better.

Goal, March 1996

TO A FAR, FOREIGN LAND

Jim Gardiner

The UEFA Cup draw is imminent. 'I'm up to my eyes at work for most of September,' says I, 'so if we're away second leg and it isn't one of those new Russian republics I should be okay to go.' I might have known; away first, in a place called North Ossetia that isn't even on my atlas. To make matters worse, the first leg is less than two weeks away and a few phone calls make it clear that arranging our own trip is a non-starter.

Having travelled to numerous European games with the club, I rang the commercial department. The club official Jim Kennefick only planned to travel out to Russia the following weekend to check out hotels and so on. Clearly this wouldn't be a cheap trip, so cost would be the chief factor on whether I could go or not (creative scheduling at work gave me the Monday and Tuesday off). As time wore on, the possibility of any Liverpool fans going looked remote. At the QPR game leaflets were passed round about an organised trip. It seemed to be officially sanctioned but was leaving from London and meant two nights in Moscow, one in Vladikavkaz and (because of the early Monday morning departure) meant a night in London too. And then there was the money – £660 *before* visa and ticket were added. Train to London, hotel, spends – the figure was zooming towards £900.

It was beginning to look like an armchair/BBC2 job. Town Travel wanted you to book by that Saturday morning, so obviously that and the cost put paid to that. The talk at the Reserves that day (2 September) was that the club itself had failed to secure a charter flight as no UK carrier would risk an aircraft in an area the Foreign Office classed as a war zone. A week before the game, it looked like LFC would have to travel by scheduled flights via Moscow. The armchair looked a certainty, but Aeroflot came to the rescue at the eleventh hour. Someone from Anfield rang to say I could travel with the club party as long as I could get down there the same afternoon with the necessary documents for a visa – oh, and the small matter of £525.

After all that, I had time to start worrying about the flight. Aeroflot? Anyone who saw that documentary a few months back would understand why I was worried. I'm not a good flyer at the best of times, but vodka-swilling pilots and planes in need of repair? These fears weren't eased at all when the travel documentation came through from the Foreign Office, along with the guidelines about Russian transport. Be wary of Aeroflot, they said. Many of the aircraft have not had proper maintenance for five years. Thanks – just what I needed to hear. I conquered my fears enough to get to Speke at 08.15 for a scheduled 09.30 take-off. A couple of large vodka and tonics steadied the nerves, and after half an hour's delay (with no explanation) it was onto the Russian Tipolev 154 aircraft. Players and officials first, then TV press and radio, then last (but certainly not least) the 43 supporters making the trip. My fears were confirmed – the plane was nowhere near the standards you normally get on club trips abroad. Not all the seats had safety belts and some of the overhead luggage compartments wouldn't close. Just to add to the unease, we took off without the usual safety lectures from the cabin crew. No complaints about the service, though; a continental breakfast was followed by a good lunch later on and there was no shortage of the old liquid refreshment – to steady my nerves, you understand.

About five hours after leaving Speke we landed – bumpily – at Beslan airport, which serves Vladikavkaz, capital of the autonomous republic of North Ossetia. As we taxied to a halt, there was the astonishing sight of several stray dogs chasing after (and barking at) the plane. As we disembarked we got our first proper look at the plane itself. Its practically bald tyres and patched-up bodywork would not have been too inspiring a sight in Speke. We knew all the stories about being so close to war-torn Chechnya, but the only real evidence of significant military activity was a number of giant helicopter gunships. Good news at the airport, as our ranks are swelled to the grand total of 45. Two additional recruits flew in from Moscow that morning: one young chap, originally from Bootle, who was serving in the Diplomatic Service in Moscow, and my old mate Peter O'Brien. Originally from the Wirral, now resident in Helsinki, he came alone and set out from Finland on Saturday evening; a 17-hour train journey to Moscow, an overnight stay, a 30-mile taxi ride to the airport and a four-hour flight to Vladikavkaz. (I haven't heard from him yet, but I hope he made it back to Helsinki all right.)

Visa formalities concluded, we passed through the spartan airport building and onto the coaches for a 15-mile ride into the city. We were allocated our own interpreter/guide, a delightful young lady who in turn introduced us to 'your KGB representative to ensure your security'. Oh . . .

hello. He spoke no English but was clearly carrying a pistol in a shoulder holster under his jacket. We were given a police escort into the city, and at every junction other policemen held up the local traffic to allow us through. Initial impressions were of a very poor city but the waves and other signals from the locals as we passed seemed to indicate we were welcome. A correct impression, I'm delighted to say.

Now then, what about a bit of culture, history and geography? No? Well, tough, here's the potted version. North Ossetia is in the deep south of Russia, about 1,000 miles away from Moscow. The capital Vladikavkaz is situated in the valley of the Terek river, at the foot of the Central Caucasian mountain range. The correct name of the city is Ordzhonikidze, a fortress town from way back (1784) which was renamed after a Russian statesman in 1931. The fiercely independent people are reverting to the old name in the wake of the Soviet Union's break-up. The population are mainly Christian, with a significant Sunnie Muslim representation, but there is no evidence of any ethnic or religious unrest you might find in other areas.

The 40-minute coach ride gave our Embassy man from Bootle the chance to give us the lowdown. He'd spoken to the local police and army commanders, assuring us of a good welcome from the people if we wanted to venture out of our hotel into the city centre. We were advised not to go on our own, though. The Hotel Vladikavkaz was a bit of a concrete monstrosity but the rooms, while basic, were relatively clean and comfortable. The bathrooms did leave a bit to be desired, and the Russians were very security-conscious; armed guards on hotel entrances and every floor occupied by the Liverpool party. After checking in, I watched a Russian TV crew interview one or two players, and then the chef who'd travelled from Liverpool to look after their food. For some reason, it took longer to interview the chef than the players! Yours truly was asked, and though shy by nature I consented to become a Russian TV star.

A long flight and two hours' time difference meant it was now early evening. The players went off for a spot of training, as we freshened up and headed for the city centre. The main street ran through the heart of the city, the centre about 500 yards away from the hotel. There were few people about; those that were gave us curious glances or shouted 'Spartak' or 'Liverpool'. Even walking about, there was none of the menace or fear I'd experienced in Moscow in 1992. The city centre wasn't much, mainly statues and monuments to the Communist era, a few shops (all closed). There seemed to be no pubs or bars, but we managed to find a small hotel. The bar there served us cans of German Lowenbrau lager which tasted all right until we noticed the sell-by date on the cans – 1993!

Time for a sharp exit. It looked like we would have to settle for a night in the hotel bar, but on the way back we saw some lights. It looked like a restaurant; we ventured in, and although there were no other customers it seemed to be a club-cum-restaurant, with a small dance floor. Nine of us sat down and it was waitress service. Again, it was canned beer, but this time it was Turkish lager. Chilled, in large cans – and well within its sell-by date. No money changed hands, and through sign language it was established we would pay on leaving. Now that is usually a danger signal – the words 'potential rip-off' spring to mind – but we thought, what with the cost of living, even inflated nightclub prices wouldn't hit us too hard in the pocket.

A few more cans of excellent Turkish lager later (the mystery of Venison, Marsh and Saunders' moves revealed?), we decided we'd had enough of the background music – time to exercise our tonsils with a few numbers from the LFC song book. The staff in the club were delighted with our efforts and turned off the music so as not to interfere with the singing. Gradually, other groups of Liverpool fans managed to find the club, drawn by the noise or by a special signal that only Reds can hear. The choir ended up 30-strong. The locals responded by giving us an exhibition of Russian dancing and naturally we felt obliged to join in. It turned into a great evening, the kind that travelling in Europe is all about, but eventually it was time to go back to the hotel. We'd seen a couple of lads querying their bill, but ours looked very reasonable (70p for a large can) so we paid up and left a generous tip. It was back to the hotel, where the other lads had stayed all night and though the bar closed shortly after we got back, just after midnight, the restaurant stayed open.

We were having a quiet beer when we spotted a couple of Russians from the club accompanied by another chap and one of the Merseyside police who'd travelled with the official party. It turned out that the 'other chap' was a colonel in the KGB, in overall charge of the Liverpool party's security. It turned out our party of nine had been undercharged in the club, and another group who had come in later (and drank less) got landed with our bill. Needless to say, they refused to pay for the club's mistake, which seemed to be a genuine one. We immediately offered to make up the difference – 70p a can had seemed too good to be true. Obviously, one man from the club thought he was on a good number because the figure went way above the proper amount. He was told where to go in no uncertain fashion. A discussion began between the Russian KGB and Merseyside's finest and the club owner – we didn't dispute the number of beers, but the cost was way over the top. They all thought we were at it, but I played a trump card; the receipt had been written on the back of a menu. I searched through my pockets, found it and sure enough the beer was about half what the owner was demanding. Our story was accepted without query, and far from paying the difference which we were glad to do, the Colonel sent the two men on their way with a few US dollars out of his own pocket. The new KGB, the new Russia!

After another good singing session (including our glorious chairman, no less) most people headed for bed around 1.30. A few hardy souls headed for the hotel casino. Well, I say 'casino' – it was one blackjack table with an old, broken roulette table in the corner. One of the Liverpool supporters, tired and emotional, stumbled and knocked over the remains of the roulette table. Nothing was said, the pieces were picked up and put back. A Moscow-based journalist was staying in the hotel (not a football writer) and he was overheard on the phone next morning trying to send a story back to England, to the effect that drunken Liverpool fans had destroyed a casino! To their credit, the football writers on the trip put their papers back home straight on the 'story' and it never saw the light of day as far as I am aware.

For the day of the game, our hosts had laid on a coach trip to the mountains for those who fancied it, but I settled for a long lay in bed before going to the stadium for a look around and souvenir hunt. It turned out to be a good decision; the sight-seeing coach broke down in the mountains, although it was towed back in plenty of time for the match. A few lads fancied a visit to the stadium and again the Russians were perfect hosts, providing us with a coach and a KGB escort. A good look round the stadium was followed by picking up a couple of match posters, club badges and match programmes. There was even time for a cold beer in the 'President's Bar' before grabbing a lift back to the hotel on the press coach. A wash, a bite to eat (everyone came prepared with biscuits, chocolate and the like rather than risk the local food), we packed and set off to the stadium again around 6.30.

Our coach drove straight up to the main stadium entrance and we were escorted in alongside the players. Liverpool fans were allocated the 'Presidential Box', no less, and as we were located just behind the TV area we were able to make ourselves heard with singing and chanting throughout the 90 minutes. After a shaky start I thought Liverpool were magnificent and two spectacular strikes secured a superb win. The tactics were right and the players were up for it – what a night to remember. The second leg showed just how vital that victory was.

It was straight back to the airport after the match. With the celebratory mood, the aircraft didn't seem so worrying now. A few drinks were consumed on the way back, but the majority just slept. A minor panic broke out when the cork from a cheap bottle of Georgian champagne made a loud bang – many thought that the plane was under attack. By 3 a.m. on Wednesday morning we were back in Speke. I was in West Derby by half-past.

I suppose I should address the Fowler-Ruddock incident. I didn't see the 'punch' thrown, but did notice a trail of blood through the arrival gate. I only learned the details a few days later. Sunday's news-papers exaggerated as usual; Robbie sat at the back of the plane and was not the worse for drink – a couple of beers at most. It appears to have been a silly prank that backfired and is probably all forgotten now, but if you want to play pranks on people it helps if you can take a joke yourself. Doesn't it, Mr Ruddock?

There were a number of memorable things about the trip. The players took all the difficulties in their stride and came up with a brilliant display. Roy Evans and his staff had the arrangements down to a tee – nothing got in the way of achieving the right result. The fans played their part and made an impression on the Russians with their flags and songs. I'd like to think we helped the players achieve the win. Last but not least was the warmth of the welcome from our hosts. They couldn't provide much in the way of luxuries but simply made our stay as enjoyable, comfortable and secure as possible. North Ossetia doesn't get much help from the powers-that-be, but its fiercely independent people lay out a warm welcome for visitors with the flagship of their independence being its love of the football team. Now where else does that sound like?

Through the Wind and Rain, October 1995

THE CLUB MASCOT

Ivor Baddiel

There can surely be no greater joy than leading your team out on to the field of play. To let the tension and adrenalin that had been building up as you waited in the tunnel burst forth when you charge out on to the pitch. The nerves are still going during the pre-match kick-about, but once the game gets under way your stomach settles and you calm down.

Undoubtedly, the orange juice you've just been given and the fact that you're now sitting in the stands help restore you to your normal state.

For those of you who are currently wondering if my senses upped and left some time ago, I am not talking about the captain, but the team mascot. Yes, it's those snotty-nosed kids who run out on to the pitch with the teams and get in the way while the pros warm up. They can barely kick the ball and you dread to think what would happen if Neil Ruddock went at them with studs showing and teeth gritted.

But let's be honest about this. There isn't a big, burly grown-up out there who doesn't experience the slightest pang of jealousy when little Johnny gets to knock the ball about with Ruud Gullit, Matt Le Tissier, Stan Collymore and the like. Most of us would have to be confined to a wheelchair in the latter stages of some awful, debilitating disease before we finally, grudgingly, gave up on the hope of being spotted and given the chance to show the footballing public what it's been missing all these years.

The sight of a child out there on the stage, nearer to glory than most of us have ever come, brings Gascoigne-esque tears to our eyes, as we think about what might have been.

However, there's glory and there's glory. If you happen to be a Brentford fan, you're unlikely to be playing ball with any of the distinguished names above, but for five (yes, five!) lucky children, the game against York City on 20 January was their big moment.

For one of the five, eight-year-old Ben Gibson, the day started at a local primary school where, together with some 50 of his mates, Brentford's Community Programme employment trainees put them through their paces. These must be the roots that everybody insists we must get back to.

After two hours of energetic activity it is all an adult can do to stagger into the shower and stand still while steaming hot water cascades down his or her back. Kids are slightly different. It is hard to believe that most of us were kids once (Peter Beardsley and Iain Dowie are the exceptions), each with enough energy to light up more than half of London; but we were.

This lot could probably solve the world's energy crisis on their own. As they come inside for lunch, courtesy of Pizza Hut, I am reminded of the Poll Tax riots. As some foolish, thoughtless idiot shouts: 'Anyone for seconds?' a herd of deranged elephants on the rampage enters my mind. I'd forgotten the old maxim. Never work with kids, animals or Brian Clough. The footy games, lunch and all that goes on at Griffin Park, are most ably organised and overseen by Brentford's Football in the Community Officer Lee Doyle and his team of hard-working volunteers.

'It's always really nice to see how children react in front of crowds,' says Lee. 'My two six-year-old cousins were mascots and they ran out and waved to all the crowd, and jumped up and down and just lost it, really. We try to look after them for the whole day so they'll feel relaxed and avoid too many nerves.'

With lunch still gurgling away inside him, Ben is whisked off to Griffin Park and into the Football in the Community offices, where he meets his fellow mascots. Tammy, Harry, Bobbie and Lauren – all flanked by proud, beaming parents – are, at this stage, showing little sign of anxiety. Harry's calm exterior, however, belies some inner tension. When asked if he would like to be a professional footballer, he confidently answers in the affirmative. When asked what position he would like to play he replies: 'Manchester United.'

Next, it's off to the dressing-room to meet the players. I'm almost as excited as the kids and curse the fact that I left my autograph book at home. A quick check to make sure there are no unpleasant tackles to be seen and we're in and mingling with the mighty Brentford. Incredibly, the children are still managing to contain themselves, as they file round getting their programmes signed by one and all. Don't the professionals find it all a bit annoying?

'No, it's good. It gets them involved. They get to know what goes on on the inside, and it gives them a nice day out,' says Brentford's rising star Robert Taylor. 'It's no bother having them out on the pitch. If they want to have a kick-about with us, they're quite welcome to. We don't shove them out of the way. You find time to fit them in while you're warming up. I was a mascot for Norwich against Ipswich many years ago, when I was seven or eight years old. It was good. I went in and met everybody and shook their hands. I couldn't really take it all in till a few days later.' Sounds like one of the greatest, most memorable days of Robert's life.

'No, it wasn't really 'cos Norwich lost that day so I wasn't very happy.' Suddenly there's a commotion in the dressing-room as a Mr David Webb puts in an appearance. His attitude to the kids is suitably managerial. 'As long as they don't cause any problems, they're okay. I think it's a nice thing for the supporters to look at. In my day they didn't used to have mascots.'

As we head back to the office I can't help wondering what the children said to their heroes. Tammy, Bobbie and Lauren report that they said nothing. Ben forgot to tell Robert Taylor that he was his favourite player, but dear, dear Harry comes up trumps. 'I sort of said: "Good luck. Hope you get a broken leg." I just wanted to say it. I was joking.' Now, there's a lad destined to go far.

Still, unbelievably, managing to take it all in their stride, the children are now in the hands of the mascot looker-afterer Malcolm Hobday. It's his job to keep things running smoothly and sort out any problems. 'I had a couple of little 'uns crying once because they didn't want to do it, so I bribed them with a packet of sweets and that relaxed them. They usually go out for half-an-hour at ten past two and kick around with the players, and that generally puts them at ease for when they have to run out at five to three.'

On the dot of ten past two the by now famous five are out on the hallowed turf. The players wander out in dribs and drabs and reassure themselves of their ability by dribbling past five children and thumping the ball into an empty net. At one point, it looks as though one of the Brentford lads is chasing after young Harry screaming: 'Come here, you little . . .' but it's probably just a trick of the light.

The players roll back in at quarter to three to hear Webby's pearls of wisdom and Malcolm gathers the children together in the tunnel. Their instructions are to run out with the team and head to the centre circle for the photos.

As the allotted time fast approaches, a huddle of parents, aunts, uncles, a journalist and a photographer eagerly await the children's entrance. Sure enough, at five to three they appear and troop over to Brentford's penalty area, where they stand looking cold and bemused, doing nothing. Eventually, Malcolm's hollers get through the biting wind and rain (sadly not the roars of the crowd) and Harry, realising where they should be, leads the others to the middle. Malc rests easy.

After the photos the children once again cause angst as they march off to the wrong place, but eventually they arrive where they're meant to be and are led off to the relative warmth of the stand. They can now enjoy the feast of football going on before them, secure in the knowledge that, for them, the job is over.

It's been a long, anxious and very tiring day, but that's enough about me.

How was it for the real stars of the show?

'Good,' says Tammy.

'Fun,' says Ben.

'Good,' says Bobbie.

'Okay,' says Lauren.

'Overall, I felt we all performed well. I wasn't too happy about there being girls there to begin with, but they were good. I think the crowd really got behind us during the photograph and, even though there was a slight hiccup when we came off the pitch at the wrong place, at the end of the day it was an experience I know I'll never forget,' says Harry (okay, so what he really said was: 'Great,' but that's definitely what he wanted to say).

Total Football, April 1996

RISING DUMPS

Dave Cottrell

The landlord was a real-life Rigsby, the kind of bloke who wouldn't give you the sleeves off his vest. He accused the kid of trashing a hi-fi unit he hadn't even touched and claimed all sorts of household breakages against the deposit.

Trashing the hi-fi unit? Fat chance. So much as stare at the 'On' button and you had the biggest OAP demo outside your door since the Tories went to town on heating allowances.

After three months, the kid was at his wits' end. This was meant to be a big club, a North London giant. So why had they moved him into a grotty block of flats populated by wrinklies and run by a miser? It was time to abscond.

'All the other residents were old and nosey,' he whined. 'They complained if we had the telly on after 10 p.m. and even made us take off our shoes when we walked about. Playing music? A complete non-starter. We were supposed to be there for six months but we couldn't get out quick enough. Even then, they were peering through their curtains as we left.'

No one knows for sure what happened to the landlord. But the kid? He went on to play for England. His name was Darren Anderton.

Surprised? You shouldn't be. The Great God of Substandard Accommodation isn't fussy about his victims. Future international superstars and dead-losses destined to have their contracts terminated are all the same to him. In fact, it's a wonder he didn't also throw in a pet in this instance. All the best nightmare digs stories have a pet, whether it's a feline fairground for fleas, a canine conducting its own moonlit barkathon or just something shabby that shuffles across the floor, answers to 'Sultan' and looks like the Benetton ad they were unable to show.

Imagine you're a teenage footballer away from home for the first time. You've heard fabulous stories about digs, not least from that mate of a mate who knew a lad whose club fixed him up with an eccentric millionaire and his string of glamorous lady-friends in a stately home the size of Ipswich.

You, on the other hand, have been bundled into a stone-clad health-hazard with a bedroom colour-scheme called 'Cesspit Explosion' in the arse-end of town – 'town' being a loose definition for what amounts to a cemetery with traffic lights. A fortnight later, your ambition changes from breaking into the first team to spending the next 12 months sidestepping that sticky patch on the bathroom mat.

Welcome to the formative years of your footballing career.

Your first letter home reads something like this: 'Dear Mam and Dad. Thanks for the pear halves. Just thought I'd drop you a line to say how I'm keeping. Everything leaks in this house – the roof, the radiator, the rottweiler. I saw a rat in the kitchen the other day. I could've sworn it was waving a white flag. Yesterday I scored an own-goal and the youth coach called me a useless git. Is that carpet-fitter's job still going in Ottle?'

If you're lucky, a hundred senior appearances and a £750,000 transfer later you'll look back and laugh. But every so often, you'll wake up screaming in the middle of the night – for a chilling moment there, you thought you could feel Sultan's tart breath on your face.

Digs, so they say, are character-building. They made Peter Beardsley what he is today – twinkle-toed and toothless. Legend has it, the Newcastle striker parted company with his front teeth not on the pitch but in his bedroom in Carlisle, where he'd sit for hours wading through whole shipments of sweets from his mum.

Digs taught David Platt 'to appreciate things'. In the bad old days at Crewe, he and John Pemberton (now at Leeds) were so skint they mixed tins of beans and peas together for something to eat. Former team-mate David Pullar recalls how they'd only invite people round to their terraced house, which looked like it was under constant shellfire, if they brought plenty of 50p pieces for the meter: 'It all seemed to go on the TV and electric fire. Many a time, one of the lads would come into training the next day and ask how a programme had ended – because Platty's meter had run out before it'd finished.'

Digs, bless 'em, gave us that freak of nature, Alan Shearer. He was 16 and still, presumably, human when he swapped North-East for South Coast and began his apprenticeship at Southampton. Forced to grow up alone and unloved, he cultivated the abnormally mature persona that makes Bert Millichip look giddy in comparison.

Digs even moulded Captain Marvel, with a little help from West Midlands Travel. When Middlesbrough manager Bryan Robson kicked off his playing career with West Bromwich Albion, he stayed in positively palatial, mutant-free accommodation. But the man who now commutes by private plane to a permanently reserved hotel room had to endure a sprint relay between bus stops on the way to training every morning to make ends meet. Now we know where he got that 'marvellous engine' from.

'It might only have been pennies saved by running between stops,' he says, 'but we only got £5 a week so every little bit helped. I must admit, though, I had good digs. There's many a player who isn't so fortunate. Mine were in a decent area of the town and it was a lovely house – a nice little semi-detached with gardens at the front and back. The landlord and landlady looked after me really well.

'But I'd just left home and I missed my family. I wasn't a regular in the youth team at the time, and when you're in for extra training and you're not getting a game, you get homesick.'

Robbo's right – he was lucky. When it comes to digs, Albion are the business. They pride themselves on their reputation as a family club and the time they devote to their youngsters – something the current youth development officer, Richard O'Kelly, is keen to maintain.

One unfortunate incident sticks in O'Kelly's mind: when he discovered that the form of two lads had dipped because they were trapped in digs with a 70-year-old man, eight cats and a nose-wrinkling smell. Usually, though, the club gets it right. 'If there are problems with the lads playing or in training, it can often be traced back to the digs,' he says. 'You can tell their minds are elsewhere. The trick is to keep on top of things, to have a word with the landlady every so often and a chat with the lad's parents. You're looking for a home-from-home environment, a place where they'll be treated like one of the family. They stay for two years – the length of their YTS contract – but we'll change their digs if they're unhappy.'

Each club had its own tried and (supposedly) trusted formula. Grimsby, for instance, go for guest-houses; Coventry run a hostel close to their training ground; Wimbledon's young are abandoned in a nearby forest and brought up by wolves.

Albion stick with local families. Depending on their background, West Brom's new arrivals are allocated 'five-day digs' or full-time accommodation. Recruits from, say, the Shrewsbury area or South Wales are paired off and allowed to go home at weekends – 'Whereas we've got one lad from North Wales and another from the North East who stay together for seven days because it's too far to go home,' says O'Kelly. From his experience, two's company. Any more and 'it tends to get a bit unruly'.

John Scales will vouch for that. At Bristol Rovers, he and team-mate Phil Purnell were reluctant party hosts every weekend. The Liverpool centre-half recalls: 'On Friday nights before a game, Kenny Hibbitt, Nicky Tanner and the rest of the Rovers lads would pile round and either me or

Phil would have to cook dinner for everyone. Usually me. Let's just say *Masterchef* had nothing to worry about.'

Deeper within the Scales psyche lurks the hound from hell – a spaniel which shredded his slippers when he was 19 and had just moved from Leeds to the West Country. 'It yapped non-stop and it used to moult everywhere. I'd go for a bath, climb out and within a few steps my feet would be matted with dog hairs.'

It gets weirder. The house was run by 'a lovely woman' who just happened to be the mother of Larry Lloyd, the former Nottingham Forest defender. She'd feed the beast – the dog, not Larry – bars upon bars of Kit Kats while Scales looked on enviously and yearned for the day when he'd live in a luxury flat in Liverpool, gorge himself senseless on chocolate and hire his own spaniel hit-squad if the mood took him.

'Larry came from a rather large family. He had nine brothers and four sisters and they'd all come round on Sunday afternoons to keep us company. You remember how big Larry was? Then you can imagine it was a bit of a squeeze.'

Luxury, pal. Descend further into digs hell and you'll see Mark Stein's old bedsit in Stoke – a place so scary he had to get home before darkness fell. Milkmen, postmen and journalists crossed themselves when they ventured through the gates. Stein just had time after training to blow his wages on garlic and holy water before racing against sundown to get home.

Relief, as much as anything, accompanied Stein's move to Chelsea. But even his current club have had their fair share of horror stories. Gwyn Williams, the youth development officer at Stamford Bridge, has seen it all. He recalls one time a boy came to him with a particularly unusual problem. 'He insisted that he was being locked in his room at night by his landlord. I refused to believe him so he challenged me to come round and see for myself. It was only early evening when I knocked on the door. Sure enough, when I asked to see the boy, the landlord had to unlock him from his room. Obviously, it wasn't long before we moved him on somewhere else.'

Such cases are rare but it's Williams' job to ensure it doesn't happen again. He's overseen Chelsea's production line of young talent for 16 years – nurturing the likes of Graeme Le Saux, Craig Burley and Billy Dodds – and can reel off stories all day. 'I can't stress enough how vital it is for a boy who has come to us from a long distance away to be fixed up with good digs,' he says. 'We have to be very careful and keep a close eye on his situation and his happiness because if it goes wrong, we could end up losing him.'

He remembers fixing up Keith Dublin and Phil Priest with a landlord who was a chef at a nearby detention centre. On Sundays, when his wife wanted a break from looking after them, Dublin and Priest would go down to the centre and have lunch with the inmates – 'A great eye-opener for them and an important part of their growing-up.'

And yes, that old story was true – one player really did end up in a millionaire's pad. The lucky lad was David Lee, dispatched with his belongings to live in Dallas-like luxury in a mansion backing on to a golf club. 'I took a call from this guy who said he was a Chelsea fan and was offering to put up one of our youngsters,' reveals Williams. 'When I went round there, I couldn't believe what I saw. Attached to this great mansion were two- and three-bedroomed houses and that's where David lived. No wonder he didn't want to move out.'

He did, eventually and reluctantly, to his own digs. But he still keeps in touch and regularly plays golf with his sugar daddy, one of whose three sons is an apprentice at Brentford. 'It was a fabulous place to stay,' says Lee. 'Just about everything you could think of, they had. An indoor swimming-pool, a snooker table, tennis courts, a gymnasium, the list goes on. 'The great thing was that you were treated as part of the family, so I had full use of all those facilities. It was certainly quite a contrast to my previous digs – a two-bedroomed house with only one television. There, you had to watch whatever the landlord wanted to see. 'The other lads were quite jealous when they came around and saw where I was living. I could even bring them around for parties and stuff like that. I really did have a free hand there.'

So dream on, all you famished trainees currently scraping mushrooms off the back of the bog door. Next time, it could be you. For now, get that trouser-leg rolled up. Sultan wants to play.

Goal, October 1995

PLAYERS' WIVES

Shelley Webb

What is Alex Pursey, 23, a woman who enjoys lacrosse, who swam for Surrey, holds eight GCSEs and a business-studies qualification and – most significantly of all – was a late starter in the nightclubbing stakes, doing married to George Best, the hard-drinking, hard-living, nightclubbing football legend? Where are her scuffed white stilettos, the faintly orange tan, the big hair? Where is the inane grin? *Lacrosse?* Footballers' wives are not even supposed to be able to spell lacrosse. Or, if we can, we think it's some sort of casserole dish. In fact, we aren't supposed to do anything much, really. According to legend, we know the quickest way to the shops, are expert at what colour tights to wear with white shoes, know just how much Malibu we can drink without getting hiccups and, er, that's about it.

The stereotype runs deep. A recent episode of the ITV comedy *Moving Story*, for instance, featured a footballer's wife of quite epic frivolity – her interests included curtains and chatting up removal men. But things are changing. Alex, who married Best in a blaze of publicity, is only one of a whole team of new-look football wives – with not a highlight or white shoe in sight.

The shift is best exemplified by the marital histories of Best and his fellow football legend Graeme Souness, the former Liverpool manager. Best's former lady friends were all good-looking, bosomy and big-haired. (Indeed, the first Mrs Best, Angie, became an icon of bosomy, big-haired good looks.) The first Mrs Souness, Danielle, was built along the same – wholly enviable – lines. And both Danielle and Angie shared an almost fetishistic passion for grandiose external adornment. You could always tell a player's wife: lots of jewellery, more make-up and no conversation.

But, like the new Mrs Best, Karen Levy, the new Mrs Souness, is a different proposition altogether. She attracted much attention when she appeared decorously, day in and day out, on Graeme's arm during his court battle with Danielle earlier this year.

Yes, she is a blonde. Yes, she is beautiful. But what marked her out above all was a sober, sophisticated, expensively suited elegance not hitherto associated with soccer wifedom. Let's not beat about the bush: Karen Levy, a former Bond girl, exudes class from every pore. The perfectly glossed lips spoke volumes about the care which she had taken for her appearance in court. Danielle Souness suffered immensely in comparison.

The heyday of the old-style football wife managed to span three decades: the 1960s, 1970s and early 1980s. Footballers, as a rule, met their wives in nightclubs and had fairly low expectations – a pretty face and a dab hand with the Mr Sheen for polishing the FA Cup final medals. That and, of course, a fondness for (a) shopping, and (b) telling the tabloids about her three-in-a-bed sex romps with the manager.

But times change. The turning point was the 1990 World Cup in Italy, when football became intellectually respectable, a process helped along by *Fever Pitch*, Nick Hornby's book about his passion for Arsenal. Suddenly, it was acceptable for intelligent women to be seen reading books about football. Even *Cosmopolitan* is writing about the game: a survey in the current issue shows that women fans are even more dedicated than male ones. Footballers and their wives suddenly found themselves having to reflect this new-found kudos – and not only in the looks department.

Claire, wife of England international Paul Ince, was heavily criticised by the Italian press during her husband's recent transfer from Manchester United to Inter. It was Claire, they wrote, who 'wore the trousers' in the Ince household. The Italians were furious that she had appeared to reject sniffily a series of lakeside homes. This was not, in fact, true, but certainly Paul would never have moved to Italy without fully consulting her. Footballers' wives – hitherto considered meek appendages – could roar.

Isabelle Cantona is another who stays out of the limelight (Eric, of course, generates enough publicity for two). She has her own career as a language teacher, and her own views on life, which she has no hesitation in airing forcefully. She was, reportedly, behind Eric's recent request to leave Manchester United.

One of the best examples of the new breed is Karren Brady, married to Stoke City's Paul Peschisolido. They met at Birmingham City, where he was a player and she was – and is – managing director. She has not only been responsible – with owner David Sullivan and manager Barry Fry – for restoring the fortunes of the club, but has her own cable television show, *The Brady Bunch*. She is certainly a career girl, yet is not above posing in a pair of silky football shorts.

Old habits die hard, however, and footballers do still occasionally marry models. But even the models have changed. Ruth Gordon, the 27-year-old fiancée of Liverpool defender John Scales, did a stint as a Page 3 girl –

football's equivalent of the casting couch – but her interests include painting, architecture and the novels of F. Scott Fitzgerald.

'It's the archetypal stereotype,' she says. 'Footballer and Page 3 girl. So when somebody asks me the inevitable questions [Why do you take your clothes off? Did you meet in Stringfellows?], I inevitably reply, "I can't possibly answer that – you can't expect me to have brains as well."'

The most marked change in the football wife – and the most overdue – has been her dress sense. Gone are bottom-skimming dresses and the tight sparkly tops that were more boob than tube. We now opt for a more understated, classic designer look, of the sort that suits Rachel Platt, wife of the England captain, so well.

Perhaps continental chic has something to do with it. As more players are tempted by Europe, or play here alongside European players, maybe some of the understated style at which European women excel is rubbing off.

Samantha Jane, the new bride of the Blackburn Rovers striker Chris Sutton, carries off the designer look well – as do some of the wives who have been oases of style all along: Michelle Lineker, Leslie Ash (married to Ipswich striker Lee Chapman) and Jill Hughes, wife of Chelsea's Mark.

The change in style may well reflect a change in the footballers themselves, too. As players grow more wealthy and adapt to increasing media demands, they are becoming more sophisticated and more discerning. Suzy Barnes, wife of John, the Liverpool and England midfielder, says: 'Many wives have always been stylish – they have had to be. A footballer earning large sums of money has always been seen as a good catch.' It is not an easy life. 'You are surrounded by fans, pictures are being taken of you and you are very much on view,' says Suzy. 'When it first happened, it terrified me and I still can't get used to being recognised. But now I get fan mail telling me how beautiful my children are or how much they like an outfit I wore.'

What about me? I've never won a prize for elegance, what with my bitten-down nails and midfielder's legs, but I do have a first-class honours degree in English and History. Perhaps my time has come. Malibu, anyone?

Sunday Times, 20 August 1995

THE EVERTON COOK

Tom Watt

Allegiance to Everton or Liverpool is a defining element of family life on Merseyside. Mary Ellis can talk through the detail of her extended family and describe every member as a Red or a Blue. Mrs Ellis herself, as a youngster at least, didn't take much interest. Nonetheless, for the past 14 years, she's been cooking and serving meals every day for players and staff at Everton's Bellfield training ground. She's been in charge since 1992.

I used to work at Anfield, just casual work on a match-day, in the tea bars. And when Everton were at home I'd work at Goodison. The lady who used to be in charge here worked the tea bars, too. When she took over here, she asked me to come and work for her. I can't say I was ever a football fan, really, but I had three boys and only the middle one was an Evertonian. The others used to take the mickey, so I stuck up for him. I asked him first before I came to work here: he was about ten, then, and he'd come in with me. That was nearly 15 years ago. Anyway, after a while, my mate retired. They got a chef out from Goodison but the money wasn't good enough for him, being a young lad wanting to take the girls out and that. Then there was another fellow did it part-time until about three years ago. When he left they asked me to take over and I got my friend out to help me – Linda, who was working on the bar at Goodison, match-nights and functions.

I've seen a few come and go in my time. I was sad to see Mike Walker, the manager, leave. He'd got me a new kitchen ordered. But, you know, it's like a holiday camp out here. Everybody's friendly. The only thing that gets me sometimes is the kids. They'll all crowd into the kitchen together, wanting orange juice or toast. There'll be 20 of them at the same time and I'm terrified in case they hurt themselves, but they don't understand that, so I have to lock the door. But I really enjoy it.

I wanted a job, you know, and I only live up the road, so I can walk in or one of the players will pick me up and give me a lift in the morning. I'm here five days a week, nine until three. When I first came here, we were preparing three-course meals, steaks, chops. Now it's baked potatoes, baked beans, soup, tuna or ham pasta, savoury rice, toast. The first team and the reserves come up first. They're no trouble at all. Then it's the kids. At least on a Thursday they're at college so I get a bit of peace! Any one lunchtime, with players and staff, we'll do up to 60 or 70 meals. The kitchen's just about big enough for Linda and me, but when everyone starts coming in and helping themselves, well, all I can say is I hope I'll get my new kitchen in the close season. This one's 30 years old!

I don't know, really, about the new kind of diet. In the old days, they'd have steaks, sponge puddings, and they were okay. I mean, I went down to nine stone eating the stuff they have now! I do slip some cheese into their rolls if they ask me for a tray to take on the coach for an away game. It's the physio who'll say what they can and can't have, who's to cut out cheese and sausages and that kind of thing. Whatever I serve up, though, it goes! I've got to liking pasta, too. I eat it now instead of bread.

As I say, I've seen people come and go. Sometimes you hear about things going on. You get people talking, all the time: *What's going on down there?* But I just have to say: *I don't know. No comment!* It's interesting when you see a new player come in and, at first, they don't say a word. But a week later it's all changed and they've got to know everybody. I can't say a word against any of the players: they've got respect for me and Linda, they really have. They're really nice. We have a laugh with them, tell them how they don't know they're born, how we're going to ring up the papers about them. But what's really good is that there's something different going on every day. You'll never get bored working here.

I still work at the ground on match-days. It used to be that you had to work at Anfield and Goodison, it was the same organisation doing it. But, now, Liverpool have got their own arrangement so I just work at Goodison. I had the choice. My sister still works at Anfield as well although she's a catering supervisor at Goodison. She's worked at Anfield since 1972 and she's an Evertonian!

It's a football family, really. I had my brother on the phone from Hong Kong on Sunday, wanting to find out what was going on at Goodison. It's funny: I've got three brothers, the middle one's Liverpudlian, the other two are Everton. Of my three sons, the middle one's Evertonian and the other two are Liverpool. My dad was an Evertonian. You know how it is here. When I was growing up, our parish was all Liverpool. But the next parish, Holy Cross, was all Everton.

I never really bothered with football, myself. I don't watch it now, except on the telly. Mind you, my middle boy, the Evertonian, he lives up in Perth in Scotland now, and follows St Johnstone. Well, we went up to visit and he took us to see them play Rangers. Stuart McCall and Gary Stevens were playing for Rangers. Now, at St Johnstone, they've got this tea lady, Aggie Moffat I think she's called, and she just doesn't care! Apparently, she swore at Graeme Souness when he complained that the tea was late! It gets to half-time in the game and I've squeezed out to go to the toilet and, while I was gone – I think my daughter-in-law arranged it – it's come up on the scoreboard: *Welcome to Mary Ellis, Everton's answer to Aggie Moffat!* And I missed it, stood in this queue waiting to go to the ladies!

A Passion for the Game (Mainstream, 1995)

LONDON PRIDE

Andrew Walpole

A council-owned astroturf pitch in a backstreet of London's East End might be the last place you would expect to find a team of World Cup winners doing a spot of pre-season training.

But Stonewall FC are used to upsetting the football world's cosy preconceptions about what it takes to win at 'a man's game', because Stonewall is a gay club – the only one in the country, in fact. Don't for a minute, though, kid yourself that this is an outfit full of strutting exhibitionists with one eye on the ball and the other on the opposition centre-forward's legs. These boys can play. They have just become the gay football champions of the world, a feat which their captain Paul Barker gleefully compares to the 'other England' team's rather less distinguished record of late. 'Just think,' he says proudly. 'I'm the first England captain to lift the World Cup since Bobby Moore in 1966.'

Since that momentous day in Berlin earlier this summer, when they captured the trophy by beating the San Francisco Spikes 1–0 in the final, Stonewall have basked in the unaccustomed glare of publicity. They performed their club song to Boy George on the set of the BBC's *Gaytime TV* series, received honourable mentions in the broadsheets and turned down the offer of having their picture splashed across *The Sun*.

Now your average macho park footballer probably thinks this flag-waving for gay football is all very well but a bunch of queens wouldn't last five minutes if they had to mix it with teams of muscle-bound builders on Hackney Marshes week in, week out.

Wrong. What makes Stonewall's Gay World Cup win all the more praiseworthy is that the foundations for it were laid on the dogshit-strewn pitches of the Wandsworth & District Sunday Morning League.

And Stonewall don't just make up the numbers either. Last season their first team finished a creditable fifth in the Wandsworth Sunday League Division Three.

'You can imagine the average bloke telling his wife on a Sunday morning, "We're playing a bunch of poofs today",' says Paul. 'And then feeling really embarrassed when he comes home and says they've lost 5–0.'

You only have to watch Paul and the rest of the team in training near the Mile End stadium to know this is no idle boast. Along with team-mate Tony Woodward, he's played semi-professionally, a pedigree also matched off the field. Former manager David James was a full-back with Watford under Graham Taylor, while the club's current chairman, who prefers to remain anonymous, is a senior administrator in amateur football and has also refereed to Diadora League level.

When the club took its first tentative steps into the hurly-burly of straight football back in 1991 though, it wasn't their ability which was questioned, but their sexuality.

Initially, the only clues lay in the club name (the venue for a famous gay rights protest in New York in the '60s), their maroon shirts and the number of players who sported crewcuts. The League remained none the wiser until Stonewall were unceremoniously 'outed' by the *Daily Mirror* as 'The Queens of South London'. The club feared expulsion, but happily common sense prevailed and they remained in the League.

Not that this necessarily made Stonewall's task of being accepted by straight teams any easier. 'Our first game was against a team of psychopathic builders,' recalls Dave Williams, a club stalwart and former chairman. 'They had a real go at us and the game virtually ended up as a pitched battle.'

The following week, however, Stonewall narrowly lost to the League leaders – a crack Portuguese team – in a match which was hard but fair. The result proved a turning point and since then the club has gone from strength to strength.

Throughout last season, the players' eyes were firmly fixed on broader horizons: their trip to Germany for gay football's answer to USA '94. Could the club which fielded two teams, the London Lions and the London Apprentices, finally win a tournament in which they had finished second, third and fourth in previous years?

It's difficult to suppress the thought that football might come a poor second to the attractions of local nightlife when 400 gay footballers, representing 12 different teams from Germany, Italy, Britain and the USA, get together in Berlin.

Paul, however, maintains that all the clubs took their football every bit as seriously as real professionals. 'The Atlanta side didn't touch a drop of alcohol for three months before the tournament and were in bed by 10.30 every night,' he says.

His own more relaxed régime – 'Three pints of lager maximum and in bed by 1 a.m.' – proved more successful. After the Lions had beaten Boston 7–0, Milan 5–0 and Hamburg 1–0 in the group games, Paul scored a spectacular 30-yard winner in the semi-final against Munich which set up a final clash against the San Francisco Spikes.

This, in straight footballing terms, was England (plus a few handy Celts) versus Brazil. The Spikes had won the tournament seven times previously, and although now deemed past their best, still represented a huge test for a bunch of Sunday footballers from Wandsworth.

Not that Paul saw it quite like that. His inspirational pre-match team talk made hearts swell with pride. 'I told them, "You're younger, you're fitter and you're better looking than they are",' he says.

Which is precisely what Stonewall demonstrated – eventually overcoming their opponents 1–0. Victory provided the perfect cue for Stonewall's players and fans to show off their full repertoire of songs such as 'Go East' (well, the game was in Berlin) and 'Any Team Will Do', a reworking of the Jason Donovan number. 'We also sing ones about scoring and cruising, but they're too rude so I'm not going to tell you what they are,' adds Paul with a cheeky grin.

A month on from their historic victory, the team is back in training for a new season. The strong sense of camaraderie is obvious – even if it does manifest itself in a different way to El Tel's lads. Forget oh-so-macho nicknames like 'Psycho' or 'The Guvnor' for a start. Stonewall's players prefer monikers which betray their love of camp humour. So last season's leading goalscorer – and current holder of the 'Golden Stiletto' – Tony Woodward, is known as Wendy on account of his interior decoration looking like a Wendy House; Toby Musk is known as Tina Tantrum because of his penchant for angry foot-stamping; the tall and athletic Roger Taylor has, not surprisingly, been dubbed Two Legs and a Knob; and the club's Welsh full-back Mike Bowen is called Gladys – after *Hi-Di-Hi*'s Gladys Pugh.

The list of nicknames is likely to grow as the club's reputation for combining good football with a 'fabulous social scene' spreads. But their main aim remains attracting talented gay footballers who feel uncomfortable playing in straight teams or have been put off by the sport's macho image.

'Our message is that if you are a gay man and you love football, get in touch,' says Paul. 'After all, there aren't many park footballers who can say they have played in tournaments in New York, Los Angeles and Berlin over the past three years.'

His 15 years' experience in straight football bears this out. He still plays every Saturday in a high standard of amateur football for a team whose name he won't reveal. Although Paul has not 'come out' with his Saturday team-mates, he suspects one or two may have an inkling about his sexual preferences. 'I remember telling one of the team I was starving hungry and could kill a plate of sausage and chips,' he recalls. 'He just looked at me and said, "I should think you get enough sausage already, don't you?"'

Other players agree that it can be difficult for gays to be 'one of the lads'. 'We just want to enjoy playing for a team where we don't have to pretend after the game that we're going to go off and pull some birds,' says Roger Taylor. But what about pulling your own team-mates, or heaven forbid, a member of the opposition?

'We've brought one couple together and one of our players did get friendly with a referee during the World Cup,' says the club chairman. 'But most of the players are in relationships with "football widows".'

A post-training pint at the team's North London watering hole provides another reason why Stonewall have won the respect of their straight opponents. The drinks are on Courage, the club's sponsors. 'You should see some of the teams we play when they see Courage on our shirts,' says Paul. 'You can see them thinking, "Crikey, this lot must be good!"'

After he's presented the team with the World Cup, Courage's representative, Mr Lawson Mountstevens, echoes this view. 'Our sales team would love to give them a game,' he says. 'But frankly, I think we'd be annihilated.'

Goal, October 1995

AFTER-DINNER MINT

Bill Borrows

One hundred and twenty Yorkshiremen, shoe-horned into the kind of single-breasted metallic suits that Top Man stopped selling in 1984, shaking hands and talking bollocks, drinking bitter and smoking Henry Wintermans, are waiting to sit down to a three-course set meal with coffee and mints to follow.

There are no women in sight other than those carrying trays or plates of steaming meat and two veg to groups of tables seating small-time businessmen who have paid £25 each to listen to an ex-footballer who stopped playing before they caught the Yorkshire Ripper, telling anecdotes about his career. If they're lucky they may get an ex-manager or, on rare occasions, a manager still holding down a job.

This is the Sportsman's Dinner – a mechanism for getting middle-aged men out of the house and into their court summons suits. Some would call it Hell, but for David Taylor, owner of the Taylor Made Speakers, the agency that supplied this evening's entertainment, this is business. Taylor, who counts Ron Atkinson and Dave Bassett among his clients, is the foremost supplier of former footballers and managers to the after-dinner circuit.

Earlier today, we visited his Middlewich nerve-centre, a war office squeezed into a small airing cupboard, which gives off an air of organised chaos. Taylor is an over-stressed workaholic lurching from one crisis to another. Today's incident involves Wilf McGuinness who's unexpectedly been taken into hospital. The former Manchester United manager was due to perform tonight and Taylor is frantically hunting through his client list for a replacement. The temperature is in the high 80s outside and he's beginning to panic.

'Norman Hunter said he'd do it but didn't get the message I left on his tape and when I spoke to him he'd already made other arrangements. He's doing a golf day or something.'

A list on the desk has all the potential replacements crossed out. This is eleventh-hour stuff. Suddenly, the phone rings. It's Duncan McKenzie and he can fill in. Crisis over. Taylor exhales. Is it always like this?

'Nine times out of ten things run like clockwork,' he explains. 'But I've had a few nasty moments. The worst night I ever had,' he continues, visibly blanching, 'was when I put X [*former Manchester United player*] and Y [*former Chelsea player – the names have been withheld to protect the guilty*] on the same bill. I thought it would be a good pairing but X got there and refused to do it and Y disappeared to London because the police were after him and he was about to be prosecuted for controlling these girls . . . I've got every sympathy with those managers who had to deal with players who won't toe the line,' he confides. 'I know what hard work it is.

'I got a call from one of my players who wanted to know where Sunderland Football Club was. I says to him, "You must have played there," and he said, "Yeah, but I went on the coach." I send them all maps now.'

Taylor pulls out a wad of his players' CVs. Smith, Summerbee, Thomas, Worthington, Whiteside; the last-named's, especially, makes impressive reading: youngest player to score in an FA Cup final . . . youngest player ever in the World Cup finals (taking the record from Pele) . . . captain of Manchester United and Northern Ireland . . .

'Norman's the youngest player on the books,' remarks Taylor. 'He doesn't charge as much as, say, Tommy Smith, but he is a good name.'

Taylor works on a commission basis but generally speakers are paid according to the status they achieved as a player or manager. Consequently George Best can command £2,000 a night plus expenses and first-class train travel to the venue. Former Liverpool captain Tommy Smith will earn £500 a night for three hours' work. He'll eat and drink at the expense of his hosts and then deliver edited highlights from his autobiography to a crowd of drunk 50-year-old men who will then, inevitably, stagger up to him at the end of the night. 'Tommy,' the punters who can still operate their mouths will slur, 'I saw you play against Burnley in 1965. You were the best. You really bloody were.' And Mr Smith will say, 'Ta, mate.'

Smith might work three nights a week and, like many from his era, is now earning more than he did as a player. As Taylor succinctly puts it, 'Tommy's angle is, like, the hard man of football and he can charge a decent fee because he puts bums on seats and not every ex-player can do it.'

Taylor's clear on what it takes to make it. 'You've got to have bottle, be able to string a sentence together and talk for half an hour. Some of these guys have played in front of 40,000 people, but ask them to speak in front of 200 and they dry up.

'If they are a name all they have to do is get a script writer. The going rate is £100 for five minutes of material. It's going to cost them £600 to get the routine together, but they'll make that back at the first dinner.

'They'll get there at 7 p.m. for the pre-evening drinks and photographs with the sponsors. Dinner will be at 8 p.m., they're on their feet at 9.30 p.m. and they will do about half an hour. It's not bad money, really.'

Which probably explains why there's currently no shortage of ex-pros gagging to get on the circuit. 'I've got over 60 players and managers on my books and, if they are good, I can find them as much work as they want. I do about 40 dinners a week. The demand is insatiable.

'The only thing that worries me is whether young players today will need to do it because they're earning so much now.'

This man loves to worry . . .

Taylor's star attraction at dinner tonight is Tommy Docherty who will speak for 40 minutes. With the crowd already whipped into a frenzy by stand-up bingo and taken to nervous exhaustion and back during an auction for an autographed Wakefield Trinity rugby ball, the Doc stands up with his audience just the right side of pissed. He gives a good speech, finishing on the 'Me and Shanks at Preston North End' story and sits down. At the next table, a man is tipping a full pint of bitter into his friend's pocket for a laugh.

The poor bloke who has to follow this is Charlie Ale – Ale as in Ale & Hearty, a comedy double act which never made it past Patricroft Conservative Club. Halfway through Ale's impression of Chris Eubank ('I do impressions of sportstars and Frank Carson – all sorts, really') Tommy Docherty drains his glass, gets up and walks out. He must have a long journey home. The comic looks initially perplexed before announcing: 'Let's have a big hand for Tommy Docherty, lads, they don't make them like the Doc any more.' The audience are too far gone to realise that he has, in fact, left the building. He's a lucky man.

Ale's act goes down pretty well but then again, so much beer has been drunk that video footage of small dogs being put to death would bring the house down.

It later transpires, as is often the case, that Ale was quite a useful player in his youth. 'The sad thing is,' he explains, 'I could have been a top-notch footballer. I started out at Man City but I got a lot of knee trouble and asthma, which they can cure now but couldn't then. I went to Crewe and then Wigan and ended up back at Crewe before I called it a day at 22 or 23.'

And that is why he now earns a living entertaining the sales staff of Halifax Timber Supplies in a pub function room on a Tuesday night. Charlie Ale is the warm-down man. It's a job that pays enough to provide him with a personalised number plate (ALE 1) even if that plate is bolted on to a rusty Volvo estate.

Ale is telling us how well he thinks the evening has gone when a large man with a scrape-across haircut lurches up and sick-burps Websters and peanuts before swallowing it back down. 'Let me shake your hand, son. You're the best I've seen since Charlie Williams came on to the scene, really funny. Are you doing a tour of West Yorkshire?'

'I'm not but thanks,' says Ale, fretting because the man looks ready to throw-up. 'I'll be on Sky TV in April, though.'

'You were brilliant, mate.'

'Thanks. As I say, I'll be on Sky in April.'

'That joke about Fred West, brilliant.'

'Thank you.'

'What did you say you were on?'

'Sky Television.'

'When's that then?'

'April.'

'Sky what . . .?' The bouncers have arrived.

'On in April,' says the comic as the man is led away to be poured into his taxi. 'See you soon. God bless.'

Ale confides, 'You get a lot of that but these people are the salt of the earth. Where would we be without them?'

Probably selling five disposable lighters for a quid . . .

The party's over. By the following morning, not one of those punters will be able to recall a single joke or anecdote. For a comic, especially a bad one, that's the perfect audience.

A man in a Paisley waistcoat bursts into the toilet and fills the urinal with asparagus soup. 'Eh, pal,' he asks, picking an almond off his chin, 'do you remember me eating that?'

At this point, we make our excuses and leave . . .

Goal, October 1995

FADING AWAY

Vincent Hanna

My uncle died last week. He used to take me to football matches. We supported Cliftonville, an amateur side in the Irish League. They hardly ever won. By the age of ten I was an expert in losers' jokes. *So I says to the man on the gate: 'Two at three and six please.' And he says: 'What do you want – backs or forwards?'*

I once sat near the directors' box. They were dumbstruck as somebody kicked the ball over the stand into the street. One turned to my uncle and remarked: *'Aw Christ, there goes the gate money.'*

Gerard had the good taste to die during Liverpool v Newcastle last Wednesday, thus ensuring that his name will be forever linked with the game of the decade. That will please him.

Since I nearly had a cardiac arrest myself, I wonder at the damage the Premiership run-in is doing to community health in Newcastle. My friend Mick teaches at the university and used to make me stand at the Gallowgate end of St James' Park of a Saturday. The price he made me pay later was too high. My system can absorb only so much Newcastle Brown and Lindisfarne.

Mick called me yesterday: 'The city is stunned and morose,' he said. 'People stare into their beer and weep, the music is gone. It's like a city after an air-raid or an earthquake. All about me is the silence of death.'

'Hold on, Mick, it's not over yet.'

'We know that,' said Mick. 'But we are afraid. Manchester United are not. That's the difference. Kevin Keegan is the Camillo in our *Winter's Tale.*'

I thought: 'You know-it-all bastard.' But I said: 'Good point, Mick.' And looked it up. After Monday's match at Ewood Park Kevin bravely appeared for the cameras. His face was ashen.

'Obviously I want us to defend better, but I don't know what we could have done different tonight.' And then: 'At the end of the day if it's not meant to be, it's not meant to be.'

In *The Winter's Tale*, Leontes the king of Sicily chides Camillo for his lack of nerve. Camillo admits that he has found himself *fearful to do a thing, where I the issue doubted, whereof the execution did cry out against the non-performance, 'twas a fear which oft infects the wisest.*

Newcastle have played in a free-flowing manner. They say they don't deserve this misery, this horrible thought of coming second. But maybe they do. Going forward is not enough, neither is wanting to win. Not by itself, it's not. Champions also have to want not to lose, to hate defeat as much as they crave victory.

On 22 January Newcastle had 54 points, Liverpool and Manchester United 42. All three had played 23 games. Since then Newcastle have earned 13 points out of a possible 30. Manchester's record is 31 out of 33.

Faustino Asprilla arrived to play – and displace Keith Gillespie – on 10 February. Asprilla provides subtlety and strength in front of goal, but Newcastle's 12-point lead was earned by other means.

So it was on Monday, Gillespie came on for Asprilla after 73 minutes. Two minutes later he coaxed Kenna and Wilcox out to the right touchline. And the gap was there for David Batty to find.

But it wasn't enough. How could it be when Newcastle's execution in attack cries out against their non-performance in defence?

There is something else too. Champions are not normal people. They thrive on fear, living on the edge because that is where they are happiest. Walter Hagen once partied all night before a play-off. He was asked whether this might give his opponent an advantage. Mark well his reply: 'He may be in bed – but he ain't sleeping.'

Such seems to be the present mood of Eric Cantona, who has scored six goals in as many games. The record is eight, held by Bill Whelan, who died at Munich. Cantona imposes an icy calm upon his youthful team-mates. Not only do they cope with tension, they appear to enjoy it. The fans, the manager and Manchester also have been infected with serenity sickness. Win or lose, they are not afraid.

During the Ardennes campaign a soldier found George Patton standing in the midst of a bloody attack. He urged the general to quit the line of fire. Patton whispered: 'God help me – I love it so.'

The Guardian, 10 April, 1996

NO PLACE IN SPORT

David Meek

The line between love and anger in sport is fine, the path between passion and fury difficult to tread . . . as I was reminded by the father of a brain-damaged boy limping across the Manchester United forecourt.

I had watched the moving unveiling of the larger-than-life-size bronze statue of Sir Matt Busby, which now stands gazing out of Old Trafford towards his adopted city of Manchester.

It was an occasion full of warmth, love, friendship and all those other qualities at the finer end of the sporting spectrum. The great man's pupils had returned to pay their respects, former players who had survived the Munich air crash with him. His family, Sheena and Sandy Busby, had tugged at the rope and the bright red drape to reveal a marvellous piece of work by sculptor Philip Jackson, which has captured the character of a man who, as Martin Edwards told us, could walk with kings or commoners, and be equally at ease.

But then, as I walked away, I was stopped by this softly spoken Irishman who had also watched the unveiling, at the same time as keeping a watchful eye on his teenage son as he sought out the players for their autographs. He told me that his boy had been wearing his Manchester United shirt back home in Ireland, and because of it, had been attacked by other boys, and left paralysed down one side, his life wrecked and his engagement cancelled, along with most of his other prospects, I imagine. The point his father wanted to make was his concern for those of us working in the media who lose our balance between the passion and the fury, between the love and the anger, who write or talk with a little too much provocation and aggression.

I thought about the delightfully nonsensical tale of Geoff Hurst's hat-trick ball in the 1966 World Cup, which was picked up and taken by

Helmut Haller back home to Germany. But did the story really have to be given the xenophobic overtones with references to the 'Greediest Krauts on Earth', 'Horrible Helmut' and 'Sour Kraut'?

There are different kinds of provocation, though none as daft as that by Graeme Souness, who took leave of his senses after winning the Turkish Cup at the weekend. Now manager of Galatasaray, he ran to collect an 8ft flag from his fans, before spearing it like a war trophy in the centre circle.

The self-styled 'fans from hell' immediately rioted, the windows of both team coaches were smashed, the police waded in, and three people were wounded in knife attacks. Souness defended himself pathetically. 'We always do that in Britain,' he said. Really?

I considered, too, the cavalier approach of the advertising business these days, and Nike's latest campaign, which will fan the flames of hostility across Europe. Using high-profile players, they have Eric Cantona declaring on a poster: 'I have worked hard for English football – now it must be destroyed.' Is destroy really the right word, even in the exaggerated parlance of sportspeak?

Then there is the picture of David Ginola and Les Ferdinand staring at each other, as in a shoot-out, either side of 'Friendship Expires 6/96'. Does Euro '96 really have to be played without friendship?

Shame on you, Eric, selling your soul for this kind of money.

Maybe I will be told to get real . . . but reality for my Irish friend and his sad boy is very real.

Manchester Evening News, 30 April 1996

THE POLITICS OF FOOTBALL

David Bull

So, what's the connection between the death, in May 1995, of Lord Wilson of Rievaulx and the staging in England, come June this year, of the European football championship?

Try asking some of the revisionists–cum–forecasters. Not only have they seized upon the first event to resurrect the folklore that links World Cup football results to the electoral fortunes of Harold Wilson, but they have gone on to suggest implications for John Major as Euro '96 lands on his doorstep.

The World Cup finals at issue are those played in England in 1966 and Mexico in 1970. But let's get the sequence of events in 1966 straight. The general election was in March. England beat West Germany at Wembley in July. So those who claim that winning the World Cup helped Labour to win the 1966 election have some explaining to do.

That's not to suggest that Wilson was incapable of exploiting the World Cup victory. Prime ministers have been known to court popularity outside election campaigns. And even Richard Crossman – whose diaries document a disdain for football in general and for Wilson, the fan, in particular – reflected that the win could 'strengthen . . . sterling . . . and the position of the government'.

In a recent comparison between the 'wily' Wilson and the 'genuine' sports-loving Major, Laura Thompson (in *The Guardian*, 20 July, 1995) effectively accused Wilson of cutting short a visit to the US president, Lyndon Johnson, in order to hurry home to be photographed with the 1966 winners. Yet, you might think that the British prime minister would have attended the final, whoever was in it. And Wilson's trip to Washington seems to have proceeded as scheduled, although a Friday evening touchdown, in Ottawa, had to be 'rushed'. There was time, though, for

Lester Pearson, the Canadian prime minister, to bet Wilson $5 that England would lose and to suggest – 'half seriously', Wilson later concluded – that he board his guest's plane and join him at Wembley.

The RAF got Wilson home in time to watch England win 4–2. And we have his account of 'a great celebration at the Royal Garden Hotel', when he made his infamous appearance on the balcony with the victorious England team. The president of FIFA, Sir Stanley Rous, was not amused when the 'prime minister . . . appropriated the World Cup', although he acknowledged this as another example of Wilson's being 'so good at judging the popular mood'. If anybody deserved to join the team on the hotel balcony, Sir Stanley felt, it was Denis Howell, the minister for sport, who had 'worked hard' to stage the finals.

Lord Howell says Lord Harewood, the Football Association president, suggested that Wilson take a bow with the team. As the government was hosting the reception, that was not entirely inappropriate. Meanwhile, his deputy, George Brown, led the singing of *Forever Blowing Bubbles* – as befitted a life-long West Ham fan who had seen his lads contribute all four England goals at Wembley.

The next World Cup played two roles in the Nuffield College analysis of the 1970 election. Did it influence Wilson's choice of a date for the election? And did West Germany's revenge, in a Leon quarter-final on 14 June, contribute to his government's defeat at the polls on 18 June?

Several cabinet diaries and memoirs report a Chequers weekend in March when an election date was on the agenda, and Wilson pondered the 'risk' of clashing with the World Cup in Mexico: if England were defeated just before polling day, might the government suffer? Three weeks before he announced the risky date, Wilson appeared on *Sportsnight with Coleman*. The Nuffield psephologists interpret that as an attempt to counter, if only as a fan, Edward Heath's sporting achievements as a participant: four months earlier, the Conservative leader had skippered *Morning Cloud* to victory in the Sydney-Hobart yacht race.

Yet Wilson's motives in making two appearances at the FA Cup final – at Wembley on 11 April and at the Old Trafford replay on 29 April – appear not to have been impugned. On the contrary, this final brought him tributes, from Sir Stanley Rous and from the Chelsea chairman, for correctly forecasting a 2–2 draw at Wembley and a replay result of Chelsea 2 Leeds 1, after extra-time.

On the morning of the replay (and the eve of his *Sportsnight* appearance) Wilson discussed, with cabinet colleagues, the pros and cons of June, before heading for Euston and a fortuitous photo-call – a perfect example, for Lord Howell, of his opportunism: 'But it came out of a genuine interest in sport.'

For all his concern about the 'risk' of June, Wilson could not have anticipated the nuisance value, to his campaign, of the World Cup. The trouble began with England's warm-up tour of South America. On 28 May, Labour's manifesto was the lead story in only one daily newspaper, *The Times*. Five of the others led with the news of Bobby Moore's arrest in Bogotá. The only consolation was that the Conservative manifesto had fared almost as badly, the previous day, in competition with that alleged theft of a gold bracelet. Wilson took up the diplomatic cudgels on Moore's behalf – only to be accused, by Conservatives, of trying to win votes.

The World Cup kicked off three days later. An ORC poll found that 20 per cent of people, most of them Labour supporters, were more interested in the tournament than the election. Nonetheless, things were still looking good for Labour on Thursday, 11 June, when England qualified to face West Germany. Yet, on the morning of Sunday, 14 June, Roy Hattersley's canvassers found that their erstwhile 'rapturous' reception had given way to 'something between contempt and hostility'. This change could hardly be attributed to the events of the evening in Leon. Undeterred, Hattersley scapegoats Peter Bonetti for his failure 'to hold a shot which every elderly man watching the match on television was sure that he could have saved'. So, Labour could 'blame . . . their party's defeat on the disappointment of a football-mad nation'.

The alternative Leon scapegoat – manager Ramsey, for his questionable substitutions – was offered up when Denis Howell and Roy Jenkins held their usual Tuesday-before-election meetings at a factory along their constituency boundary. The monthly trade figures – the worst for nine months – had just been published. Wilson had shrugged them off, on the Monday, along with the Leon result: he was 'not aware that any of my cabinet were in the British [*sic*] team'. But Jenkins was still worrying, at the factory hustings, about the balance of payments. His neighbour tried to reassure him that their audience would be more concerned about the World Cup defeat. Sure enough, when Howell stood up to speak, 'They started shouting: "What about Alf Ramsey? What . . . was he doing taking Charlton off?" I said to Roy, "There you are. That's where their priorities are."'

Two days later, the electorate gave Wilson more time to go and watch Huddersfield Town – pending his return to No 10 in 1974. The onus is surely on those who link electoral fortunes to World Cup glory to explain how, within 12 months of England's failure to qualify for the 1974 finals, Wilson had won two general elections. Shortly before the 1975 FA Cup final, the last final of his Downing Street years, he joked with Bobby Moore that he was 'a bad politician but . . . a good forecaster'. So Moore asked him who was going to win the Cup. Wilson 'said he'd have to see the state of the pitch first'.

Major's reputation as a 'genuine' football fan appears not to require forecasting skills. Like Wilson, he was keen on football as a schoolboy. Each schemed to introduce the game at his rugby-playing grammar school. And both remained loyal to their boyhood heroes – unlike the fickle David Mellor, condemned by loyalists for swapping affiliations on the road to Chelsea. Being seen with Mellor at Stamford Bridge has not helped the prime minister's credibility as a fan.

But are there other lessons, in any of this, for Major? On 18 June 1995, the 25th anniversary of that 1970 election, England went out of another World Cup – to the All Blacks in Cape Town. Four days later, Major announced a different kind of election – for the Conservative leadership. Like Wilson in 1970, he has no need to call a general election this year. Yet suppose he does. Will his calculations include the European Championship?

You don't have to be a Eurosceptic to question his chances of holding the Henri Delaunay Cup aloft on 30 June.

New Statesman and Society, 1 March 1996

The Players

2

THE LOST EMPEROR

David Stubbs

Manchester United's fierce title claw-back since January can be ascribed almost entirely to their talismanic Frenchman. There was his Yeboahesque advance, swerve and volley against Arsenal, his mazy run and soft yet lethal left-footed goal against Spurs, that vital header against QPR when he coolly left it till the 93rd minute of normal time to find yards of space where no one else would have to ghost into behind the defence. Then, there were vital goals against Newcastle, Coventry and Man City.

However, his role in his side's title charge has been about more than goals. His poise, vision and coolness have lifted the entire team. The way he subdued an incoming ball with a single, contemptuous nudge of his thigh, the fearless way he despatched every penalty with the bored, routine efficiency of a postman delivering gas bills, those heat-seeking crossfield passes. All this was reminiscent of his form back in 1994. Only then he didn't have the added difficulty of Andy Cole getting in the way.

What's most remarkable is that he's managed to hit form without hitting people. Or stamping on them, drop-kicking them, spitting at them or suggesting to their faces that they are laughably deficient in their appreciation of Baudelaire. He's even been seen to intervene with Roy Keane like a one-man peacekeeping force, when the pugnacious Irishman threatened to deck some hapless opponent for looking at him.

When Cantona returned to the Premiership back in October it looked for a while as if, with his fiery rage quelled, he'd ceased to burn on all cylinders. He had a series of quiet games, didn't score much, didn't make his presence felt. It made you wonder if his temperament had been not a blight on his footballing genius but a necessary fuelling of it.

Now we know that's not the case. Now we have the dream Cantona, all talent and no tantrums. How has this transformation been wrought?

Lobotomy? The close-cropped legionnaire's haircut suggests as much but there are no scars. Maybe having to do retake after retake of that bit in the Nike ad where he says, 'I know that violence is not acceptable' ingrained the message like a tattoo on his consciousness. Who knows?

What's for sure is that all of this has boosted his chances of a return to international football, with the probability that he will be included in the French squad, if not automatically the team, which comes to England for the European Championship. Manager Aimé Jacquet hinted as much in a recent interview in *L'Equipe* magazine.

Yet in France they remain cool about Cantona and the prospect of his rehabilitation. While we've been in raptures, they've been indifferent. *L'Equipe*'s Alain Constant admires Cantona's skills, yet sees him as superfluous to the French scheme of things. 'As far as most French supporters are concerned, the national team is excellent without him. Most people think they should leave him out. They're unbeaten for 20 games and a lot of that's down to those who've replaced him – Zidane of Bordeaux, and Djorkaeff. They may not be very famous in England but over here they're really big, big stars. Even playing behind those two, Martins of Auxerre is fit, so Cantona wouldn't be the first choice there. It's a bit strange for us when we read in the English newspapers that you're astonished Jacquet could even consider going to England without Cantona, because for us, it's just not a big deal.'

What's more, there's scepticism about Cantona's current spate of saintliness. Is the violent moodiness in him extinct or merely dormant?

'I wouldn't bet a penny on his behaviour,' says Constant. 'He's a very strange guy, he always has been. I'm surprised he's kept out of trouble for so long. Maybe his daily life is a lot smoother and quieter and easier than it was in France.'

If all this seems a tad churlish it's worth remembering that Eric did not, of course, leave France on entirely amicable terms. 'Everyone connected with French football is a liar and a cheat,' he declared on coming to this country. 'They are all against me. The game is rubbish.'

The series of contretemps which led to his departure from France are now legendary and still make for excellent light reading. He was accused of leaving 'a trail of excrement' at the various clubs he moved to and from. At Auxerre he thumped international goalkeeper, Bruno Martini. He moved on to Montpelier where he assaulted team-mate Jean-Claude Lemoult with a pair of size-ten boots. He was on the receiving end at Marseille when, during a charity match, the crowd mistook a skied shot for comedy causing him to rip off his shirt and flounce off in high dudgeon. At Bordeaux he missed training because, he explained, his dog had died. This poignant variation on 'the dog ate my homework' didn't impress the club and he was fined. He was fined again after referring to national coach Henri Michel as a 'shitbag', and again at Nîmes for throwing the ball at the referee's head. At the subsequent disciplinary hearing, he turned on his accusers, branding them 'idiots'. Asked to repeat his remark he did so, approaching each individual member of the committee by turn and shouting 'Idiot!' in their face.

To the keen observer, a pattern seems to be emerging here but, as Cantona explains, it was not he who was in the wrong, but the rest of the French nation. French referees were at fault for 'whistling too often', a flaw they were especially prone to when footballs were being bounced justifiably against their head. 'A year later, people have realised it was me who was in the right,' Cantona observed of his behaviour. Sure enough, video evidence does suggest that Bruno Martini was guilty of assaulting Cantona's fist with his chin.

'In France he wasn't that successful and he wasn't that popular,' says Alain Constant. 'He was known mainly for being a bad boy, not as a unique footballer. Yeah, he was good but so were half a dozen others. In the end he was fed up with the French press, the French public, French opinion.'

Perhaps we've always been guilty of romanticising Cantona. French footballers had previously been a rarity in this country. In the mid-'80s Didier Six had a spell with Aston Villa and none of us can forget the sensational impact made by Ollie Bernardeau at Chesterfield. The approach of these flamboyant Frenchmen, however, was greeted with the kind of misapprehension with which the 19th-century citizens of Hartlepool greeted a crateload of monkeys washed up on the North-East coast. They hanged them for being French spies. And Cantona was a particularly weird one.

He began to cultivate the image of himself as a 'cultured' footballer in the broader sense of the word quite early on. When he came to England, he declared himself a poet, a painter and a student of the works of the anarchist Leo Ferre and Rimbaud among others. While this gave *The Guardian* the opportunity to make the old Rimbaud/Rambo joke about 500 times (and it is indeed true that when he came to Leeds, fans besieged him with photos of Sylvester Stallone after he had expressed his admiration of the French author), much of the footballer/philosopher guff was taken, surprisingly, at face value in all sections of the British press. An early photo did the rounds showing Cantona in a potting shed wearing a deerstalker flanked by his faithful hounds hunched over an easel and canvas daubing an semi-abstract landscape. This ought to have raised the suspicion that here was a *poseur par excellence*. Cantona is reminiscent of Chris Eubank in this respect (except he threw more punches than Eubank).

The British media, however, were impressed, intimidated even, by this unnerving show of highbrow endeavour. He was allowed to get away with a whole bunch of guff. 'I love life passionately,' he declared in the *Daily Mail*, 'like a true Gaul.' 'My paintings express many dreams and power,' he said in *The People*, shallowly. Even the broadsheets allowed him licence to bullshit, their sportswriters having long wished for a footballer who might, perchance, understand their reference to Ovid in their reports on the Sheffield derby. *The Daily Telegraph* admired that 'He speaks of *simplicité*, *vérité*, *beauté*, *integrité*, *politesse*, *spontaneité*.' They forgot to mention *banalité*. *The Independent* gushed at his 'chic', his 'élan', his 'brooding, abstract paintings' and his poetry 'about liberty and the search for freedom', wandering alone, no doubt, in fields unencumbered by the presence of pedantic referees niggling him in reference to some player he'd just poleaxed.

There was actually very little substance to Cantona's musings. 'I like Rimbaud because he has the spontaneity of a child,' he said. Frequently. Truth is, Cantona adopted culture the way a moody adolescent clutching a Sartre novel does, in a spirit of morose self-importance, mumbling about life being so unfair. All that vague nonsense about 'passion' was sixth-form stuff. His other heroes were Jim Morrison and Mickey Rourke – big, sulky, overgrown kids with a persecution complex, posing 'existentially' on Harley Davidsons. 'They hound me, they hounded Van Gogh,' was the subtext.

Truth is, Cantona is as truly a philosopher as Camus was truly a footballer. Not much. As Camus's death in 1960 in a car crash demonstrated, he couldn't handle corners. But Eric was accepted, not least out of the naïve notion that his embracing of 'higher' culture was somehow typically French. Not so, according to Alain Constant. 'When he made that remark about the seagulls and trawlers we laughed too.' So it wasn't some obscure quote from Proust, then? 'No! Everybody just thought it was ridiculous. No one tried to interpret it, it was just a case of "Nobody disturb him, this guy might be dangerous".'

The French, in truth, are as philistine as the Brits, in spite of the Louvre. Their equivalent of *Spitting Image* featured a caricature of Cantona as the misunderstood painter/poet thoroughly lowbrow in its derision.

What's more, whenever Cantona flared up there was much, quasi-racist talk of his 'Gallic temperament' almost as if his behaviour was to be expected from a typical, hot-blooded Frenchman. Again, Constant begs to differ. 'No! Not at all! I mean, sure, people from the South of France are supposed to be a bit more exuberant and, true, he comes from the South of France but no, he's unique, he can't be compared to any other Frenchman!'

Maybe Cantona is a mystery to us for the simple reason, he doesn't speak English. 'Yeah well, he's a mystery to us, too! No one knows what he's really like. Myself, I don't think he's that interesting a person. Some players you can talk with outside the game, but not Cantona, he was never like that.

'For people over here who don't know too much about football, Cantona is seen as an "intellectual", whereas Papin is seen as an idiot. And the truth is, in fact, that Papin is not such an idiot and Cantona is not such an intellectual. Still, I don't care about that so long as he can play.'

Cantona has repeatedly declared his love for England over France but Leeds fans still remember that barely had his serenade of *I Don't Know Why I Love You* on the steps of Leeds Town Hall died away than he promptly pissed off back to France prior to skipping to Manchester United. After the Matthew Simmons incident, he again made a dash for his homeland, having to be winkled out of a Paris hotel room by a mollifying Alex Ferguson. In spite of the 'trail of excrement', in spite of the mutual *froideur*, he still seems to regard France as his bolt-hole.

Italy has always been another option. Indeed, on 12 April last year he accepted a deal to quit Man United and join Internazionale of Milan for £3 million. Terms had been agreed and that was that, Harry Harris was able to exclusively reveal in the *Daily Mirror*.

Well, not quite. For, as Harry Harris was able to exclusively reveal in the *Daily Mirror* on 28 April, Cantona eventually agreed on a £1.5 million deal to stay at Man United. Alain Constant is convinced he wouldn't have hacked it in Italy.

'I wonder how he would cope in Italy? I wonder if he'd be as brilliant as he is now? I wonder how he'd cope with the fans and the opponents, because they're tougher − not necessarily physically, but the pressure is more vicious in Italy. England is definitely the right country for him.'

True enough. The relative lack of spatial awareness of Premiership defenders does seem to give Cantona the sort of advantage Superman had over earthlings under the British sun. Moreover, Manchester United is probably the right team for him, and Alex Ferguson the right manager. His near-paranoid siege mentality matches Cantona's own. Ferguson will always publicly defend his players against whatever ludicrous odds. He defended Cantona to the hilt, against accusations that he stamped on Phil Babb for instance, against the brickbats of Jimmy Hill, calling the chinny-one a 'prat'.

Leeds' Howard Wilkinson would never have done the same, you suspect, nor would any French manager. Given such stout barricades, Cantona seems finally to have settled down, flourished and even matured. So surely the time is right for reconciliation with his home country?

Not quite, says Alain Constant. Memories are too long in France. 'I don't think he should be in the team right now and that's the general opinion over here. Cantona had his chance for years and years in the French team, sure, he did well in the qualifiers and the friendlies but never in the big games.

'Platini called him a big man in small matches but a small man in big matches. The 1992 European Championship was a disaster and only three years ago, he was a part of the team which lost to Israel and Bulgaria. People haven't forgotten that.

'But I'd bring him along in the squad and if the French find themselves in trouble, as I think they will, then bring him on for the last 20 minutes to save the game. He is unique. He has physical as well as technical strength. And he can win a game on his own.'

Constant remains ultimately blasé about the man we idolise, romanticise and deify, leaving one with a depressing sense of the gulf between Premiership football and its continental counterparts.

'I don't think people in France really care so much about Cantona these days. Sure, we put him on our cover – but it was a very quiet week and we've got to fill the papers!'

Goal, June 1996

RUUD GULLIT

Ian Stafford

The owner of the most famous dreadlocks in world football leaves Mark Hughes and Dennis Wise to their lunch-table banter and wanders over with an accommodating couple of cups of tea.

Even now, six months into his Chelsea career, you still perform a double-take as Ruud Gullit approaches. Maybe it was because our meeting was on the back of Chelsea's best display of the season, in which they dumped Newcastle United out of the FA Cup thanks, largely, to an inspired performance from you-know-who, but his happy demeanour is such that he would make the Cheshire Cat look depressed.

It is hard to believe, really. With great respect to the perennial sleeping giants of West London, if you had predicted three years ago that the former Dutch captain would play for an English side, you would have put money on Manchester United, Liverpool or Arsenal.

But to leave Italy for a two-year contract at Chelsea? 'I let my heart speak for once,' he says, grinning and understanding how odd, at least in theory, his decision sounds. 'The first impression is usually right, and my first impression of Chelsea was very sharp. I needed a new challenge.

'I loved many aspects of playing in Italy, and could have stayed for another couple of years, but you have to know when enough is enough. I'd won everything playing for Milan and Sampdoria, but I needed to go.

'That's why my motives for playing in the Premiership for Chelsea are probably different from, say, Dennis Bergkamp or David Ginola. My concern is not to win a whole lot of cups, but just to do something different and face a new challenge.'

Yes, but why Chelsea? 'Well, it was Glenn Hoddle,' he explains, opening up a package to reveal a pile of reggae CDs sent to him by a record company. 'He's my type of player. In Holland we couldn't believe how little England played Hoddle. If he'd been Dutch, or Italian, or French, he would have won a hundred caps. From the start I knew Glenn's intention, otherwise I wouldn't be here now. "This is the way we're going to play," he said, and that was the challenge.'

Did he know anything about Chelsea? 'I'd heard of two players, but knew absolutely nothing about the club.' You mean to say you don't know the words to 'Blue is the Colour', Ruud? Gullit gives a quizzical look at such double Dutch. But I thought you chaps know everything about the English game?

'That's normally true, but not me,' he replies, lifting his hands in a semi-apology. 'I never supported a team as a kid, not even in Holland. I never collected autographs or had posters on my walls. For me it was the beautiful game itself. If a game is boring on TV, I always turn over and watch a film instead. It's not that I'm disinterested, it's just that football has to be good. I see it as a fast-moving games of chess, in which I'm required to think two or three steps ahead. That's the fascination for me.'

Of course, others suggested different reasons when his surprise move was first announced. One of the most popular theories was that the 33-year-old was injury-prone and a shadow of the man who, in the late 1980s, was arguably the most gifted footballer in the world. Chelsea were merely providing a lucrative field in which to graze in the twilight of his career.

'First you need to ask yourself if you can still do something,' he answers. 'The truth is that I left Italy as still a good player. If I didn't think I could meet the challenge I wouldn't have done it. It was the same when I left Milan for Sampdoria. They all said I had knees of crystal and couldn't play two games in a week. Then I had a great season with Sampdoria, we won the Italian Cup, and everyone said: "What's happening, how can this be?" I feel so fit and good right now, which is why I must take advantage of my situation.'

What, then, were his first impressions of Chelsea? 'Well, I have to admit, when I saw Stamford Bridge for the first time, it was before the start of the season, and the place was in a mess. I did begin to wonder, but as soon as I played there I knew everything would be okay.'

And off the pitch? 'It was a bit like the first round of a boxing match at first. I could see that the players were all sizing me up and seeing what I was like. But as soon as they realised that I was one of them they were okay. I don't go on about my career, but when they ask me about Milan, as they quite often do, I explain the Milan way of doing things.'

Six months on and Chelsea, led the Hoddle and Gullit way, are fast becoming an attractive force in the Premiership. The game knows it, the crowd sees it, but, most important of all, the team realises it. This, for Gullit, is as satisfying as anything else he has achieved in his career. 'We are getting better all the time and I'm enjoying seeing it happen. Every day I'm very happy to be a Chelsea player because I'm having fun. The foundation's now being laid. Success will definitely follow, but it will still take some time yet. For me, winning something is always the dessert. The creation of this is the main course.

'You can see on the faces of the Chelsea players that they are doing something now that gives them so much pleasure. They know they're better now than a few months ago, and they understand that there is much more to the game than just kicking the ball into the box and hoping that somebody might score.'

Is that how Gullit judges the English game, then? 'Not any more, no. England is learning. It used to be so different to Holland. Here the youngsters seem to be taught about the physical side, but in Holland they only focus on the technical aspects of the game.

'Rule one for the youth coach is never to win cups, but to simply get the youngsters into the first team. He has to make them better players and if an individual is good enough to play for the senior team ahead of the rest he will stay in the youth team so that the others will learn from him. At Chelsea, too, the youngsters are now concentrating on technique and skill, and you can see how much they are enjoying themselves as a result.'

But what about the Premiership? After all, Gullit was widely reported to have said to an Italian journalist that he thought there were only three decent players in the whole League.

'No, that's not true,' he insists. 'I never said that. Neither did I say, by the way, that I wanted to become a manager of an English league club. I have no idea what I will do because I'm enjoying myself too much at the moment to think about it. Actually, I think there are many skilful English players.' Such as? Gullit laughs. 'I'm not going to say who because I'll get into more trouble if I leave anyone out.'

With perfect timing Dennis Wise appears with some match-day tickets for his Dutch colleague, and can't resist a dig. 'Talking more bollocks, are we, Ruud?' he asks, displaying an impressive range of vocabulary. 'We're all shit and Ruud Gullit's the greatest.'

Do you get on well with your new team-mates, then, Ruud? Gullit laughs again. 'They all know me well enough by now to understand these things,' he answers. 'No player has ever asked me if I said it, or why. Instead they just poke fun at me. But I enjoy their company. I play a lot of golf with them and I sometimes go out to the pub with them. It all provides the freedom I get out of playing my football in England.

'It's so different to Italy. If you are playing on a Saturday, after a Wednesday game you go home and prepare for the weekend. Here, you go out for a few drinks. You can't do it in Italy. You have to be professional, go home, sleep and focus on the next game. The Italians wouldn't believe the players here on the day of a game, talking about tickets and using their mobile phones.

'It's because I lived my life so seriously over there that I now feel so free over here, playing for Chelsea, living in London, going to gigs and the cinema and just having fun.'

Just about the only hiccup, so far, in Gullit's adventure at Chelsea were the accusations, mainly from one Vinnie Jones, that he dived in order to get the Wimbledon player dismissed. Gullit gives his side of the story.

'If someone wants to hit you in the face, and you see it coming, what do you do? You try and avoid it, don't you? It's the same in a game. When someone's coming at you with both feet, you have to go up in order to avoid the tackle. If you don't, he'll break your legs.

'Even when you jump, they still hit you, but it's not so bad. I said to him: "If I stay on my feet, what do you think will happen? You'd break my leg. Would you be happy then? I don't want you to get the red card, but I don't want a broken leg either." He accused me of diving when he didn't even hit me. But his attitude was wrong, so you have to punish this attitude.'

Apart from that, then, it all seems to have gone exceedingly well for Gullit. He likes the football, and he likes the life. In which case, I wonder, does he wish he had come to England eight years ago, rather than joining that tin-pot outfit from Milan? Gullit gestures dramatically with his arm. 'You can't say that, you know,' he replies. 'What happened happened.'

Then he leans forward in order to share a secret. 'Let me put it another way. In Holland, we have a saying: "If your grandma had a penis, then she would be your grandpa".'

First we had Eric Cantona's seagulls and sardines, and now we have this slightly less cryptic offering from Gullit. He's been smiling for the past hour, but now Gullit's roaring with laughter as he ambles off, clutching his CDs by his side.

The Independent, 22 January 1996

STEVE McMANAMAN

Martin Thorpe

With Hoddle retired, Waddle and Barnes close, Le Tissier in hibernation and Gascoigne as mercurial as ever, there is a job vacancy: wanted, the most talented English player of his generation. One applicant stands tousled head and slightly stooped shoulders above the rest.

The sight of Steve McManaman running at defences has become one of the few home-grown thrills in a Premiership increasingly dominated by foreign pyrotechnics. The red No. 17 shirt billowing on his back, arms pumping, hair bouncing, a turn, a twist, maybe a step-over just to get the defender thinking. And while he is, a sudden burst of speed that whistles McManaman past the startled player and within range of hovering team-mate or glaring goal.

Such fearless audacity has been at the heart of a youthful resurgence at Liverpool which this season sees them one game away from Wembley, still with a shout of the league and last Wednesday led to the man himself making his eighth appearance for England as the build-up begins to Euro '96, which will be the biggest test yet of McManaman's maturing talent.

What with a choice of caps, a mop of hair topping a scamp's face, and spindly legs protruding from short trousers and disappearing into ring-topped socks, McManaman looks rather like a grown-up Just William. Perhaps he stows a catapult in his kit bag.

But despite the looks, McManaman, at 24, is reaching the stage in his career when he needs to prove that the sporadic flings of a youthful winger which originally made everyone sit up and notice can be translated into the consistent swagger of manhood. The signs are encouraging.

All the early excitement over McManaman's arrival in the Liverpool first team five years and 227 games ago was doused by his disappointing season in 1993–94 amid criticism that he drifted out of games all too easily.

But since Roy Evans has succeeded so stylishly in bringing the team back in step with Liverpool tradition, McManaman has blossomed in his new free role, a dashing presence among his dashing peers.

One person who has watched over the Bootle boy's rite of passage is Steve Heighway, an Anfield great who knows a bit about running with the ball. As Liverpool's director of youth development, he oversaw McManaman's rising career as a teenager and knew from early on which position would suit him best. 'Our early match reports on him, back when he was 17 and 18, recommended that he be played as a free man,' says Heighway, 'though he did a lot of his best work when he was wide – not actually standing in wide positions, but arriving in them, if you like.'

And, says Heighway, it is Liverpool's way to adapt a team to a player's strengths. 'Liverpool have always had players who can run with the ball, but McManaman is a one-off, and because he is a one-off he has defined his own role. That's always been the way here. You bring your own talents to the club and if those talents are good enough, Liverpool will encourage them and assimilate you into a team.'

McManaman's role is simple: to find space and attack defences. 'His biggest strengths are his pace, touch and his ability to run with the ball,' says Heighway. 'He's very direct, likes to get at defenders and probe until he finds a team's soft centre.'

Of course, it is the exhilarating burst of speed that twinkles the eye. 'His particular quality is the quickness with which he receives the ball, turns and starts running at people. He's got a lovely awareness of what's behind him and he's probably the best in the country at playing in and around players and between sections of a team. That comes from a natural feeling for space. He's always on the half-turn, slightly sideways so he's got a good awareness of what's around him.

'Many times he doesn't even stop the ball when he's receiving it, just lets it run, gets on a half-turn and is immediately attacking defenders. That's what makes him so difficult to pick up, and of course we've got a nice style and system of play here that appreciates his talents, surrounds him with other great players and allows him to express himself.'

Not even man-marking seems to stop him: Leeds tried in the sixth-round replay and McManaman replied with two goals. 'It actually suits him in a way,' says Heighway. 'He's got great stamina and won't stop running, so if you do man-mark him he'll take you all over the pitch.'

But McManaman does have weaknesses. For one, he is very right-footed. So although his main element of surprise is speed, the direction he takes is obvious. If he is out wide left, for instance, he will always cut inside, which could become a problem against better defenders. The other weakness is his finishing. 'If he scored more goals he would be a world-beater,' says Heighway.

In keeping with his growing maturity as a player, McManaman has taken it upon himself to sign up for extra shooting practice with Robbie Fowler and the goalkeeping coach Joe Corrigan.

'I know goals are important,' says McManaman, 'and I need to improve. So Robbie and I stay behind with Joe after training and go through regular 30-minute sessions shooting from different positions, angles, dropped balls, everything.' It is beginning to work: so far this season he has scored ten goals, more than in the whole of last season.

So what of the future? 'You can never say how far a talented player can go,' says Heighway, 'because he is so reliant on his team-mates. But McManaman's a very exciting player. There is nobody in English football like him.' As CVs go, not bad.

The Guardian, 30 March 1996

DAVID GINOLA

Amy Lawrence

'GIN-OOO-LA!' Arms outstretched, with a beaming smile, this is how Geordies greet one another. Strolling around town the day after Newcastle had beaten Middlesbrough, the refrain 'Gin-ooo-la!' (to the tune of 'Toon Army') was everywhere. Hanging in the air like an echo, ricocheting off every building in every street. 'Gin-ooo-la!' at the bus stop. 'Gin-ooo-la!' outside the bakery. 'Gin-ooo-la!' in the dole queue. If you had no knowledge of English dialects, you could be forgiven for thinking the word *Ginola* was Geordie for 'hello'.

Olivier Godallier, Ginola's friend and agent, isn't sure if he should be amused or alarmed by the Newcastle public's adoration of his man. During a morning stroll in town, fans were throwing themselves to their knees, gasping, 'We are not worthy,' when Monsieur Ginola walked past. 'David doesn't want to go into the city because everyone is bowing: "Gin-ooo-la!"' Godallier imitates the Toon faithful. The man himself tries not to let such adulation interfere with his desire to lead a (relatively) normal life. After all, Ginola is pretty used to public attention. Last season in France, he was unquestionably the biggest football personality. Yes, bigger than Cantona. He has his own phone information line, computer service, fashion calendar, range of merchandising, watch deal, and tie-up with clothing designers Cerutti . . . Not that all this has given him an ego problem.

Let's get this straight. As well as being indecently skilful, intelligent, cheekily amusing and startlingly handsome, Ginola is astonishingly down-to-earth. *Faux de mieux* indeed.

He keeps his ever-growing popularity in cool perspective. 'I don't think I am a hero for the people,' says Ginola. 'Now I am David Ginola. In a few years maybe I'm nothing. It's very important and I never forget that

107

because now I play football, people enjoy it, it's very good. Maybe in five years I will stop football and go back to the South of France with my family and have a normal life and all the responsibility and the pressure around me is finished. I know that.'

Ginola is sitting comfortably in the bar of his hotel in Newcastle. He sports a beige polo shirt, beige and white checked shorts (short shorts, European-style, not the baggy, knee-length English variety) and a pair of loafers. Very Tyneside. Ginola has never felt the need to conform. Although his first concession to the north-east lifestyle is his decision to learn Geordie, never mind English. Peter Beardsley has questioned his motives, but Ginola insists he isn't taking the mickey out of his Newcastle team-mates' vocal talents. 'Who, me? No . . .' he says with astonishment. 'I just know some words in Geordie. Lee Clark taught me.' C'mon then, David, let's hear it . . . 'Sheers mayte!' he sings. Everybody in the room tries, unsuccessfully, to stifle hysterical laughter. Imagine Inspector Clouseau in an episode of *Auf Wiedersehn Pet*. Ginola loves it. He does an encore: 'Allreeet?' Everybody cracks up now, including Ginola.

He has adopted the lighthearted spirit of the Newcastle dressing-room as easily as he has slotted into the team. 'There is a very funny atmosphere,' he says. 'All the players laugh and joke. It's different on the pitch – very serious. The players work very hard and when you finish, enjoy life. I think it's a good mentality.'

He's in England to have a good time. But he has something to prove (and something to win). A handful of French critics doubted his choice of England – saying he'd never last the season – and of Newcastle. The French were as mystified by his move to St James' Park as the British would be if Andy Cole had signed for Lens. French knowledge of the Magpies is limited, but they're learning, as news of Newcastle's fantastic early-season form filters across the Channel. After a handful of games, Ginola must be writing very smug postcards home. Honours have already gone his way (the first Carling Player of the Month award) and he is setting the pace for Player of the Year.

Did he always know he'd be a professional footballer? 'Yeah. *Exactement*,' he says, nodding, stroking his jaw as he listens attentively. He confided his ambition to a friend when he was seven years old. Good as David was, his friend didn't believe he'd do it. 'I am from a village, not a big town. A great football player never comes from a village,' Ginola says now. But aged seven, such logic couldn't deter him. 'I said, "Okay . . . but I'm sure I will realise my dream." Now when I go back to my village I meet my friends and they go [he whistles] "It's fantastic".'

When he was a small boy, practising football on the sundried pitches of Sainte Maxime, he didn't pretend he was Michel Platini or Pele. Young David didn't have football heroes. 'I read *Batman* and *Superman*,' he says. 'They are superheroes. But not a footballer because it is a job.' He thinks about hero-worship and smiles: 'My hero is my boy.' Andrea, David's energetic, seven-year-old son runs around the hotel in his black and white Newcastle shirt bearing the No. 11 (Ginola's number for France and for PSG) and A-N-D-R-E-A in big letters on the back.

Surprisingly he doesn't see himself as a talented player: 'I never think about talent.' He smiles broadly: 'I just think about always giving my best, working hard, training. After that you win and become a great player. Talent? If the crowd or the journalists say, "*Ohh, magnifique*" it's for the crowd and for the journalists.'

It's all about attitude. Confront him with the old chestnut about only turning it on in big games, and Ginola is a mite frustrated. 'I don't want to know the people who say that because they don't understand what I think about football or what I think about life,' he says. 'I think in Bolton or against Middlesbrough it's not a great, great game. I try to play my best football always.' This (and the small matter of Eric Cantona) are the questions Ginola gets asked *ad nauseam*. He shrugs. It's all quite boring and he doesn't know what all the fuss is about.

But this is the new Ginola. It's not the Ginola who was once described as 'a monster' by a team-mate. He admits a screamfest with referees, opposition, and even his own players used to be an integral part of his game. His career stuttered in the early days because he was too easily distracted. His unquestionable talent was undermined by a questionable temperament. Even after he signed for PSG at the age of 24 there were games when yelling came easier than passing. Now he realises he was winding himself up more than the opposition: 'I say: "Oh, shut up, David. There is no reason to shout like this." Now I say nothing.'

Aside from easing the strain on both his blood pressure and voice box, the new improved Ginola is a far better player. Defenders who try to provoke him don't get any change. 'They attack me all the time and I always stand up and say nothing,' says Ginola, ever so pleased with himself. 'They think: "What do I do to stop him?" It's better. When the referee blows the whistle to start the game, my mind is closed. I forget everything. Only the ball. The game. My partners. Everything I think is more inside. More philosophy of life, you know?' Whoops! A touch of the Erics there, David.

Still on the 'Are you Eric in disguise?' theme, Ginola contemplates what makes football so wonderful: 'Generosity. Respect. For yourself, for your partners, for everything in the game.'

A video tape convinced Ginola that St James' Park was the place to be. As the Frenchman didn't know the Magpies very well, Kevin Keegan gave him a video of Newcastle's season 1994–95 highlights. 'I think it's a good team, with Andy Cole before he went to Manchester,' says Ginola. Player and manager didn't have lengthy talks but Ginola was struck by Keegan's positive thinking. 'He's very good *psychologique*. The coach doesn't have to speak a lot. Sometimes a good word at a good moment is the most important thing, as effective as a big speech. At the beginning he just wanted to show me the pitch.' A shrewd move by Keegan which, obviously, didn't have anything to do with the language barrier.

It could have been very different. Ginola might just as easily have been examining the pitch at the Nou Camp or Highbury. A host of clubs were banging on Paris Saint Germain's door for him. Ginola was keen to play in Serie A but got fed up wading through Italian agents' waffle. Arsenal and Barcelona ended up as Newcastle's closest challengers. Johan Cruyff was desperate for the Frenchman to join him. But Ginola worried that although Cruyff wanted him, the chairman and directors didn't. Knowing the volatile nature of the Spanish club, he thought better of the move. 'I didn't want to go to a club where the people see me like this [he frowns] and say: "I don't know why you're here." I prefer it in Newcastle knowing all the people want me here. They look you in the eye and say: "I want to play with you."'

The Arsenal bid was millimetres away from luring Ginola to Highbury. A mix-up with phone-calls meant Arsenal vice-chairman David Dein was waiting for Ginola to contact him while preliminary finances were being agreed with Newcastle. Dein finally tracked Ginola down (in Holland) the night before he was due to fly to Newcastle to meet Keegan for the first time. Ginola explains: 'David Dein called us in a hotel in Amsterdam and spoke with Olivier and me for one and a half hours at two o'clock in the morning. He said to Olivier: "I want David. Arsenal is good for him." I knew the story before with George Graham.' (That's not *the* George Graham story – Ginola is alluding to the former Arsenal boss's attempt to buy him). Both the Magpies and the Gunners agreed a fee with PSG but Newcastle offered Ginola a wage deal Arsenal couldn't match. 'There are so many things in the deal on the money side,' says Olivier. 'You don't go somewhere if you don't have the price you think you can get somewhere else.'

Ginola takes up the story: 'When he [Dein] phoned it was too late. He had a problem on the right side of the midfield and said: "David, we have this position," and I said: "No problem. But it is too late." "You sure?" "Yes." Olivier told him I was already going to sign with Newcastle, and David Dein said: "Okay. Good luck." He is a very nice man. If everyone in football had his mentality there would be no problem in football.' Did Ginola want to go to London? 'Yeah,' he says. 'They spent a lot of money on Bergkamp and Platt. No money for me!' Ginola laughs. He isn't going to worry about it now.

A month into the season he's still finding his feet in the city of Newcastle (if not on the pitch at St James' Park). 'Paris is one of the most beautiful cities in the world,' he says. 'To live in Paris is a great thing for a Frenchman.' A man used to the Parisian lifestyle will have to substitute *vin rouge* and croissants for brown ale and chips with curry sauce. He isn't too fazed: 'I didn't choose Newcastle for the weather or for the city. I chose it for the football. I'm not 34 years old and going to play in another country for the sun, the sea and the city. Maybe in five years. Now I want to play in the League here because I think that it is one of the best in the world. It's important to me to win something. The Premiership and maybe one cup.'

He sips his drink. Pineapple juice (pronounced pin-apple), no ice. He comes from the Platt rather than the Rush school of continental transfers. He started to learn English as soon as the deal was struck, and his *anglais* is impressive. 'It's a big adventure for me because Newcastle is not the South of France. I'm hot-blooded, you know, like Italian. It's very different but it's okay.'

The fanaticism of the Toon Army makes it hard for him to explore his new surroundings. 'Sometimes you want to go out, maybe in Metroland in Newcastle, you want to stay quiet with your family. It's very difficult because people don't understand that you want to be cool for a moment and not sign autographs. It's life. You must sign autographs for the people because they love you and they can't understand if you say: "No, I don't want to sign." They say: "Why? You're my idol. Why can't you sign?"'

Things are looking up for the Ginolas. They have found a house – hotel living has been hard on David's wife Coraline, cooped up with two small children and little understanding of English. 'You want to have your proper life. Go back home and close the door and say: [he exhales deeply] "Okay. It's cool now."'

Ginola just wants to play football and win trophies. He'll play anywhere on the pitch. Well, almost anywhere: 'I think I can play everywhere but I am better now on the left side. Maybe one day *libero*. Why not? I'm sure I'm not a goalkeeper.' His virtuoso trickery deep in defence during Newcastle's victory over Middlesbrough showed how comfortable he is with the ball at his feet in any situation. With his arrogant flicks, confident touches and clever vision, he taunted any Boro player who dared come near. 'Come on then . . . have a go if you think you're good enough. If you want the ball, you'll have to do better than that.'

Lineker and the lads on *Midweek Sports Special* drooled over such fine footwork, turning defence into attack in dazzling style. But Keegan won't deploy him as a sweeper just yet. Not when he can cross like a dream, dribble past opponents at will, and drift in for the odd wondergoal. An epidemic of right-back manic depression is sweeping the country with the news that Ginola is still working on his technique. 'I enjoy training with the ball,' he says. 'But long runs? No. I don't like.' He smiles cheekily. This may be his attempt to ensure that Howard 'cross–country run' Wilkinson doesn't bid for him but it is more likely to be evidence that Ginola, like many creative players, prefers to train with the ball.

When Keegan first showed off his £2.5 million capture, Newcastle fans didn't know what to make of Ginola. They knew what to make of his wife after pictures of the clinching couple were smacked all over every newspaper. (Toon fans serenaded the midfield man with: 'Get your wife out for the lads.') But who, they thought, is this Ginola geezer? Is he any good?

Some 5,000 curious fans checked him out at his first day of training. Andy Wraith, editor of the fanzine *The Number 9* was one of them. 'A lot of people didn't even know who he was. He was full of ball tricks but you don't expect him to do that in a game.' Then the Premiership started. 'What can you say, the man's a genius. Everything he touches turns to gold,' he says. But Wraith returns to earth to point out that the boy is tackle shy: 'Ginola doesn't tackle at all. Newcastle fans like players who get stuck in.' Oh. It seems Ginola has an imperfection (albeit slight) after all.

Even more revealing is that, after the initial honeymoon period, his team-mates have started to throw him the odd frustrated glance. When Newcastle played Manchester City, an unmarked Ferdinand moaned at Ginola who had ignored his call and blazed a long-range shot over the bar. 'If Ferdinand can stick it in from six yards, Newcastle fans are going to prefer that to Ginola scoring one in ten from 30 yards,' says Wraith. But when you are dealing with an *artiste*, this comes with the territory. And with Keegan's almost reckless attacking strategy, Ginola needn't fear reproach.

First Cantona, now Ginola . . . can we expect to see more French footballers hopping on a one-way Air France flight to find their fortune in England? 'We have opened the doors for some other players because English football is one of best in the world,' says Ginola. 'Why not? They go to Italy and Spain, why not to England? I am very impressed by English football. I like it.'

If things don't work out, Ginola's swoonworthy looks mean he can always find work as a model. He is one of the few footballers who don't object to the touch of a powder puff. At the end of *FourFourTwo*'s photo-session, he made a point of personally thanking the make-up artist. Imagine Iain Dowie shaking the hand of a woman clutching tubes of Clinique, saying: 'Thank you for the make-up.'

Olivier reveals the key to Ginola, the footballer and the man. If you are jealous of his magnetic appeal, he will lose interest. But 'if you love him, he'll give you everything'.

FourFourTwo, November 1995

THE BOY FROM BRAZIL

Richard Williams

'You should see his boots,' Steve Gibson said. 'They look like something you'd hang from the mirror in your car.' And as the tiny figure of Oswaldo Giroldo Junior disappeared into a scrum of camcorders and sombreros at the Riverside Stadium yesterday morning, Gibson's £4.75 million investment suddenly looked terrifyingly fragile. The thought of the 5ft 5in Brazilian's scheduled meetings with Neil Ruddock and Tony Adams in the midst of an English winter was enough to raise a shudder.

For Gibson, the chairman of Middlesbrough Football Club, this was a precious day. About 4,000 people turned up at the new £20 million stadium, built on redundant dockland, to welcome Juninho, captured from São Paulo by Gibson and his team manager Bryan Robson in the face of competition from such metropolitan giants as Internazionale of Milan and Arsenal of London.

Some of the fans, bursting with pride and anticipation, had been at Teesside International Airport on Monday, when Juninho and his father touched down in Gibson's private jet on the last stage of their 15-hour journey from São Paulo. Yesterday many more assembled outside the stadium for the official presentation of the player to his public, whose colours – the scarlet of Middlesbrough and the bright yellow of Brazil – shone through the grey light as the early-morning drizzle died away.

Brazilian flags and scarves were waved alongside the local favours, and with equal enthusiasm. Several small boys wore the shirt of the world champions, with Juninho's name and the No. 10 on the back. That is his national squad number, although the replica shirts in which Middlesbrough will do a lucrative business over the coming months will bear the No. 25. (John Hendrie, Middlesbrough's existing No. 10, was yesterday reported to have offered to sell it to Juninho for a week's wages

– the Brazilian's wages, that is, which means something in the region of £13,000.)

Through improvised banners and placards the people of Middlesbrough tackled basic Portuguese in an attempt to make him feel at home. '*Bem-vindo*,' they proclaimed. Welcome. Other exiles added their encouragement: '*Os Brasileiros do Teesside te saudam.*'

There was a three-month-old baby boy brought by his mother in a pram, and a couple in their 60s who had first seen the Boro just after the war, when the great Wilf Mannion was the team's brain. But most of the crowd was of school age, which swiftly led to criticism from the leader of Cleveland County Council, who felt that the club could have arranged the event for later in the day, out of school hours, instead of suiting media deadlines.

Some individual establishments, however, took a more relaxed view. 'I can understand young people wanting to be part of something like that,' said the deputy head of St Peter's Roman Catholic School, Mrs Jean Pickup, 'although we'd have to take a dim view of anything that cuts across the work we're doing to raise our attendance figures.' She paused. 'It's a pity he doesn't speak Spanish,' she said, 'since that's our foreign-language speciality.'

Fifty students of Stockton and Billingham College of Further Education made no attempt to disguise their presence. Blowing whistles and banging a variety of percussive devices from tin lids to plastic water barrels, they filled the air with a thunderous samba rhythm that may have owed less to finesse than to the traditional English virtues of commitment and work-rate, but which was otherwise distinguishable from the samba schools of São Paulo only by the fact that the girls kept their T-shirts on. Formed as long ago as Monday morning, the band set the scene for the arrival of Juninho, who saluted his new fans from the balcony before making his way down to the pitch for a photo opportunity with his new manager.

'I believe the lad will enjoy his football with us,' Robson later told a press conference. 'We try to pass the ball around, which will suit him. He's a tough character, he wants to be the best player in the world, and he'll work hard to achieve that. That's the kind of player I want in my football team. He can handle the pressure. As the number-one player in Brazil, he's under pressure anyway. He'll cope. When I watched him play in São Paulo, he was being marked by a beast of a man who got away with murder compared to what defenders are allowed to do here. And our winters are milder now.'

Robson and Gibson are acutely sensitive to the jibes of southern commentators who find it hard to understand the player's reasons for joining an unfashionable club in the supposedly frozen North.

'I don't think it will be so terrible,' Juninho observed through an interpreter. 'It's not Siberia.' His first impression of the area, he said, was 'fantastic'.

But Gibson, the 37-year-old haulage millionaire behind the Boro renaissance, sees it as a smear campaign. 'Did you read that article in the *Evening Standard*?' he said, his anger visibly rising. 'It was a disgrace. He criticised our females, our landscape, our weather. You have to ask what was the motive behind a story like that.'

There was also a resentment about Monday's story that the Football Association was intending to investigate the role of agents in the transfer negotiations. 'We'd like to put paid to that one right away,' the club's chief executive Keith Lamb said. 'We dealt directly with São Paulo Football Club, and with Juninho's father. We've been absolutely right and proper in all our actions. I think it's just mischievous speculation.'

'This club doesn't break the rules,' Robson added, and his words were given extra weight later in the day when the FA issued a statement clearing Middlesbrough of any suggestion of impropriety.

Robson was asked if the language barrier might present problems in training. 'If you've got a really intelligent football brain,' he said, 'it doesn't matter what language you speak. You'll automatically work well together.'

The auguries are good for the relationship between manager and player. Juninho confirmed that it was Robson's personal intervention, and his willingness to travel to São Paulo for discussions, that swung the decision in Middlesbrough's favour. 'That's what made the difference,' he said, observing that the thought of joining an English club had not entered his head until last summer's visit for the Umbro Cup.

After yesterday's ceremony Juninho was taken off to Ayresome Park, now used as a training ground, to meet his new team-mates. Government regulations mean that he must fly home again this week while his work permit is processed. This, Middlesbrough have been told, will take anything between ten days and six weeks. They would like him to make his début away to Manchester United a week on Saturday, although the current unavailability of tickets for away fans during the rebuilding at Old Trafford means that Middlesbrough would erect a giant screen for a live transmission at the Riverside Stadium, for which Gibson would expect a crowd of 15,000. But a début at home to Leeds the following Saturday, 4 November, looks more likely.

The 22-year-old player's impact on the club's finances is already being felt. Season-ticket sales have risen from 21,000 to 27,000, an immediate source of £900,000. Gibson says the turnover will double this year, to between £14 million and £15 million.

Events such as yesterday's run the risk of arousing unrealistic expectations, but Robson and Gibson would be right to believe that, in terms of status, this transfer is the most significant by an English league club since the arrival of Ardiles and Villa at White Hart Lane in 1978.

Klinsmann, Roy, Gullit and Bergkamp all arrived after their services were no longer required in Serie A; the same goes for Yeboah and the Bundesliga. The case of Cantona was more complicated. But, with the arrival first of Ginola, who was wanted by Barcelona, and now Juninho, the prosperity of the Premiership has been endorsed. And something about little Juninho's presence yesterday suggested that this, too, will be a promise fulfilled.

The Guardian, 18 October 1995

FERGIE'S FLEDGLINGS

Richard Williams

On a dark, wet winter's night three years ago I sat in the main stand at Gigg Lane, Bury, and watched Alex Ferguson's reserves struggle through the clinging mud, failing to get a result against the bigger and more experienced Leicester City 'stiffs'. Ferguson was not worried. In the starting line-up was a bullet-headed midfielder with a knack of scoring goals. Paul Scholes, 18 years old, Salford-born, had barely graduated from a successful youth team. On the bench were a fresh-faced winger, David Beckham, a 17-year-old east Londoner, and a quiet, watchful centre-back, Gary Neville, just 18, born in Bury.

It was the month in which Ferguson realised that the arrival of Eric Cantona just before Christmas had given United the missing ingredient which would enable them to win the delayed league title.

The Frenchman was not the last of his big buys, of course, but the effect of Cantona's contribution did mean that the years of chequebook team-building were over. Having created his first version of United by splashing out on the likes of McClair, Donaghy, Schmeichel, Webb, Ince, Pallister, Irwin, Kanchelskis and Keane, now Ferguson could allow the club's own talent to come through.

Three years later that trio are fixtures in the Manchester United first-team squad, along with their contemporaries Nicky Butt and Philip Neville − raised, like them, in the Old Trafford youth programme, reinvigorated by Ferguson when he took over the managership in 1986. The elder Neville brother, indeed, is a certainty for Terry Venables's European Championship squad.

'We thought they were certainties, those three,' Ferguson said. 'Absolutely no doubts that they'd make first-team players. It goes in cycles. I can go back to my schools football, and that's what I remember.

Suddenly one school or one area would have a great group of players. And with clubs, you'd notice that it was the ones that worked hard with their youth teams. When I went to Aberdeen, the first eight players I signed all made the first team. And six of them went on to represent Scotland, either at full or Under-21 level.'

Young players have had a special priority at Old Trafford since the days of Duncan Edwards and the Busby Babes. 'We've always worked particularly hard at it here. That particular youth team of the early 1990s represented a high point in terms of intensity: we managed to get a group of players together from different parts of the country, and they became a team. And now you can look back and say that there were one or two decent players, talented boys who've gone on to make useful careers for themselves elsewhere, who couldn't get much of a look-in.'

It was instructive to get out the team sheet from that reserve match in the early weeks of 1993 and see, alongside Scholes, Beckham and Neville (and the more experienced players Les Sealey, Lee Martin and Danny Wallace) a clutch of less familiar names. Ferguson described the destinies of the seven who had not made it into his first team.

'George Switzer? We knew his height would be against him. He went to Darlington, and now he's with Hyde. A popular boy, the kind it breaks your heart to let go. Kieran Toal – a very intelligent boy. He had a bad injury, went to Doncaster, had another injury and now he's studying law at university. Brian Carey went to Leicester for a quarter of a million. Patrick McGibbon is still playing centre-half in our reserves. Simon Davies is in the reserves. Craig Lawton broke his leg and went to Port Vale. Still there, doing well. We released Robert Savage, he went to Crewe, and I believe he has a Welsh cap now.'

Ferguson was quoted recently as observing that, if the Bosman ruling had been made two or three years earlier, his 1993 title-winning team would have won the European Cup. Their coherence was disturbed by the need to juggle the foreign players.

'No, I didn't say that,' he interjected. 'What I said was that I felt we'd have had a good chance.' But does the freedom to buy and select un-limited numbers of foreign players mean the end of a thorough youth policy at a club such as United?

'Absolutely not. In fact we're going to extend our plans. We'll be spending a lot more money on the youth programme.' How will it be spent? 'I'm not going to tell you that. Our Centre of Excellence is . . . excellent.

'The problem is the FA blueprint. I'm only allowed to take boys from within one hour's travel of Old Trafford. So, in effect, the FA are encouraging a parochial attitude in a club that has to compete on a world stage. It's a total waste of time. And what it means is that every club that has a youth programme is breaking the rules, but doing it under the guise of community work. Some clubs have half a dozen schemes going, up and down the country.' United themselves have two regional centres, in Belfast and the North-east. The Ulster scheme has yielded Keith Gillespie, McGibbon, a 22-year-old central defender from Lurgan, and Philip Mulryne, an 18-year-old Belfast-born midfielder. David Healey, a 16-year-old centre-forward from Downpatrick, is another showing promise.

'He'll be called up this year,' Ferguson said, adding to the list the name of Jonathan Macken, an 18-year-old Manchester-born forward who did not come through the Belfast scheme but whose Irish ancestry has already won him a schoolboy cap.

The school in the North-east, originally run by 'Pop' Robson, has been slower to bear fruit, understandably so in the light of increasingly self-confident competition from the local giants Newcastle, Middlesbrough and Sunderland, now alert to the need to hang on to the talent on their own doorsteps. Robson, in fact, is now in charge of the Roker Park initiative.

One cannot help thinking that the capture of Ryan Giggs was vital to this evolutionary process, one in which the immediate needs of a championship-chasing club have to be balanced against the development of sometimes fragile young talent. Snatched at the eleventh hour from the clutches of Maine Road, Giggs became the club's leading prodigy and assumed a senior role in the youth team, an experience which has turned him into a positive role model for the young players now entering the first-team squad.

In one or two cases, Ferguson pointed out, family background has been helpful. 'The Neville brothers, their background is right. Their father is the commercial manager at Bury, their mother was a talented athlete. Excellent. No problem. Chris Casper's another one.'

A centre-back, now on loan to Bournemouth, Casper is the image of his father Frank, who knocked in goals for Burnley 20-odd years ago before moving into sports kit manufacture.

The whole experience of bringing young players from the youth scheme into the first team has, Ferguson says, 'gone better than we expected. At this place you never know with young players. The style, the demands, the expectations . . . as well as talent with a football, a boy needs certain qualities of character to succeed here. And the boys we've brought in over the past couple of years, they've done exceptionally well. No failures at all.'

Kevin Keegan, by contrast, is still at the stage of buying talent. Only Steve Howey and Lee Clark, of Monday's squad, are products of the youth scheme, although the plans the manager has hatched with the enthusiastic assistance of Sir John Hall should ensure that when these two clubs meet again in, say, ten years' time, their squads will contain a fair proportion of talent nurtured in the old-fashioned way.

The Guardian, 2 March 1996

LES FERDINAND

Ian Ridley

It is 14 years since that Norwegian television commentator seemed to invoke every famous English person except Sherlock Holmes upon whom to heap shame after his team had humbled the givers of the game 2–1 in Oslo. Now not even Eamonn Holmes would wonder how they did that if they were to repeat the result on Wednesday.

The roles are reversed. Norway, conquerors of Graham Taylor's confused collection just over two years ago, have recently been hardened by European Championship qualifying and, before that, World Cup finals. Both have been denied England, one by their hosting of Euro '96, the other by ineptitude.

This England, though, should go to the Ulleval Stadium with more optimism and organisation than the one which saw Gary Pallister and Lee Sharpe vying for the left-back position, even allowing for the absence of potential first-choice players such as Gascoigne, Platt, Beardsley and Le Saux.

The draw with Colombia last month offered hope of inventive football beyond the English stereotype of direct industry at which Norway are the more proficient these days. 'We have got to face facts and we have not been successful playing our way,' said the England coach, Terry Venables. 'Someone, somewhere has got to be a bit bolder.'

Venables has already indicated that his formation will be similar to that for the Colombia match. That comprises a back four out of which and into midfield a defender should be expected to step when the opportunity arises, and a front six led by a spearhead striker around whom mobile players rotate to find gaps in defences. Thus are we close to Venables's *modus operandi* for the European Championship finals. Having been most influenced by Milan, Brazil and Ajax in the last couple of years, he intends England to adopt the best elements of all three; the back-four cohesion of the first two and the front-six fluidity of the latter. 'We expect England to be a lot better now,' said Oyvind Leonhardsen, Wimbledon's Norwegian midfield player, scorer of one of his country's two goals against Taylor's toiling troupe. 'We know they will be better prepared and hard to beat.'

In defence, Pallister and Stuart Pearce could replace the injured Steve Howey and Le Saux (Gareth Southgate and John Beresford may have been risked at Wembley but probably not against Norway's totem strikers in Oslo) and Robert Lee could take over from Gascoigne in midfield. The main question, once easily dismissed, is whether Alan Shearer will retain his place as leader of the attack. The burden of carrying Blackburn on his manful shoulders so far this season appears to have wearied him, now without a goal in eight international matches. Typically, on Friday he was playing down talk about loss of confidence, remaining defiantly positive, but he has not looked comfortable in the Venables system.

Now Les Ferdinand appears a more than viable alternative, in form with nine goals, having shrugged off persistent injuries, and looks in Newcastle's line-up, which bears similarities to England's, an even more vibrant force than at Queen's Park Rangers. The move to a big club has helped him, Venables has said, a statement that might have been read with interest by some players, Matthew Le Tissier, for example.

Of all the strikers now clamouring for attention in the Premiership, Ferdinand looks the most complete English example. His pace matches Robbie Fowler's, his shooting Stan Collymore's and his control surpasses Andy Cole's. Not even Shearer can match his heading ability and astonishing hang-time in the air – natural, he says, rather than worked on.

His link play may not yet quite rival Teddy Sheringham's, for Tottenham at least, but Newcastle's influence is beginning to tell on him after an initial brief period when he was unused to laying the ball off to the variety of attacking midfield players, rather than flicking it on, and they unused to his need for the occasional ball played over defenders.

Ferdinand's main problem down the years has been his own lack of self-belief, probably fostered by his early experiences in the game. The scouting and apprentice systems missed him and he played in the non-League with Hayes until he was 19, working as a van driver and painter and decorator. Then QPR found him. 'You go from looking at all these big-name players in sticker books and the next year you're one of them,' he said. 'It can take a long time to belong and it probably took me a bit longer than it should.' First Gerry Francis informed him of his potential, now Kevin Keegan has convinced him of it, he added. It flickered for England under Taylor; for Venables it could now catch fire. It will be a surprise if Shearer is not the starter on Wednesday but we should also see Ferdinand given a decent time to impress.

Independent on Sunday, 8 October 1995

STAN COLLYMORE

Karen Buchanan

'If I felt now that I'd be stuck at Liverpool for the next two years and just be average and just go through the motions I would give up football tomorrow without a doubt.' Stan Collymore, the most expensive player in British football, slides back into his voluminous black leather sofa. He fiddles nervously with his fingers as he continues. 'I spoke to Paul Stretford, my agent, and said: "Look, Paul, between you and me, I don't think it's going to work." He says: "You can't say that, we've just got here. You'll be trapped; nobody will be able to afford you." I said to him: "I take your point, but think about it: if it's not going to work, it's not. It's not one of those things where you can, say, give it a couple of years and then say, well, at least you gave it that." He says: "Fair enough, we'll have this meeting with Roy and see what he thinks." But it's just not going to happen.'

Stan Collymore, Liverpool's most expensive summer signing, says he'll go if he and Liverpool can't resolve their differences and they are currently discussing different options. But who would have him? At £8.5 million, he knows few clubs could afford him. But he argues it would be in Liverpool's interests to drop the price dramatically and get as much money as they can for him sooner rather than later. Where would he go? 'God knows! At the moment I feel like "where do I go, what do I do?". I certainly don't feel that by leaving me out he's taking the pressure off me.'

Collymore's much-vaunted move to Liverpool went wrong right from the start. Incredibly, the player claims that he and manager Roy Evans never sat down during the contract negotiations and discussed Collymore's role. But, I suggest, surely he could have forced the issue? 'I thought I was going to sign for a club with better players who would give me even better service than anywhere I'd ever been before. I thought, yeah, they play a patient build-up, but obviously if they're going to spend that kind of money they're going to use my strengths. I never sat down with Roy to discuss the plan. You've got to understand the mentality of football, of football supporters and the press: if a player's doing well, he's great; if he's not doing so well, he's not great, so it never comes to this stage where anybody analyses anything. It's as black and white as that.'

He feels aggrieved that when he joined Liverpool nobody spelt out to him what was expected of him. There were, he claims, no discussions involving how Redknapp and McManaman would try and bring him into the game. He's obviously bemused by this approach. 'I don't know of any other industry that would lay out £8.5 million on anything and then not have some plan from day one of how they're going to use it, or pre-plan to think, is it worth buying this, anyway? You'd think people would think it through before they go ahead and do it, even if it's a £20,000 transfer.'

But no one did and Collymore and Liverpool aren't working out. Two months down the line, Collymore's only played five League games. He scored two sensational goals at the start of the season but we are speaking the day after he came on as a sub against Manchester City in the Coca-Cola Cup. For six minutes. Which makes Collymore a very expensive seat-warmer. And leaves him feeling bewildered.

It's easy to feel sorry for him, but haven't we been here before? At Forest he touted the line that he just wanted to feel appreciated, for the manager to play to his strengths. At Anfield, it appears, it's the same story. He's in danger of making a career out of being a square peg in a round hole. But 'twas not always thus.

Collymore frequently returns to the subject of Southend during our interview. 'I'm sorry to bring it up again,' he apologises, 'but I keep going back to that because it's the happiest I've been. It's the nearest I've got to being treated like a "big boy".'

There were three main reasons why he was so happy at Southend. (1) the management team understood his strengths. (2) they used them on the field of play. (3) Colin Murphy and Barry Fry listened to his views. Collymore needs to be needed. He needs to be loved, appreciated. He needs to be understood and to be given space. At his first club, Stafford Rangers, manager John Williams told him he'd got ability but that he, Williams, wasn't going to be the one to bring it out. Collymore's reaction was: 'Sod you!' Williams' successor, Chris White, spent five to ten minutes a day with the youngster. It made a huge difference. At Crystal Palace Steve Coppell took the time to bother with him. Then he met Colin Murphy who took him to Southend: 'It was the only time in my career that I've had anybody say: "I've watched you and I feel that what you've got to offer when you're playing at your maximum will make us a better team," and actually utilise that.'

At Forest he complained that he wasn't getting enough of the ball, enough chances. The record hasn't changed with the move to Liverpool. His detractors argue that he's a selfish, lazy, whining, arrogant egotist who wants a team to be built around him and isn't prepared to compromise. But doesn't he have a point? You don't pay £8.5 million so you can mould a player, you buy the finished article. And it's surely a false economy to ask a fine artist to decorate your lounge. 'What would you rather see?' asks Collymore. 'Someone running around and building a character for themselves based on fighting and being rough and kicking people or a lazy git who'll get the ball and score an amazing goal? What do you pay your money for? The fees that I've gone for suggest that people want something different. If I can't find the platform to do that, then hopefully I'll keep plugging away till I do, whether that be in Division Four or Division Ten of the local park league.'

As a youngster, Glenn Hoddle was his hero: 'If Glenn was a 21-year-old now, managers would be asking him to combine doing what he does with chasing back and tackling and it would take away from his natural game.'

His disillusionment with the cautious nature of English football is a constant theme. Collymore would rather thrill fans than frustrate opponents. 'I never wanted to stop other players from playing, I wanted to excite. In the game now, especially at the top level, there's not enough genuine positive thinking, there's not enough players willing to go out and say: "Sod this! I'm really going to have a go at somebody and be attack-minded." The teams that do are successful, like Manchester United.

'I would rather play in a team that go out and genuinely get beaten 2–0 but have been really positive and been beaten by a better team than draw 0–0, sit off all game, 'cos I think you're kidding yourself then. That's easy for me to say but the manager will turn round and say we're playing for points and at the end of the season these points are going to get me the sack. Or not. And if we stay in this division it's worth £3 million more to us than if we go down to the First Division. I can understand it, but maybe money has destroyed everything good.'

Stan Collymore is very intense. He talks a lot. Earnestly. And he's very opinionated. A good PR company would advise keeping his mouth shut a bit more. But Stan's not in the game to be liked: 'I say what I feel I have to say. Some people obviously don't like me because I have an opinion. They're the manager and you're the player so you don't get the chance to have your say. Maybe it'd be great for all managers to have a group of players that they send out and they'd do exactly what the manager wanted. You can't underestimate money in all of this, a lot of players get into a team and if they're on a good contract they don't want to be saying anything.'

Money is something he claims not to be interested in so long as he's got enough for a house and his family. He squirms a bit before revealing that he's on £12,000 a week: 'It's never been for the money. People might say that's a load of rubbish – "he can afford to say that".' Of course he can. But he argues: 'It hasn't made me any happier than I was five or six years ago: if somebody said, "Would you play for half what you're earning now and be dead spot on happy?" I would.'

He's certainly not too full of the joys of spring at the moment. Mindful of the European Championships next year, he's keen to get back on top of his game. At the moment he's way off: 'I feel I'm using 10 to 20 per cent of my capability and I don't mean in effort. That's scary. Obviously you want to be 100 per cent all the time, but if you're not and you're being given the opportunities, you can put it down to a bad day. If you're not 100 per cent and you're not getting any opportunities, then there's something fundamentally wrong.'

He's still unsure why Evans paid £8.5 million for him. 'Maybe because we've got a squad of 25 with 18 internationals, maybe they don't feel there's the need to get the best out of me. Maybe the mentality at Liverpool is that if they get a pool of good players, they'll use them at different times, in different circumstances. Maybe Roy's thinking we might come across five or six different circumstances in a season, injuries, suspensions, teams playing in a different way. Maybe that's his thinking. It certainly wasn't in my thinking. At Forest when someone got injured, there wasn't always the same calibre of player to stand in for him. That wasn't a thing you could worry about at Liverpool 'cos of all the players there, but I didn't expect to think I would be one of those sorts of players.'

Aside from finding himself the most expensive reserve player in the country, his move to Liverpool hasn't been quite what he expected. 'My ideas on big clubs have changed: you think you're going to something far superior in every way. I thought the training would be as good as, if not better than, at Forest.' Certainly Anfield training has its idiosyncrasies: Collymore was called in the day after his six-minute Coca-Cola Cup appearance purely to take a bath with the rest of the lads. 'I think it's because they don't trust players so late in the week, they keep their eye on them. It does drive you nuts, but that's the way it is.'

Collymore hates the 'dictatorship' nature of gaffer-player relationships and feels there should be more input from the players, who, after all, are the ones who have to put the system into practice. 'I feel that I've got good ideas about football but because I'm a player, people think "He's just a player". Unfortunately most people think footballers are stupid and thick and haven't got an idea about anything. Some players don't help that image, there's no doubt about that – even at Liverpool, there's been times when I've wanted to say, "Look, this is so obvious", but you have to be mindful of all the other stuff. Abroad they're a bit more used to player power, especially in Holland.'

If players in this country were given more of an opportunity to discuss their views, Collymore reckons he wouldn't be in the woeful position he is now: 'From the outset I feel it should be done, especially with a new

signing, especially one who's cost a lot of money and who could potentially have a great influence on the team. You'd think that, the first day,
you'd go into the dressing-room and the gaffer would say: "This is
whoever, this is what he can do and let's go and put that into practice on
the training pitch." But that hasn't happened. It's very odd. It's one of those
professions where nobody thinks about anything, it's like: if it happens, it
happens and that's it. For me, that's not good enough, but I've got to work
in that system. It's very frustrating.'

Another thing he finds frustrating is the misconception that he's a thug:
'The "bad boy" thing is a load of rubbish.' He denies that Colin Cooper
hit him for not running for the team, but admits: 'Yeah, I'll hold my hands
up and say that maybe [punching Alf-Inge Haaland in training] was one of
the incidents that perpetuated the myth. We were training and his studs
must have gone down my Achilles tendons half a dozen times if they went
down once and I just turned around and says: "What the ****ing hell
d'you do that for?" And he said something and he said it again and he said
it again. What did he say? Eff off. So I just hit him once and he went
down,' he giggles. 'But that's happened a thousand times at a thousand
clubs. There was the thing with Robbie Fowler and Neil Ruddock
coming back from Russia. Razor hit Robbie 'cos Robbie cut his trainers
up, but as soon as it happened it was over. It's one of those things.'

He feels that his whole 'bad boy' image has been built around the fact
that he's outspoken. And the unseemly rows with Nottingham Forest
manager Frank Clark earlier this year haven't helped: 'I don't regret what
I said, because they blew it up. But he [Clark] could have had me and
Bryan [Roy] in the office and had it out [after the game against Spurs,
when Clark accused the pair of not pulling their weight]. He said that me
and Bryan Roy were almost cheating. That game I thought he was
particularly unfair to both of us. If it had happened behind closed doors,
who knows . . .? I went to Liverpool for three main reasons. (1) Forest
agreed to sell me, which was the main reason. (2) A desire to play for one
of the really big clubs. (3) The ongoing arguments with Frank Clark.'

He's hurt at the way he was treated by Clark, even though at an early
age, he says he learnt not to trust people in football. Rejected by Walsall
and his beloved Wolves (despite 16 goals in 20 youth-team games), his
move to Crystal Palace was marred by mickey-taking from the
predominantly south London boys. A sensitive soul, Collymore found it
difficult to adjust and didn't like playing out wide. When Colin Murphy
wanted him to play up front for Southend, Stan jumped at the chance.
That was the one seriously happy move of the lot but soon he was off to
Nottingham. He admits he should have socialised more with the players at
Forest, but around that time his sister Andrea died of cancer and understandably he spent much of his time with his mother and family.

It's hard to reconcile the image of Collymore as Norman No-mates with the reality of seeing him perform in public. Sure, at Forest at the start of last season he sat alone in the canteen and didn't seem to mix that well. But at Anfield in August Stan was the centre of good vibes. Joking with David James (who's DJed round at Stan's six-bedroomed Cannock abode at a barbecue), holding hands with Jamie Redknapp (he wanted Stan to finish our interview and come and play), laughing with Steve McManaman. And what about the Stan Collymore who signs endless autographs for fans, who's softly spoken but honest, polite and adores his family? None of this fits the 'bad boy' image.

Stan the Man is full of contradictions. An intriguing talent, an intriguing personality. Outspoken, but down to earth. He still lives round the corner from his mum, and relies heavily on her and his mates to keep him sane. He's going to need them if he's to turn things round. 'I'd hate to look back and say: "For the sake of a couple of medals here and a trophy there, I neglected relationships." That would be even worse than not achieving. Football's very important and for a long time it's been one of the most important things in my life, but you have to put it into perspective.'

FourFourTwo, December 1995

FROM THE CITY GROUND

Richard Forest

Turn the clock back just over a year. It is Sky's live Monday night game and Stan Collymore has just run from inside his own half, beaten the Wimbledon team and netted a screamer from 30 yards to give Forest a 2–0 lead. 'He had absolutely no right to score from there,' screeched Andy Gray, seemingly on the brink of orgasm.

Maybe he didn't. But that pearl of wisdom from the ever enthusiastic Scottish pundit more or less sums up Collymore's main strength as a player – the rare ability to receive the ball in the most innocuous positions and yet still end up scoring a goal. In this respect he is almost unique, with only Matt Le Tissier and perhaps Tony Yeboah able to touch him out of all the forwards in the Premiership when it comes to this quality.

In his two seasons at Forest, Collymore scored 50 goals in just 76 games – an astounding strike-rate made even more remarkable by the fact that a large percentage of them were scored in spectacular fashion. The afore-mentioned strike against Wimbledon and his goal away to Manchester United a few months later immediately spring to mind.

It is therefore little surprise that Collymore was a big crowd favourite at Forest. Even if Forest were playing extremely badly, whenever he received a ball in the opposition's half, the expectations of those in the City Ground would suddenly rise. Although my feelings regarding Collymore have been pretty irrational since the rather ungracious manner in which he left for Liverpool, I can't deny that he is the most prodigiously talented player I have ever seen in a Forest shirt. He has it all – pace, skill, strength, good vision, heading ability and two good feet. When on top form Collymore really is unstoppable. Okay, £8.5 million is a hell of a lot of money, but in today's inflated transfer market in which a striker as mediocre as Chris Armstrong is worth £4.5 million, I would say that he is well worth it.

Unfortunately, as part of the bargain come Collymore's various idiosyncracies. In this respect it could almost be said that he has as many weaknesses as he does strengths. On the field he has a dodgy temperament, a habit of going for goal instead of passing to unmarked team-mates in better positions and, most frustratingly, a tendency to show little interest in games that are either insignificant or not on TV. Off the field Collymore is a psychologist's dream; his departure from Forest was ultimately the result of what appeared to be a severe attitude and ego problem. He just seemed to think that Forest were no longer big enough for him, that he was a big fish in a small pond.

Although Forest had lost their best player, I almost felt quite smug as Collymore signed for Liverpool claiming he had at last found a pond of appropriate size and was about to take the footballing world by storm. After all, as well as the fact that it gave Frank Clark a lot of money to improve the team, I was convinced that, despite Collymore's undoubted ability, with all those idiosyncrasies he would fall flat on his face under a stricter régime at Anfield and would want to come back to the City Ground within two years. A few months on, his indifferent start at his new club has done little to disprove my convictions.

Whether he will come crawling back like the prodigal son remains to be seen. Many other Forest supporters might disagree but I would still welcome him with open arms, such is his ability. Having said that, who needs Collymore when you've got Jason Lee . . .

Forest Forever

ALLY McCOIST

Sue Mott

Ally McCoist is a danger to himself and to others. Don't ask me how I know, I just know. A person could go out for an innocent swift half with the record-breaking Rangers striker and be found wandering along the banks of the Clyde three days later with no memory of events after 1963 and someone else's car keys in their grip.

There is scarcely a disco or a racecourse or a centre-half in the whole of Scotland that has not suffered at his hands and at least one of the reasons Graeme Souness went to Turkey must have been to put as much space as possible between him and his *bête noire*.

Other players of his ilk get into trouble. You think of Gazza's exploits in Indian restaurants or Duncan Ferguson (wearing one earring and a flower behind his ear) assaulting a fisherman on crutches. McCoist escapes virtually scot free. Hamilton Sheriff Court once had the temerity to fine him £150 for assault but otherwise he is as securely zipped into Teflon as Ronald Reagan once was. Nothing sticks.

There is a good reason for this. McCoist is smart. Not so smart that he won *A Question of Sport* when invited to stand in as captain for Ian Botham lately ('Wait till you hear this . . . I'm telling you . . . we're nine points clear – not five or four or six – we're nine points clear and we got beat on the last picture!') but he possesses that classic combination of bright, boyish and incorrigible roguery that melts the opposition. Even the Catholics like him in Glasgow.

Last Saturday he became Rangers' most prolific scorer of Scottish League goals, breaking the 57-year-old record of Bob McPhail. As the ball went in off the post from 25 yards against Raith, McCoist celebrated his 231st league goal with two fists raised to the sky.

'That record meant everything. Oh, everything,' he said over the first bottle of New Zealand chardonnay. 'You think how long that record stood. Fifty-seven years. *Phewww.* I wanted it ever since I broke my leg in 1993. That was the one I was really, really striving for. I wouldn't have admitted it before. But I'll admit it to you now. That's an amazing record.'

McCoist has broken records before, but usually for keeping people waiting. His sister, a former Great Britain handball international, bought him an 'Ish' watch for Christmas which has no minute or second hands. Actually the hour hand, pointing to 'oneish', 'twoish' etc, is pretty redundant in his case as well.

As I sat on and on in reception at Ibrox, all polished wood and muted blue, waiting for our man to appear, even Paul Gascoigne felt moved to provide coffee and sympathy. 'There you go, pet,' he said. Richard Gough walked by. 'Who are you waiting for . . . Coisty,' he said, seamlessly answering his own question.

Two and a half hours later (which is not bad) he was ready. It makes you wonder how the BBC managed to get him to the *Question of Sport* studio in Shepherd's Bush before the audience went home. 'Ah well, I flew down the day before for the Chelsea-Newcastle game so there wasn't really an excuse.

'I was nervous, being captain for the first time. I'd be lying if I said I wasn't. But Big Bill* was just fantastic, such a big gentleman, and once I had a couple of glasses of wine it loosened the tongue and I really, really enjoyed it. You get the chance to meet people from different sports that you not so much idolise as have great admiration for.' Except Sam Torrance, who McCoist blamed totally for losing.

There is an irony in the fact that McCoist has become a national figure only by appearance on a TV quiz show. His renown in Scotland is profound, but after a spell, short and sour, as a teenager at Sunderland he has largely been hidden from English gaze behind Hadrian's Wall.

'I just didn't perform at Sunderland. I was definitely too young when I went down. I wasn't good enough.' Plus, he might have added, his room-mate was the debonair and dangerous Frank Worthington who, one suspects, taught the young Glaswegian a thing or two.

'My only regret is for the Sunderland fans, who were so good to me it was embarrassing. That's why it was very important to me to score home and away for Rangers against Leeds United in the "Battle of Britain" a couple of years ago. It proved a point to myself. It was a wee personal thing. A bit selfish really. It stopped all the whispers about me only being good in Scotland. I honestly think Big Mark* and myself were one of the best partnerships going.'

McCoist is of the Max Miller school of strikers. The cheeky chappie that pops up when least required by opponents to slide the ball in the net from a yard. He is small by striking standards, only 5ft 10in, but he is sturdy, astute and can talk a hulking great stopper into abject submission.

His heading is rather suspect but as a fellow player once said, 'I think he's protecting his face for his next career as a TV star.'

But before he is unleashed, all grin and eyelashes, on our unsuspecting screens, he would like to win his 50th cap for Scotland, preferably when Scotland play England in the European Championship.

'I'd give anything to play in it but I'm not kidding myself. I know I'll have to be scorin' regular for Rangers because Big Fergie'll* be there, Durie's* absolutely flyin' and Wee Spenny's* playing well.'

Does this mean he's fourth- or fifth-best scorer in Scotland? 'I didn't say that,' he shot back with the split-second timing of Gerd Muller.

McCoist's record in football is one of astonishing consistency. All his managers have hit him, including the present incumbent, Walter Smith. 'Oh, Walter. A lot of people don't realise that Walter can be equally if not more aggressive than Graeme Souness. Honestly. Walter was my manager at Under-17 level and my first run-in with him was when I locked him out on the hotel balcony in Monaco. Well, it got to the stage where I was terrified to let him in because I knew he was going to batter me senseless. In the end, I hid in a room next door and got someone else to let him out, but I don't have to tell you the end of the story. He got me later and battered me absolutely senseless.'

It was the on-going war of attrition with Souness, however, for which McCoist became notorious. Many a nickname was accrued in this period. 'Dudley' they called him after one particular roasting from the manager: 'You were a dud at St Johnstone, a dud at Sunderland and you're still a ****ing dud,' roared Souness. McCoist sat on the bench so often, his team-mates re-christened him 'The Judge'.

'Looking back on it, I probably didn't do myself any favours. I should just have shut my mouth and taken it. But I was always coming back with these smart or funny jibes and that would get him even more annoyed. I honestly don't hold any grudges, though. I believe, rightly or wrongly, Graeme and I could be good friends now he's not my manager.'

That thumping sound in the background is probably Souness pounding on the chairman's door in Turkey begging for a new five-year contract.

Can he see that arriving on the bench at St Mirren with a pot of tea and two cups would be somewhat galling to the gaffer? 'But it was perishin',' he said, blue eyes wide with innocence. 'All right, maybe I'm genuinely wrong sometimes. Maybe I should be a little bit more serious . . .'

Pause for true story. Daley Thompson once played in a charity match in Gateshead with Ally McCoist. He'd never heard of him and McCoist played so horrendously, the Olympian thought he was some insurance salesman or other who had paid to play with the stars. McCoist explains: 'Actually we were out the night before with Crammie* and his hospitality was making me suffer.

'. . . But I believe I'm very serious at the right time. There's nothing more important to me than my football. But it doesn't help having guys like Durranty* and Gascoigne about, come on.'

You will not be surprised to learn that McCoist and Gazza get on. 'Famously. I think he's an intelligent boy who likes to let people think he's stupid. He's brilliant with kids and he doesn't have a bad bone in his body. But to counter all that, he does some stupid, ridiculous things. That's what makes him so interesting.'

Known in the dressing-room as 'Taylor and Burton', Gascoigne and his girlfriend Sheryl attract the keen interest of McCoist. 'Sheryl's a lovely girl. And he's a different man around her. I mean, he's in love. He's really in love. He's the last person you'd expect it from.'

But then McCoist has a keen interest in a lot of things: skiing, Super Bowl, China (the country as opposed to plates), the Olympics, golf and, especially, horseracing. He part-owns a yearling called Paldost (for Paul, Ally, Dougie and Stuart, the members of the syndicate) and a gelding, Samartian, that is running over hurdles at Ayr next Saturday. His first horse, Fishke, had a bad knee ('a bit like me') and doesn't run anymore. ('Very much like me.')

'I'm the only player in the Premier Division who goes down injured with old age,' he said, contemplating his 34th birthday this year. This has not stopped Motherwell, rooted to the foot of the Premier Division, expressing an interest in his services. He doesn't fancy it, though. After 13 years at Rangers, 313 goals, innumerable deckings and more bottles of assorted brews than France exports in a year, he is pretty attached to the place.

'I don't want to go out on a whimper,' he said. No, the whimpering is usually done by his companions as evening and brain cells surrender to darkness. Don't ask me how I know. I just know.

*Glossary of terms: Big Bill = Bill Beaumont; Big Mark = Mark Hateley; Big Fergie = Duncan Ferguson; Durie = Gordon Durie; Wee Spenny = John Spencer; Durranty = Ian Durrant; Crammie = Steve Cram.

Daily Telegraph, 20 January 1996

JEFF ASTLE

Michael Heatley

There was a time when the sturdily built six-foot Jeff Astle let his feet do the talking. A bargain £25,000 buy from Notts County in 1964, he served Albion for a decade, picking up five England caps and winning FA Cup and League Cup-winners medals during his stay. Goals in every round of the Cup in '68 plus a season atop the First Division scoring chart brought records galore and rather more than a footnote in WBA history. Now, though, it's other records and notes that interest him.

'It's incredible how it's taken off,' Astle admits with a smile. 'Last night's *Derby Telegraph* had me on the front page, not the back page – two pictures of me in that Ziggy Stardust thing I wore when I sang "The Wonder of You"!' This, he admits, was the most outrageous of all his outfits: 'It took me about two hours to get the stuff out of me hair!'

The costumes, he explains, are as much a surprise to him as the viewers. 'When I get down there I say, "Bloody hell, not *that* . . ."' It was a similar, surprising story when the 'Jeff Astle Sings' cult started. 'Frank Skinner used to idolise me when I played at West Brom, and he phoned me up and asked if I'd like to go on the show. The following week I went down and Frank's hand was trembling: he'd never met me, you see.

'He introduced me to everyone else and when they'd finished talking he threw me a big piece of paper and said, "Here y'are, Jeff – that's what you're singing." I said, "You *what?*" And it was "Love Grows Where My Rosemary Goes". Some people think it's the best one I ever sang . . .' It took off from there, and 19 weeks later we're talking record releases.

Skinner's belief that Jeff, 53, could add a musical dimension to the show was no fantasy – because back in his heyday he'd teamed up with Carl Wayne, the non-hairy singer from The Move ('he married Diane out of *Crossroads*,' Jeff offers helpfully), to cut a single, 'Sweet Water'. 'Carl used

134

to come to our house sometimes when I was at West Brom.

'I thought it was a lovely song,' he continues, 'but I don't think it had the publicity in those days. People were more bothered about Jeff Astle playing football than singing. But it was a catchy tune, I always liked that song.' The B-side hasn't been included on the new release since it's an instrumental version: suggestions that pop connoisseurs might consider it the better side provoke uproarious laughter. 'The pianist will, that's for sure!'

Jeff's own musical tastes are, he admits, fairly middle of the road – so when Julian Cope's record company asked him to perform the former Teardrop Explodes star's hit at their sales conference, even the unshockable Astle was, for once, nonplussed. 'It was called "Try Try Try",' he earnestly explains, 'and I'd never heard of it 'cos I don't listen to that kind of *Top of the Pops* music much. They sent me a tape and I learned it at home.' Sadly Cope wasn't in the audience to hear his mangled masterpiece, but everyone else went bananas.

'I sang "Sailing" and some of the others from *Fantasy Football*, and they all got out their lighters and waved them,' says Jeff, wide-eyed. 'They were brilliant, singing with me and clapping, and when I went off I saw this group who were going on next. The head [sic] singer came up to me and said, "How the fookin 'ell d'you expect me to follow that?"'

So does Jeff agree that 99 out of 100 football records are simply awful? 'They've got a cult following, haven't they?' he insists, neatly ducking the question. '"Back Home" was ever such a catchy tune. I've told people it's being re-released and they say, "I remember, *lovely* song . . ."' He bursts into the opening bars. 'Blokes my age remember it well because it was Number 1 for quite a while.'

The album on which it appears was cut by the England 1970 World Cup squad with Jeff, who'd been a star of the local church choir before swapping hymnbooks for football boots, very much to the fore. 'The World Beaters sing the World Beaters' was the original title, partly because England were the holders at the time. Maybe it's also because songsmiths Bill Martin and Phil Coulter were the men who gave us Sandie Shaw's Eurovision 'classic' 'Puppet on a String' – which, along with the likes of 'Sugar Sugar' and 'Lily the Pink', is one of the low . . . er, *high*lights. Whatever, Jeff was a leading vocalist in a team whose overall tone-deafness was as legendary as their ball skills.

Even if his singing career takes off, Jeff's unlikely to give up his day job – he owns a successful industrial cleaning business that sees him working up to seven days a week. He can, though, always make time to watch his beloved Baggies. 'I finish Saturday dinnertime to go to the matches, and when there's one at night I work round my jobs – because I daren't miss a match at West Brom.'

He's not that impressed by First Division football, though: 'The grade's not as high as when I played.' As for Albion's promising start transferring into promotion, Jeff hopes so, 'but I can't see it just at the moment until we get some money pumped into it like what's happening nowadays at the top clubs. I think Alan Buckley's doing the best job on what he's got.' Even so, 'The team's looked very good so far this season, it's surprised me, really.'

If Jeff doesn't see a return to the top flight, where he scored his goals back in his 1960s–1970s heyday, without money, then finding a benefactor must be the next step. Now Eric Clapton, we hear, is a famous fan who could maybe be a source of funds. And that would throw up all sorts of musical possibilities.

Matchday, October 1995

WILF MANNION

Bob Holmes

PORTUGAL 0 ENGLAND 10
Friendly International: Lisbon, 27 May 1947

Born in Middlesbrough on 16 May 1918, Wilf Mannion wanted to become a shipyard worker but possessed a refinement more suitable for *Swan Lake* than Swan-Hunter. Robust but with a poise worthy of the ballet, he was an artist with a football, his deft brushstrokes illuminating the bleak landscape of the industrial north-east. Soon hailed as the best boy footballer since Cliff Bastin, he was snapped up by Boro as if he was the Kohinoor diamond.

Mannion first revealed his sublime skills with South Bank St Peters and signed amateur forms for Boro in September 1936, turning pro the following January. Of a generation for whom the outbreak of war could not have been more untimely, the 'Golden Boy' made his mark immediately hostilities ceased. Having won four wartime caps, he linked with other similarly deprived legends to earn just recognition and rave reviews in the post-war era. He scored a hat-trick in a 7–2 win over Northern Ireland in his first full international and notched two for Great Britain against the Rest of Europe. But 26 caps was scant reward for an undoubted genius and said more about his brushes with authority than the quality of his rivals.

At 5ft 6in and 11 stone, he boasted one of the best shots in the game, while his perception was almost psychic; his passing being so accurate and perfectly weighted he could find his colleagues in a crowd – and suddenly they would have space. After retiring prematurely in 1954, he had a second coming with Hull City six months later before winding down in the unlikely outposts of the lower leagues.

'Mannion is Mozartian in his exquisite workmanship,' wrote Donny

137

Davies, of *The Guardian*. 'His style is so graceful and so courtly that he wouldn't be out of place if he played in a lace ruffle and the perruque.'

With locks as golden as his first touch, he was bound to be eulogised, but for Wilfred J. Mannion the white shirt of England and the company of fellow maestros were quite enough. Alongside Messrs Matthews, Mortensen, Lawton and Finney, Mannion felt completely at home and this fabulous five were probably the finest forward line ever to wear the three lions. However, when they played together for the first time – against Portugal in Lisbon – the portents were not good.

'It was an end-of-season tour and we had just been beaten by Switzerland,' Mannion recalls. 'England were not supposed to lose to anybody in those days so you can imagine the stick we got from the press. Stan [Matthews] had had one of his rare off-days and the reporters had really got on to him.' The team for the Portugal match was picked on the plane – over the Pyrenees – and Finney came in for his début, replacing Langton who had a knock. 'In Lisbon,' remembers Mannion, 'we met an Englishman, Bob Kelly, who had been helping the Portuguese, and he warned us that they had their best side for many years. He said they were "very quick and clever", and also told us that we might struggle in the intense heat.' As if that were not enough, it was felt that both Matthews and Lawton would be up against it – their respective markers reputedly being measured at 6ft 2in and 15 stone.

As the teams came out, the setting could hardly have been more spectacular: a magnificent natural amphitheatre whose marble steps were teeming with a 65,000 crowd. Clad in the colours of the kaleidoscope, they were full of anticipation as the old masters took their bow. But there had already been drama, with England manager Walter Winterbottom concerned that two members of his team had soaked up too much of the festive atmosphere. Mannion remembers: 'Tom Finney and I had been sitting on the beach at Estoril in the boiling sunshine while the others had been sheltering under umbrellas. Walter disapproved. He said: "It's for mad dogs and *not* footballing Englishmen to go out in the midday sun." Nor did he take kindly to our excuse that we were used to it after serving in the Middle East and Italy in the Eighth Army! But neither Tom nor I felt any effect and in 13 seconds we went in front. And I had laid it on.'

With the shirt-sleeved crowd still settling, Mannion crossed for Lawton to hammer home. This goal was scored with the 'heavy' British ball and the England party looked on in amazement when it was replaced by the lighter, larger continental ball. But that was not all that was changed. Heartened by his goal and relishing his partnership with Mortensen, Lawton put the Blackpool man through for the second, a terrific right-foot drive, after eight minutes. Three minutes later, Lawton went through on his own and in the 21st minute Finney opened his international account following a clever move down the left.

'After this,' chuckles Mannion, 'they changed the goalie – without telling anyone, not even the ref. Walter went to the touchline and skipper George Hardwick protested, but the ref did nothing. At 4–0 up, we weren't too bothered and Frank Swift said: "Well, you'll just have to put another four past him." Before half-time, Lawton had got three himself, and we might have eased up after that but when we went in at the break, we got a dressing-down. Old Iron Man, Wilf Copping, a real disciplinarian, told us: "No slacking. Herbert Chapman always used to say that slackers never got anywhere. Keep on until their net is full of goals."'

That message and the lessons of Switzerland sank in. Instead of weaving pretty patterns which got them nowhere, England delivered a powerful punch at frequent intervals, demoralising the home side into further unsanctioned substitutions before they were finally counted out. No one enjoyed their football holiday in the sunshine more than Mannion, who prised open the home defence at will, while Lawton was a revelation alongside Mortensen, both players collecting four goals. Matthews, who made four, added one himself and ran the home defence ragged.

'Everybody scored but me,' says Mannion, 'but I played deep behind Lawton and Mortensen to collect the loose material and keep the link between them. We were unstoppable and even had two goals disallowed. It was a marvellous performance, one of the best ever by an England team. But old Kelly was right – the Portuguese *were* clever and quick, and never gave up. It was just masters against pupils.'

Portugal: Azevedo, Cardoso, Feleciano, Amaro, Mereira, Ferreira, Correira, Arajuo, Peyroteo, Travassos, Rogeiro.

England: Swift, Scott, Hardwick, Wright, Franklin, Lowe, Matthews, Mortensen, Lawton, Mannion, Finney.

My Greatest Game (Mainstream, 1995)

JIM BAXTER

Robert Philip

Alan Baxter was eight before he discovered who his father really was. 'My dad was talking to this man he'd met while we were on holiday on the island of Rothesay. We were on the prom and the rain was lashing down but they stood laughing and joking for ages. Then, as he turned to go, the stranger said to me: "What's it like to be the Son of God then, eh?" I'd been three when my dad retired, so up until that moment I had no idea he was so special.'

If you, too, missed the age of miracles, let me try to explain exactly why Jim Baxter was so special. While Liverpool idolised The Beatles in the 1960s, Glasgow worshipped Slim Jim. If Paul Gascoigne is worth £4.7 million, then you could not buy Baxter today for £9.4 million; if Faustino Asprilla is demanding £30,000 a week, then Baxter could have asked for £60,000. Think of Glenn Hoddle at his very best . . . then multiply that image by two. Like George Best, he was more rock star than footballer, a beauty queen on each arm, a betting slip in every pocket and, most destructively of all, a drink in every pub. Like Asprilla, according to the lurid tales from Italy and Colombia, Baxter burned the candle at both ends then torched the bit in the middle.

He never trained or practised, he scarcely won a tackle in his entire career, his right foot was only there for symmetry, he never headed the ball, he stood 5ft 11in but weighed only 9st 12lb, and he moved at nothing faster than regal elegance. Yet the stranger's revelation was uttered without fear of thunderbolts from above; Jim Baxter was indeed a football god. A swivel of those narrow hips, a dip of that slender shoulder as he drifted in on goal and entire defences would leap out of his way like shell-shocked passengers abandoning a sinking ship. He scored twice on his first appearance for Scotland at Wembley in 1963 and played keepie-uppie underneath the twin towers four years later when he toyed with Sir Alf's world champions. No marvel was beyond his power.

Thankfully, the last miracle was reserved for himself, a second liver transplant in 1995 saving a life he had done his very best to destroy through alcohol. 'I was offski, there's no doubt about that,' reflects Baxter, now 56 and though maybe not the svelte figure of our sepia-toned memories, still a remarkably leaner and healthier Slim Jim than the bloated apparition he became when booze had him in its murderous grip. A glass of Highland Spring mineral water, rather than a Highland malt, accompanies the fillet steak he is attacking with relish, although the second new liver he was given is working so well he admits to 'a wee glass of champagne every now and then at hame, like'.

Glasgow may belong to Jim Baxter, but the lilt remains that of the Fife coal-mining community of Hill o' Beath where he worked down the village pit during the week and turned out for Raith Rovers on Saturdays until Rangers paid £17,500 for his blessed genius in 1960.

'Did I think I was dying that time? Oh aye, I was away. It really was a miracle I came through that. I was lucky, I got a wee break there right enough . . .'

The combination of drink, gambling, two ill-advised transfers to Sunderland and Nottingham Forest, plus Rangers' snooty refusal to grant him a testimonial — 'Och, I was only there five years,' he says with unflinching loyalty — means Baxter lives in modest retirement on the south side of the city over which he once reigned supreme. If he had been allowed an agent, he would have earned — and probably spent — millions.

In 1963, when he played alongside Lev Yashin, Ferenc Puskas and Eusebio in the Rest of the World team who met England at Wembley, Baxter was earning a meagre £35 a week at Rangers, yet there is nary a shred of bitterness at the riches currently on offer to every Tom, Dick and Faustino. 'I think Puskas was on two grand at Real Madrid even then. But, no, I don't envy Asprilla, Ginola or Cantona what they're earning — why should I? I was a slave during my time at Rangers but the game's changed. In my day the directors had all the power, now it's the players, and good luck to them.

'Having said that, there's very few who actually deserve it. The foreign lads apart, there aren't that many great players about. Gascoigne could still make it and Giggs is marvellous — really marvellous — but the Raith Rovers team I left in 1960 would probably win the Scottish championship today. But, no, I've no regrets. I was dead two years ago and was brought back. I've got two terrific sons and a great partner so I really am the luckiest guy in the world. I started off with nothing down the pits and went on to have a life money can't buy. I messed up my marriage and my liver but that was inevitable the way I was going.'

From as far back as he can remember, Baxter's weekends were spent playing his beloved fitba' and bevvyin'; since there was only one full-sized ball in Hill o' Beath, everyone joined in. 'Forty-a-side. Until the big boys came out the pub [here he mimics the swamp monster from the black lagoon] in their great size-12 wellies. When you get the ball and there's 39 miners chasing you, you've got to have a wee bit of skill to survive.'

Even on a crowded, muddy pitch resembling the battle scene in *El Cid*, Baxter's shimmering brilliance could be seen by all through the gloom. At 17 – by which time he had been one of the big boys in the pub for some years – he signed for Raith Rovers and received £250. 'My mum was the proudest woman in Scotland because I bought her the first washing-machine in the whole of Hill o' Beath.'

Still a month shy of his 21st birthday, Baxter joined Rangers and joyously surrendered the last vestiges of self-control. 'After Hill o' Beath, Glasgow was Las Vegas. People might wonder how I went off my head. But one day you're a Raith Rovers player who cannae pull the birds at the Cowdenbeath Palais. Next day you come through to Glasgow and the girls are throwing themselves at you. It was a wee bit o' a change in fortune and I certainly wasn't letting it go by. I was a rascal, all right.'

On many an occasion, Baxter would still be trying to sober up three hours before kick-off, yet despite these well-publicised excesses, only Alex James before or since can challenge his position as the king of Scottish football. The eyes, usually sparkling with mischief, moisten at the notion. 'You don't know how that makes me feel, you talking about me and Alex James in the same breath. It was only when I thought I was dying I realised what I meant to people. I got cards from all over the world. Messages of affection from Hong Kong and Australia, from Sean Connery and Billy Connolly, from Rangers fans and Celtic players, from grannies and weans [children] I've never even met. Every time the post arrived at the hospital I was in tears.'

The greatest or not, however, Baxter was paid the same as everyone else during the golden days at Ibrox. And so at the end of every season he would approach the Rangers captain, who would approach the manager, who would approach the directors with his claim for a wage rise. That was the way things were done. He insists he was not asking for Puskas's two grand a week, merely a 'few quid more than those less-gifted. I mean, we were all paid equally. Which is a bit like paying Frank Sinatra the same as the Alexander Brothers.'

He almost went to Spurs as Danny Blanchflower's replacement but Rangers backed out of the deal at the last minute, and when Inter Milan showed an interest Rangers refused to part with Glasgow's most glamorous citizen – so the Italians bought European Footballer of the Year Luis Suarez from Barcelona instead. 'Suarez,' repeats Baxter softly and without a hint of conceit, 'he wasn't in the same league as me.'

Only a precious few ever were. Playing in what Scottish coach Craig

Brown calls the 'spiv's role' – Baxter prefers to describe his position as 'attacking nomad' – he wore the No 6 shirt but roamed wherever he chose with the purpose of tormenting the opposition and entertaining the congregation. When the great Gianni Rivera checked into Hampden Park for a World Cup tie against Scotland in 1965, Baxter began the festivities by nutmegging the Italian golden boy in the first minute. 'Hey, wee man,' he shouted across to Billy Bremner, 'one down, nine tae go.' Bremner stopped keeping count after Baxter nutmegged Rivera the sixth time. The Glaswegian expression 'dead gallus' (cocky/sharp/bold/tough/flash/nonchalant) might have been coined especially in his honour.

'I had great inner confidence on the field. As soon as I got the ball I was the guv'nor. It didn't matter who I was playing against, Pele or any o' them. I could make the ball talk. Some days, if I wanted to hit a pass 25 yards 6¾ inches then I would hit it 25 yards 6¾ inches.'

Baxter's close friend, Dave Mackay, was a willing crony through many a long night's binge, but whereas the Tottenham captain would work it out of his system by training harder than anyone else, Slim Jim preferred to sleep it off under the covers. 'Dave warned me I'd pay the consequences eventually and sure enough I did. Lots of people offered me advice but I loved the booze, it's as simple as that. I just loved getting boozed up.' Might he have been even better or might his career have extended beyond the age of 29 had he bothered to train? 'Nah, I don't think so. Remember, everything I did on the pitch was off-the-cuff. Sheer instinct. If I'd been a good boy, maybe a' the swashbuckling stuff would have got stifled. I was just a happy-go-lucky guy who would come out of the pub, lose four or five hundred pounds on the horses, pick a fight with somebody – maybe get battered in the mooth – then win back the five hundred quid the next day. That's how I looked at life and still do . . . it's too precious to waste being sensible.'

Though the Baxter legend began to spread alarm bells throughout England – Don Revie, Matt Busby and Bill Shankly were among those who decided they could not afford the sleepless nights – in Scotland he was loved as no other after he routed the English at Wembley in '63, scoring the opener with a deft chip over Gordon Banks from a tight angle which floated over the line like a snowflake, and the winner from the penalty spot. 'I'd never taken a penalty in my life but Dave Mackay handed me the ball and said, "Here, put this in the net". So I did.'

In '67, Baxter mesmerised England again (Scotland winning 3–2) but the decline was imminent. He finally raised some money by leaving Rangers for Sunderland and then Forest – 'two bad teams' – before returning to the Glasgow club on a free transfer in 1968 and a second marriage which lasted one season. 'I had all sorts of offers when Rangers freed me but it wouldn't have been fair. I wasn't the Baxter of old and I couldn't cheat people. I might have been a bit of a scoundrel in my private life but I'd always done an honest day's work on the pitch, so I retired.'

Though there are no mementoes in his flat — 'the boys have all my medals and I think I gave away most of the caps and shirts when I was drunk' — there is a lifetime of memories. Like the golden night in the Prater stadium when Rangers beat Rapid Vienna 1–0 in the European Cup with Baxter touching new heights even by his greatness. He ended the night in hospital, an Austrian defender snapping his priceless left leg in the last minute. 'Ach, I couldn't blame him, really . . . I'd been taking the mickey something terrible.'

Many will tell you he was never quite the same again after that injury but the evidence of Wembley '67 suggests otherwise. 'I went downhill because I left Rangers and went to a bad side, simple as that. I would never have wanted to leave Rangers if I hadn't gambled away all my money. I'd bet on anything. Fifty quid the next man to walk in here is wearing black shoes, that kind o' thing. The bevvy did my liver in and the gambling did my brain in. Was it a waste of talent? In a way it was. But ten years of me was maybe enough. I was lucky enough to be able to play a bit of fitba', but when all's said and done, I was just a human being like everyone else.'

Though he inherited his father's left foot, Alan Baxter chose a different path: a fee-paying school education followed by a career in estate agency. 'I could never have made it as a footballer. Nigel Clough and I were born in exactly the same week in March 1966 and look how difficult it's been for him. If your dad's Picasso you don't want to be a painter-decorator. Imagine what it would have been like running out on the pitch as the Son of Baxter . . . the Son of God?'

Daily Telegraph, 5 February 1996

DENNIS BERGKAMP

Chris Lightbown

Scene 1: Arsenal v Inter, Thursday night; even by the standards of pre-season expectations, Highbury is electric with anticipation. A roar greets the announcement of David Platt's name, but uproar greets that of Dennis Bergkamp.

The man is here. The £7.5 million transfer man. The £25,000-a-week man. The gifted Dutchman who plays like an Englishman.

Klinsmann? Cantona? Forget it. They were the fanfare, whereas Bergkamp's arrival proves that the best in the world will come not just to notch up an English season or escape disciplinary wrath back home, but because they believe England is the place to be.

If Bergkamp's transfer works, incredible vistas open up. More world-class players will come here in their prime, finally giving our clubs the mixture of English attitude and foreign skill which professionals say is the ultimate blend.

More. Arsenal will gain kudos in Europe's corridors of power, giving them and any English clubs following in their wake more influence over the shape of the inevitable European league.

More still. If Bergkamp and the players who follow in *his* wake integrate their skills with our pace, opponents will have to follow suit. For English pace will never be able to contain such a blend and should youngsters emulate it, a period of playing like this could haul English football back to world supremacy.

All this from one man? As the crowd roar their recognition at Highbury, Bergkamp remains utterly oblivious, brusquely kicking a practice ball into touch. His body language screams of irritation with the hype, and desperation to get on with the real thing. Which is oddly reminiscent of Bergkamp's last appearance on an English pitch.

Scene 2: Aston Villa v Inter, 29 September 1994. Bergkamp, playing for Inter, stands with hands on hips, glowering at colleagues who yet again have left him stranded up front, shouldering ridiculous levels of responsibility. Minutes later, Villa score and Inter, the holders, are on their way out of the UEFA Cup.

Bergkamp's transfer to Inter was meant to be the jewel in a package of measures aimed at breaking AC Milan's grip on Italian football. But everything that could go wrong went wrong. When Bergkamp would not talk to the Italian press, they talked to his gardener, who said Bergkamp was a withdrawn individual who rarely bothered with Italians. After just 11 goals in 52 League games, Bergkamp was on his way to Arsenal, damned for being Inter's problem because he had failed to be their solution.

Scene 3: Highbury, Wednesday lunchtime. Arsenal are having their team picture taken, but with access restricted to the club's official photographer. A cool breeze wafts through the empty stands. Bergkamp, said to be the cold fish nobody can reach, is chatting to Ian Wright, said to be the ultimate extrovert. If he is ever going to open up, surely it will be here, in the citadel?

Soon after, Bergkamp sits in a quiet room, behind the directors' box. There's no point in tiptoeing around. Does he realise that many people are alienated by the transfer fee and wages he attracts? 'I can very much understand that. I think football is now over the top in these things, but what can I do?' Bergkamp replies. 'I know the other way, too, because in my neighbourhood in Amsterdam and in my family, are people who are not doing too well, so you will never hear me talking about my own situation because I know it's big money. But what can I do?'

Bergkamp's body more than fills the chair, but not in an English player's sprawl. There's a relaxed neatness in his physical presence, just as there's an effortless dignity in his manner. The Dutch way.

Ajax, he says quietly, almost didn't happen. Their youth system wanted him at around eight years of age, but it was dominated by 'parents with fur coats and little dogs, you know, the people who aren't rich but pretend to be rich'. Bergkamp's father, an electrician, didn't like that and neither did Dennis: 'Ajax didn't give their boys tea at half-time. I played football for fun and they looked like a school for just getting results.'

Nevertheless, at 12, he joined Ajax. 'Normal people', whom Bergkamp felt at home with, had come into their youth system, and he got the usual Ajax treatment. A right-winger-cum-striker, he was played in every out-field position, he says, 'partly to educate me, partly to check what my best position was'. At 17, 'small and skinny' as Bergkamp was, Johan Cruyff made him a professional and a first-team player.

Normality swept on, through names like Gullit, Rijkaard and Van Basten. Through Dutch honours and international caps. Through a partnership with Wim Jonk, who could place a pass on to Bergkamp's toe from 40 yards, and into a style of play we barely recognise. Imagine Shearer's goalscoring and selflessness combined with Beardsley's deftness and you start to see what Arsenal have paid for.

Thursday's game showed that Bergkamp's strength lies more in his balance than in his physique. As for his skill, it will work like this. In the seventh minute, Bergkamp was deep in his own half, surrounded by opponents in a position where it would have been awkward for Arsenal to lose the ball. But he wrong-footed his markers by rolling a foot across the ball, then swept off in a direction which defied his body's position and solved the problem with a simple lay-off. Genius so meshed with simplicity that you could not see the joins. Which is perfect for Arsenal. But their team, any English team, will take a long time to blend that sort of play with theirs, let alone raise their standards nearer to his. Will we, the demanding public and media, grant both parties such time?

Back to the quiet man in the quiet room. Bergkamp's reserved manner is what the Dutch call normal but we call insular. His voice tone remains the same whether talking about the nightmare of his two years in Italy or that thunderous, slashing goal in Rotterdam which effectively stopped England qualifying for the 1994 World Cup. ('Er . . . sorry about that.') The footballer's black humour is there; you just have to pick it out from the dry manner.

The Italians, by and large, didn't, and the task they gave Jonk and himself – that of hauling Inter from defensive mania back to national supremacy – got more complicated when they answered Latin hysteria with Dutch stoicism. Inter wanted a god, a saviour or at least a miracle-worker, but Bergkamp says this was rather difficult when the midfield wouldn't move up quickly enough.

Yes, he says, he still thinks of himself as a Dutchman but what he really means is that he doesn't think of himself as footballing Eurotrash, soaking up the ways, playing and otherwise, of whatever country pays those wages. His contract is for four years, no mean commitment; his manner is the same whether talking to the cleaning lady or the chairman, and his emotions flow where he believes they belong, into his private life and his work. The Dutch way. No hype. If we understand that, he could well spark the revolution. But will we?

Sunday Times, 13 August 1995

TEDDY SHERINGHAM

Olivia Blair

'WHAT ISSEEEELIKE?' screamed the irate Spurs fan down the line to Bob 'The Cat' on Radio 5's *6-0-6* show. 'Dunno,' replied Bob. 'I'll tell what he's like,' retorted the caller, who was making that miserable post-defeat journey back down the M6 from Boundary Park on a frozen Saturday afternoon. 'He's a bloody carthorse, that's what he is.'

That was back in December 1992. Three years on, and the carthorse has become a thoroughbred. Ready Steady Teddy . . . Sheringham (© Jonathan Pearce) has finally made Gary Lineker's No. 10 shirt his own. You know it by the noise around N17 on matchdays. BT (Before Teddy) the talk was all about 'Ooh Gary Gary, Gary Gary Gary Gary Lineker'. Last season Spurs fans walked in a Klinsmann wonderland. But this season there's no doubting who is the King of White Hart Lane: 'Ooh Teddy Teddy, Teddy Teddy Teddy Teddy Sheringham.' That's who.

Teddy Sheringham is boiling hot in front of goal right now, the third-hottest striker in the Premiership. This afternoon, however, he's freezing cold; far colder than earlier this morning when Gerry Francis put the Spurs squad through a shortened Tuesday sprint session. We're in the middle of a photo session on the roof of one of Leicester Square's highest buildings. And it's snowing. And although Terry Venables is currently naming his England squad for the friendly against Portugal just a long ball away at Lancaster Gate, Sheringham is more worried about his 'Rudolph' (red nose) and not being on *FourFourTwo*'s cover than whether his name will be on El Tel's list. Because he knows it will be.

There's a certain swagger about Sheringham now, that wasn't there in the days when even Tottenham's fanzine, *The Spur*, had cause to ask: 'Who's that string-haired baboon in the blessed Gary's shirt?'

'How come they can get on the cover and I can't?' he asks indignantly, pointing to previous covers of Diego Maradona and Roberto Baggio. The irony was sweet. Sheringham may not be blessed with football's sexiest ponytail or deftest hand, but he has now taken his first small steps towards silencing his critics.

After 11 caps and almost as much stick as John Barnes got during his 78 caps, 'England expected' against Switzerland at Wembley in November – and Sheringham finally delivered. To such an extent that one report described Wembley as 'Sheringham-gripped'. If Steve Stone was the rough diamond, Sheringham was the polished gem who at last proved his worth. Technically he appeared on top of his game, holding the line and linking with Alan Shearer so intelligently that one newspaper journalist compared the performance to one of Sheringham's boyhood heroes, Kenny Dalglish. He must have felt like doing a Swiss roll, such was the praise.

Strangely not. 'That's nice,' he says demurely of the Dalglish comparison. 'But footballers are their own worst critics and I didn't play that well. My touch was off for the first 20 minutes and I lost the ball a lot, which was frustrating since one of my biggest assets is keeping possession. The difference was that we scored three goals and I scored one of them, a very good goal. If I hadn't scored people would still be saying: "Is he really the one to partner Shearer?" It's given me a little bit of breathing space.'

But the criticism has been so fierce over the years that Sheringham has adopted his own defence mechanisms. His manner is aloof and diffident, his wit sharp. He likes to give the impression he is made of stern stuff. Even so, the odd chink appears in that ice-cool armour. 'When I got into the England squad, so many people said I wasn't good enough that I started to think it might be true.' No wonder, since he's constantly had to prove himself in better company. At Millwall he regularly went to youth- and reserve-team games to identify with the club and win over his critics. And in his early days at Spurs he was the target of boo-boys who doubted his ability to follow in the footsteps of legendary goalscorers like Greaves, Chivers and Lineker.

Like his first club, Millwall, Sheringham is from the 'no one likes me, I don't care' school of football, rated by managers and players, slated by fans. In his defence, he says: 'Of course it's nice to be liked by everyone but in football there's always someone who hates you and someone else to whom you're a hero. Maybe it's because I'm not the eye-catching type of player fans think should be playing for England. But I do my job efficiently and that doesn't always mean running 40 yards, going past six players and smashing the ball into the top corner. Those are dream goals but they're not my style.' So what is his style? The eyes narrow: 'That'd be telling. But Gerry and Terry appreciate me and so do the players around me. That's all that matters to me.'

Sheringham's style has often been described as awkward. And he's been mistaken for the archetypal target man because of his aerial ability. But to label him is to miss his point: he may not be a classic centre-forward, but he's certainly an all-round one; his portfolio of goals ranges from volleys to chips, long-range drives to tap-ins, and headers like the peach against Switzerland. Certainly Venables has never doubted Sheringham the way his predecessor Graham Taylor did. Sheringham had scored 12 times in eight matches for Spurs, yet Paul Warhurst got the nod against Holland in April 1993. When Taylor did eventually pick Sheringham, he could only justify it by saying: 'Well, coincidentally, Sheringham was born in 1966, the year we won the World Cup.'

Venables, conversely, has always maintained – to those who are infuriated by his alleged penchant for picking Spurs players and would rather see him partner Shearer with the strength of Les Ferdinand or the raw talent of Robbie Fowler – that: 'Ted is genuinely two-footed, as good as anyone in the air, the best around at bringing others into the game, and he scores goals. If he had a change of pace he'd be right up there with the best in the world.' In his diaries Alex Ferguson described Sheringham as 'the best link player', and admitted he was the striker the United players would most like to play with after Andy Cole. Sheringham's team-mate Darren Anderton says: 'I don't know what the fans see, they must be watching a different game because Teddy's the best.' Jürgen Klinsmann simply said: 'I know Teddy to be a striker of the highest order.'

It was alongside Klinsmann last season that Sheringham blossomed. Between them they scored 52 goals, Sheringham the foil for Klinsmann and the main man behind the German's opening-day party-piece at Hillsborough. 'We talked about the dive and agreed it would make people laugh. Now everyone's doing it. But it's not the special Klinsmann dive, is it?'

Cynics claimed Sheringham disliked not being top dog at White Hart Lane, and exchanged knowing smiles when he was still doing his lap of honour at the final game of the season long after the Klinsmann *aufwiedersehens* had all been said. Sheringham's obvious admiration for Klinsmann suggests otherwise: 'You learn things from every player but when you see someone world-class you have to sit up and take notice. I loved playing with him and didn't want to see him go. His whole attitude was so single-minded; he knows from his years of playing for Germany that you might only get one chance, and he's always there to take that chance. He would always make the keeper work or put the ball in the back of the net. That's what makes him a cut above the rest.'

Sheringham was genuinely unhappy with Klinsmann's departure (and the subsequent departures of Nick Barmby and Gica Popescu) but claims his alleged unhappiness at Chris Armstrong's arrival was just press hype. On the pitch the pair have already scored more goals than Sheringham and Klinsmann had at the same stage last season, and their partnership is further proof of Sheringham's adaptability. 'We're like chalk and cheese, really; you couldn't find two strikers less alike. But it's a combination of styles that complement each other. When I played with Nigel Clough at Forest we were both slow, intelligent players whom intelligent centre-halves could combat, but now centre-halves are wary of me and wary of Chris's pace too, and have to be on their toes all the time. It's up to us to try and outwit them.'

Outwitting defences is something at which Sheringham has become adept. He has a shrewd air about him which, because of the way he is dressed – head to foot in black – makes him look like a cat burglar, as ready to unlock the nearest front door as the nearest defence. He's lean and sleek, with angular bone structure and his predatory eyes are so small it's hard to tell their colour. This is what gives him what he calls 'my moody look', or what someone else once described as a 'Clint Eastwood gaze'.

Sheringham is more your thinking man's footballer than your working man's. He admits that, because his game isn't based on pace and power, he has to think about what he's doing rather than just doing it: 'I get moody, sometimes even if I've played well, because I've spent so much time thinking and geeing myself up for those 90 minutes that I'm too engrossed in what I'm going to do and what he's going to do and where I'm going to go if I get the ball and where he's going to go. It's so intense that there's a comedown period after the game that's quite bad, really, hard to take. I know if I didn't have a drink after the game I wouldn't sleep that night. And the bigger the game, the more I worry.'

He first started to worry when, playing in a Millwall youth side alongside a certain left-winger called Neil Ruddock, he found himself struggling to keep up with the game: 'It was a real low point. I was only 17 and I remember going to my coach Roger Cross [now Francis's assistant at Spurs] and saying: "Roger, I don't know where to run." Teams were pushing up and playing offside, our midfield players were running through and stealing the limelight and I was lost. Roger was a great help because he'd just finished playing as a striker. It was a learning process, about adapting to different styles and situations, and I realised that it isn't just about doing what you're good at but learning what others are good at too so you can stop them.'

Over the years he's found it hard to accept he is one of the best and feel comfortable alongside fellow top-class players. During early England get-togethers he said he'd look at a player and think 'Cor, he's mega', then: 'Hold on, I'm in this collection of players because I'm pretty good too.' It was back to proving himself again, even if that meant the bright blue Mercedes with which he announces his arrival on the White Hart Lane forecourt.

At Millwall, the young Sheringham's already fragile ego took a battering from then manager George Graham who was critical of him for always trying to score spectacular goals: 'I really thought he had it in for me. It wasn't until John Docherty arrived at the Den and said the same thing that it started to sink in.'

Practice began to make perfect: 'I used to stand in front of a mirror studying exactly what I did with the right foot, then mirroring it and doing the same with my left. When you look in the mirror you realise what you're doing wrong. I had to sit up and take notice of what they were telling me and it was then that my game really took off.' Graham didn't appear to think so; he tried to loan Sheringham to Swedish side Djurgaarden, and Aldershot, as well as trying to offload him to Brentford for £5,000.

But Sheringham went on to become the Lions' all-time top goalscorer, scoring 93 goals from 1984–91, 38 of them in his final season at the Den under Bruce Rioch, who brought him and Armstrong together at the Den 'for the future'. And that future saw the duo combine to sink Rioch's Arsenal in the most recent north London derby.

Nottingham Forest parted with £2 million for his talents at the end of the 1990–91 season, but after he'd moved on to Spurs, Sheringham's absence from the City Ground seemed to make Brian Clough's heart grow fonder. When Forest's 'too-good-to-go-down' side went down at the end of 1992–93, Clough admitted: 'I shouldn't have sold Edward Sheringham.'

There had been talk of tactical rows between manager and striker and Sheringham describes Cloughie's ideas as 'unbelievable'. He explains: 'His philosophy was that you had to get as much rest as you could for Saturday so we'd train for 20 minutes on a Monday then he'd say: "Go home and put your feet up, son, I'll see you on Thursday." There were times when we wanted to do extra shooting practice but when he said we'd finished, we were finished. He didn't improve me skill-wise but worked on my footballing brain. My dad taught me football was all about simplicity and Cloughie was a great believer in that. He'd say: "Get the ball, control it, pass it and always play the way you're facing."'

Sheringham got a Rumbelows Cup runners-up medal and a Zenith Data Cup winners' medal with Forest but at club level that's as good as it's got so far. Ask him for his highlight to date and you'll get that gaze again, then a broad smile: 'Scoring for England at Wembley. But the disappointing thing is that I've never won anything except the Second Division championship with Milwall. I mean, beating Arsenal is always nice and I won the Golden Boot, but that's something that in a few years someone might see in my house and say: "I forgot you won that." It's not something people remember in your club's history. Something lasting.'

That 'something lasting' was odds-on to come his way in last season's FA Cup. But Francis's team came a cropper in the semi-final against an Everton side whom Sheringham believes 'wanted to win more than us'.

The FA Cup defeat was a double blow. Soon after the game came the first rumours that Klinsmann would quit White Hart Lane at the end of the season – and begin the break-up of a team that Sheringham believed could have challenged for the title for the first time in 35 years. But then he'd seen it all before. The Millwall side which won promotion to the then First Division in 1987–88 lost first Tony Cascarino, then Terry Hurlock, then Jimmy Carter. 'Life goes on, teams evolve,' Sheringham said at the time.

But what about the current Spurs side who, whisper it, are being compared to the boring, boring Arsenal side of George Graham's era? Are they really championship material? Sheringham, who followed Spurs from the terraces as a kid and admitted recently that he 'hates Arsenal with a passion', gives a 'you better believe me' look: 'All that stuff about the long ball, that's fantasy. There's no doubt we were very entertaining under Ossie [Ardiles] but we're in this to win things and we never would have. We'd have been so good if we'd worked on the back four because our front six were dynamite. But the defence wasn't consistent. It was very frustrating. Gerry sorted that out and we can play the short stuff and build from the back now. But when you've got players as quick as Fox and Armstrong you have to use their pace.'

Francis picked up Ardiles's mess following a League Cup defeat against struggling Notts County which Sheringham admits 'was one of the worst results of my career'. That kind of débâcle is unlikely to happen under Mr 'Methodical' Francis who is a hard taskmaster: 'He often gives us a rollicking at half-time, he's even gone mad about certain things if we've won. A few of the players can't understand how he isn't happy with that but I can remember George Graham saying things to me like: "You let him have a free header after 25 minutes, didn't challenge him." And I'd be like, "But boss I'd just run . . ." and he'd say: "No excuses, that's your man, mark him." It's perfectionism. But those minor details can mean the difference between winning and losing.'

Sheringham has never been short of that precious commodity: confidence. He relishes the big occasion and expects to score in every game he plays. You can tell by the way he celebrates, the characteristic head back, arms aloft salute followed by the 'told you so' point to the crowd. He's arrogant, but what striker isn't? By the same token he sincerely believes that England have a real chance next summer. He's already talked about warming up for Euro '96 in June by scoring Spurs' winner in the FA Cup final at Wembley in May.

Venables has no shortage of respect for Sheringham and the feeling is mutual. Sheringham won't be drawn on his feelings for Alan Sugar (suffice to say that he was probably closer than most to following Neil Ruddock out of White Hart Lane after Sugar sacked Venables as chief executive) and he was thrilled when Venables got the England nod.

'Terry's trying to run England like a club side and he's succeeding. All top players recognise him as a great coach and tactician, just unbelievable little details, fine-tuning which makes all the difference. He gives me a lot of freedom, I mean, even though I'm playing just off Shearer, I'm really a striker, and he says if I want to join in the play then I can, as long as Shearer goes wide or short and we make sure one of us is in the box when the ball comes in. You can get the ball off the right-back then give it back to him and slowly jog round while it goes out to the right or left wings, but still be in the box when it comes across and it's like, how did he get there? That's the art of it: timing.'

You get that gaze again when Sheringham says he hopes he hasn't reached his peak yet. Presumably he's hoping to reach it next June, or possibly just before when he wins his first major club honour with Spurs. If that hope isn't fulfilled within the next couple of years he might be tempted to search elsewhere for the elusive silverware. But right now he's staying put: 'It took me a long time to get to Spurs but this is the club I want to play for, the club I want to make great again. I just hope everyone here feels the same.'

The Saturday after that freezing photo session Sheringham is off again in search of his quest, to make Spurs great again. Spurs beat Queen's Park Rangers at White Hart Lane with Sheringham scoring after just three minutes. They win 1–0 and Rocket Ronny Rosenthal plays a rare blinder. But the chants outside the ground are for one man, and one man only: 'Ooh Teddy Teddy, Teddy Teddy Teddy Teddy Sheringham!'

FourFourTwo, February 1996

THE ENGLAND TEAM

Gary Lineker

For Terry Venables, England's extended winter break, which ends this week after three months of inactivity, hasn't sheltered him from the storms of publicity that seem to blow up around him. This time it was his resignation that provoked the headlines, and the game on Wednesday will be his first in charge since announcing that after the European Championship he will concentrate more on those on the bench than those on the pitch.

I know that the quarter-year wait for the next fixture has been hugely frustrating for the England manager, especially when you consider the encouraging signs of his team's most recent performances. His quest for continuity had been spoiled and it still seems hard to believe that the FA couldn't have conjured up a game somewhere in either January or February. So, with just over two months to go, England start their preparations for Euro '96 with a home game against Bulgaria – a tough and ideal test against one of Europe's premier teams, who have themselves an outside chance of winning the Championship in June.

For Venables it will be a relief to get his squad together at last and re-establish the way he wishes his team to play. It certainly won't be easy. Yesterday the Premiership continued and today there is not only the Coca-Cola Cup final but Manchester United against Spurs in the league. Therefore, in just a couple of training sessions, Venables must rejuvenate tired players and organise the 11 men he chooses.

It's nearly as difficult to guess what his starting line-up will be as it is to remember the names on his last team-sheet. For me it will be just as interesting to see the system he operates as the individuals who will endeavour to make it function. The time to experiment is running out and if he wishes to try something different, it has to be during this or next month's game against Croatia.

The area in which he may wish to explore an alternative is at the back. Venables has always favoured a traditional four defenders playing closely together (flat back four) which, if well regimented, can be difficult to break down. The England chief is superb at marshalling this particular defensive format, although I've a feeling, and a hope, that he's ready to try playing a more flexible three at the back. Many Premiership sides are currently playing this way – some of them, it has to be said, without a great deal of thought.

A couple of teams though, notably Liverpool, have used the system to enhance their attacking game. Two requirements are essential if it's to be a positive rather than a negative transition. First, the three central defenders must be prepared to contribute to the team in their opponents' half, which means, of course, that they have to be capable of maintaining possession. The naming in the squad of the likes of Mark Wright, Ugo Ehiogu and Gareth Southgate suggests that Venables may be contemplating giving a chance to footballing centre-halves as opposed to our customary 'head on a stick' variety of defender. Even Paul Ince might be worth trying out in this position. The self-proclaimed 'Guvnor' could well become exactly that if he showed the necessary discipline and desire to play the role. I don't believe he possesses the technical capabilities to be England's playmaker in midfield, but as a defender he has sufficient passing ability to supply the more gifted players in front of him.

He could also push himself into forward positions if England were faced with a team wary of sending more than one man up front. If Venables does adopt an alternative defensive strategy, it is vital that the wing-backs, as they are now called, play as wide midfield players as opposed to defensive-minded full-backs. Under this system, the emphasis must be for them to provide the width going forward as well as a balance defensively. It's physically the most demanding role of the modern game and one in which we appear to have a shortage of talent, especially on the left side. Steve Stone has both the engine and the appetite to play on the right, and Rob Jones, although naturally right-sided, is playing well on the left for Liverpool and would be a candidate, along with the more defensive Stuart Pearce and possible even Philip Neville. A recovery by Darren Anderton would certainly ease concerns about Venables's problem position. He believes Anderton could play on the left if fit.

In midfield Venables will be enormously encouraged by the progress of Paul Gascoigne. It was always going to require time free of injury for Gazza's game to reach its former levels. He's been outstanding for Rangers in recent weeks and his fitness is still improving. He still has a tendency to leave his brain in the dressing-room, but if he could control his emotions, as he did for much of Italia '90 under extreme pressure, he would once again be England's most influential player. He's been constantly written off and branded a gamble not worth taking, but if England are to be successful in the summer, the inspiration, I feel will have to come from Gascoigne. The only other midfielder in the country who could introduce the flair that England will need is Liverpool's Steve McManaman. His brilliant performances this season surely mean that he'll be given the role he enjoys with his club. In his international appearances to date he's been stifled by being the wide-man, a fate that previously befell his team-mate John Barnes. Giving the chief responsibility for width to the wing-backs would allow McManaman the freedom to inflict the kind of damage that has been commonplace in the Premiership. Some people may argue that to play Gascoigne and McManaman would be too much of a luxury. In a 4–4–2 formation I would agree, but playing three at the back with an extra man in midfield would alleviate any defensive frailties.

Alongside the creators in the midfield anchor role could be Jamie Redknapp, Robert Lee, or Ince, whom I suspect will not be risked at the back by Venables. Lee's real strength is getting forward into goalscoring positions, rather like David Platt, whose strike-rate for England is such that, now he's approaching full fitness, he will enter the equation. Redknapp would be ideal, as his consistent ability to feed McManaman and Gascoigne would be invaluable. He has very little match practice of late following injury, however. It would be ironic if Reknapp plays despite Michael Thomas and John Barnes, neither of whom are in the squad, keeping him out of the Liverpool team.

Now to my favourite, and perhaps the most contentious, area: the forwards. I'm convinced after his fine performance and goal against Switzerland that Teddy Sheringham, if fully fit, will play. He is much admired by the England manager and this could be the opportunity to discover if he can overcome his lack of pace against the man-to-man marking that the Bulgarians may employ. Sheringham will offer the team depth which is imperative from at least one of the front men.

Venables has always known this and probably tried Alan Shearer and Les Ferdinand together, not solely because of injury but to placate the media and prove the point – possibly to himself. Against Portugal the twin strikers were exposed as being too similar and too predictable. So who will play up front with Sheringham? Will it be Shearer, Ferdinand or Robbie Fowler? I don't think Ferdinand will play. Despite his obvious attributes, he still remains an erratic finisher, particularly with his left foot. Shearer continues to score goals by the bucketful in the Premiership and may well go on to do the same for England. But in his last performance in the white shirt he looked low in confidence and a rest might ease the pressure. He could always come back later, full of determination with a point to prove.

I would love to see Fowler given a chance to display his awesome finishing repertoire. There's no question in my mind that he is the most complete English goalscorer around. He creates space for himself in the box to score from close range and he's deadly accurate from distance. He also appears to be gifted with a big-match temperament, so crucial in international football. If he can bridge the gap that clearly exists between club and country, and I expect he will, he could become one of the greats. I already believe that he has more potential than the Dutch star of the future, Patrick Kluivert. Give him a go now, Terry, and we could have a rare gem shining for us in Euro '96.

The Observer, 24 March 1996

3
The Managers

GLENN HODDLE

Glenn Moore

It is a risk, but it is a justified one for the doubt is not about the man, but the timing. At 38, Glenn Hoddle would be the youngest manager-coach England have had. He has just five years' managerial experience and has won nothing more substantial than promotion to the Premiership. Already Don Howe, arguably the most experienced coach in the game, has wondered aloud if Hoddle will feel he is ready.

It is a valid question but, in plumping for Hoddle, the Football Association have chosen potential rather than achievement. They hope he will emulate Franz Beckenbauer, who led his country to World Cup success in his first management job. A less encouraging precedent comes from France, where Michel Platini's initially promising stewardship ended in failure at the last European Championship.

The irony is that the FA, in putting their faith in Hoddle, have made a decision their managers refused to take when he was a player. Hoddle, though the most extravagantly gifted midfielder of his generation, was never successfully harnessed to the England team. He won 53 caps but rarely played in his position of choice, roving the centre of midfield. He was thus unable to make the mark upon the international stage that he could have.

This did not stop him becoming one of the most admired players of his era, however. Read any of those instant profiles of footballers, and to the question 'favourite player as a boy' the answer will invariably be 'Glenn Hoddle'. Not just in England either – a whole generation of Dutch players grew up admiring him – and many of his contemporaries, in England and Europe, accord Hoddle a rare respect.

Having such a reputation helps when trying to inspire, cajole or instruct international players, who can have big egos and wallets to match. Terry

Venables has it – that is evident in the way the players listen to him and the way they work on his ideas on the training ground. The previous incumbent, Graham Taylor, did not command respect so easily and seemed uncomfortable handling the most talented players, like Paul Gascoigne and Chris Waddle.

Hoddle is at ease with such players and they look up to him, even Ruud Gullit, who Hoddle not only attracted to Chelsea but also persuaded that he should not play at sweeper. Instead Hoddle has played David Lee in that position, bringing the best from a player who had languished in Chelsea's reserves. He has also promoted Michael Duberry who, with the Nevilles, has emerged as the best young defender in the country.

In midfield, Dennis Wise has flourished and John Spencer has been convinced, against his initial judgement, that his best position is just behind the centre-forward, not leading the attack.

They each fit into a system which is more continental than English. Three central defenders, wing-backs on the flanks of a flooded midfield and, usually, a lone striker. When it all clicks, as against Middlesbrough early this year, it is a treat to watch. Hoddle's commitment to the system is such that all Chelsea's teams play that way, right down to the youth sides. It means when young players like Duberry or Jody Morris come into the side the adjustment is that much easier.

While similar to Venables's vision, it is not as advanced. The England team which played Croatia was genuinely European in approach with attacking midfielders on the flanks, not defenders, and a sweeper behind two mobile markers, rather than three centre-backs.

Maybe, with the better players available to England, Hoddle would also adopt such an approach. His assessment of players has improved – early transfer mistakes like Paul Furlong and Mark Stein have been followed by the successful signing of Dan Petrescu and Terry Phelan.

There is the criticism that, as yet, he has won nothing. But the ability to win the League is not necessarily what is required for England – look at Don Revie's respective records for club and country. National management is about winning a series of one-off matches culminating, hopefully, in an intense but short tournament. Hoddle has shown, through Chelsea's successful cup runs at home and in Europe, and, earlier, through Swindon's success in the play-offs, that he has the ability to organise teams for specific tasks.

It could be good news for Matthew Le Tissier, another player inspired by Hoddle as a youngster but one of the few with similar ability. Hoddle himself was regarded as a special talent from the moment he fired past Peter Shilton from 25 yards on his Tottenham début in 1976.

He also scored a stunning goal on his England début against Bulgaria three years later but was then dropped for the next matches. It was the story of his England career.

At White Hart Lane he attained the status of a legend and won two FA Cup-winners' medals. After 11 years, and more than a century of goals, he moved to Monaco where he won the French championship in his second year. In 1991 he became player-manager of Swindon. After two successful years he moved on to Chelsea.

Despite early struggles, Hoddle refused to modify his playing style and he has been rewarded with the creation of a stylish side which has engendered real optimism at Stamford Bridge.

Should he take the national job, the self-belief he showed in that first season will be vital. Chris Waddle, his former Spurs team-mate and singing partner, said: 'He's very determined and sticks to his beliefs. He is bound to get criticised but I think he is big enough to handle it.'

He will need to be, because criticism, both personal and professional, goes with the job. There will be intense scrutiny of his private life – he may have become a dedicated Christian but, as David Ginola found out at the weekend, there are newspapers which do not mind rattling skeletons from a decade ago, even innocent ones.

There will also be criticism – often uninformed – of his team. This is the danger in the FA going for someone who, to an extent, will be learning on the job. He has the ability to become a good England manager but it may take time to be translated into results. Where England are concerned, time is not available.

The Independent, 2 May 1996

ALEX FERGUSON

Hugh McIlvanney

In any fair discussion of Alex Ferguson's record as a manager of football clubs, the word greatness is now inescapable.

Manchester United's season is still poised this morning between extremes of possibility, with strong hopes of completing an unprecedented second double in the League championship and the FA Cup haunted for at least a few more hours by the danger that all their strivings could leave them empty-handed. The odds are, of course, against such an outcome (Ladbrokes quote United at 1–10 to win the title) but even if devastating scorelines at Middlesbrough and Newcastle today are followed by defeat in the Cup final against Liverpool next Saturday, Ferguson's achievements since last summer have surely lifted an already extraordinary career to a level which demands that he be compared with the best managers the game has known.

Frank Clark, whose own work in charge of Nottingham Forest has attracted much admiration, recognised the scale of those achievements when he said last week: 'What Alex has done this season is incredible.' Clark went on to marvel at how rapidly, smoothly and successfully Ferguson had transformed his team, jettisoning players as important as Ince, Hughes and Kanchelskis and bringing through young footballers to fill the gaps without suffering more than the odd stutter in competitive momentum. If it had been suggested nine months ago that he could restructure his team so fundamentally and win the championship at the same time, many might have been inclined to point out, with an indulgent smile, that the feat was about as probable as a grand-prix team replacing an engine during a race. The bonus for all at Old Trafford is that there now appears to be no reason why the latest model of the red machine should not go charging on to a clutch of further honours over the next few years.

It can be said, without fear of inaccuracy, that such a prospect does not delight everybody in the land. Manchester United have devoted supporters in every corner of Britain, and in most countries of the world, but their army of well-wishers must be outnumbered by the many who want to see them awash with disappointment. No doubt the bitterness felt towards United by supporters of other clubs has a variety of origins, ranging from resentment of the glamorous aura that has surrounded their name even in periods when their performances were miserable, to some kind of amorphous backlash against the sentimental warmth accorded to them in the decades after the Munich crash. What is undeniable is that a lot of these ill-defined animosities have hardened around the controversial figure of Ferguson.

For those of us with deep affection and respect for him, it is often a jarring experience to encounter the depth of contrasting feelings he stirs in other people, although the reasons for hostile reaction are plain enough. Principal among these are the vigour with which he presses the Manchester United case in any argument (a tendency that in the past has produced attempts to justify the unjustifiable) and the public perception that, for all his success, he is constantly on the lookout for complaints and excuses – is, in short, a whinger.

That definition is too harshly simplistic to have any real validity but the injustice of the judgement contains an irony, since Ferguson is exposed to it by a passion for the cause that can make his own view of events simplistic in the sense of being profoundly unobjective.

People who do not know him well can scarcely imagine the ferocity of commitment he brings to his job. The workaholic hours, and the voracious appetite for detail, are only part of it. Running through everything he does is a blood-heat current of combative energy that seems, if anything, more powerful at the age of 54 than when he was stunning Scottish football in the 1980s by thrusting Aberdeen ahead of Rangers and Celtic. It is a drive that has carried United, in less than ten years, through a revival bordering on the miraculous. We should remember that, given a slight difference in results at the end of a couple of seasons, they might be bidding for their fifth championship in a row instead of their third in four years, and be challenging for a third rather than a second double. Ferguson's triumphs owe much to clear-headed thinking about football matters, and especially to the soundness of his long-term planning, but when he is speaking publicly it is the fervour that tends to take over, and a lifelong inclination to let whatever is on his chest come out through his mouth frequently pitches him into disputes. Occasionally his friends want to leap forward and gag him but the chances are he would get his points across in sign language.

In any case, for some of us, the private Ferguson's warm openness, generosity and humour will always effortlessly outweigh the damaging effects of ill-advised utterances. And then there are the talents he brings to management, his inspired effectiveness and positive style. Even the absence so far of a European Cup win – which reflects English football's shortcomings more than his – does not exclude him from the company of such as Stein, Busby, Shankly, Nicholson, Paisley, Clough and Ramsey.

When we talked last week of the photo-finish in the Premier League and the thrills promised by confrontation with Liverpool at Wembley, he conveyed an impression of enjoyable excitement, not debilitating tension. 'What happens in the championship is bound to have a tremendous impact on our morale in the Cup final,' he said. 'If we win the title I'd be up to play at Wembley myself. But if it all goes wrong at the death, all the horrors of last year – when we were on the verge of the double and finished with nothing – will come back into the players' minds. I'll have a hell of a job lifting them to face Liverpool. But I believe we'll get it right at Middlesbrough and go bouncing into the final.

'We know we'll have to be at our best there, because Liverpool have done better than anyone else against us in the League this season. I couldn't field the right team to play against them when we lost 2–0 at Anfield. They slaughtered us then. In the 2–2 draw at Old Trafford, for the first 15 minutes we constantly looked as if we would score and I thought we had a similar superiority in the last 20 minutes, but for that long spell in between they outplayed us. Their system of using three centre-backs has given us bother, but we have coped with it pretty well by adopting much the same shape, pushing our full-backs on top of theirs. My main feeling about the final is that it will be a brilliant game. Both teams are full of footballers, players with personality and pride. I'm really looking forward to it.'

The same is not guaranteed to be true of two or three prominent members of his playing staff. When injury put the splendid Bruce on the sidelines, he had just betrayed hints in the midst of an alarming defeat at Southampton that, at 35, he might at last be losing his heroic battle with the calendar. With May functioning so well as the replacement in central defence, and selection liable to be swayed by the thought of how Fowler's quickness of mind and limb could exploit Bruce's slowness, it is reasonable to speculate that the big Geordie will miss the final.

Ferguson brims with compliments for Bruce's contribution and all the others that have created United's astonishing season, from the crucial midfield dominance of Keane to the wonders of Schmeichel. 'The goalie is different class – the best in the world and getting better all the time,' the manager said. 'He is lightning quick for such a big man. What a bargain at half a million!'

At the opposite end of the team, Cole has never been accused of representing a bargain. Ferguson remains sympathetic to his £7 million man, but the alternative partnership of Cantona and Scholes can hardly be disrupted after its recent successes: 'I had to give Scholes his chance and I had to do so in his best position. The boy prefers to play a little bit off the front-man, as Eric does. So I played Cantona up, knowing he had the experience to cope with the adjustment more easily. Eric is strong enough to play as a target-man and still come into spaces when the midfield men run through. I gave Scholes his chance against Forest and he took it. So he made a case for himself. When I was a young centre-forward my father used to say, "If you can keep scoring, the manager can't ignore you".'

Being ignored is not one of Alex Ferguson's problems.

Sunday Times, 5 May 1996

ROY HODGSON

John D. Taylor

First impressions count for a lot in football, so it's full marks to Roy Hodgson who, on his opening morning as Inter coach, amazed his players by referring to them all by their Christian names. Having already found favour with the national press just hours earlier by answering questions in Italian, French, Swedish and English, Hodgson certainly got off on the right foot.

But of course, to win over Inter's fickle fans, the relatively unknown Englishman has to do more than just talk a good game. To justify his £600,000-a-season two-year deal, he needs results, with a UEFA Cup placing already the minimum requirement this season.

Hodgson was the first choice of club president, Massimo Moratti – a man who shares a curious love-affair with all things English. It was Moratti's persistence that eventually prised Paul Ince from Manchester United. And it was Moratti who, after winning control of the club midway through last season, singled out Hodgson as successor to Ottavio Bianchi.

Although Hodgson wasn't on the official Italian team coaches' foreign roster – a fact which made him legally ineligible for the job – Moratti named him Technical Director to bulldoze his appointment through. The 48-year-old Croydon-born boss is the first Englishman to coach in Serie A since former Newcastle player Jesse Carver at Roma and Juventus in the 1950s. He'll be expected to stand up and deliver, but producing the goods against the odds is something Hodgson has done before.

The son of a London bus conductor, Roy was a journeyman defender with Crystal Palace, Gravesend, Ashford, Carshalton and Maidstone United. Earning a weekly wage of just £30, he used to believe people were failing to realise his playing talents. Now he honestly admits he just wasn't good enough.

There were more setbacks when he joined his pal Bob Houghton as assistant manager at Bristol City. 'The problems were Friday nights and Sunday mornings – knowing we were going to lose on a Saturday and then reading about it the next day! Inevitably, the club went bust and I ended up on the dole. From then on, my football career could only go one way.'

And it did. Hodgson returned to Sweden, where he'd already won the League title twice with little-fancied Halmstad. Malmo hadn't forgotten what he'd done and offered him a lifeline. Hodgson repaid their faith by winning them five consecutive titles and gaining the club regular places in Europe – ironically knocking Inter out of the Champions' Cup in 1989 – as well as lifting two domestic cups.

That success brought him a move to Swiss club Neuchatel Xamax and eventually to the notice of the Swiss FA, who were impressed with his coaching pedigree. 'When they made me national team manager four years ago, I had been involved in 36 European ties,' he says.

Hodgson's career continued to progress as he led Switzerland, for the first time in 28 years, to a place in the 1994 World Cup finals in the US and to qualification for Euro '96 in England. He was first approached by two unnamed Italian clubs 18 months ago, but in October '95 Moratti finally stepped in to make Hodgson an offer he couldn't refuse. Typically, Roy wanted to continue in charge of the national team until after this summer's tournament – confident he could do both jobs.

But the Swiss decided otherwise in December, appointing Portugal's Artur Jorge to lead them in the Euro finals – a decision which Hodgson found upsetting. At least he can now concentrate fully on the task awaiting him at the San Siro, and he's under no illusions about how tough the job will be. Inter have been a sleeping giant since their last Scudetto win in 1989, and very much the poor relations to city rivals Milan.

'The moment you sign for a club like Inter – as happens at clubs like Manchester United, Liverpool or Arsenal in England – people expect great things. You're hailed as a messiah if things go well but hung out to dry if they don't, with 50 TV stations and 100 scribes telling you where you went wrong. I was prepared to take that risk and move into the big pond, even if there are big fish waiting to eat you . . .

'There will be bad moments. But sometimes you have to live with defeat in football before you eventually get things right. It's difficult in Italy, because football fans are either sad or euphoric. There's very little middle ground. We're in a boiling pot where people expect us to win all the time.'

Just two weeks into the job, Hodgson and his new charges were plunged straight into the cauldron when they faced Milan in the 130th city derby. The result – a 1–1 draw – was a face-saver, but it couldn't disguise the rebuilding job ahead.

The question on everyone's lips upon Hodgson's arrival was whether there would be a regular place in his new-look team for the San Siro's other Englishman, Paul Ince. Hodgson made it clear from the outset that the former Old Trafford star, himself struggling to adjust to life in Serie A, would receive no special favours. 'There are loads of good players in Italy and Paul is one of them. It's not so much whether he has the qualities but maybe whether he wants to dedicate the next two years of his life completely to the club.'

Ince had a tough start at Inter, twice winning a sports magazine's 'Donkey of the Week' award in Serie A, and Hodgson quickly realised that the player had got a battle on his hands to establish himself in front of the critical home fans.

'They see Paul very much as a typical English player and that can be a bit of a problem at first. English players now start at a real disadvantage because of a few failures in the past. Even if he'd scored five goals in his first five appearances he would have probably only got mediocre ratings . . . In England, people are more generous with foreigners. They have a better chance than anywhere in the world. In the UK, a foreign player will start at plus two – in Italy, it's minus two.'

But Hodgson was pleased at his first glimpses of Ince. 'He shows a great desire to do well and is an honest player. The standard of play in Serie A is very good, so he must be given a little time to find his feet on and off the field.'

Hodgson too needs time, but he hasn't got a lot of it. He admits that Moratti has made it clear that he expects the club to be challenging for the title by next season.

First impressions are important, but it's a lasting impression that Roy Hodgson wants to make. It shouldn't be too difficult for a man who's already hauled himself from the backwoods of non-league clubs to one of *the* jobs in football.

Football Italia, March 1996

KEVIN KEEGAN

Joe Lovejoy

The first thing you noticed among our friends in the north was how the atmosphere had changed. On my last visit to Newcastle, a month ago, the mood was bullish, celebratory even. They were going to win the championship, no sweat. Four demoralising defeats later, the belief had dissolved, and before yesterday's events at the Dell, any talk of Manchester United doing their own Devon Loch was dismissed as fanciful nonsense.

At the training ground in Durham last week, Kevin Keegan and his court jester Terry McDermott did their knockabout best to lighten the mood, but the old bright-as-a-button response was missing.

Keegan had been the first to sense it. 'We've all been a bit low this week,' he said. 'It's been a bad few days in terms of morale. Any human being going through what we've been through would have spells thinking, "Lady Luck has deserted us".'

In the pubs and clubs of the Bigg Market the statistics were trotted out like a cribbage of despair. A 12-point lead had become a six-point deficit in the space of ten games. Keegan had promised them it would not happen again, but for the second season in succession the team had let slip a title-winning position.

A few weeks ago it would have been heresy, and not just in Newcastle, to criticise the man many would still have as England's next coach. Now, with televised tears replacing the exultation, the phone-ins and local papers were telling a different story. In two days spent on Tyneside in the aftermath of the latest glorious failure at Blackburn, I could not find a single person who still believed the championship was 'on'. Losing it, which is how they saw the situation, was spoken of like a bereavement by many. Dereliction that bordered on the criminal was the near unanimous verdict.

Downhearted yes, disaffected never. Not for the first time, those devoted fans were reacting rather better in adversity than their team, and in a touching gesture of solidarity, some 3,500 turned out to watch the first training session after the Ewood débâcle. Newcastle's must be the only training ground with its own fast-food van, Beardsley the only player who spends up to 40 minutes after each session patiently signing autographs.

Keegan said it is a mystery to him where it had all gone wrong: 'We played well against Manchester United and lost, well at West Ham and lost, again at Liverpool and lost, and now at Blackburn and lost again. We've had a bad patch, results-wise, but performances have remained good. It's a fact of life that you don't always get what you deserve.'

Every one of those 3,500 could probably put him right. Not since the French in 1940 had anyone defended with so little conviction. Even the honour guard in his black-and-white army accept that England would be murdered if they tried to play Keegan's way. The problem he finds so mystifying is transparently obvious to everyone else.

Newcastle attack like dervishes but defend like Mr Magoo, all clustering in search of the ball, oblivious to the basic tenets of the zonal-marking system in which they are notionally deployed.

Like another famous leader, Keegan insists he is not for turning, and that he would sooner leave than betray his principles. He, too, is paying for his intransigence. The cussed determination which saw him exceed all expectations as a player threatens to have the opposite effect on his managerial career, or at least this early part of it.

There is a fine line between single-mindedness and bloody-mindedness and Keegan is straddling it in absolving certain forwards from defensive duty, and refusing to reinstate Gillespie to the right wing, where he clearly gives the team a better balance.

Misjudgements, both. On the eve of the Arsenal extravaganza, Keegan said: 'I'm not going to ask Ginola and Asprilla to defend. I want to challenge people to play us, because we pass it at a pace other teams cannot live with. There is not a side in the country that can do it.'

Liverpool could, and did.

He was even wider of the mark, in the same interview, when he suggested that for Newcastle's supporters, attractive football meant more than results. He told *The Times*: 'Newcastle fans say, "Let's have a great game" first, and then, "Let's hope we win".' The pictures of those distraught faces, after a truly great game, contradicted him in spades.

Preoccupied with attacking football ('When Don Howe was coaching the defence with England, I lost interest after a few minutes'), he needs someone better than his present cast of thousands (McDermott, Chris McMenemy and Arthur Cox all assist him with first-team coaching) to work on a last line as effective as the Maginot. Don Howe, come to think of it, would be a good choice.

Better organisation would undoubtedly help, short term, but a proper solution probably requires a change of personnel. Total football is all very well, but too many of Newcastle's defenders seem to be forwards by inclination and reluctant to perform their primary function. Beresford and Barton, with their harum-scarum charges, look like frustrated Ginolas, Albert a would-be Beckenbauer. An Adams or a Pearce would not go amiss.

For the time being, at least, Keegan will have none of it. He does not take kindly to criticism (who does?), but few managers flip quite like he did over some innocuous remarks Ferdinand made, while on England duty, about the difficulties of forming a partnership with a maverick like Asprilla. It is clearly a sensitive subject. When Keegan was appraised of Vinnie Jones's suggestion in Friday's *Daily Mirror* that the purchase of the Colombian had cost Newcastle the title, it brought an abrupt end to the briefest of press conferences.

Early in the season, when things were going well, reporters sprightlier than I were invited to train with him at Durham. These days all requests for interviews are brusquely refused, the strained media relations evident in a dig after the Blackburn game, when he said: 'I haven't changed my approach, nor will I. You guys can come up with any number of reasons why we keep losing. Now that we've conceded a couple late on, you'll probably say we are not fit enough. I thought the balance was okay – even by my adventurous standards.'

The sarcasm, and the attitude behind it, was a pity. One of the things Keegan has got right recently is that there is universal admiration for his basic approach, and what he is trying to do. With the obvious exception of Middlesbrough and Sunderland supporters, Newcastle are just about everyone's favourite 'other' team, and the press, overwhelmingly, share this goodwill.

In mitigation, Keegan is still learning the managerial ropes. After just four years he is, to some degree, the victim of his own success, in that he transformed a team heading for the old Third Division into title aspirants well ahead of schedule. It took Alex Ferguson six and a half years to take the holy grail to Old Trafford, and he came to the job with the benefit of a championship-winning apprenticeship in Scotland.

Keegan, given Sir John Hall's continued largesse, is destined to get there in the end, but after 69 years, the fans are increasingly impatient. Fanatically typical is Dominic Hourd, a 26-year-old charity worker who kicked out in frustration when Liverpool's late winner went in 11 days ago, and accidentally killed his budgie. He has written to Stan Collymore, demanding compensation.

Lock up your pets this afternoon. With Dwight Yorke in town, it could be the Magpies' turn to have their feathers ruffled.

Sunday Times, 14 April 1996

BIG JACK
BEATEN BY FEAR

Eamon Dunphy

As soon as Jack Charlton announced his team last Tuesday the writing was on the wall. Knowledgeable professionals knew there was simply no way a team containing four full-backs could survive against Holland. Perceptive football fans also knew that Charlton had made a grave mistake.

He had selected a team that reflected not the talent at his disposal but his own rather curious personality – and his own enduring dislike of anything that smacks of originality or daring.

To describe the selection of two full-backs to occupy the wide midfield positions as defensive would be an understatement. The decision was absurd. It was cowardly, it reeked of fear. The signal sent to the Dutch must have been reassuring: they knew they would not have to defend their flanks, they could concentrate instead on attacking Ireland for 90 minutes knowing that goals would inevitably come.

Charlton was asking the impossible of the two full-backs designated to play as wide midfield players, Jeff Kenna and Terry Phelan. Kenna has played wide for Blackburn, with some success, in the Premiership. But playing for one of the better teams in the English league bears little resemblance to facing Holland at international level. More pertinently, Blackburn never had the option of playing Jason McAteer instead of Kenna. On Wednesday McAteer, dashing, accomplished, daring, a threat to Holland, spent all but the closing 15 minutes of the game on the bench.

When Charlton eventually sent McAteer on, the Liverpool player transformed the game, creating alarm in the Dutch defence . . . and, with a superbly flighted cross, Ireland's best chance of the night which Tony Cascarino missed connecting with by a matter of inches.

It is an open secret that Charlton doesn't like McAteer. Off the field this gifted young player possesses the kind of irreverent exuberance that is reflected in his play. Jason is an original. A free spirit. Unafraid. No respecter of reputations, as the great Italian Paolo Maldini discovered at the Giants Stadium, when McAteer took him to the cleaners during the last 20 minutes of Ireland's most famous victory during last year's World Cup.

The case of Jason McAteer is the perfect illustration of Charlton's mistrust of originality, of his narrow mind and fearful spirit. Jason cannot be trusted to obey orders. He won't be bullied. Therefore he is no use to Jack Charlton.

The decision to play Terry Phelan on the left side of midfield was laughable. Phelan is a good full-back, quick and aggressive. He is notably limited with the ball at his feet, which is where it was on Wednesday night. Watching him struggle in vain to cope with the problem Charlton set for him was painful. The idea is to humiliate the opposition, not your own players.

Ray Houghton is a great battler, a player blessed with the spirit for the important occasion. For Liverpool, Aston Villa and Ireland, Houghton has been an inspiration to his team-mates in so many difficult games. He is a wonderful player, the quintessential good pro with an acute footballing brain. Houghton lifts any team he plays for. And although he is not a goal-scorer, he scores goals when they are most needed. He torments defenders. As recently as last April at Lansdowne Road, Houghton played a major part in turning the game against Portugal Ireland's way. He was superb. He would have made an incalculable contribution to the cause last Wednesday. Charlton decided to leave him on the bench.

Perverse? Worse than that. This preference for Phelan over Houghton offended football reason. Thus, this important game was lost before the Irish team left the dressing-room. Commenting before the game, John Giles and Mark Lawrenson both expressed disappointment and bemuse-ment at Charlton's team selection. Two great, vastly experienced players, who know the game backwards, know the demands of a great occasion such as last Wednesday, know as well how utterly demoralising dressing-room life can be when the governing imperative is managerial folly and fear.

The folly of a limited coach who has never really known how best to deploy the wonderful players available to him, the fear of a bully confused by talent, determined to mask his confusion by projecting the image of sturdy conviction. In public relations terms that act has worked, worked beyond his wildest dreams, elevating him to the status of national hero at the expense of the true heroes, a magnificent generation of Irish players whose like we will never see again.

Last Wednesday night at Anfield the Irish football team looked de-moralised from the moment they entered the arena. Although we fer-vently hoped that those magnificent professional players would avoid humiliation we knew, as in their hearts they did, that humiliation was a possibility. Fortunately, it was not a débâcle. Narrowly, by the width of a goalpost, by virtue of the unfathomable courage of every one of those players, a defeat of epic proportions was avoided.

We can only guess how good the Dutch really are, for they and their wonderful, instinctive striker Patrick Kluivert never had to break sweat to prevail against a team disarmed by a fearful manager, bewildered by tactical folly on a scale unprecedented even by the bizarre standards previously set by Big Jack.

Three Irish players deserve special commendation. Tony Cascarino was magnificent. For 90 minutes his intelligence and honesty when confronted by a hopeless task was inspiring. Paul McGrath was simply his heroic self. John Sheridan has been the butt of much anger but he displayed an admirable degree of moral courage last Wednesday, attempting valiantly to remain true to his footballing nature. He erred to concede the first goal, but he erred trying to do the right thing. Yes, the truth is complex, but not something to fear. Except in an atmosphere contaminated by sentimentality.

For this observer, two contrasting memories of the Anfield game will long endure. After the game the Irish supporters offered a moving tribute to their team and the man at the centre of all this, Jack Charlton. This spontaneous eruption of emotion vouched for the indefatigable good nature of Irish sportsmen. The loving affinity between fan and player was never more engagingly evident.

The Dutch and English people present were beguiled by this manifestation of grace in adversity. This we can celebrate. But not what followed. An ugly scene which illustrated W.H. Auden's maxim that 'private people in public places/are so much nicer than public people in private places'.

The other side of Irishness was witnessed only by the few who see this story from the inside, who see the ugly consequences of sentimentality. Having just been acclaimed by the fans outside, Jack Charlton entered the press room to account for the business of the night. Baby was brooding, ready to explode with petulant anger. Faced with a polite question about his future he humiliated a journalist who has recently experienced hard times, a decent man trying to do his job.

Then, as is lately the norm, Charlton proceeded to lay into his players who, he claimed, had failed to execute his orders. A colleague courageously inquired if this didn't imply some problem with the instructor. The question was couched in deferential terms by a gentle man, respected in our business for his singular good manners.

Charlton glared menacingly at his inquisitor for an instant . . . then uttered an obscenity before storming out.

Independent on Sunday, 11 December 1995

BILL SHANKLY

Stephen F. Kelly

I could swear I saw him recently. In the dusk of an autumn evening as menacing clouds rolled in across the Mersey. The last man out of Anfield, switching off the lights, slamming the door shut, then shuffling across the carpark towards the Shankly Gates. And before heading off down the Anfield Road, pulling the gates to and locking them securely. Gates almost too heavy for a man of his age. Then off home towards West Derby, a squarish figure in his white mac, the little tough guy, a slight stiffness in his walk, the legacy of 60 years of football.

Connoisseurs of the early Cagney would recognise the style. There goes a satisfied man you might have thought as he disappeared into the blackness of the chill November night, duties done. Tell us you haven't gone, Bill. Tell us you're still there keeping an eye on things.

Maybe it was Shankly, maybe it wasn't. In the half lip of a dull moon, you could never be sure. It was probably just the old memory playing tricks. But others have felt his presence too, stalking the corridors, sitting in the corner of the dressing-room or preparing to play five-a-side at Melwood. Shankly is as alive today as he was 30-odd years ago. Make no mistake. Bill Shankly is more than just a legend. He has become a part of the fabric of Liverpool, as unmistakably Liverpudlian as Cilla Black, the Beatles or *Brookside*.

Shankly is everywhere, immortalised in graffiti on the walls, his name etched on Liverpool shirts and still chanted from the Kop. Young kids, born years after he died, have been reared on tales of his exploits; old men who watched and cheered his teams of the '60s and early '70s can never forget the joy and pride he brought to their lives and to the city. His off-the-cuff remarks were immortalised in print. Shankly is a legend never to be forgotten in this part of the land.

'I came to Liverpool because of the people,' he claimed. 'They have a fighting spirit with fighting blood in the veins, but mixed with it is a tremendous kindness. They will threaten your life one minute and give you their last penny the next.'

There may have been more than a smattering of romanticism in his words, but they caught the mood of a city where sentimentality is as thick as the salt in the sea breezes. To understand how Shankly manipulated that sentimentality, you also need to understand Liverpool and its people.

Liverpool was well capable of being just as obsessive, bizarre, emotional and contradictory as Shankly. They were almost one and the same character. He spoke of the dreams of those on the Kop. But he was also full of loyalty, as fundamental a Liverpool characteristic as any. Nor could you pigeonhole him. He was anarchic, subversive and always ready to speak his mind. And of course he was witty. He could so easily have been born a scouser.

It was little wonder they soon took him to their hearts. Shankly was charismatic, a spokesman, voicing their thoughts and speaking their language. All that power. In another man, it could have been frightening. It was a good job he had so many likeable qualities. It's hard to think of anyone in British life, let alone a sportsman, who commanded as much affection and respect, and who could manipulate his audience like Shankly.

Talk to any of the older Kopites and they will tell you the same. 'He was one of us, a man of the people, a Kopite. He understood us, and we shared the same passion for football and Liverpool. He wanted the team to win as much as we did. He wasn't like today's managers with their gold medallions, sleek cars and fast women, taking a few backhanders here and there for players. He was a man of principle, who loved the game more than anything.'

The respect was mutual. Said Shankly, 'Occasionally, I would have a walk around the ground before a match, and I went into the Kop one day, before it had filled up. A little chap there said, "Stand here, Bill, you'll get a good view of the game from here!" I couldn't take him up on that offer because I had to look after the team. The encouragement the supporters have given the team has been incredible. When there is a corner kick at the Kop end of the ground, they frighten the ball!'

Shankly was a messiah who arrived at Anfield just as the city was set to burst on to the world map. It's hard to think of anyone else, who so captured the hearts and minds of Liverpool people. The Beatles may have brought international acclaim to the city, but once they had achieved their glory they were off chasing the Yellow Brick Motorway to fame and fortune, preferring the suburban squirearchy of Surrey, or the glens of Scotland, to the chaos of Liverpool. But once he had arrived, Shankly, the man from Ayrshire, was here to stay: he was never embarrassed by his fame, nor did he shirk the responsibilities it brought.

He was the ultimate obsessive: fanatical not just about Liverpool Football Club but about football in general. He'd buttonhole fans in pubs, cross swords with journalists in remote corridors of Anfield, argue with his players in the dressing-room and then urge them all on from the bench. All he ever wanted to do was talk football, to be involved with the game.

And no game was less important than any other, whether it was Wembley, the San Siro, or a five-a-side at Huddersfield with the dads. Even before his death, he was an icon, elevated to the loftiest position, a god who couldn't be knocked down. It's hard to find anyone with a sour word to say, or indeed a story that shows Shankly in a harsh light. There are hundreds of anecdotes about him. Anyone who met him has a tale, and the stories are nearly always amusing, bizarre, the stuff of legend.

But of course there was another side. Nobody could be as dedicated without having forfeited something. There's a picture of Shankly taken by Liverpool photographer Steve Hale. It's one of those memorable photographs, instantly recognisable, of a victorious Shankly walking triumphantly around Anfield. There he stands before his beloved Kop, Liverpool scarf tied caringly around his neck, the emperor greeting his subjects. Shankly has an old-fashioned face, grey and seamed, a boxer's jaw, a welterweight's shoulders. But it is his eyes. Look at them. Staring, almost frightening, into the wilderness. The eyes of a man obsessed. There is a mystical messianic quality that cannot easily be explained away.

As a player, Bill Shankly was the archetypal Scottish half-back, aggressive, punishing, but always honest. With his short-cropped hair and middle parting, he was a terrifying prospect for any forward, even if it was Matthews or Lawton. He was the leader on the park, motivating his fellow players, urging them on. It was hardly surprising that, when he retired, he should immediately land himself a managerial job.

His career took him across the wastelands of English football, from Carlisle to Grimsby, then to Workington and on to Huddersfield before finally he rolled into Liverpool. Shankly spent most of that time in the Third Division North, hardly ideal preparation for his later success. Yet those places shaped his philosophy and style of football management. But none of his achievements could have come without his loyal bootroom lieutenants at Anfield, particularly Bob Paisley, whose wise, unassuming counsel kept Shankly in check.

Shankly was also the last of a dying breed. By the time he came to retire, football had moved on from the 1930s. Tracksuited managers, agents and sky-high transfer fees had taken over. The old loyalties had all but disappeared.

In Shankly's day, they shook hands over a deal and toasted it with a cup of tea. By the 1980s, the lawyers were drafting the contracts, the agents doing the talking, and the champagne corks kept popping. Shankly would have hated it all, though no doubt he would have been every bit as successful. However, the game of the 1990s was not the same honest game that he had played.

As a manager, he will always rank among the best. Only Busby and Stein could compare. They were all out of the same mould, growing up with the same set of values, from backgrounds where adversity bred backbone. But Shankly was a one-off. No other manager in the history of the game has been as idolised by the fans. Busby was loved and respected for all his success, but never idolised. Busby did his talking on the football field. Shankly did it wherever he was. For Shankly, football really was much more important than life or death.

On the last day of the Kop on Saturday, 30 April 1994, more than 44,000 fans came to Anfield to celebrate the end of an era. It was an occasion dedicated to Shanklyism. The old banners of the 1960s fluttered in the breeze, and scarves dating back to the days of Hickson and Yeats had been pulled out from bottom drawers, as the chants and songs of a past era were once again aired.

The Kop, in full cry, belted out choruses of 'She Loves You' or 'Go Back to Ital-ee'. Many of its younger inhabitants were not even alive when their fathers had sung the same words in the '60s. Yet the songs have been lovingly passed down over the years, each one learnt by a new generation.

That day, one by one, the great players of the past were introduced to the crowd – Albert Stubbins, Billy Liddell, Phil Thompson, Tommy Smith, Kenny Dalglish and so on. But they saved the biggest cheer for a woman, Nessie Shankly, widow of Bill. As she tottered across the pitch leaning on the arm of Joe Fagan, a roar erupted from the Kop. 'Shank-lee, Shank-lee, Shank-lee,' they wailed to the tune of 'Amazing Grace'. It was their way of saying thank you to Bill Shankly's widow, after all those years when she had to share him with Liverpool. Twenty years on since he left Anfield, and still they had not forgotten him.

Shankly: The Biography (Virgin, 1996)

JACK CHARLTON

Paul Rowan

The IFA's worst fears were realised when it tried to recruit the Bolton Wanderers midfielder, Jason McAteer. McAteer, who had a grandfather from Co. Down in Northern Ireland, had come to the attention of the former Northern Ireland international, Bryan Hamilton. Hamilton had been working as a sports journalist for a local radio station on Merseyside and had interviewed McAteer on a number of occasions. When Hamilton was appointed to succeed Billy Bingham as Northern Ireland manager, he immediately stated that he did not share the same objection as his predecessor and let it be known that he regarded McAteer as a legitimate target. The story then appeared on Teletext that Northern Ireland were chasing Jason McAteer. Having opened the door, Hamilton was trampled over by two more powerful suitors.

Jimmy Armfield knew that he was up against a formidable opponent when he went to Bolton on behalf of the FA to offer Jason McAteer the chance to play for England. He, Maurice Setters and Jack Charlton went back a long way. Armfield had been in the same army regiment as Setters when they did their national service together in the mid-1950s. Even then, Setters had to do the spade work, cleaning out the stables at Chelsea Barracks, while Charlton's stint includes a period coaching the British army team out in Hong Kong.

Charlton and Armfield had spent much of their footballing lives together. As a full-back, Armfield had spent the latter part of his England career playing alongside the obstreperous centre-half from Leeds United. At Lilleshall, they had argued vehemently about who should go after the ball when it was kicked over the full-back's head. Charlton had argued that Armfield should run back rather than he run over, and had won the argument in the end.

Charlton had views on a lot of things, which is why the *Daily Express* employed him as a columnist, with Armfield, now a trained journalist, as the ghost-writer. Armfield had been writing up Charlton's column for ten years before he got the job with the FA. Even when Charlton was out of work, and seen as yesterday's man, Armfield persuaded the *Daily Express* to keep paying him when they wouldn't be getting a column. The most difficult part of it was always tracking Charlton down on the telephone as he was on the move incessantly.

When Charlton's name was linked with the Irish job, Armfield became his *de facto* publicist, briefing Irish journalists and FAI officials about the type of man they were considering taking on board. It was Armfield who phoned Jack at his hunting lodge in the Yorkshire Dales to let him know he had got the Irish job. And then Armfield gave the number to the FAI so that they could get in contact with him.

Now Armfield, in his new role as technical consultant to the FA, was doing a job for the new England manager, Terry Venables. Armfield had spotted a couple of promising boys at Bolton, the right-sided midfielder Jason McAteer, and the centre-half Alan Stubbs. On Armfield's recom-mendation, Venables went to see them at Highbury in the fourth round of the FA Cup, when Bolton beat Arsenal 3–1. He decided to pick the two players for a forthcoming England B international against Northern Ireland, and dispatched Armfield to Bolton to inform them of the call-up.

Armfield rang the Bolton manager, Bruce Rioch, to make the arrangements. He was then informed that Jack Charlton was also trying to recruit McAteer and was planning to come to the FA Cup quarter-final game against Oldham on Saturday. Armfield arranged with Rioch to see the two lads on the day before the game; it was an arrangement that Rioch was happy with, as he felt it would give McAteer and Stubbs a boost before the big Cup game the following day. Armfield then drove down to Bolton; Burnden Park was familiar territory to him; he had been manager there in the mid-'70s before taking over at Leeds. He sat in the manager's office and called the two players in separately. Armfield told McAteer that Terry Venables had sent him over to ask if he would play on the England B team in a fixture they were trying to arrange against Northern Ireland. McAteer replied that he would be happy to play. He particularly looked forward to playing with Stubbs, who was his best friend.

'He left knowing that I'd be playing for England,' McAteer says, 'and the next thing he sees is that I'm playing for Ireland.'

In the dressing-room after the Oldham game, McAteer shed a few tears. It was the end of a long Cup run, a 1–0 defeat because of a soft goal in the last five minutes of the match. Waiting for him outside was Jack Charlton.

'I said to Jason what I said to all of them. "No pressure. We want you to play for us, but we're not looking to force ya, and if you want to come in and look and you like it, and you decide you want to qualify for us, we'd be delighted to have you." If they qualify for two or three countries, we do that with 'em. And we say, "Listen, there's no hassle. If you decide you want to go play for England, that's your business. But we think you'll like the Irish. Plus the fact that there is an international career with the Irish that might not be there for you with the English. We have only 30 players to pick from, England have three thousand players to pick from." '

Charlton offered McAteer a place in the team for a forthcoming friendly game against Russia, part of Ireland's build-up for the World Cup, but he wasn't looking for an answer on the spot. He told McAteer to think about it for a few days and then get back to him.

It was a difficult choice for McAteer to make. 'I'm English, and it would have to be England, I suppose,' he told the Bolton *Evening News* at the time. 'I'm still young and there will be other World Cups. But Jack has dangled an enormous carrot in front of my nose.'

For guidance, McAteer turned to his parents and to Bruce Rioch. His mother, Thora, whose parents were Welsh, wanted him to play for Wales. Rioch had been in a similar dilemma to McAteer; he was also born in England, but played for Scotland, the country of his father. Rioch told McAteer that he would have to make up his own mind, but said he would find it easier to get established with Ireland in the long term.

McAteer dismissed Wales and Northern Ireland. 'The two biggest ones as I would see it are the Republic and England. That's when you start worrying. If it's just one, like England, then there's no problem. And when Jack asked me, flippin' heck, it was one of the toughest decisions I had to make since me options in school.

'With England it was like a B international and there have been hundreds of good players who've played B internationals and not gone any further, and it was just, you know, Ireland was a full cap, and I think I can get into the Irish side much quicker than I can with England in my position, because with England it's all blocked off with the likes of Gascoigne, Platt and Batty in there. They're all there or thereabouts, like. I've found that there's no back of the queue with Ireland, it's whoever's playing well that gets in.'

Armfield was left shaking his head. 'I can't understand an Englishman wanting to play for Ireland,' he said. 'No matter how hard I try, I can't understand it.'

The Team That Jack Built, 1995

FRANK CLARK

Mark Staniforth

At Nottingham Forest's spartan training ground, the wind is whipping off the adjacent River Trent and swirling around the weather-beaten cones and goalposts with considerable venom.

A clutch of YTS lads who thought they'd got the easy option by getting injured are moaning into their tracksuits about being employed as ballboys to the first team.

Stuart Pearce is tearing around like an absolute nutter. At one point he unintentionally leaps into the way of a team-mate's goal-bound rocket, diverting it round the post. Mark Crossley chuckles cautiously. You get the feeling he would have laughed hysterically had it been anyone else. The small knot of dads with kids, YTS ballboys and journalists immediately shift position. We thought we'd got it right to go behind Stuart Pearce. Apparently not.

Surveying it all is Frank Clark, the gaffer. He disallows one of Pearce's team's goals. Pearce fires expletives in Clark's direction. The thought enters my head that that would never have been allowed to happen under Brian Clough. Perhaps not. But perhaps Cloughie went a bit too far at times.

Watching the squad training together and then eating together in the club's banqueting suite afterwards, one senses a healthy, mutually respectful team spirit, a squad free of prima-donnas, a perfect happy medium.

Nottingham Forest are the only British team left in Europe.

Frank Clark is surprised: 'Surprised and disappointed, in fact,' he says. 'I thought the others would have done better, particularly in the UEFA Cup with the strength, on paper, of the representation that we had. I don't know why they failed – I didn't see the games – but it is very difficult in Europe these days.'

Since the horrific capitulations of their Premiership rivals who all, with the possible exception of Everton, succumbed to teams they were expected to beat easily, Forest have been the lone standard-bearers for England in the UEFA Cup.

Few clubs have better pedigrees to be so. Forest have one of the best records of any English club in Europe, thanks to their two European Cup wins in 1979 and 1980. Ironically Malmo, overcome in the first round of this season's UEFA Cup campaign, were also the conquests in that first final, in which Frank Clark played. But Clark doesn't strike you as a man who scrabbles around for good omens. Things have, he admits, changed a bit since all their Premiership rivals tumbled out: 'I don't think it's different in terms of pressure – we've certainly had a bit more exposure since we became the last English club in Europe. The spotlight's become a bit brighter but it's not a problem. We're not doing it for England, we're doing it for Forest – for ourselves, for the club and for the supporters.'

The theory that their continued involvement in Europe will affect concentration on the rather more mundane business of carving out a top-three spot in the Premiership doesn't wash with Clark: 'We're aware of it and we'll make sure it doesn't happen,' he says. With Bayern not rolling into town until March, the players have every reason to throw themselves into the domestic programme, unafraid of picking up any niggling injuries which could have kept them out of the glamour tie, and anxious to cement their place in the side in time for the big one.

'I was delighted that we got drawn with Bayern,' says Clark. 'There are no easy draws in the quarter-finals of any cup competition. There were some illustrious names in the hat and we were just delighted to be in there with them. There is a danger that Europe might affect our concentration in the Premiership, but it's something we're aware of and we'll have to deal with it and make sure it doesn't happen. We're a long way behind Newcastle, but we've got to just try and win the next game and not be concerned about anyone else.'

Clark is talking so candidly about battling for titles and championships less than two full seasons after taking them up from the First Division. This is testament to the great change the club has enjoyed since the new broom started to sweep out the cobwebs which were beginning to gather at the end of Brian Clough's gargantuan 18-year reign.

The club has regained its synonymity with slick, passing football, and its permanent position among the Premiership top dogs. Outside the Midlands, hardly anyone hates Nottingham Forest.

Clark has made it look so easy since resigning his managing director's post at Leyton Orient and heading north in the summer of 1993. But he had a hell of an act to follow: Nottingham Forest wasn't just associated with Clough, it was Clough. Didn't Clark feel a bit overawed by his predecessor; a bit wary of breaking all his routines and ideals?

'No,' he says, 'I suppose the people outside saw it as a hard act to follow but I've never seen it that way really. This job came and I've tried to manage the club in the way I think it should be managed, without paying any attention at all to who's been the manager in the past. When I first came here, everything was in a routine but I wasn't worried about changing it. I just did it in the way I thought it should be done. If it was different it was different, if it was the same it was the same. It wasn't a conscious decision whether to change or not.

'It's only difficult in that he's set certain standards that coloured people's expectations. The expectations of Forest's supporters are high because of the standards he attained, and that's the kind of level that we have to aspire to. That's the only difficulty about following Brian Clough.'

But Clark's title claims have been devalued by the departures of Stan Collymore and, this season, Lars Bohinen, to supposed 'bigger clubs' for reasons of glamour and money. Nobody leaves Newcastle or Manchester United for that reason.

'It's frustrating and disappointing,' Clark admits. 'I felt if we could have kept the side together that finished the last bit of last season we could have had a real go at it this time round, but there you go. It was all about more money with Lars. Stan saw Liverpool as a bigger club than us. He saw it as a good career move – I think he got carried away with the glamour that's attached to Liverpool. Money-wise, we made it clear that we would have matched any offer that he got from Anfield. But Stan will eventually succeed at Liverpool, there's no doubt about that.'

Meanwhile, Forest fans have taken a new hero to heart. Steve Stone is the unlikeliest of saviours for Terry Venables. When the going got tough for Tel at the tail-end of last year, Stone popped up with a string of dazzling displays on the right side of midfield which captured the headlines. Even his easy-to-make-a-pun-on surname was spot on. Stone's rise to international stardom is all the more miraculous when you consider that he has had to battle back from three broken legs since signing for Forest as a trainee in 1989. Clark enthuses: 'Steve's success rubs off on the whole squad to a certain extent. The more internationals you have, the better it is for the image of the football club. As far as the players are concerned they're delighted for Stoney because he's such a popular fellow. I've seen a gradual improvement in him since I came to the club. He's worked very hard on his game and particularly the areas where he needed to improve. That, allied to his character, temperament and physical ability, have turned him into a very good player. I'm sure the experience and exposure he's had with England will make him an even better player. It doesn't happen to everybody but Stoney has taken it very well.'

To replace Collymore directly, Clark went where others have feared to tread in the close season and raised countless eyebrows by signing Andrea Silenzi from Torino. Silenzi thus became the first Italian from Serie A ever to play in English top-flight football. Let's be honest: up to now he's done nothing to suggest that he won't be the last as well. Silenzi hasn't had much luck, being dogged by a string of minor injuries, and finding it hard to break back into the team when fully fit because of the exciting form of the other strikers in the squad, most notably the super-dreadlocked Jason Lee.

But Clark remains unruffled over the question of whether he has any regrets about the ground-breaking transfer. 'All signings are gambles, wherever they're from. Bryan Roy came from Serie A and he's settled in. Andrea's just been unfortunate. He missed the early part of the season so he wasn't quite fit when the opportunities came around to get into the team. Others got the opportunities instead and they've taken them very well. Ideally, he needs a run of five or six games in the first team but it wouldn't be fair of me to turn round to someone like Jason Lee and say, "You've got to be out because I've got to give Andy six games." He's got to be patient and wait for his chance.'

There may be little scope for more groundbreaking transfers in the future. A handful of days before this interview, the results of the Bosman affair were cemented by the European Court. The ramifications will hit clubs like Forest particularly hard; Clark is the first to admit they cannot compete money-wise with the likes of Newcastle and Manchester United. 'No wonder Sir John Hall's in favour of it,' Clark says pointedly. 'He needs it so Newcastle can get all the best players because they pay the biggest wages. United, Liverpool, Everton, Arsenal, Tottenham – they pay wages that we just can't compete with. If they don't have to pay transfer fees, players will just go to whichever club pays the most.

'I would just like people like Rupert Murdoch and the European Commission to stay out of football and leave us alone. We had a perfectly good retaining transfer system that was vastly superior to that on the Continent. I don't blame Bosman, I blame the club. What they tried to do was disgraceful. They wouldn't let the boy go, they put a massive transfer fee on his head and they halved his wages. That's immoral and you can't possibly justify that. But you couldn't ever do that in England. If you had a player and you tried to halve his wages, he'd become a totally free agent, and that's good, that's an effective mechanism against abuse of the system. And I don't think you'll find one player who had complaints about the system.

'It's all been absolutely blown out of the water because of an immoral act by a Belgian club and some lunatic ruling by the European Court or whatever it's called. It's turned the game into a total and utter shambles. You try and get guidance from the FA and even they don't know. One day this is the law and the next it isn't, and that is. The game is in total chaos.'

Total chaos. A state which has never been further from Nottingham Forest's heart.

The Game, February 1996

RON ATKINSON

Jeremy Novick

Ron Atkinson first unleashed Big Ron on his suspecting public in 1978 when, after taking them out of Division Four as champions, he left Cambridge United to manage West Bromwich Albion. It was there he made his reputation and set the standard that was to hold him in good stead for the rest of his career. With a team that included the late (great) Laurie Cunningham, Cyrille Regis, Tony Brown, John Wile, Derek Statham and Alastair Robertson, West Brom set the game alight by playing fast, joyous football that sparkled as much as their manager's fingers. In his first year in charge there, the statistical record spoke for itself: played 53, won 30, drew 16, lost 7. Goals for 96, goals against 45. There was an FA Cup semi-final, too, where WBA were beaten by the eventual winners, Ipswich.

The statistics might have had their own eloquence, but the manager wasn't taking any chances. Headlines like 'TORA! TORA! TORA! – THAT'S OUR NEW CLUB MOTTO!' flowed quicker than the soccer. The back pages loved him. So did the critics. 'Atkinson is one of those football managers who impress, initially, through presence as much as presence of mind,' said David Lacey in *The Guardian*.

Ron tasted life in the Big league and liked it. And why not? After a career scrabbling around in the lower reaches of football, to be a headline-maker must have been sweetness itself. As a midfielder who looked as if he belonged on a rugby pitch, Ron had spent most of his playing career with Oxford United and had been the cornerstone of their dramatic rise out of the Southern League and into the real world. 'The Tank', he was called. Maybe if his playing career had been a little more sparkling, he wouldn't have felt the need to compensate later when he was successful.

'When I was seventeen and on the Villa ground-staff, I bought myself a car, a Ford Anglia. Paid £34 for it. I used to drive to training in it and some mornings I'd see Jackie Sewell and Peter McParland standing at the bus-stop. Now they were real big-time; I mean, Sewell held the British transfer record and McParland had won the Cup for Villa practically on his own. "Jump in," I used to say. "And mind the upholstery." They might have thought I was a real flash bugger, but they never said a word.' It was just an idea.

Big Ron's still compensating. He's always structured his training sessions around competitive five-a-sides, partly to inspire the team to new levels of fitness, but more importantly so that he can play himself. His eagerness to play the game is legendary – 'It's the highlight of his week' is a common enough comment – which is curious until you remember his inauspicious playing career.

'He threw himself into those games. He was the centre of the action and if he was injured or ill – which was extremely rare – we wouldn't play, it was as simple as that. I don't think he could bear to watch us play football if he couldn't join in.' Needless to say, he took the penalties. 'He absolutely loved it. He placed the ball very deliberately, then walked back with a swagger and crashed it in. He never failed. If the goalie saved it then he had moved too soon and it would have to be retaken.' We can all take the piss out of Big Ron, his ego and those five-a-side games. Only that was Liverpool stalwart Phil Thompson talking about the late Bill Shankly. And who's going to take the piss out of Shanks? So maybe we shouldn't be so cynical. Maybe it's just a man who loves football playing football.

'Pressures? What pressures? Perhaps I'm wrong, I don't know. Perhaps I enjoy things too much.' The zenith of this period was a dazzling 5–3 victory at Old Trafford. No wonder there was no pressure. There was something else that Albion became known for – their Three Degrees. The name is a giveaway.

For a working-class sport, British football in the 1970s was riddled with a racism of the most ridiculous variety. Black players, it was said, lacked 'bottle'. They couldn't compete. They lacked the appetite for the physical aspect of the game. It is to Atkinson's eternal credit that he turned this nonsense on its head. Inheriting Cunningham and Regis, Atkinson went back to Cambridge and bought Brendan Batson to complete the set. 'I don't care if a player's black or white or green with purple spots. If he can do a job for me, he's in the team.' It was, at the time, a brave thing to do. Regis says now, 'Looking back, it must have taken some courage to sign the third black player. Three black players in one team, there was no such thing at the time. It was unique.' Whatever other -isms Big Ron may have bought into, racism wasn't, and still isn't, one of them. Sexism, though. That's a different matter.

Examples of his sexism are rife. When he arrived at Sheffield Wednesday he was interviewed by *Sunday Times* journalist Sue Mott. 'Can we expect less of the long ball game now at Hillsborough?' she asked him.

'Blimey,' he replied. 'You're the first bird I've met with an FA coaching badge.'

'I can't stand women talking about football,' he said famously. 'I don't know why, but it grates on me. They shouldn't interfere.' Or, as he said in 1989, 'Women should be in the kitchen, the discotheque and the boutique, but not in football.' The discotheque? The boutique? These words existed in 1989? Backing up his view is one of his best, most familiar stories. He's manager of Aston Villa. 'I'm at the ground one day when Terry Cooper walks in. He's managing them at the time and he's got this young girl, Karren Brady, with him who's just been made managing director of Birmingham City, God help us. She's very pleasant and she says what a nice ground it is and what a good team we've got and how I must be really proud of them all, but particularly proud of my son who's playing so well. Now this throws me a bit, and I say, "My son?" very casual. And she says, "I've heard a lot of good reports about your Dalian." Now that's what I mean about women and football.'

It was the inspirational Albion side that really attracted United in 1981. Dave Sexton was a good coach but, like a dog to its owner, his United team had started to resemble his outlook. Steve Coppell, a thrilling winger in Docherty's day, had become a sensible midfield support. Ray Wilkins had lost all interest in being butch and had discovered the joys of the five-yard pass to a colleague in whispering range. United were nothing if not United and they needed a bit of flair and *joie de vivre*. Old Trafford was, as Sir Bobby Charlton said, 'a theatre of dreams' and United needed a minimum of 36,000 paying dreamers every week to stay in the black. More, they needed to recapture the joy of the Docherty era, preferably, though, without the earache. Big Ron'd sort it out. No one mentioned that he was fourth choice after Bobby Robson, Ron Saunders and Lawrie McMenemy.

Ron? As Tommy Docherty said all those years before, he'd have walked to Old Trafford. If Ron had never had a go at United, he'd never have been able to look His Bigness in the face again. It was a marriage made in the print room. At his first press conference there, Ron set out his stall. 'Gentlemen, you can have my home number, but please remember not to call during *The Sweeney*.' Such chumminess.

In a League of Their Own (Mainstream, 1995)

TOMMY BURNS

Ian Stafford

Just over a year ago a red-haired Scotsman took it upon himself to go to school. Packing a small bag, he set off first to Amsterdam, where he spent three days, watching, talking, listening and learning.

Six weeks ago he was off on his travels again, but this time to Turin, where he continued his education in a short, but effective visit to the old capital of Piedmont. His teachers were a little surprised to see him. After all, they were not used to the British, and especially a Scotsman, wanting to study their ways, but they were nevertheless delighted to help out.

Safely back home again, the lessons learned from these trips are being repeated to a new class of eager pupils. Slowly a new language is being taught, and the results are there to be seen by everyone. After the worst period in their history, a time during this decade when only failure was known, and extinction a possibility, Celtic Football Club is a force in Scottish football again. Suddenly life is looking a great deal rosier for one half of Glasgow.

For this the club must thank two men: one a businessman called Fergus McCann, who provided the much-needed financial rescue package, and the other, a visionary called Tommy Burns.

It was Burns who took it upon himself to sneak away in midweek to spend a few days in the company of those Dutch masters, Ajax, and then, later, with Juventus. It is no coincidence, therefore, to find a Celtic team now breathing down their Old Firm rivals' necks for the championship, defending the Scottish Cup and adopting a highly technical, passing game.

'I knew, because of my lack of credentials and experience, that I had a lot more to learn about being a manager before I could go to my players and show them a new style of play,' Burns admitted, sitting in the Celtic boardroom, surrounded by the glittering success of dim and distant years.

'The people at both Ajax and Juventus were pleased to see me, and couldn't have been more helpful. I spoke to the coaches man to man, because it was important for me to learn from these people. Ajax proved to be more technical, while Juventus were physically strong and organised, but both were tactically advanced. It was an education.'

And what did Celtic mean to them? 'Well, it meant what it meant in the late 1960s. A great team, 30 years ago. But I want a Celtic team to make an impact in Europe in the 1990s, known for our success and for the way we play.'

Such words could not have been uttered 18 months ago. Celtic had not won a trophy, any trophy, in the 1990s. They were not only playing second fiddle to Rangers, who have totally dominated Scottish football during their rivals' decline, but were also bowing to the likes of Motherwell. The board had self-destructed, and had just been kicked out by the fans, while Celtic had just appointed a 37-year-old former player whose experience of management amounted to two years as the player-manager at Kilmarnock.

Enter Tommy Burns. As a player, he had won everything in Scottish football during his 17 seasons at Celtic. He had cleaned Bobby Murdoch's boots, sat shoulder to shoulder with Billy McNeill, and played alongside Kenny Dalglish and the exuberant Charlie Nicholas, but after he left in 1991, he watched the decline with sorrow. 'It didn't bother me that Rangers were doing so well,' he said. 'I have no interest in them at all. But I see Celtic as an entirely different club, with a different mentality and different principles. Celtic have been compassionate and good to the poor and, most of all, they are the people's club. It took the fans to put the wrongs right. They have become more bitter and angry, until they organised demonstrations and boycotts in order to get the people running the club out. And they were right to do so, because there was no direction at the club.'

Celtic's position seemed even worse once Burns stepped back through the Celtic Park doors after a four-year absence. 'I felt the club's condition was terminal. They were heading for oblivion, and it was only when I came here that I discovered why. The majority of the players had become detached from the people. The fans soon realised this, and when they coupled this with the poor results, there was a general sourness about the place. The atmosphere just wasn't right.'

Anything else? 'Yes, for many years the club has lacked a leader. I'm not just talking about Fergus McCann, but someone who was aware of the football side, of how important the club was and is to the people, and how badly the club needed an infrastructure.

'The biggest problem was that nobody realised just how big this club can be in terms of support. If ever there's an example of this, it's the amazing fact that, on the back of losing to Raith Rovers in last year's

League Cup final, Celtic enjoyed the biggest share issue scheme in the country. The club should have been asking itself how it could be the very best, not just in Scotland, but in Europe.'

So it was some step to take from Kilmarnock to a giant in crisis. Presumably, Burns must have felt that accepting the job at Celtic would be some test? 'Now that,' he replied, 'has to be the understatement of all time. I didn't have the credentials, and I knew the chance had come very early, but I had to take it. It was my dream club to manage, and I felt that if I turned it down someone else would step in and turn Celtic round. You don't get too many chances like that in life.'

On the basis that Burns could hardly have made matters any worse, he set to work, changing the infrastructure of the club by appointing his own hand-picked personnel, and creating a new mood.

'The first thing I noticed was the unhappy atmosphere and, basically, I felt I had to start from scratch. I had to make it a place where people were comfortable to work in. I brought in Billy Stark as my assistant, David Hay and Wally McStay from Sligo, people of integrity, who had the interests of Celtic at heart, and not themselves as individuals.

'The players used to go home after training. Now they have lunch together afterwards. The TV's on, they're talking and laughing, and there's a wee buzz in the air. They even have music in the dressing-room now, whereas before they just sat and stared at each other.

'Celtic were going to discard players like Pat Bonner. When you have someone who's played in World Cups, broken national records, and been through the whole club, you don't let them walk away, but keep them as part of the set-up. I also introduced two sessions of training a day, where we concentrate on the technical side of the game. Consequently, we now play a totally different style to last year.'

And they are getting results. It is looking that the championship race, strictly between Rangers and Celtic, will go down to the wire this season, which represents a remarkable transformation for Celtic and one which even Burns is surprised about.

'We've got to this stage a lot quicker than I expected, and that's down to the attitude of the players, and the atmosphere. But we've reached a critical part of the season now, and all the progress we've made will be forgotten if we come second to Rangers. For me as a manager, I know I've taken this club a long way, and winning the league would be a fantastic bonus, but to the fans, anything else than becoming champions would be considered a failure. You see, they've been waiting too long for success. What's happened at Celtic has been unacceptable.'

Incredibly, Burns felt the axe was hovering over him after Celtic lost the League Cup final last year to lowly Raith. 'A few people turned against me,' he admitted. 'Had we not beaten Airdrie to win the Scottish Cup, who knows what might have happened to me? I knew I was on shaky ground.'

So what kept you going, and what have the experiences of managing Celtic taught you?

This turns out to be an easy question for Burns to answer. 'I've learned how much depends on God, because there's no doubt about it, he's carried me through the past 18 months. There have been very, very difficult times here, but I've been able to turn to him with my thoughts and prayers, and to find my strength.'

Burns, obviously, is a Catholic. 'Yes, but although that's relevant to the Celtic supporters, it's not important from a club viewpoint,' he argues. 'We don't look at non-Catholics in any different light to anyone else.'

Does he put everything down to his faith, then? 'God has helped me see things straight and reach what seem to be the right decisions.' Even going to Ajax? 'I consider that to be divine intervention.'

Scottish football abroad, both at club and international level, could have done with some divine intervention over the years. Burns pulls no punches over the reasons why a nation that has produced so many outstanding individual players has always under-achieved.

'It's because we've never had the right leaders, at club or national level, who can make their teams tactically aware, show them a successful way of playing, and make the players believe in it. We've never had a Capello or a Sacchi, who are real students of the game.'

I suggest that Andy Roxburgh probably saw himself as a student. 'Where's the proof, though?' Burns asks. 'The proof's in the results.'

Point taken. So you are not stopping at just a return to winning ways in Scotland, then?

'That's the short-term plan, but the eventual idea is not only to play in Europe, as Rangers have done, but to become one of the main contenders. That's why there's much work still to be done.'

Which is why Burns will go AWOL again before the end of the season, choosing another European city, and another football classroom to further his education.

It is 5.30 in the evening as I leave Celtic Park, rapidly emerging as the finest and biggest club stadium in the country. Burns won't be home for some time yet. The man is on a mission, not only for himself but, it seems, for his club, and the whole of the east end of Glasgow.

The Independent, 7 February 1996

TERRY YORATH:
A WELSHMAN IN BEIRUT

Robert Fisk

It's strange the way Terry Yorath fits into Beirut. Maybe it's the craggy face of the former Wales manager that matches the bullet-splashed walls. Ask him to step out of the taxi for a few minutes and he'll stand for pictures beside the ruins of a 15-year war as if he grew up here, hands in pockets, eyes sliding in familiarity over the wreckage of hotels and shops and homes. Maybe it's the understanding of tragedy. The war that killed 150,000 people here had only been over 19 months when Terry Yorath's 15-year-old son died in his arms in their Leeds back garden.

Not that the Lebanese footballers he now trains to play for their country speak of their personal suffering any more than the 46-year-old Welsh manager of the Lebanese national football team. 'The Lebanese don't talk to me about the war,' he says. 'I'll ask Hussein, my driver: "Did this incident in the war happen over there?" or "Was this where so-and-so was killed?" and then he'll tell me. But he won't offer any information. Sometimes the Lebanese see the photograph of Daniel in my wallet and they'll ask who it is and I'll say it's my son and then I hear Hussein saying something to them, whispering to them in Arabic, and though I don't understand him, I know he's telling them that Daniel is dead. But they won't ask me why or what happened to Daniel. They are silent.'

Terry Yorath wouldn't mind telling them. Maybe Lebanon has tamed him, blunted a traditional team manager's fury in a land where losing your temper can sometimes get you killed. You can tell how much he has learned since he arrived last June – or just how easily he fits in – by the way he says goodbye to the taxi driver who has brought us back from the old front-line ruins. Most westerners would have ignored the driver. But Yorath jumps out of the car, thanks him profusely for the journey and shakes hands. Is Yorath always this nice, I wondered?

He had better be, in a country whose individual football teams still painfully reflect the country's sectarian divisions. The players in Ansar (Partisans) are almost all Sunni Muslims, in Nejmi (Star), they are Shiite Muslims, in Hekmi (Wisdom) Christian Maronites. Most Sunnis, of course, support Ansar, Shiites Nejmi, Maronites Hekmi – which is why the riots that sometimes follow matches are as sinister as they are violent. Into this little nightmare strode Terry Yorath seven months ago.

Of course Yorath had been in charge of an international team before, managing the Welsh for five years until the controversial decision not to renew his contract in 1993. Even the in-fighting that job exposed him to was little preparation for what awaited him in Beirut.

'It was pointed out to me quite clearly at the very start that I mustn't get involved with one sect or another,' he says. 'The problem is that Ansar is such a strong team that people say the football federation is on the Ansar side because Ansar have seven players in the national side. Yes, of course, for this reason the national side is dominated by Muslims. But we make no distinction when we choose players.'

Is that why, I suggest archly, he has three Armenians among the national players, to add a few more Christians to the team? 'We need the Armenians because they're the best footballers. They are pros, they play the game to the best of their ability. They know I'm absolutely going to crucify them during training.'

If he has avoided the sectarian traps – which he clearly has – Terry Yorath admits that Arabic can be a problem. 'A lot of people speak English, of course, but you can find that people just don't understand you. I've learned that I can't take too literally what the Lebanese say to me in English. I always have to check. A Lebanese will say "Yes" to me when it's not what he means – because people say things here that they think you'll like to hear.

'But football is a language all it's own. I draw pictures on the blackboard and they all understand. They know football terms. You know, the other night I was up till one in the morning with some of the team and we were all talking to each other in our own languages and though we didn't know the other's language, we understood each other.'

Such conversations are given an exotic twist by the fact that Yorath's official translator is from Moscow, translating Welsh-accented English into Arabic via Russian. Nor is his work made easier by the fact that of the 14 teams in Lebanon's premier division, only four have grass pitches. In summer, Yorath will be training again in dust bowls, starting at five in the evening to avoid the day's heat, pushing the 25 or 30 players available to the national team for the Arab Games that are intended to be another symbol of Lebanon's recovery this summer and which will climax the last seven months of Yorath's current contract.

Meanwhile Yorath has been travelling in Lebanon. 'I found it exciting going down to Sidon. The guy who was showing me round stopped at one point and pointed up to the hills and said, "There is Israel." He didn't mean the area Israel occupies [below Jezzine]. And a few days ago, Hussein was driving me through some narrow streets in Beirut and he suddenly left the car and went off to some shop. And there I was all on my own in the car in this crowded street and I remember thinking: "A few years ago, if I'd been sitting on my own here, I'd have been very, very frightened".'

As it is, Yorath's only personal problems have been the time it takes to get through to his wife Christine in Leeds on the phone and the loneliness he admits to suffering in his bachelor flat at Khalde, just down the highway from Beirut airport. The ghost – or perhaps the very presence – of his dead son never leaves him. Daniel, who was about to sign up for Leeds United, died of hypertrophic myopathy, a rare heart disease, while playing football with his father in 1992. Only a year later, Yorath lost his contract as Wales manager. A large photograph of Daniel sits on Yorath's sideboard, along with pictures of Christine, his other son and two daughters. 'I don't think of him being gone. I feel he's still with us. Of course I think about him a lot.'

When Daniel died, Yorath would not move the football he was playing with from the spot where it fell in the garden. We were driving through the edge of Beirut's old front-line, past shell-smashed façades and rivers of sewage, his eyes all the while running back and forth over the ruins. Was it still there, I asked? Was the football still there four years later? 'The dog moved it and the wind moves it but it's still there. It moves around. It's strange but we still keep his room tidy and one day the girl making the bed swears that a pillow had moved from the bed to the floor when she was out of the room.

'Yes, loneliness comes when I miss my son. I often think of him when I see kids here of 13 or 14. And I often wonder if Daniel had been born here in Lebanon, would he have been a footballer? I guess it's God or fate. At home, I only have to glance at his picture to feel lonely. But, you know, I can't understand people who, when they lose someone who is dear to them, how they will let that person just drift away.'

In this, the holy month of Ramadan, Yorath is woken each morning at four o'clock by a drummer alerting Muslims to take their pre-fast breakfast. 'This guy goes banging this drum very loudly just below my flat. The first morning I woke up, I hadn't got a clue what was going on and was going to ask him to pipe down.'

With team members who will be fasting, Yorath, who was capped 59 times by Wales, has to oversee three international matches during Ramadan – against the Emirates, Ecuador and Bulgaria. Unlike British players, the Lebanese all have jobs to maintain – Yorath has a travel agent, a bank clerk and an airline official among his squad – and forcing them to acknowledge their errors on the field can be a painstaking task.

Yorath remembers how Lebanon has changed him. 'I'm much more patient than I ever was before in my life,' he says. 'And I've learned how to make a smashing stew.'

The Independent, 5 February 1996

GRAEME SOUNESS

Ron Scalpello

'Gala-TASARAY! Gala-TASARAY!' A swirling cacophony of sound floods the senses, absorbing everyone into its contagious energy. It's 6 p.m. in Fenerbahce Stadium, Istanbul, two hours before kick-off and 20,000 Turkish fans are already busily thumbing their way through the Byzantine book of passion and intimidation to create the sort of dark atmosphere that chills the heart of any unprepared Western observer to the core. Chinese crackers tap-dance across the stadium racing track's red tarmac, fireworks ignite high above its open-roof before arching across the city's burnt-orange sunset, riotously spraying the impressive skyline with pinks and greens.

And the beat goes on, 'Gala-TASARAY! Gala-TASARAY!', driven by a small man with a large bass drum. Another one, wearing a luminous yellow jacket, stands aloft an improvised podium conducting a bopping mass of heads like a devilish game-show host while a mist of gunpowder settles across the pitch. Eleven silhouettes stand on the race track looking lost, bewildered and slightly confused. It resembles a scene from *Apocalypse Now*, especially when the Turkish tactical support raise their reinforced shields to protect the Galatasaray players from the hail of coins thrown by the Fenerbahce fans.

And this is a friendly. The first game in the Turkish Journalists' Federation Cup when Istanbul's equivalent of Arsenal, Tottenham and Chelsea line up against each other in a pre-season mini tournament. Galatasaray and Fenerbahce are opening this year's triangular event with the losers playing last season's Turkish champions, Besiktas. The trio are the fiercest rivals who not only dominate the Istanbul football scene but share most of the domestic honours.

The interest and passion surrounding tonight's game has been intensified by the arrival of foreign blood. Graeme Souness is in charge and has secured Dean Saunders, Barry Venison and Mike Marsh for his Galatasaray team. Fenerbahce, not to be left out, have acquired the mercurial Dalian Atkinson from Aston Villa and are now coached by Brazilian World Cup winner Carlos Alberta Parreira. Expectations are high and either side's defeat could have a drastic effect on team confidence and on season-ticket sales.

Souness's arrival confirms the growing status of the Turkish league as it continues to attract foreign internationals with Germany's Stefan Kuntz and Norway's Ronny Johnsen lining up for Besiktas and Nigerian centre-half Okechukwu Uche dominating Fenerbahce's defence. The Brits' migration is seen as an overwhelming endorsement of Turkish football's technical development in the global arena and a confirmation that their domestic teams are now taken seriously in European competition. Hope is rising that Turkey will grace next year's European Championship with the national team, coached by ex-international Fatih Terim and con-structed around the graceful skills of Torino-based Hakan Sukur. The side are currently heading their group and impressive victories against Sweden and Switzerland have left them needing only victory against Hungary to ensure qualification.

Just visible through the sulphurous haze, three familiar, slightly pallid faces stare curiously out, joined together by a fear of the unknown. They belong to British mercenaries Saunders, Venison and Marsh. They're shaking their leg muscles, trying to maintain some professional cool and a 'seen it all before' air. But they haven't, not like this anyway. There's apprehension performing an awkward dance in their eyes that gives them away.

Mike Marsh looks like a nervous teenager who has been thrown off the school bus in the middle of the night a million miles away from home. His move here from Coventry seems even more startling when you consider that his excuse for leaving West Ham was that he was 'homesick' for his native Merseyside. Dean Saunders chews his gum with exaggerated confidence, smiling at the passionate, melodramatic hyperbole 'Die For You' which is emblazoned across the swaying red and yellow Galatasaray banners. And what does the high priest of British fashion, Barry Venison, make of it?

'It's forkun' mad, man, forkun' mad. They were throwing cans of beer and bottles at the bus when we came through. I've never seen anything like it,' he replies, with his resolute Geordie accent fraying badly at the edges.

Of course he is only half right. Dean Saunders coolly reflects on the unabated bedlam emanating from the stands with a more rational and apt analysis: 'It's the same all over the world, they're a bit more passionate, that's all, especially about this game. This game is all they worry about.'

Is it the equivalent of a Liverpool-Manchester United game?

'No, it's more bitter and twisted than that.'

Saunders isn't taking into account that this is the land where you can receive a long prison sentence, starve and sweat away the days in solitary confinement in a Turkish jail, probably the Bayrampasa, for merely burping in public. Alan Parker's shocking, jaundiced *Midnight Express* offers a view of an oppressive country which is not without substance. Especially when you consider that Turkey is currently under investigation by a European delegation for gross human rights violations against Kurdish activists and the police force recently curbed stone-throwing street riots in an impoverished district of Istanbul with restraints that left 15 dead.

The Turkish police authorities, groomed on extremism and political unrest, are a malevolent law unto themselves and are best avoided at all times as 217 Manchester United fans found to their cost on 3 November 1993, complaining of police brutality and wrongful arrest in the pages of *The Guardian* following their deportation. This does not justify the hysterical coverage Galatasaray received from the British sports press when they audaciously out-played United at Old Trafford and proceeded to knock them out of the European Cup in the return leg by preventing them scoring at the now infamous 'Welcome to Hell' Ali Sami Yen Stadium. It should be remembered that the police that night didn't stop with the club's fans, wading into both Eric Cantona and Bryan Robson in the players' tunnel after the match.

The xenophobic projection of Galatasaray fans as a vicious brand of Asiatic tribesmen craving English blood relies on hostile stereotypes that presents Istanbul as the footballing heart of darkness, distracting from that club's achievements. It seems their only crime is mastering the technique of making away teams feel as if they are playing against 12 men. And the miasmatic whirlpool at the stadium is little different from the welcome produced at Elland Road when United play there, or Upton Park when Paul Ince braved the East End abuse last season.

With deeply buried phobias bristling close to the surface, the inclination is to believe everything you've ever read about Turkish football, but this is a country madly in love with the game. It exists in the cafés, the taxis, the papers, in the blood. Bandanas, colourful ribbons, T-shirts, large whirling flags, moshing queues, the smell of spicy kebab stalls and scorching Mediterranean sun all add to the ritual pre-match carnival.

We're constantly mobbed wherever we go, our presence generating fresh waves of singing and clapping or requests for photographs. I try to converse with a bunch of teenage Fenerbahce fans queuing up with increasing impatience by asking them what they think of Dean Saunders. There's a pregnant pause before one of them leaps to the tape recorder and yells, 'I FUCK Saunders.' A common tongue found at last. And Venison? 'I FUCK Venison,' he laughs, receiving a round of applause. And Atkinson? 'No, I don't fuck Atkinson. I love Atkinson.'

Ten minutes later, the queue becomes a little too enthusiastic as they approach a police check-point. Their excitement is soon dampened by a police officer who launches into the crowd swinging his truncheon with ruthless abandon smashing legs with sweeping blows that make the stomach churn. Calm is restored, eyes mist over and painful, burning tears are fiercely fought back as legs are gently rubbed, but no one is arrested. The schoolyard logic of crime and punishment prevails. You're bad, you get whacked, you stop being bad. Simple, and viciously effective.

Back inside the stadium with still an hour to kick-off, Graeme Souness is sitting on his own in the dug-out. Looking like a disconsolate lost tourist, reflecting on life's cruel blows, he seems oblivious to the stadium's carnival. It's almost as if he's reliving the recent career that has seen him on the front and back pages of the press for all the wrong reasons in the last three years. A triple heart bypass, a public divorce and his acrimonious departure from Liverpool must have left him bruised and battered but there's a peaceful aura about him now. He agrees to an interview with friendly, accommodating politeness. I comment immediately on the incendiary atmosphere.

'Well, I've been involved in just a couple of games so far and the atmosphere is always incredible but this is maybe more special than other ones because, historically, they are such big rivals.'

Inevitably it puts the manager and his new players under intense pressure but Souness is phlegmatic about the hothouse scrutiny they will inevitably sustain: 'There's a lot of pressure in football today because the stakes are so high and there's a lot of money involved in football and with that is pressure. Everybody handles it differently.'

Why then did you choose to make your return to management with Galatasaray when you would have had the pick of clubs back home?

'I said that I didn't want to work again in England and I fancied . . .' he pauses, creasing his tanned face, '. . . well, that's not true, I thought I was finished with football. It would take a lot to bring me back as I was so disillusioned. But I thought maybe a job abroad, so I met these people and they gave me an interesting offer. Fortunately, I've always played and managed clubs that have been passionate and these supporters, as you can see, are passionate about their football. It excites me.'

So how far can you take Galatasaray, to the UEFA Cup final perhaps?

'We have a very hard game in the first round. It's meant to be a preliminary round, which means it's supposed to be easy. We've drawn Sparta Prague who are actually the champions in their league. UEFA, in their wisdom, have put them in the UEFA Cup.'

Why did you go back for Saunders given the problems he had during his tenure at Liverpool?

'He's a proven goalscorer, and I think he'll score goals in Turkey. He's already scored goals in the pre-season friendlies and I'm sure he'll score goals when the season starts. He is the right character, the right price and the right man to do the job.'

For someone who has been involved in football for so long and one as committed to winning as Souness, it must have been extremely difficult to walk away from home.

'Well, I went to Liverpool with great expectations,' he says staring at his feet. 'It wasn't happening for me, it wasn't happening as quickly as I wanted it and I was disappointed with certain things there. In the end I thought it was the best thing to do – and the best thing for the club for me to leave.'

Everyone seems to forget that you won the FA Cup with Liverpool.

'Well, I was there two and a half years, I won the Cup and I think it was generally accepted that the club had to have major work done to it. I think I was only halfway through doing that.'

There was a lot of speculation that you ruffled feathers at Anfield, changing too many practices too quickly, reversing successful methods. Would you agree?

'No. Not true. It's not true. If anything, I didn't change enough.'

Is that why you quit England?

'I just see this as an exciting challenge. Seeing the way football is out here, you could be here six weeks or six months. I'll see how it goes. I'm enjoying what I'm doing and as long as that continues I'll be here.'

How did you lure Venison out here when he'd just broken into the England squad?

'I think he was like I was and maybe Deano was too. When you come out here, you realise how big football is in this part of the world. We in England tend to think we are the best in everything, but unfortunately, that's not the case anymore, and I'm not just talking about football.'

So do you think England's on the sorry slope of economic and social decline?

'Well, we're getting into a whole different field now,' he replies awkwardly. A ball conveniently flies towards the bench, Souness instinctively leaps out of the dug-out and plays a meticulous ball straight to Marsh's feet. It's tempting to scream 'SOUNESSSSS!'. He runs back, a broad smile on his face, and winks, 'The old reactions are still there,' before dashing off.

Suddenly I'm reminded what many managers have said about nothing comparing to being out there on the pitch. In fact, we all want to be out there, deep in the centre of a beautiful game, in the unconditional ambitions of the fans who are investing in the dreams they still share and have craved all their lives. That couldn't be more true than here, in Istanbul, where the essential spirit of the game is everywhere – in the noise, the mayhem and the unrestrained naïvety and infectious passion of the fans. Graeme Souness could not have picked a better place to rediscover the same dreams that took him down to London to play for Tottenham at the tender age of 15.

Unfortunately, following an evenly balanced first half, Galatasaray lose 3–1 after their defensive frailties are cruelly exposed, and Saunders is reduced to a solitary shot. Beneath the stadium, after the game, the paparazzi are gathered outside the dressing-room doors. Police SWAT groups run up and down tight, claustrophobic hallways, where dour yellow lighting and dank, dripping pipes resemble a bunker scene at the end of the world.

Venison is having a hard time with the press, one of the local commentators remarking, 'He is so heavy and so slow.' The ex-Newcastle man is subsequently blamed for tonight's defeat, which is not fair but it's clearly taking Venison longer to adapt than the other British exports. Souness defends his team to the Turkish press with the standard line from the manager's phrase book, 'I will never criticise any of my players publicly but the goalkeeper will not be happy with the goals that we gave away and on another day he would have expected to save them'.

We arrive back at the hotel at the same time, and Saunders is fiddling in his purse to provide the doorman with a tip but cannot find enough small change. 'I'll sort you tomorrow, okay? I'll sort you tomorrow,' he tells him. Souness overhears the exchange and laughs, 'You'll never see that.' We walk through the swing doors together and he confides, 'I was disappointed tonight.'

I tell him that I thought the third goal looked a great strike from where I was standing, which was, granted, at the opposite end of the stadium. 'Oh no, the goalie was a fucking sack,' he replies succinctly before retiring for the evening.

The following night, a relaxed Dean Saunders sits in the hotel lobby. He has a thin, diminutive, Peter Pan-like physique and a mind that flies around numerous topics with vivaciousness. He is preoccupied with finding a house in Istanbul for his heavily pregnant wife and his family and spends ten minutes explaining the trials and tribulations of being a father and a soccer player. Subsequently, his conversation is split between the stop-start existence of professional football ('One minute, you're playing for one club, they choose to sell you and the next day you've got to move your family, find a house and report for training') and scoring goals ('I've scored in the last three games. I'm on a roll').

Like Souness, he has had a difficult couple of years, ending with a disappointing season at Aston Villa. He diplomatically answers questions about Ron Atkinson's sacking with, 'I wasn't too keen about the way things were going at Villa.'

He also started last season facing a heavily publicised High Court case over a tackle which put an unfortunate end to Paul Elliott's playing career. It was a case he finally won but which still left a taint on a previously unblemished and successful career that has seen him develop from a YTS apprenticeship with Swansea into one of the most expensive strikers in the land. All he is prepared to say on the topic is, 'If Elliott had won it would have been the end of football as we know it. Every footballer in the country would have, in the back of their mind, the fear of being liable for every tackle that they went in for.'

Saunders doesn't have a reputation for being a vicious player and it is difficult to reconcile the damaging accusations of being a vindictive professional who deliberately set out to hurt an opposing player with this man-child who faces me now.

Did you have any reservations signing for Souness again or coming to Turkey, Dean?

'No. During my time at Liverpool I never once criticised him. I was obviously disappointed about not being selected for games but I just got on with it. As for Turkey, I came out here last year for a holiday and really enjoyed it. I was concerned about my wife though, but Graeme said they have babies out here too, and it made me think, really. I also thought it might put an extra couple of years on my career, like it did for Chris Waddle, as the warm climate is good for the muscles. I've also always wanted to play abroad and I thought that this would be my last opportunity, really.'

Souness is nothing like I imagined him to be . . .

'He's a different man. At Liverpool they used to call him the Rottweiler. He's changed.'

Is there anything that keeps you awake at night?

'I don't think there's a footballer who doesn't think about what they will be doing at the end of their playing career.'

How about outside of football?

'Well, I'm reading Ian Botham's autobiography at the moment and he describes visiting the children's wards and seeing all these perfectly normal children suffering with leukaemia. I just hope that my children are always all right and healthy, really.'

On that note, he leaves for the confined opulence of a lavish hotel room that is currently doubling as a home for him and his family.

The following day, he is darting across Besiktas' back four at the Ali Sami Yen Stadium desperately trying to carve out an opportunity. However, another, different Galatasaray goalie has the sort of 45 minutes that careers seldom recover from. After two amazing howlers that leave Galatasaray two down after 20 minutes, the hapless keeper starts headbutting the post, drawing blood in the process. His mind has gone and Souness quickly pulls him off to spare any further embarrassment. He slopes off behind the goal and arrives at the bench crying his eyes out. Galatasaray finally lose 3–0.

On my last night, Graeme Souness invites me over for a drink and we spend the whole evening talking about women, players, big games that he's played in and life in general, as you do when you're away from home with a pint in your hand.

'I used to be the man who wanted that car, that woman, that life; there was always something I was after and now I'm perfectly content with what I've got,' he states.

And on his most memorable game: 'My last game for Liverpool, in the European Cup final, before I went to Italy.'

He proceeds, comically, to explain the painful defeat at the hands of Besiktas. 'There's really not a lot you can do when everything you've planned during the week dissolves in the first 20 minutes. There are very few players who can carry on regardless but my heart went out to the goalkeeper. I was tempted to leave him on until half-time, but we could have been 5–0 down by then,' he laughs. 'Did you see him head-butting the post? I've been in football all my life and I've seen things here in the last six weeks that I've never seen before. Whatever happens out here, it's an experience.'

I know the feeling.

Goal, October 1995

THE VOTE OF CONFIDENCE

Shaun Campbell

The transition from football manager to job seeker is often quick but seldom painless. Step one: the losing streak. Step two: the vote of confidence. Step three: the sack. Managers fall into two categories: those who have been given the bullet, and those who have pulled the pin. Many have qualified for both.

On stage or after dinner Malcolm Allison can make the whole thing sound funny: 'The owner of the club had never been in football before – he was a solicitor. It was really a personality clash. He had no personality.' And that's five months with Fisher Athletic summed up in a surefire laugh. But on the phone, the 'Fedora'd Favourite' paints a darker picture: 'You seldom get any warning. The chairman comes up to you, says they're going to sack you, and that's it.'

The warning signs (if there are any) take different forms. Most obvious is the losing streak. It doesn't even have to be a long run, it just depends on the circumstances. Terry Venables had coached Barcelona to a league championship and a European Cup final. But when they lost four of their first five matches in 1987 and Real Madrid had a 100 per cent record, Venables knew the game was up. The Nou Camp stadium was full of fans waving white handkerchiefs; when that happens, it means there's a job vacancy at Barcelona.

Managers often only realise they're due for the chop when they hear that someone else has been approached for their job. Venables walked out of his first managerial post at Crystal Palace in 1980 after learning that the board had been talking to Howard Kendall. In fact the Palace board talked to almost everybody: in the next four years the club hired and fired five managers.

Jim Smith recognises, in retrospect, that his Birmingham managerial career was bound to end in tears the moment Ron Saunders left Aston Villa. City were down in the dumps while Villa were heading for the European Cup. Smith was having a shave when he got the phone call telling him that the chairman wanted to see him at the ground at ten o'clock. His first reaction was to cut his throat but, with the touching optimism that characterises all football managers, he 'surmised that the meeting meant one of two things – the sack for me, or the chairman had become so disillusioned that he was quitting'. When Smith saw the chairman's Rolls-Royce parked outside the boardroom rather than the office he knew which way things were going to go: 'It was like a death in the family. I think I drank a bottle of brandy that day, but you wouldn't have known it. I was still as sober as a judge.'

Perhaps the most obvious warning sign of all is the name on the chairman's door. If you manage one club where it's Jesus Gil, and another where it's Doug Ellis, then you're just asking for trouble. 'Sacking a manager is as big an event in my life as drinking a glass of beer. I'd hire 20 managers a year if I wanted to – 100 if necessary' – that's how Atletico Madrid president Jesus Gil accounted for his dismissal of Ron Atkinson. BFR had been there just 96 days and the club were lying third at the time.

The manager's job at Halifax is another that should carry a Government health warning. Jim McGrath took the challenge on in 1991, becoming the club's 23rd manager since the war and the seventh in ten years. He said it wasn't the fact that his name was written on the door in chalk that made him feel uneasy; it was the sponge on the string handle. McGrath soon got the bullet and described the experience as being 'so bad that I received a letter from *Reader's Digest* saying I hadn't been included in their prize draw'. But then he knew what it would feel like – two years earlier he had left Preston exactly as he had arrived, 'fired with enthusiasm'.

The vote of confidence is often the clincher. 'Let's kill off the rumours that Ossie Ardiles's job is on the line,' said Newcastle chairman Sir John Hall to the press. 'If he leaves it will be of his own volition.' Three days later Ardiles got the boot.

Explaining this abrupt U-turn, Hall said: 'When I said that Ossie's job wasn't on the line I meant every word. But we ran some projections through the computer which confirmed that this club would not exist if we are relegated.' Yeah right, so it was actually a computer that got Ossie fired.

Tommy Docherty believed in getting his retaliation in first. Having resigned as QPR manager after just 29 days he joined Aston Villa, at that time rooted to the bottom of the Second Division. Where they stubbornly remained. Eventually the board decided to act. After a seven-hour meeting, throughout which Docherty was asked to wait outside, Ellis emerged with the news that the board had given him a vote of confidence which told the Doc all he needed to know: 'Thanks, chairman, I'll pack my bags and clear out now. A vote of confidence from you lot is the kiss of death.'

It's a funny story until you learn that he didn't pack his bags. But he might as well have done. The man that the Villa fans had christened Doctor Doolittle hung around for a week. Then he got the boot.

On this occasion Docherty was fired for the main reason managers lose their jobs – poor results. But other things can also do it. Docherty's career with Manchester United ended thanks to his affair with the physio's wife. George Graham took money he shouldn't have. And Big Mal introduced a topless model into the team bath at Crystal Palace. 'I thought it was just a joke thing,' says Allison of the day in 1976. 'A funny thing, like. The chairman didn't want to fire me but I think the FA said I had brought the game into disrepute and he had to do it. It was an unusual situation.'

Of the usual situation – not winning enough matches – Allison says simply: 'They never give you time to do your job. To build a good team takes at least three years and not many clubs will wait that long. They want immediate success.'

Don Howe would agree. After being sacked by QPR in 1991 he said of chairmen in general: 'Their definition of success is making money as quickly as possible. You talk to them about development, about how three-quarters of Arsenal's team have come up through the youth system, and they say: "Great, let's have a youth policy, and in the meantime could you win us the FA Cup?"'

If it's not poor results (or 'indiscretions') that bring down managers, it's often arguments with chairmen over players and, inevitably, money. 'Most directors put very little money into a club,' says Malcolm Allison. 'And the moment they're in financial difficulty the first thing they want to do is sell the players. They never think about firing themselves.' Allison went to court in a last-ditch bid to stop the transfer of players from Middlesbrough in 1984. He lost.

Mark Lawrenson was another victim, but there's a crushing inevitability to his story. Lawrenson was managing Oxford which then, like Derby, was controlled by Robert Maxwell. Money – and players – were going to Derby. Lawrenson threatened to quit over the sale of Dean Saunders but Cap'n Bob was quicker on the draw: 'No one resigns on the Maxwells. You're fired.' Lawrenson left football management for a saner life.

No one was ever as safe in the manager's chair as Brian Clough at Nottingham Forest. Even in 1992, as his long reign drew to its sad end, he could afford to quip on his way out of a meeting: 'I've just been upstairs to give my chairman a vote of confidence.' But Clough had had a taste of the boot – although typically he managed to come away from his 1974 sacking by Leeds in triumph, negotiating a £90,000 golden handshake.

Few managers get fired as comfortably as Clough. Allison says he only got compensation from one of the 'four or five clubs who fired me'. There are several disputes about manager's compensation terms currently in the courts, including Brian Horton's with Manchester City. But the managers are now getting organised, putting some semblance of security in their work.

'Whenever there's a dispute between the manager and the club it's generally because the contract hasn't been precise,' says John Camkin, secretary of the League Managers Association. 'Many of them simply aren't worth the paper they're written on. Every manager who changes clubs has got a mate who's a solicitor, who says, "I'll do it for you." But football is such a specialised business and a lot of contracts that have been drawn up have just been useless when it comes to a termination settlement.'

The Premier League now registers the contracts of its managers. 'The registrations will not be transferred to any other club until the first one has been adequately compensated,' says Camkin. 'And they don't get registration unless the termination clauses are set out very clearly in very simple words.' The Football League is resisting such a scheme although, as Camkin points out, it's the managers of these clubs who are invariably involved in disputes.

But what's it like, being fired? What really happens in the boardroom? Do they look each other in the eye? Are there blazing rows? Or is it just a few mumbled words and then the walk down to the training ground to say goodbye to the players?

'It was like opening a book I've read before. I knew the lines,' said Norman Hunter of his dismissal as coach of Bradford. John Toshack took it on the chin when Real Madrid canned him in 1990. 'I admit that I'm to blame for our performances this season,' he said. Adding, with just a hint of bitterness: 'Just as I was to blame for the 108 goals we scored last season.' When Coventry sacked him Jim Sillet said it felt like his house had just been bombed. Barry Fry felt rather differently after being sacked from Barnet for the seventh time by Stan Flashman: 'I'm absolutely gutted. The man is a complete and utter shit, a disgrace to the game.'

But as Fry proves, managers keep coming back for more. Ten years on from Docherty's walkout from QPR (after an argument with chairman Jim Gregory over players), he was back. It lasted a year. Gregory invited Docherty into his office and said things weren't going too well (QPR had missed promotion by four points) and that it was time they parted company. 'I don't think you should go, Mr Chairman,' said Docherty. 'I think you're doing a great job.'

Gregory laughed. Then he fired him. Then, after the players had pleaded on his behalf, he took him back. Then, early the following season, he fired him again.

Docherty had already been through the mill of a sacking at Manchester United, by all accounts one of the least funny things that can happen to a manager. Docherty had succeeded Frank O'Farrell, who had come to the job in 1972 inheriting the ageing remains of the great team of the 1960s. The club was in turmoil: one day Sir Matt Busby would insist that George Best must leave, the next he would bring him back over O'Farrell's head. Results were awful. On the day United were thrashed 5–0 by Crystal Palace the decision was made and Docherty was offered the United job during half-time in the Palace boardroom. Three days later O'Farrell was instructed to attend a board meeting.

'We are relieving you of your duties,' said chairman Louis Edwards. When O'Farrell asked why, he was told 'no reason'. United promised to honour the remaining years of his contract in full but O'Farrell, who had resisted being pushed to resign, had to go to court for the money. He even had to sign on at the Labour Exchange to show that he was looking for work. 'I had been working since I was 15. I never had to sign on in my life. That hurt,' he said.

O'Farrell's sacking came just two years after the messy affair with Wilf McGuinness. Promoted from coach to manager when Sir Matt Busby moved upstairs, McGuinness was given only a few months at the wheel. Two days after Christmas in his first season Sir Matt sent for him. According to one account he said: 'Wilf, things haven't been working out. The directors have asked me to take charge again.' According to another he said: 'Wilf, you've been at the club since you were a small boy. For over 18 years you've given this club your all and I don't know how we could get by without you. But we're going to give it a try.'

McGuinness started banging his head against the wall. He refused to quit and said they'd have to sack him. United wouldn't give him back his old job as Sir Matt's right-hand man. Finally he left. The shock caused his hair to fall out. He was only 33.

George Best recently asked him if he was still bitter about his sacking. 'Of course not,' he replied. 'A lot of time has passed since then. After all, it was 22 years, three months, two days, one hour and 24 minutes ago.'

FourFourTwo, November 1995

BOB PAISLEY

Stephen F. Kelly

He was a wily old fox. But always a loyal one. Shankly would tell some story to the press and have them falling about at his famous one-liners. Paisley, quiet in the background, would turn to a journalist and, with a big grin on his face, whisper: 'I told him that one this morning.'

But there was never any bitterness. They were like a double act. Shankly, the front man: inspirational, ebullient, charismatic, always coming out with a memorable quote; Paisley, merging into the background: more thoughtful, the tactician, ironing out all the problems before Shankly ever got to hear of them.

He arrived in Liverpool in May 1939 from Bishop Auckland as a 20-year-old and never left. But he had to wait seven long years before making his début for the club. In between he served in the army, fighting Rommel in the desert and then riding into Rome on top of a tank as part of the British liberating forces. And years later he returned to the Italian capital leading another army, this time to capture the European Cup.

He wasn't the greatest wing-half but he was tenacious with a never-say-die attitude that made him popular on the terraces. In his first season at Anfield he picked up a league championship medal but the nearest he came to any other honour was making an FA Cup semi-final against Everton in 1950. He shouldn't have played that day but he stepped in to take over from the injured Laurie Hughes and scored a vital goal. When it came to the final he was back in the reserves. But he took it stoically, the way he took life, never complaining, just glad to have played his part. The lesson served him well. Years later he understood what it meant to have to drop a player.

When Shankly retired he hadn't even considered Paisley a possible successor until someone on the board suggested it. 'Aye, I suppose so,' said Shanks. Paisley never wanted the job either. He was happy doing his bit in the bootroom. But when called upon he wasn't going to turn it down. At his first training session as the manager he called the players together and told them: 'I never wanted the job but I'm here, and that's it.' Weeks later Shankly was asking for his job back: Paisley would have given it up gladly but chairman John Smith was not going to turn the clock back.

At first they all compared him to Shankly but he was his own man. He didn't change things around much. He carried on the same way except that now he was free to put one or two of his own ideas into practice – even though the players could hardly understand his Geordie twang most of the time. But he was the supreme tactician, conning Bayern Munich by playing the unknown Howard Gayle; conning Spurs by making his players stand up when extra-time was called for at Wembley in the League Cup final; conning St Etienne by bringing on the match-winning David Fairclough late in the game; conning Celtic into selling him Kenny Dalglish. 'We'd better get out of Glasgow before they realise what they've done,' he said as he stepped into a car to take Dalglish back to Merseyside.

He could spot a good player when he saw one although he often left it to the scouts to make the decision. He never saw Ian Rush play before signing him but simply trusted in chief scout Geoff Twentyman's judgement. (After all, Twentyman and Paisley went back years.) But he did pursue the likes of Dalglish, Souness, Lawrenson, Hansen and Nicol, all world-class players, himself. Any manager who signs men like that has to be special.

He was like your favourite uncle, wandering around in his slippers and cardigan, secretly giving you a shilling to buy a few sweets 'but don't tell your Mam'. Like Shankly before him he continued to live a modest life, in the same semi-detached house, with the same friends, the same family car. Maybe it was because he and Shankly came from similar stock, mining communities where adversity bred backbone. As honest as they come. His only vice was a flutter on the horses and then it was a mere £1 each way.

'Loyalty', that's the word. 'We never drop players at Anfield, we just move things around a bit.' Shankly may have said it but Paisley dreamt it up. And yet he will always be underestimated, always in the shadow of the god Shankly. But he was a star in his own right. Three European Cups, six league championships, three League Cups and the UEFA Cup. His triumphs say it all.

FourFourTwo, April 1996

The Teams

4

THE AJAX WAY

David Lacey

Artur Jorge and his clip-on moustache belong to Central Casting. They are usually to be found half-hidden in an doorway just up from the marshall's office, waiting to shoot Wyatt Earp.

Jorge is the manager of Switzerland. This week, as he prepared, along with Terry Venables, to check out some of his country's Dutch opponents in the European Championship by watching Ajax play Borussia Dortmund in the Champions' Cup, he gave the usual foreigner's view that English teams should stick to what they know best.

England beat Switzerland 3–1 at Wembley last November. 'When they played fine old English football they played very well,' quoth Jorge, 'but when they tried to play the ball around European-style they were not very difficult to contain.'

It would appear, then, that in trying to attain the standards of technique and intelligent team play which Ajax produced in Dortmund, England are wasting their time. Much better, surely, to rely on those timeless virtues of speed, power, stamina and the will to win. The reality, of course, is that these qualities alone never won anything.

Venables would make a good Doc Holliday, even without the cough. His knowledge of dentistry may be sketchy but in a football argument few are quicker on the draw. It was, therefore, no surprise to find that during a long discourse on the Ajax performance Venables should have gone some way towards convincing listeners that in order to play like this it is not necessary to be born within kicking distance of a tulip field.

'It's amazing,' he said, 'Ajax are the best club side in the world and I don't know anyone playing the same way. That's unheard of, because everybody copies success.

'I think this [the Ajax way] is the way forward and we can do it,' he added. 'It's not just about experience. Ajax are putting 18-year-olds in there and playing the best football in the world. And it's not only about developing good habits in young Dutch footballers from seven upwards. Litmanen, George and Kanu [a Finn and two Nigerians] have only been there two years.'

Venables believes that anything is possible provided intelligent coaching finds an intelligent response. And since he won the Spanish title for Barcelona with Steve Archibald, his predecessor having failed with Diego Maradona, he can speak from experience.

Yet how many English teams, with the obvious exception of Liverpool over the years, conform to Venables's description of the way Ajax play? 'The same things appear all the time,' he said. 'It's like a recurring dream. When they win the ball they all go off to their positions. The back three keep the ball until everybody's ready, then they'll go. It looks slow but the ball is the pace.

'They draw you in, then they hit you. If you play two up against them you'll never win. They'll always be coming back at you. Their wingers do the job of full-backs. And they can only do all this because they're intelligent people.'

Should Venables manage this summer to convince Gareth Southgate he is another Danny Blind or persuade Dennis Wise he is, in reality, a dormant Edgar Davids, then the next Government should consider appointing the retiring England coach Secretary of State for Education.

There is, however, still far to go. In Monday's match against Manchester United, Newcastle produced an inspired cameo from the Colombian Faustino Apsrilla but the only domestic football of the week to approach, even remotely, the Ajax performance was played in the eight minutes it took the newly anglicised Liverpool side to score three against Villa.

Yet there is no need to despair. In Dortmund a Dutch colleague, asked why Ajax had lost 2–1 to Vitesse Arnhem at the weekend, replied that the winners had 'played like an English team'.

Perhaps Jorge had a point, after all. But Olde Englishe football belongs on Boot Hill.

The Guardian, 9 March 1996

MANCHESTER UNITED

Keith Dewhurst

When I watched Manchester United from the terraces at the end of the 1940s, ancient-seeming men in the crowd would describe the previous great United side, the one that between 1908 and 1911 won two championships and the FA Cup.

Later, when I was first married, I lived round the corner from Vince Hayes who played left-back in that team. He had untidy white hair, a brisk manner and a limp from the badly set fracture that ended his career and sent him to coach in Germany, and as we walked uphill with shopping bags he would talk about the team and its two superstars, centre-half Charlie Roberts and outside-right Billy Meredith. By then I was myself a travelling reporter with United, because our paper's man Alf Clarke had been killed at Munich. When the team was on the road during that time out of time, I spent many late nights with the acting manager Jimmy Murphy, who would ply me with whisky, sugar, hot water and a million anecdotes, not least those about him picking the brains of pre-1914 coaching gurus. One journalist colleague, old Ivan Sharpe, had played against Meredith's United. Another, Brian Glanville, wrote about Vittorio Pozzo. The manager when Italy won two World Cups in the 1930s, Pozzo had studied in Manchester and said that what inspired him was the memory of that attacking team in red.

Now I must seem ancient to teenagers myself, and I do rumble on about the 1948 Cup-winners, and how Jimmy Murphy coached them by walking the players through the moves in the pre-fabricated gym that stood between the railway and the bombed Old Trafford stand.

All of which is itself a bit of a rambling introduction to the notion that what seems to me to be the most interesting thing about United is the fact that their attacking style and their belief in ballplaying class have persisted for most of this century.

If you think this wildly partisan, let me say that I believe that Manchester City have shown the same long belief as well, and that it is something in the character of Manchester itself, its international importance before 1914 and its survival power since, that has created the urge towards beautiful football. That United have become a world legend while City remain hostages to fortune is due to luck and management. During United's pre-1939 crisis years there were men at the club with memories of the past and visions of the future. They began a youth policy in the late 1930s, and in 1945 were shrewd enough to engage Matt Busby.

I have met or worked with many famous people in my lifetime but Matt Busby was the most charismatic and remarkable. Even his charm, ruthlessness, political skills and genius for publicity, however, could not have sold a duff product. Torino lost their team in an air crash but it is their local rivals Juventus who are the legend, and the reason is the beautiful football. It is the beautiful football that must defy death, not a lot of percentage play and hard men at the back; because the most difficult thing, and the one that Busby always attempted, is not just to play beautifully. It is to play beautifully and win.

Alex Ferguson's achievement, and that of the board who backed him, is to have done this in the era of corporate decision-making and financial mega-pressure: they would not sell the replica kits, remember, if people in faraway places did not dream the dream. To realise that the shapes of the dream are marvellously the same, look at one tiny detail. There is a mannerism that all the good home-produced players share, which is that as soon as possible in the game they put their foot on the ball, but in a very particular way: shoulder dropped, head up and looking to settle themselves and establish a tempo. This was taught them by Brian Kidd and Nobby Stiles, who were taught by Jimmy Murphy, who had it from men of that Golden Age before the change of the offside law in 1925, and the worldwide spread of defensive football.

My ideal United squad I have chosen as a team and not necessarily as the 14 best individuals. It would play in a modern 4–4–2 formation with Duncan Edwards as a centre-back. Coming forward he would be a tidal wave. Law and the inspirational Tommy Taylor would be the nominal front two, playmaker Crerand and Robson the nominal midfield, Charlton the great fetcher and carrier. Opportunities for rotating the play would be enormous. Byrne, for example, would be the perfect overlapping full-back, and if people today saw Johnny Carey they would marvel at the classic serenity of his play. Keane and Cantona are on the bench for versatility. Others had more specific brilliance, perhaps, and Johnny Morris and Johnny Giles were geniuses; but they needed to be linchpins, which I suspect is partly why they were sold. Others died or, like 1960s full-back Bobby Noble, retired before maturity. Finally, if I was allowed only one player, and he had to save my life with a goal before morning, it would of course be Denis Law.

Southampton programme, 13 April 1996

COWDENBEATH

Robert Philip

*Prayer never seems to work for me on the golf course. I think
this has something to do with my being a terrible putter . . .*
Dr Billy Graham

At the depths of Cowdenbeath's suffering, Rev Ronald Ferguson gathered
the players around him before their latest ordeal, bowed his head and
sought divine intervention. Fivescore weeks had passed since the worst
team in Britain had won at home, the longest famine in the history of
world football. The result: Cowdenbeath 0, Montrose 1.

'Ah, but it takes time for these messages to get through,' explains Rev
Ferguson with a gentle smile. 'That was 23 March 1994. Ten days later – on
Easter Saturday – we cuffed Arbroath 1–0 and after 38 successive home
games without a win our prayers were answered.'

Though he presently serves the congregation of St Magnus Cathedral,
a 12th-century church of stunningly beautiful simplicity looming over the
picturesque alleys of Kirkwall on Orkney, the townspeople and footballers
of Cowdenbeath where he grew up under the grim silhouette of the Fife
coalmines are forever in Rev Ferguson's heart.

On Saturday afternoon, therefore, as her husband prepared the sermon
he delivered from the pulpit yesterday morning, Christine Ferguson plied
him with regular updates on Cowdenbeath's fortunes at the foot of League
Division Three via Ceefax (1–1 at East Stirling). There, in the
comfortingly cluttered office of his manse, an assortment of football
memorabilia is awarded space alongside the shelves of biblical tomes.

A knitted teddy, resplendent in the blue and white of Cowdenbeath, sits
atop Rev Ferguson's writing desk, and a faded sepia photograph of the

late, great 'Hooky' Leonard (of whom more later) is pinned to the back of the door; in another corner lies a stack of mail from some of those who have delighted in *Black Diamonds and the Blue Brazil*, the minister's affectionate and often poignant book about coal, Cowdenbeath and football which has become a publishing phenomenon.

'Dear Ron,' wrote Scotland manager Craig Brown, 'I thought when I read *Fever Pitch* by Nick Hornby that I had enjoyed the best book on football in recent times. However, having found myself engrossed in your book, I now know better . . .' Brown is not alone. And if you do not believe in miracles, then explain how a tract about the least supported club in the land (average attendance 250) has sold almost 2,500 copies.

In the foreword, Erik Cramb, Church of Scotland minister and official chaplain to the Tartan Army, notes: 'For years I have felt an enhanced status in the presence of Ron Ferguson. There are not many people in the world a Partick Thistle fan can safely patronise; thus a friend who is a Cowdenbeath supporter is a rare treasure. One night, when we sat discussing the future of the world as clergymen are prone to do, Ron got talking about his dream of writing a book about the Blue Brazil. Even if this sounded barmy beyond belief, I was drinking his whisky at the time, so it seemed reasonable to hear him out.'

Whether over a glass of whisky or a harbourside lunch of Orcadian haddock and chips, Ron Ferguson is worth hearing out whatever the subject . . . So does the existence of Cowdenbeath FC – or, indeed, Hamilton Accies and Hartlepool – prove God has a sense of humour or that He believes suffering is good for the soul? 'You do develop a theology of suffering, fatalism, endurance or whatever. But you also learn to appreciate the humour that goes with supporting clubs like Cowdenbeath. After a century of failure you don't expect anything else. Even the nick-name – the Blue Brazil – is absurd. Now, I don't think Rangers or Celtic supporters can laugh at themselves. Football to them is a serious matter.'

While the great battalions of Rangers and Celtic fans march to the beat of triumphalism, those who follow Cowdenbeath and their lowly ilk wallow in romanticism. If Robbie Burns had been a footballer he might have played for the Blue Brazil . . . with Laurel and Hardy at wing-half. 'There's something more humane about it, isn't there?' continues Rev Ferguson, who lived under the shadow of Ibrox Stadium while preaching in Glasgow for eight years. 'I actively encouraged my two sons to support Cowdenbeath rather than Rangers. I find the religious bigotry and arrogance associated with Rangers disgusting. Bigotry really angers me. To sing vile songs in the name of religion is appalling. It's anti-human. I feel very angry the Rangers management have put up with this kind of thing for years. The whole Rangers–Celtic, Protestant–Catholic thing is evil. It's racist and I hate it. It diminishes Scottish life. It stunts people and Rangers, in particular, have a very serious case to answer.

'When we lived near Ibrox I resented people assuming I approved of all that stuff just because I was a Church of Scotland minister. The Rangers–Celtic bigotry is actively dangerous to people's lives and neither club can hide inside its hospitality suites. What can be done? Well, Rangers chairman David Murray should take a stand against the garbage which masquerades as songs for a start. He should come out and say "this is no longer tolerable in a civilised society". It might cost them some supporters . . . but supporters they can well do without.'

To paraphrase Tony Blair, therefore, can you be a Christian and a Rangers or Celtic supporter? 'I seriously believe it's hard to be both. Obviously you can do it, but I think you're under an obligation to protest about the racism. I feel quite disquieted when I see people laugh it off for it can't be laughed off. To many, some of the big clubs have become a substitute for the Church. The "hymn" sheets are handed round and everyone has his or her own favourite chant or song.

'The connection may not be immediately obvious but it's interesting to compare the mood swings among huge crowds. A Palm Sunday-like atmosphere when the team's winning and anger when it's losing. So just as the multitude called for Barabbas to be released, a football crowd can turn into a lynch-mob against its own players. The cruelty is unbelievable.'

Blessedly, this is a tale of a good man's love of football, not his abhorrence of internecine hatred; and so we return to the empty terraces of Central Park where Ron Ferguson spent his childhood ('Just like I gradually become conscious of being in a pram, I became conscious of being *there*') while listening to his father's wondrous tales of James 'Hooky' Leonard, the George Best of the 1920s Cowdenbeath team.

'A legend,' remembered Rev Ferguson in his book, 'a genius . . . a folk hero . . . when will we see his likes again? Hooky scored 84 goals but his indiscipline was as bad as his ball skills were brilliant. He was suspended for missing training and demoted to the reserves for "failing to keep himself fit on Friday nights".' There are others like Hooky who 'swagger, strut or limp' through the pages of *Black Diamonds and the Blue Brazil*: centre-forward Peter Lamont, nicknamed 'Sumo' because of his uniquely 'athletic' physique, and Egyptian inside-right Tewfick Abdullah, who was accorded the ultimate honour when a local greyhound owner named a whippet after him.

'We've had a couple of great players, a few good ones and some fairly terrible ones,' confirms Rev Ferguson affectionately. Asked to present the trophy at last season's Player of the Year gala supper in Wee Jimmy's Bar, the padre found himself shaking hands with a player who had appeared in only a handful of first-team games. 'Because he played so seldom, he won by inflicting the least damage on the team. But the fans have always loved any player – good or bad – who wanted to play for Cowdenbeath. Of course, some were so bad no one else would have them.

'In the old days, the team were all the miners had for entertainment. On Saturday afternoons they went straight from the pithead to Central Park, their faces covered in coal dust. Crowds of 18,000 were not unusual. The mines are long gone now, of course, and so are the crowds.' As the packed supporters' buses leave Cowdenbeath for Rangers and Celtic every Saturday, so only a couple of hundred diehards remain, including Rev Ferguson when parish duties on Orkney permit. 'If the club didn't exist it would be like a bereavement to those who still showed up each week. You realise the total irrationality and sentimentality of the whole thing but it's life's blood stuff for all that.'

Before deciding on a career in the Church, the young Ron Ferguson saw duty as a trainee reporter on the *Cowdenbeath Advertiser and Kelty News* where the joy of covering his beloved Blue Brazil ('I even got to travel on the team bus . . . bliss') was tempered by the anguish of waiting at the top of the mineshaft – notebook and pencil in hand – after the latest pit disaster. 'I suppose that's why Cowdenbeath will always be home. So much of me is still there. I've no family in the area now but I knew so many heroic characters, larger-than-life miners. A harsh life. And a lot of them paid the price of that way of life . . .'

Though he chose the Church over journalism, Rev Ferguson, whose best-selling biography of George MacLeod (founder of the Iona Community) was shortlisted for the Scottish Writer of the Year award, has published several books, poems, regular newspaper and magazine articles and is now planning his second stage play. But it is through the magical pages of *Black Diamonds and the Blue Brazil* that he has achieved global celebrity. 'The day Cowdenbeath broke their hoodoo in '94 and finally won at home, the phone went at half past one on Easter Sunday morning. It was Hooky Leonard's son from California. A real American with a Scottish burr. He told me Hooky had run away to Gretna to get married, fathered 11 children, moved to the States and died at the age of 54. His son had read my book and been really touched by it. He'd obviously been drinking – and of course old Hooky himself was no stranger to the demon drink – but was deeply moved his father had been immortalised. It was a surreal incident, but then I suppose Cowdenbeath's entire history has had an air of the surreal about it.'

Surreal is the word. When Cowdenbeath won promotion to the old First Division – talk about miracles? – in 1970, Ron Ferguson was studying for a Masters degree at Duke University, North Carolina. 'It was bad enough I couldn't get to the games but how was I to find out the results? The Blue Brazil aren't exactly hot news in the *New York Times*. So, first game of the season I searched every paper in the library and, finally, there they were – the Blue Brazil . . . in the sports pages of the *Jerusalem Post*.'

Daily Telegraph, 22 April 1996

MANCHESTER CITY

Sue Wallace

I don't care who 'lacked pace' or who 'closed down their defence', or who laid it on for whom, and I rarely spot who's offside. I'm not a football tactician or factition – I'm a football romantic (and that doesn't mean I fancy the players). I go to every game expecting to be entertained, uplifted, thrilled (steady now!). I sit with my youngest son in the Family Stand at Maine Road – so close to the pitch that I can smell the grass, the sweat and the embrocation (and that's just the guy sitting next to me).

I used to be in the Kippax stand but, unlike the purists, I don't mourn its passing – for me it was a dark, gloomy place, where I peered between some gawky six-footers, like some sneaky Peeping Tom. But I loved the Kippax for its sense of solidarity, and I wept when, in the 'SWALES OUT' campaign, the stand's inhabitants sat down in silent protest – thousands of them. Awesome. The new stand is magnificent, but as oddly out of place in its surroundings as the FA Cup in a car-boot sale. It will take some years to restore the sense of camaraderie that glued the many and varied factions into one amorphous mass.

Meanwhile, from where I sit – forever hoping that City will win a corner, so we can give a verbal pat-on-the-back to the much-maligned Nicky Summerbee – I revel in the elegance of Keith Curle; the cool intelligence of Kit Symons; the determination of the recently revitalised Summerbee; the boyish enthusiasm of Flitcroft; the durability of the 'man for all positions', Ian Brightwell; and the emerging magic of Kinkladze.

Watching a game, I hate to see obvious set pieces (we're no good at them anyway) – although I look forward to the day when I see City take a well-rehearsed corner, and score. My favourite team is a mixture of the greats from the late 1960s and players of recent years – and, yes, I would pick Nicky Summerbee ahead of his dad. The period in between is less personal to me, having had to settle for second-hand information. I need to witness a player's breath in the floodlights to have him on my team. However, I'm not really keen on meeting players in person. I don't want to find out that they're normal-sized human beings (well, apart from Niall Quinn, that is). I want my heroes firmly where they should be – up on a pedestal. Our household is just recovering from one of the hardest years we've known – the 'Dad is City's fan on the Board' year. As Dave struggled against great odds to make the role a success, our home became the 'House of Horrors'. The phone never stopped ringing; Dave was never in; we lost touch with friends; the press and TV walked all over us (thank God for local radio, who were always considerate and charming, and Sky TV who at least offered remuneration); and worst of all, Dave was put in the miserable position of having to argue, on behalf of the fans, with one of his footballing heroes, Francis H. Lee. It's one thing to fight your corner with a guy who made his fortune selling 'tellies', kitchen furniture or scrap metal. But how do you handle an ex-England international, a soccer superstar, a hero you'd prefer to keep on a pedestal? But I digress . . .

Apart from our manager (and I'm reserving judgement on Mr Ball), we have no particular affiliation with the Saints. We do have a couple of friends who are Saints fans and we share a surname with Danny, Rod and Ray. Once, when Danny was living quite near us and playing for some other North West team, we had a phone call asking for Danny Wallace (our eldest son's name). It was some minutes before it dawned that this was some sad rag – but for a little while at least we had a taste of what it must be like on that proverbial pedestal.

We once made an out-of-season pilgrimage to The Dell, when we were staying in the area – other people have holiday snaps on sunny beaches, for us it's empty football stadiums. But my first proper visit was May 1993.

We'd planned to make a weekend of it (romantic, huh?), but himself had a mishap at work and was escorted home on the Friday afternoon, draped over a pair of crutches, his leg in half a mile of crepe bandage. The trip was off. Dave couldn't drive. And I had no licence. We cancelled the hotel and slumped into a cloud of gloom, until he had the bright idea of asking if there were any spaces left on the Supporters Club coach. There were. We were sorted. It was a glorious day; we had a smashing seat in the West Stand; City fans were on great form, and we won 1–0. Worth the effort, but not much chance to sample the sights, as it was straight back on the coach, to be home before closing time. My first trip on a supporters' coach, and probably my last.

Eventually, last season, we did make a weekend of it – but we stayed in London, because Dave was on the telly next morning. Maybe *this* time . . .?

Southampton programme, 30 December 1995

ASTON VILLA

Lord Howell

I was born into the family of Aston Villa. So were my wife and our four children. My father first took me the mile from home to Villa Park in 1933. My wife first went with her father in 1938. In the mid–1960s I took my three sons and daughter to their first games. Our eldest grandson (ten) attended his first Villa match (v Everton) last month. The other two will follow soon. They already wear the shirts.

My brother and I were allowed to go to reserve games without an escort. We would stand by the tunnel where the players came out and would hold out our autograph books, hoping for a player to take them back to be signed. We then had to wait after the match to collect them. I was there when referee Snape sent off 'Pongo' Waring, which caused the only crowd trouble I can recall before the war. And I was there for Frank Broome's memorable goal against Charlton Athletic in an FA Cup replay in 1938. He collected the ball in his own half, ran with tremendous speed in a huge half-circle to the Charlton penalty area and slotted it in at the far post, all along the ground past Sam Bartram.

I stood at the top of the Holte End for our record attendance of 76,588, an FA Cup tie against Derby in 1946. I was with two old school friends – we were by then in our early 20s – one of whom fainted early on. The men around us lifted him overhead and he was passed down to the front, where he soon recovered but remained. Derby went on to win the Cup in that first post-war season. Villa had themselves won the cup – the League North Cup – in 1944. In the second leg of the final, we beat a Blackpool side with six great stars, including Stanley Matthews from Stoke. A vivid memory – as is our Wembley final win over Manchester United in 1957. Peter McParland scored a wonderful goal from a great run and cross by Johnnie Dixon. Best of all was winning the European Cup in 1982. I was in Rotterdam to see a goal by Peter Withe and a superb, early substitution, when Nigel Spink came on for only his second game.

Although I joined the list of League referees in 1956, I was still able to see the Villa from time to time. And I always did some training with them. That was how I became a great friend of Joe Mercer, Villa's manager from 1958 to 1964. He would call me and say 'we're having a practice match tomorrow. You had better come down and get fit'. Or he would have me running with the 'Oldies' – all much younger than me – or with the young lads, including George Graham.

It was in that same period that I came to admire Ted Bates, whom I still meet for a chat when he travels with the Saints to Villa Park. Our association goes back to a famous cup night at The Dell in 1963, when I refereed the sixth-round replay against Notts Forest, in which the Saints came back from 3–0 down to draw 3–3. A George Kirby goal began the fight-back and Peter Grummitt, Forest's keeper, scored an own goal for the second. He was looking for Kirby and took his eye off the ball. It hit him and went in.

The Forest manager blamed me for not protecting Grummitt. I suspect the FA checked with George Reader, the World Cup referee, who was present. Anyhow, they stood by me, but had to replace me for the second replay because I was abroad on a parliamentary delegation. Jack Taylor refereed Saints' 5–0 win at White Hart Lane. A year later, Labour won the election and I became the first Minister for Sport, with responsibility for the Government's involvement in the 1966 World Cup. It was a real thrill to include Villa Park in the grounds where the matches would take place.

There have been lots of thrills. But, as one of my favourite poets says, 'your joys have to be measured against your sorrows'. And there have been plenty of sorrows. They began with our relegation from the First Division in 1937. But, under Jimmy Hogan, our manager brought over from Austria, we were back within a year, with the finest Villa team I can recall: Biddleston; Callaghan, Cummings; Massie, Allen, Iverson; Broome, Haycock, Shell, Starling and Houghton. They restored our pride and gave us enormous pleasure – despite the intervention of war. Seven of them played in the Cup-winning side of 1944.

Five of them are in my All-Time XI. They include Frank Broome of that famous goal and Bob Iverson who scored the quickest goal I've ever seen – in six seconds. George Cummings, the finest left-back, had a wonderful sliding tackle, even if he frightened the opposition. Alex Massie was a right-half in the classic Scottish tradition. Matt Busby told me he was the best wing-half he had ever played against. And Ronnie Starling, a great dribbler, could put his foot on the ball and slow down the game – a lost art today.

Southampton programme, 20 November 1995

HEREFORD AND BRAZIL

Frank Keating

The scorer of the World Cup's finest goal dropped in to town this week, by fluke on the very day that Hereford United were drawn in the FA Cup against the comparatively high-flying and haughty Hotspurs. There is a connection, too, a palpable link.

A quarter of a century on, Carlos Alberto, captain of Brazil and scorer of that voluptuous curtain-call goal at the end of the 1970 final against Italy in Mexico City, is in prosperous good shape, full of the joys, and in the trim. He passed through London to film for the hoorayingly inimitable BBC2 series *Fantasy Football League*, which comically clatters down the tunnel to begin its new series on 22 December. The great man stars with the programme's ubiquitous butt Jeff Astle, which is like asking Lester to kick home the winner in the Donkey Derby.

The vivid image of Carlos Alberto's eruptively emphatic score, which sealed Brazil's victory by 4–1, has ever since been lodged in the souls and spirits of those of a certain generation as the very best of the bunch, and the certainty of its place atop the pantheon was confirmed in the recent poll on BSkyB television which also pronounced it the World Cup's best of the best.

The once straight-backed defender with the puma's stride remembers the goal, of course he does. Clodoaldo's compelling dribble out of defence, Jairzinho's take and turn and caressing pass to Pele, mid-pitch inside-left and 25 yards from goal . . . but as the Italian defence bristled *en masse* behind its sandbags, Pele does not run at them but senses the express thundering through the station on his right and, like a meticulous carpet-bowler, serenely rolls the ball into its path.

Carlos Alberto, at full steam ahead, has no need minutely to alter stride or direction as his instep convulsively meets the ball and in a blink the missile is nestling in the netting behind the ambushed and astonished Italian goalkeeper.

Was it, for Carlos Alberto as well, the best ever? 'The best ever? There were so many. Well, I played 11 years with Pele at Santos. You cannot pick just one as the best among so many.'

He remembers the finest match of those epic finals being Brazil's narrow win over England, 'although a few days later, for the first half-hour against Romania, we were playing so beautifully we looked at each other with wide-open eyes, saying, "Wow! Isn't this great." After that, although we won 3–2, we played like shite, like manure.'

Which latter could be a reason Hereford United (with its dinky ground alongside the cattle market) muscle in on the conversation. But it isn't. The link is another poll, the best televised goal of the FA Cup. The winner fulminated from some fuzzy faraway footage on a glistening mud-slurp winter afternoon at rustic Edgar Street, two years and a million miles from Mexico's midsummer sun and colour and Carlos Alberto.

Hereford were in the Southern League in 1972 when Newcastle United swaggered down for the Cup. Their stripy strut stopped when, late on, Ronnie Radford's 40-yard screamer billowed the Newcastle net. Hereford presented Radford with a rose-bowl as thanks for the goal, and he still keeps it in pride of place in his Leeds home. He is 51 now, and a joiner.

'Apart from the rose-bowl, the warmest recollections are still all in my mind,' he says. 'In midfield, I pushed the ball through to Brian [Owen], and when he gave it back I thought "ooh aye". I always liked a sudden dig. No rhyme nor reason to it when your instinct sniffs a chance, is there? You don't think about it, nor look up to place it. Just head down and good contact. If it's on and you can see them white sticks, then have a go at getting it between them.

'Mind you, down the years quite a few screamed over the bar that I hit from far out just as well. Okay, almost as well. That day I just caught it perfect, it flew in – but it only became famous because the telly was there.'

And still they fly in, by the netful and from all round the world. Only yesterday the Australian Damian Mori, playing for Adelaide City against Sydney United, claimed he had equalled the record for the fastest goal – four seconds from kick-off, set by Jim Fryatt of Bradford Park Avenue 21 years ago.

Still they fly in . . . but none so savoured as Carlos Alberto's – nor, come to that, Ronnie Radford's.

The Guardian, 8 December 1995

BRIGHTON

John Duncan

They're mad. And they freely admit it. But as the official Brighton supporters' bus – 29 on board, six to pick up at Kempton – left the 7 a.m. Goldstone Road gloom for their match at York City five hours and 260 miles away, anger, depression and bitterness were only barely concealed by the boundless and groundless optimism that fuels every travelling supporter. For Brighton, however, this season may be the road to nowhere, a highway on which the club are currently breaking all speed limits.

More than anything, Brighton fans want to be sitting on coaches for ten hours next season as well, even to watch their side lose 3–1 away as they did at York on Saturday. They desperately desire the privilege of other days like the Burnley match where, their bus having broken down, they arrived at half-time to find Brighton already 3–0 down.

'Well, yes, we may be a bit mad,' said Peter Henry, 38. 'I suppose once you're into a thing it gets in your blood. A lot of people have strange habits – my brother collects Marc Bolan recordings, so you could say he is addicted as much as we are. But if Brighton ceased to exist I don't know what I'd do.'

That possibility is scarily close because, say supporters, of the wretched mess caused by the people who run the club, and their behind-closed-doors deals. The board may (or may not) have already sold their ground to developers. The board may (or may not) have found another site. The board may (or may not) have a plan to get the club out of the financial mire.

Now the FA is taking an interest after the club declared they were contemplating sharing with Portsmouth, 43 miles away. The FA has the power to kick Brighton out of the Football League if it does not get the answers it seeks, yet the information the club are giving the FA is 'confusing'. 'The problem is that nobody knows what the board are up to,' said Tim Carder, who, as well as occupying seat 5A on the coach, spent 15 years co-writing the club's unofficial history, *Seagulls!*. 'They are pursuing their own agenda in all of this but nobody knows what it is. What exactly are the board's motives? Are they in the best interests of the club? I think most Brighton supporters would say that at the moment we don't believe they are.'

Nothing the club have done has bathed them in glory in recent months. When Liam Brady, the manager who resigned in frustration this week, negotiated a free minibus for the youth team recently, it lay idle because the club would not put it on their insurance. Brady asked the supporters' club to find the money.

Although the local council seems willing for the first time in 50 years to help – it has commissioned a report, due next month, to identify a new site – the club are pursuing their own options in secret. It appears the Brighton board has not so much buried its head in the sand as stuck it in an oven and switched on the gas.

Sylvia Linney, seat 15D with the smokers and tearaways, has spent more money than she cares to remember following the Albion. At 74 she is only 20 years younger than the club itself, but with 69 years of dedication she finished 'work' – 'I help the old people' – on Friday, packed her sandwiches and set off.

Wouldn't she have preferred to stay at home? 'No. Never, never, never. But I'm very sad that somehow somebody has had the power to ruin a club like this. I would be shattered if the club went out of existence.'

If the board contained anyone with the dedication and gentle discipline of Liz Costa, 53, who organised the coach, the club might have faced up to the undoubted problems somewhat earlier. Mrs Costa counts the heads, sells the soft drinks, organises the sweep (Q1: Who will get the first corner today? Q2: Will a replacement ball be required?) and doles out soup from a well-worn flask at half-time.

She feels as dumped on as everyone else. 'It's outrageous and completely hypocritical to expect us to follow them week in week out and not give us anything in return. All we want is to know what's going on.'

She shares that desire with most of the 200 Brighton fans who had travelled to York, their gallows humour down to a fine art. When York's supporters started chanting for the removal of their own chairman, Brighton's faithful pitched in with a chorus of 'We hate our board more than you, more than you'. When you listen to what successive boards have done to the club, it isn't hard to understand why.

The Guardian, 27 November 1995

GLORY, GLORY, CANVEY ISLAND

Paul Hayward

Canvey Island were on their way to a 2–2 draw with Brighton yesterday and their dug-out was throbbing. Tony Mahoney, substituted, emerged still sweating to suck on a well-earned Silk Cut. Jeff King, the manager, issued an urgent tactical instruction to his aides. 'Get some of those people off the top of those toilets,' he said. 'It could be dangerous.'

As King gazed wistfully across the Park Lane ground, with its 3,500 tightly packed souls, he had cause to reflect on the vaunted romance of the FA Cup first round. Ignoring the taunts from Brighton supporters about the size of his waistband; King could dream of a trip to the Goldstone Ground for the replay a week tomorrow, while hoping that the Canvey Island 'khazis' did not collapse before his men arrived to clear the roof.

So goes it in ICIS League football, where the 'press room' is a raised platform of planks, reachable only by way of a creaky stepladder, the club shop shares the same dimensions as a telephone kiosk, and the physio has a habit of shouting 'quality!' when he is pleased with one of his players. The only bung you would hear of down here, in one of Britain's less glamorous seaside spots, is a tenner for the postman at Christmas.

'I have never known Canvey Island to be the attraction of as much media attention as this,' wrote King, a local nightclub owner with a good-time girth. The truth is he had probably never known Canvey Island to be the 'attraction' of *any* media attention. Certainly, Anne and Nick were unlikely to invite club officials on to the daytime television sofas after Canvey Island had won the Essex Senior League (football, not darts).

For Liam Brady, King's counterpart, this was a second plunge into the nether regions of non-League footy. Last year, Brighton went out at the same stage to Kingstonian. If Alan Harding, the Canvey No. 12, had beaten the Brighton goalkeeper with a fierce shot in the last five minutes then Brady might have been scanning the ICIS League for a new job. In an inversion of the natural order, the Seagulls are currently being dumped on regularly from a great height.

Brady, remember, has graced the finest footballing lawns of Italy with the likes of Juventus and Inter Milan. With the Goldstone Ground sold to property developers, his club are about to join the ranks of the South Coast homeless. If Brighton still has a pleasant seafront, the industrial skyline of Canvey Island puts you in mind of southern Silesia, yet prettiness and tradition count for nothing on a bumpy Essex field in November.

How they enjoyed their brush with proper football, this self-proclaimed 'Yellow Army' of postmen and brickies and bouncers (why are they never surgeons or teachers or gamekeepers?). The club were happy to welcome 'the Mayor of Castle Point and other distinguished guests' and were duly apologetic about squeezing Brighton into a visitors' dressing-room that measured 12ft by 12ft. Another 'khazi', to quote King again.

At the end of a week in which football has made even boxing seem about as seedy as an episode of *Postman Pat*, it was something of a relief to observe such snorting endeavour under a warm sun. We become so inured to the idea of football as a business, as a means of fighting over money, that it jars in the mind to see the game played for nothing more grand than boasting rights in the pub, or the chance to win some award at the club's annual dinner dance.

At places like Canvey Island, a less complicated and less mendacious spirit prevails. Before the game, Glenn Pennyfather, a Canvey midfielder and a former professional with Southend, Crystal Palace and Ipswich, was reflecting cheerfully on last week's 5–0 win over Tilbury. 'It really should have been 6–0,' Pennyfather said, but Steve 'Herman' Porter, who scored Canvey's first equaliser yesterday, had missed a penalty. His excuse, said Pennyfather, was that 'his hair was in his eyes'.

The usual caper of showing press passes was dispensed with in favour of an 'awright mate – in you go' approach. Almost all the baiting and hating came from the Brighton end, where the deckchair-striped shirts carried echoes of the *Titanic*. If the FA Cup first round is the great democracy then Brighton, not Canvey Island, is the rotten borough. There were times yesterday when you could hardly tell the teams apart.

Others had helped Canvey Island enjoy their day. In his pre-match notes, King declared: 'I would like to thank Concorde Rangers for not making us fulfil our Eastern Floodlit League fixture last Tuesday so that we could prepare for this, our biggest match ever to be staged at Park Lane.' A round of drinks for Concorde Rangers, whoever they are.

For Brighton, in contrast, facing possible extinction, a thick storm is rolling in off the Channel. Twelve years after the club reached an FA Cup final against Manchester United, they are letting in water second from bottom in Endsleigh League Division Two, and the Football Association are investigating a controversial change in the club's constitution that allowed the board to profit from the sale of their ground.

With a team who looked yesterday as if they would do no more than cope in an ICIS League, Brighton must have a claim to be the most wretched club in Britain. It was only 30 years ago that they were attracting crowds of 35,000 for FA Cup ties at the Goldstone. We will go on wondering how any group of company directors could have presided over such a dramatic collapse in the 12 years since Brighton's big day out at Wembley.

From Alan Brett, Canvey Island's second scorer, came this withering thought: 'I was really disappointed with Brighton. I thought they would be much better than us, but the supposed gap in class didn't show.'

'What do I think of Brighton?' said Jeff King. 'I think the beach is all right.' Then he probably went off to check the toilets.

Daily Telegraph, 13 November 1995

TORQUAY DIARY

John Ley

This morning Torquay United sit eight points adrift at the foot of the Endsleigh League. Twice this season they have conceded eight goals in a game, they have not won in the league since September, nor away from home since April. The drop into the GM Vauxhall Conference beckons.

In November, Eddie May became the club's 15th manager since 1980. The position has an average life expectancy of 13 months.

Last weekend he and his team made the arduous journey from Devon to Yorkshire to play Doncaster Rovers. No overnight stops, no hotels and not even a pre-match meal for the Football League's worst club.

Torquay may be short of points, but they have plenty of problems. They begin on Friday, when the players and staff arrive at Plainmoor for their eve-of-match preparations.

FRIDAY
9 a.m.: Paul Compton, ten years a servant of the club, arrives. He was manager three years ago and is now assistant to May. Compton looks perplexed. The West Country storms have rendered the pitch useless and he needs somewhere to train. 'God knows where,' he says. 'I'll find some-where where we'll have to scrape the dogshit off.'

Instead, he calls a local school who have an all-weather pitch. 'Guess what I want?' he asks the secretary at Audley Park School. The pitch is free, and the day is off and running. Or so they think.

9.30 a.m.: May arrives to be confronted with the news that Ashley Bayes, Torquay's only goalkeeper, has been violently ill. 'He'll be okay, boss,' assures Compton. 'He's like the fella in *Monty Python's Holy Grail* who wants to carry on fighting after he's lost both his legs.' Bayes does not possess such powers. He has glandular fever.

Despite the setback, Compton sustains his enthusiasm throughout the weekend. On his desk is a scrap of paper with the words: 'The harder I work, the luckier I become.'

9.40 a.m.: Compton takes 19 players to training, May visits chairman Mike Bateson, hoping to resurrect a deal to sign Chester goalkeeper Ray Newland.

Missing from the squad is Rodney Jack, a young striker from the West Indian island of St Vincent who is playing for his country in the Concacaf Gold Cup in America. Jack is from the same Lambada Club of Barbados which also produced Gregory Goodridge, whose summer sale to QPR could earn Torquay £350,000.

One player to catch the eye in training is Matt Carmichael, a trialist who has spent three days trying to impress May. On Thursday night, his club called to say they wanted him back. Though May has been promised Carmichael for a week he agrees to return him – to tomorrow's opponents, Doncaster.

10.45 a.m.: May arrives at the training session to announce the signing of Newland on a free transfer. The former Everton apprentice will become the 37th player to represent Torquay this season.

11 a.m.: Breaktime at the school, but only passing interest from the children. One youngster walks past with the words: 'You're shit, and you know you are.'

'People think we are crud,' says an older boy, 'but we're the strongest team in the league.' As he returns to school, he explains: 'We must be, we're holding up the rest of the league.'

Not for the first time, I witness the good humour of a town and its football club. From the teenaged fans to the chairman, there is a remarkable bonhomie and animosity against those doom and gloom merchants who want Torquay to struggle.

11.59 a.m.: Back at the club, secretary Dave Taylor completes Newland's registration with the League one minute before deadline. The chairman, meanwhile, is drawing up a list of the Conference teams whose grounds are good enough for League membership.

'I thought about bunging Stevenage £200,000,' says Bateson, a self-made millionaire with a self-made sense of humour to match. Stevenage's stadium is not up to standard, and if they were to win the Conference they would not be allowed into the League: Torquay would be safe.

Bateson, who collects exotic birds, rolls his own cigarettes and boasts a tattoo from his days as a Scots Guardsman, started a double-glazing business in his home and sold it for £6 million. He bought it back later for £2 million and sold it again for another profit. Now he is full-time at the club.

In the corner of his office is a 3ft ventriloquist's dummy, resplendent in club blazer and tie. 'That's Algernon,' he announces. 'He can be a foul-mouthed bastard at times. He comes in handy if I want to be abusive to other directors.'

12.30 p.m.: The players are back and the team talk takes on greater significance. They are made aware, by May, that, after half a season, things have to change. 'We've got to be more professional,' says the manager.

And Bateson, asked to sit in on the talk, adds: 'I will back the manager and there will be new players coming in, but you have to pull your socks up.'

SATURDAY
7 a.m.: A coach collects 46 fans for the trip to Yorkshire. A drink and a quiz game – the pitches are too wet for the usual pre-match game between the fans – are planned in Doncaster.

8 a.m.: Physiotherapist Damian Davey cannot travel; he has glandular fever too, so Compton must assume the role. The first player arrives at the ground. Jose-Luis Mateu Pinto is a Spanish university student who wants to learn English. In Spain he played for Castellon; after a lengthy injury, he is to play for Torquay for the first time. He arrives with a pillow under one arm and a rucksack on the other. 'Eet eez a long way,' he says, already protected against the rigours of regular marathon journeys.

Striker Richard Hancox is next to arrive, with a guitar. He strums 'Homeward Bound', but Bateson's vocal rendition is hardly Simon and Garfunkel.

Bateson is armed with wine, cheese – and slippers. Six other directors travel, while five players will meet up at Doncaster.

8.34 a.m.: The coach sets off on a five-hour, 300-mile trip, picking up player Tom Kelly at nearby Ashburton. Food for the journey is packed lunches comprising a Mars bar, banana, apple, pot of yoghurt, piece of cake and a sandwich. Midfielder Charlie Oatway produces a video of *Only Fools and Horses*. The players sleep; the directors have already started their first card school of euchre, a West County mix of bridge and whist.

1.30 p.m.: The bus arrives at Belle Vue, a dilapidated ground ravaged by fire during the summer. Newland is already in the dressing-room and is introduced to his team-mates by Paul Ramsey, the Torquay captain. 'I don't know any of them,' admits Newland. 'But when Torquay rang, I had to say yes. It's a job.'

2.15 p.m.: May, whose managerial experience ranges from Norway to Saudi Arabia and Kenya, delivers his pre-match talk. Outside, the Torquay fans arrive. One of them is Graham Tanner, who left home after the Torquay bus departed and will be home by the time they return to Devon. The only difference is that he lives in Helsinki, having flown from Finland to Manchester and finished the journey by cab to Yorkshire.

2.30 p.m.: Another fan, television presenter Helen Chamberlain, spots May and gives him a kiss. She left London at 11 a.m. after finishing a programme and will be on air again in the morning. Dressed in black leather trousers and Torquay shirt, she says: 'I've got a good feeling about this one.'

The Glasgow branch of the Torquay supporters' club is on the terraces, as is Trevor Wood, a fan for 18 years and chairman of the supporters' club for ten years. 'I've probably travelled 200,000 miles with them,' he says. 'Let's face it, before Plymouth and Exeter were relegated, our local derbies were Hereford, Walsall and Wycombe.'

3 p.m.: Referee Eddie Wolstenholme blows the whistle. 'Here we go again,' says May.

Torquay start well. Newland clears one attack with his head. 'Bloody hell, I've signed a centre-half,' says May.

Half-time arrives and the signs are good. Doncaster emerge first for the second half. I inform May that Carmichael has just been brought on. 'I thought he would,' he says.

All is well at the back, but in attack Torquay are shy. Mateu does his best, but looks confused when May barks the order: 'Get on his left peg.'

In the 71st minute, a Doncaster corner. The defence slips for the only time and, predictably, Carmichael scores.

The energy is sucked out of Torquay's players. The final whistle extends Torquay's run without a win to 15 games – two short of their all-time record.

May is in the dressing-room. He is angry. 'We talked about this yesterday. There are players here who are unprofessional. You can't expect the defence to keep you going all the time.

'I'll tell you this: I'll get it right. I'll do what I have to do. You've had your chance, and this is it. I'll bring in the personnel to get us out of it.'

No names are mentioned, but the strikers look concerned. Tempers are raised and May encourages the players to speak their minds. Alex Watson, younger brother of Everton captain Dave, and Oatway respond. 'We've got 20 to go,' says Oatway, 'then it'll be 15, then 10. Before we know it, we'll be out the League.'

'We've got to realise what's happening before it's too late,' says Ramsey. A moment for quiet reflection follows.

7 p.m.: The coach stops in Ashby-de-la-Zouch to order fish and chips. With 20 minutes to wait, some players go for a drink. Watson and Oatway have had more time to reflect.

'I've been a painter and decorator and a part-timer,' says Oatway, once of non-League Yeading. 'I had a good living, but I wanted to play full-time. I don't want to go back to training two nights a week and having to travel on a cold Tuesday night to Slough. I wish some of the others realised that.'

Watson, who played in a Charity Shield game for Liverpool at Wembley, adds: 'It's a different world from Liverpool, but I'm a footballer and I play at whatever level I can.' Indeed. Premiership players earn up to £20,000 a week. Torquay players average £450.

Back on the coach, May and Compton consider attacking options. They will return to Bury in an attempt to sign striker Phil Stant this week.

Meanwhile, the directors have forgotten the defeat, for now, and as we reach Devon start trying to lift the gloom by singing. 'Things Can Only Get Better' and 'The Only Way is Up' echo out.

11.40 p.m.: The coach arrives, more than 15 hours and 600 miles later, back to another storm. The vice-chairman goes back to the club office to drop off some equipment. While the fans, now back from their 17-hour jaunt, enjoy a glam-rock evening downstairs in the club's Boots and Laces pub, Mervyn Benney looks at Algernon and says: 'I'm sure I saw him smile just then.'

Daily Telegraph, 15 January 1996

The Games of
the Season

5

LIVERPOOL 4
NEWCASTLE UNITED 3

Michael Parkinson

I think Liverpool versus Newcastle was probably the most entertaining game I have seen. It was an occasion when football lived up to its description as a beautiful game, the Premier League enhanced their reputation and even the factory of hyperbole that is Sky Sports could not invent anything to exaggerate what we were witnessing.

Even as I watched the vivid movement of continuous attack and counter-attack, the small voice kept nagging that there would be some who didn't approve. Sure enough, we were told that this was the kind of game the crowd loved but managers hated. Even the two men who concocted such an intoxicating event were inclined to sober assessment, indicating there were more pragmatic ways of winning the championship.

They are undoubtedly right but no one who saw the game will need reminding of the difference between two teams seeking the glory of winning rather than sharing ethereal defeat. Such was their all-out commitment to victory that neither contemplated a draw as a satisfactory result. In the end, it might have been the fair conclusion but somehow it would not have been fitting. This was a dead heat demanding a winner and a loser and if that sounds Irish I can only say the players understood it perfectly. There was no crowing from the victors. They knew they had been taken to the very limits of their skill and stamina by opponents of equal talent and commitment. Similarly, the Newcastle players, while feeling thwarted by the result, realised they had been equal partners in a game of such spirit and quality, it even aroused admiration in the legions of the disenchanted, like myself, who had imagined the game long since lost to dimwits and dullards.

That Sir John Hall felt it necessary to defend Kevin Keegan is a depressing reminder that while things might be improving on the field of play, little changes on the terraces – or, indeed, in the press box. Those who seek to blame Keegan should Newcastle not win the championship fail to understand the significance of his achievements, not just at Newcastle but for English football as a whole. Those who argue it has been easy because Newcastle have a rich patron should remember that money doesn't necessarily bring entertainment. Arsenal and Blackburn are wealthy but it has been a long time since anyone has suggested that they were a joy to behold.

What Keegan has brought to football is a realisation the game must be entertaining. The fans and the community as a whole have responded and the result has been the clearest possible demonstration of the part a team can play in the life of a city and its rejuvenation. When Keegan says he won't change the way Newcastle play because that is how the game should be played, he is not only challenging those blockheads and numbskulls who have ruined our football in the past, he is also lighting the way ahead.

In the final analysis, the link between spectator and team is not about the amount of silverware in the trophy room. What is burned in the minds is the intimate and everlasting joy of watching great players demonstrate their skills. The problem with our national team is not that they don't win trophies but that they compete in such an unenterprising and unappealing style. The same can be said of our cricket team. It's not losing so much as the manner of doing so which is the worry.

If the Football Association merely wanted to put a smile on the face of the England team and their fans it could do no better than appoint Kevin Keegan as manager. I am not saying we would win the World Cup but we would certainly have fun losing it. In the unlikely event of Keegan taking over tomorrow, I wonder who he would pick up front: Ferdinand or Fowler? On the evidence of what we have seen this season, the Liverpool player is a class apart from the pack. I have to go back a long time to recall another with his instinct for scoring goals. We can only hope that Robbie Fowler finds a more sympathetic England manager than did Jimmy Greaves.

What Newcastle's defeat by Liverpool set up was the perfect season's end. The three best teams in the Premier League are neck and neck and that is how it should be. Newcastle's 12-point lead was always a false representation of the true facts. There is only a whisker of difference between the three and whoever wins will have the satisfaction of knowing they did so against opposition of the highest quality, which is how true champions should be judged.

In the meantime, anyone meeting Roy Evans and Kevin Keegan should buy them a large drink and thank them for contributing so significantly to the gaiety of the nation. It was a good job I was watching on television. Had I been at Liverpool, I might have hugged Graham Kelly or embraced Sir Bert Millichip. It was that good a game.

Daily Telegraph, 6 April 1996

JUNINHO'S DEBUT

Richard Williams

He'll be all right. In fact on Saturday's showing something will have gone badly wrong if, by the end of the season, Juninho has not been generally acclaimed the best player in the English league.

You could have filled a notebook with the things he did in his first Premiership game, almost all of them constructive and pleasing to the eye. At 5ft 5in and just over nine stone, all deft movements and speed of thought, this is a purist's footballer; yet he gave no impression of being a member of an endangered species. The bruises on Yeboah's lower legs this morning will show that Juninho fears nothing and, if he can play like this in his first match for three weeks, against a muscular Leeds United keen to make amends for their midweek humiliation in Europe, he can shine anywhere, any time.

Although he may look like a fourth-former, he is 22 years old and an established member of the world's best team. That experience showed in his composure throughout the match and in the way he dictated the rhythms and angles of Middlesbrough's play. His touch allowed Fjortoft to give the home side the lead after ten minutes and he provided enough openings to have made the game safe before Deane scored a fortunate equaliser on half-time.

It helps, perhaps, that Bryan Robson's Middlesbrough team consists primarily of young players with commendably well-proportioned egos. No one was out there trying to prove that his skills were the equal of those imported from São Paulo at a cost of £4.75 million. In fact Barmby was probably too self-effacing. When he learns to capitalise on the prompting of his new team-mate, which he can do simply by following the example of the admirable Fjortoft, he will be an even greater asset to his club and, by extension, his country.

Juninho started the game on the right side of midfield but it was only a few minutes before he drifted across to the left. Thereafter he roved back and forth, always ready to make the sudden sprint followed by the rapier thrust. It is this habit that will inevitably lead to comparisons with Osvaldo Ardiles, who did his most damaging work when moving past one defender, drawing others and sliding the ball through at a murderous angle to give his striker a better than even chance of beating the last man in a sweeper defence.

It took Juninho five minutes to put Barmby through with a pass measured between two defenders; then the Englishman's control betrayed him. Three minutes later Juninho was fouled for the first time in England. Inevitably the culprit was Carlton Palmer, that embodiment of the honest vices and questionable virtues of the domestic game, thereafter jeered by most of the 29,467 who set an attendance record for the Riverside Stadium.

After ten minutes the ground witnessed a moment that old men will still be recounting to their grandchildren halfway through the next century.

Pearson, the Boro captain, began the move with a pass that stranded the horrified Kelly and let Juninho glide past McAllister. The Brazilian's through-ball did not do all Fjortoft's work for him but it guided him goal-side of Jobson before he flipped the ball over the outrushing Lukic.

Six minutes later a sweet Juninho dink over the Leeds defence gave Fjortoft a simpler opportunity to beat Lukic but Barmby was adjudged offside. The Brazilian's menace was acknowledged by two fouls within a couple of minutes, a scythe from Pemberton and a trip by Palmer, earning two of the game's seven bookings. But then Yeboah, striving mightily, won the ball in the Middlesbrough half and sent Whelan down the right. A driven cross eluded all but Deane, who stabbed at the ball on the six-yard line and saw it bounce home between two lunging defenders.

Both sides lost coherence in the second period, although Juninho illuminated the half with a swerving dummy to Barmby and a stunning touchline turn that dismantled the already subdued McAllister. Having been cautioned for felling the massive Yeboah in an attempt to rectify his own mistake, he was substituted with ten minutes to go. He flies to Buenos Aires today to represent his country in a friendly against Argentina and will be back to play at least half of Sunday's exhibition game against Sampdoria at the Riverside, where on Saturday we saw enough to convince us that he lives up to every word of the billing. Don't miss him.

The Guardian, 6 November 1995

CANTONA'S RETURN

Ian Ridley

Here's the plot. We'll have him laying on a goal after 67 seconds, then rallying his team after they've been outplayed and equalising with a penalty, before scoring the winning goal in the last minute. No, you're right. We'll save the last-minute winner for another episode. Don't want to give them too much too soon.

Thus did the actor out on loan, as one of his heroes, Jim Morrison, once sang, return to centre stage after eight months of suspense and suspension. Curiously he seems, during that time, to have become an even better player, such is the stoking of the legend, but this was good enough. All the touches and flicks were there, if a little rusty. The eye for an opening remains that of a footballing eagle.

'He has done well,' Alex Ferguson, the Manchester United manager, said. 'He was tired at the end of it but he can be well pleased with his performance and his stamina. It's a credit to his preparation and how he looks after himself.'

Most were drained at the end of an emotionally exhausting day. It began hours before the kick-off, with Sir Matt Busby Way throbbing with buyers and sellers of inventive merchandise: red and white confetti, French tricolours. His autobiography was going for only £5 but this had less to do with lack of popularity or the end of the Net Book Agreement; more that everyone had it already.

On that famous forecourt underneath the Munich memorial some wore onions round their necks, berets on their heads. Here could be found his father, Albert, signing autographs, after a demanding two-day drive from Marseille, necessitated by his fear of flying.

Inside it was a love-in attended by 34,934, some of whom were not

244

journalists. Sadly few from Liverpool had obtained tickets. They played the music from *The Magnificent Seven* for him, 'Welcome Home' and 'I Want You Back' by, appropriately, Take That. He entered, last in line and tracked by his own TV camera, to the theme from *Rocky* and joined the other players in holding aloft a banner saying: 'Let's kick racism out of football. Respect all fans.' All except Matthew Simmons, Old Trafford was thinking.

Soon there was the cross for the goal but United then stood back in satisfaction for an hour, his cushioned passes and positional astuteness not used well enough, until the penalty, stroked home with the customary aplomb. Any worries about him taking it? 'Who was going to get it off of him?' Ferguson said.

There was never any danger of trouble involving him, with uncharacteristic best-behaviour tackling prevailing; it was the tamest North-west derby he could remember, said Ferguson. Even with Neil Ruddock in opposition, though one tangle had him throwing his arms up at him mockingly, even with a player on the field – in footballing terms the game's star – called Fowler, he was always in control. Chelsea in three weeks' time could be the first real test.

Before then, United have three goals to try and retrieve at York tomorrow night. Will he be risked? 'I'm saying to myself . . . I wonder,' Ferguson said. He may be pondering the words of a T-shirt on sale: 'Rage is temporary, class is permanent.'

The Independent, 2 October 1995

MANCHESTER UNITED 5 NOTTINGHAM FOREST 0

David Lacey

Manchester United are almost there. Newcastle's race is almost run. Far from going to a play-off, the Premiership may not even last the distance.

An initially nervous but ultimately commanding performance against Nottingham Forest at Old Trafford yesterday, rounded off by one of Eric Cantona's more regal gestures, has left Alex Ferguson's team sitting on their haunches just short of the winning post and gazing back down the straight.

Newcastle are still in view but Manchester United's 5–0 victory has left them six points in front and seven ahead on goal difference. Unless Kevin Keegan's players take at least four points from tonight's match at Leeds and Thursday's at Forest, the contest will struggle to stay alive on the final day.

Should Newcastle lose either, Manchester United's third Premiership title in four seasons will merely be a celebration delayed. In those circumstances Newcastle would have to win the other game by a margin comparable to that achieved at Old Trafford yesterday simply to give Manchester United something to do at Middlesbrough next Sunday while Tottenham are at St James' Park.

Yesterday Manchester United ultimately played like champions. They owed much to Giggs, Cantona and Beckham. Significantly they owed an equal amount to Scholes. It was United's biggest home win since their 9–0 thrashing of Ipswich 13 months earlier. In that match Andy Cole scored five times. Yesterday he watched on the bench as Scholes calmed Old Trafford's nerves with the first of two goals United scored in four minutes shortly before half-time, and then playing significant parts in another two without actually touching the ball.

In the Leeds game, after another series of misses, Cole had been taken off by Ferguson to ironic cheers from the stands. Yesterday the United manager explained that, once he had decided to use Scholes up front, it was a simple matter to leave Cole out, the first time he has been dropped. Not that £7 million strikers are ever easily discarded, but Cole will be wondering about his place for the FA Cup final against Liverpool on Saturday week.

For half an hour Forest's crowding of the midfield and stifling of space in the approaches to goal looked like frustrating Manchester United to the point of desperation. United's final passes were either predictable or awry. Giggs, having moved inside, with Sharpe wide on the left, was only a spasmodic threat. Hereabouts the only clear chance created by United saw Sharpe hurl himself full-length at Beckham's centre only to glance the ball wide when a straight header would surely have beaten Crossley. When Sharpe did meet a half-cleared corner with a well-struck shot low towards the inside of the right-hand post eight minutes before the interval, Crossley made an excellent one-handed save.

By now Ferguson's decision to reverse the roles of Giggs and Sharpe, moving the Welshman back to the left, was starting to have an effect. In the 41st minute it led to United taking the lead.

Lee, whose poor control as Forest's lone striker regularly set off United counter-attacks, gave the ball away and Keane immediately found Giggs in space. Haaland was outwitted on the byline by a drop of the shoulder and a wiggle of the hips and Scholes deflected Giggs's waist-high centre past Crossley with the natural scorer's aplomb.

Three minutes later Manchester United scored a second in extraordinary fashion. Beckham took an indirect free-kick near the left-hand byline and cracked the ball towards the net. Crossley, though he could have let the ball go by, instinctively punched it clear to Cantona, whose attempt at a volley from the right screwed back across the area for Beckham to head in. Between the free-kick and the goal the ball had not touched the ground.

The rest, for United, was a victory parade. Nine minutes into the second half Cantona threaded the ball out to Irwin, Scholes dummied over the low cross and Beckham drove in his second goal.

After 69 minutes Giggs gathered a return pass from Cantona, spotted Scholes haring through the middle and, in trying to find him with a through-ball, scored himself as the pace of the pass beat Crossley.

That would have been enough for Old Trafford but Cantona was not done. He collected a ball from Sharpe, ran at a retreating Forest defence and trapped a rebound from Chettle on his chest before hooking Manchester United's fifth goal past Crossley.

'I'm mentally prepared to wait until next Sunday,' said Ferguson, 'but if anything happens in between I'll be grateful.' He knows that a lot has got to happen now to deprive Manchester United of another championship.

The Guardian, 29 April 1996

FA CUP SEMI-FINAL

LIVERPOOL 3   ASTON VILLA 0

Martin Thorpe

It has been quite a week in quite a season for Robbie Fowler. Voted PFA Young Player of the Year last Sunday, awarded his first England cap on Wednesday, the Toxteth Terrier topped off the lot with two goals yesterday to confirm Liverpool's renaissance as a major power and propel them into a mouthwatering final against Manchester United.

Aston Villa did not deserve to lose by three goals. They dominated large chunks of an entertaining game but crucially lacked someone with Fowler's finishing power and perhaps a necessary element of luck. Taylor was denied a penalty for what looked like a first-half foul on him by Scales, and James prevented a second-half equaliser with an improbable reflex save.

Villa, behind after only 16 minutes, bounced back well and, led by the buzzing Draper, hustled and bustled the passing momentum out of the Liverpool midfield, especially after the interval, but just could not find the net.

Fowler struck again three minutes from time with a sumptuous volley, and McAteer added an unfair third in injury time.

There was no dishonour in Villa's defeat. Brian Little's achievement in turning last season's relegation contenders into Coca-Cola Cup winners, with its accompanying place in Europe, and possessors of a Premiership top-four place has been one of the wonders of the season.

But they could not suppress another wonder of the season. Fowler, with his old head on young shoulders – he will be 21 next week – took his goal total to 33, five now against Villa in three games and at least one in every round of the Cup. Geoff Hurst will recognise the increasing irresistibility of Fowler's late run into the England reckoning for Euro '96.

Despite both sides playing the continental sweeper system, it was the good old set piece which put Liverpool ahead. Townsend fouled McManaman on the left and Redknapp speared a cross into the Villa area. Fowler, stooping low, produced a diving header which rocketed the ball into the corner of Bosnich's goal. Again there was a touch of bad luck for Villa; Southgate had just come back on to the pitch after treatment to an injury and was slow in picking up the striker.

Five minutes later the England defender had to be substituted but Villa made light of the loss. They might have had a penalty when Taylor was sandwiched by McManaman and Scales, the latter stretching his leg across the midfielder's chest.

Then James made a brave block when Yorke, a yard out, got what had looked like a conclusive touch to Ehiogu's header. But then Villa's finishing let them down. Draper shot over, Milosevic shot wide, then was put through on James but allowed the keeper to shepherd him away.

After the interval Villa picked up the same script: Townsend, Draper and Taylor disrupting Liverpool's passing movements; Staunton fired over, then James made his wonder save, Milosevic's header finding Ehiogu a yard out but the keeper somehow managing to hold his shot.

If anything that was the turning point. Slowly, ominously, Liverpool came back into the game. Bosnich had to be quick to block Fowler's pounce on McGrath's underhit back-pass, the 36-year-old veteran redeemed himself with a great tackle to thwart Collymore, who seconds later skewed another inviting chance wide.

Barnes already had his fourth FA Cup final in his sights when his sublime strike from 30 yards was touched on to the woodwork by Bosnich before, finally, the second goal came. Staunton headed out Redknapp's free-kick but only to Fowler, who teed up a volley and rifled it past Bosnich off the far post.

McManaman's run down the left set up an easy close-range third for McAteer and that was it. The Villa fans rightly offered their defeated heroes a chorus of thunderous applause as they trooped off, while a familiar and colourful sight was in full display in the magnificent new stand. The flags swirled, the scarves stretched head-high, *You'll Never Walk Alone* rang out. Liverpool were back and in the FA Cup final.

The Guardian, 1 April 1996

FA CUP FINAL

MANCHESTER UNITED 1   LIVERPOOL 0

David Lacey

One inspired passing shot amid much repetitive baseline play settled an otherwise uninspiring game of doubles at Wembley on Saturday and spared everybody a tie-break. No wonder the Duchess of Kent, who does not wear thermals to watch this sort of thing at Wimbledon, gratefully stretched out a frozen hand to greet Eric Cantona as soon as he approached the Royal Box.

Cantona's second most famous kick in English football had just completed Manchester United's second Double in three seasons, adding the FA Cup to the Premiership title won six days earlier. The Double used to seem beyond the reach of the most accomplished teams, United among them, but now, like Everest, it is becoming a well-conquered peak.

United are the first club to achieve the feat twice but will surely not stop there. Since a Premiership plutocracy was created, the wealthiest club have won the two major domestic honours five times out of a possible eight and have been runners-up twice.

Not that it has all been about spending power; Andy Cole, an expensive error at £7 million, proved as much on Saturday. Success in football will always be about talented players soundly managed, and under Alex Ferguson United have won nine trophies in the 1990s, not counting two Charity Shields.

Wisely, in his latest moment of triumph, Ferguson managed to keep a sense of proportion. 'It is tempting to think that nothing could be better than today,' he said, 'but there's that challenge to do better in Europe next time. And it's going to be better, I'll tell you that right now.'

It needs to be. Unless United make a bigger impact in the Champions' League than they have done so far then the latest triumphs will be short-lived.

Another Double for United means that Liverpool will be competing in the next Cup-Winners' Cup as FA Cup runners-up. Theirs was a strangely withdrawn performance. Maybe the fact that they had been winding down in the Premiership while United were winning it played a part in conditioning the teams' approach; United were urgent throughout but Liverpool rarely shook off their languor.

The more the match was hyped as the final to end all finals the more disappointing the overall spectacle was likely to be. Riveting it was not. It was more like watching riveting.

Had James not pushed aside Beckham's goal-bound shot in the fifth minute the match might have opened up and Wembley would not have had to wait until five minutes from the finish for something significant to happen.

Yet the moment Ferguson announced that he wanted his players to have fun at Wembley, an afternoon devoid of this commodity was virtually guaranteed. Fun be damned. He wanted to win the Cup again and did so with a game plan designed to stifle Liverpool's passing in general and the influence of McManaman in particular.

Keane was crucial to the scheme of things, producing one of the best midfield performances ever seen at Wembley. His industry, covering, positioning and tackling ensured that McManaman's runs were largely diverted into culs-de-sac. Only McAteer, wide on the right, made regular progress. As a result, Collymore and Fowler were starved of service. Neither disturbed Schmeichel's afternoon and only Collymore forced the Dane to make a save.

Against Keane, Liverpool needed a greater physical presence in midfield than Barnes and Redknapp could provide. Yet Thomas only appeared once a goal had been conceded. Rush's farewell appearance was announced with 20 minutes remaining but the exhausted Barnes, not Collymore, should have gone off.

Cole had left seven minutes earlier. His poor first touch had seen half-chances for United slip away during their early period of domination and his eventual replacement by Scholes was inevitable. Cole hardly looks the man to strike fear into European defences next season.

The goal followed a sloppy sequence of events which typified the game; a missed tackle by McManaman, a misplaced pass by Butt and a sliced clearance from Babb that gave United a corner on the right. As Beckham prepared to take the kick Cantona was hovering near the penalty spot. Then, as the ball came over, he backed off in anticipation.

Previously James had caught everything, as well as keeping out an earlier far-post volley from Cantona. But now, in going for the corner, he was not quite all there. His punch lacked weight and simply dropped the ball to where Cantona was lurking in the arc.

Showing the same mastery of body control as when he gave his kung-fu demonstration at Crystal Palace, the Frenchman volleyed a shot through a thicket of players and into the net. A few minutes later he completed his rehabilitation in football by receiving the Cup and a Duchess's congratulations.

To the sub-species who spat on him as he was mounting the steps to the Royal Box Cantona offered nothing more than a withering look – which would have been a wiser response at Selhurst Park.

The Guardian, 13 May 1996

The Business
of Football

THE MAN WHO REALLY SIGNED JUNINHO

Cynthia Bateman

Ian Wilson speaks in the way Brazilians play football: he is fluent, articulate and quick. And his technique has become polished since it became known he is the man who first brought Juninho to the attention of Middlesbrough.

There had been a rumour that the man who wrote the letters to Bryan Robson and the chairman Steve Gibson promoting Juninho as the right player at the right price for the club was a Boro supporter living in Brazil. But now on the streets of Teesside Wilson has been dubbed Super Scout.

So how does a Darlington tax collector, whose closest association with Brazil was coffee and nuts, have the nerve and know-how to send Robson scurrying to São Paulo?

'I have been following Brazilian football since I was seven,' said the 49-year-old. 'There weren't many homes with television sets then but my grandparents had one and I watched Brazil play England. Even at that age I was struck by the different way of playing. They were so skilful. Much later I got a video of that game and I now realise how naïve they were then. They were just emerging as a footballing nation but even so the way they played fascinated me.

'Then in 1958 Pele emerged and, for a lad of my age to see him come along at 17, it inspired you. I followed Brazilian football thereafter – for the last 37 years.'

After decades of gleaning snippets of written information, the advent of satellite television put Brazil in Wilson's sitting-room and he has become an authority on Brazilian players and clubs. He refers to the Brazil national side as 'we' and 'us'.

He is a lifelong Boro supporter and used to be passed over the heads of the crowd down to the front like other boys at the old Ayresome Park ground. 'I followed them through all their trials and tribulations but nowadays the town is alive.'

When Bryan Robson took over, Wilson wrote to draw the club's attention to the quality on offer at reasonable prices in Brazil. 'It was the financial aspect more than anything. We have bought one of their best players for £4.5 million. How could you put someone like Romario on the same pedestal as, say, someone like Collymore? There is no comparison. Yet Liverpool paid £8.5 million for Collymore.'

Juninho was the top name on Wilson's list and Robson, already interested in Brazilians playing in Europe, remembered Wilson's advice as he watched the 22-year-old against England at Wembley last summer. Juninho, acknowledged as one of the most exciting players in the world, was everything Wilson promised.

Steve Gibson replied to Wilson, who is delighted the chairman still keeps his letter in his briefcase, and is not the least bit fazed that he has not had direct contact with Robson. 'Mr Robson has more to think about than meeting somebody who wrote him a letter. He is a busy man.'

There has been no invitation from the club for Wilson to meet the player and he does not seek one. He will not even see Juninho make his début. 'I'm committed to watching my son play in the Teesside League. But my heart will be with them.'

It is reward enough that Juninho has signed. 'I am overjoyed,' says Wilson. 'To get a Brazilian footballer on Teesside is like a god walking in on us. It has given us a new lease of life.'

But does he not feel an awesome sense of responsibility to see Juninho succeed? Not a bit of it. 'Juninho is fabulous. His vision is such he will do things the supporters have never dreamed of,' he said. He is not concerned about the 5ft 5in Juninho's physique: 'I just have a personal feeling referees might protect him.' Nor has he any misgivings about the climate: 'I saw a Bundesliga match in which Dunga was playing for Stuttgart and Jorginho for Bayern. It was five below but they still stood out.

'And I estimate he will be almost self-financing in a year's time. Boro sold 5,000 season tickets on the strength of his transfer and then there is merchandising.'

The rebirth of the Brazil national side is producing new crops of players at grass-roots level, he says, and by the 1998 World Cup 'we will see Brazil returning to the glory days of the past'. In the meantime he has a list of current young players well worth a look by any managers with two or three million pounds in petty cash. The one he would like to see join Juninho at Boro is Ze Elias, a brilliant young midfielder who captains Brazil Under-19s and is currently with Corinthians. One can almost see the letter now: 'Dear Mr Robson, may I draw your attention to . . .'

The Guardian, 4 November 1995

NICE LITTLE EARNER: ERIC HALL, AGENT

Derick Allsop

Barely a Route One ball from the FA's headquarters is the home and office of Eric Hall, football agent and as such apparently the Nemesis of the authority. We are just off the Edgware Road, in, would you believe, Star Street.

Hall works from a tiny basement room, his simple desk facing a television permanently tuned in to Teletext. Remote control in one hand, telephone in the other, cigar in mouth: the image he is happy to portray. So, too, is that of the fast-talking Mr Fixit: London Jew, loud clothes, urgent mannerisms. A small man, he delights in being called 'Monster' and adding 'ish' to a word for special effect. All part of the image, all part of the sell.

He has also been portrayed as a parasite and a cancer. Usually referred to as football's 'most controversial agent', he has been accused by an England striker of giving agents a bad name. Some of his clients, agitating for transfers, are said to have been afflicted by 'the Eric Hall hamstring'. He is quite partial to 'Mr Pickford – the removal agent'.

Whatever his image or his label, he has more than 30 players, including Dennis Wise of Chelsea, Tim Sherwood of Blackburn, Dean Holdsworth of Wimbledon, and Jamie Redknapp, Neil Ruddock and John Scales, all of Liverpool, on his books. And he is busy. 'I'm a one-man orchestra,' he says. 'My role in the game – it's an old cliché of mine now – is to make the poor players rich and the rich players richer. And give them the right advice, of course.'

Hall is relatively new to handling footballers, but then he is relatively new to football. 'I've been in this business only about seven years. Showbiz I've been in since I was 11 years old and I'm over 50 now. I've been around showbiz people all that time. I was a child actor, a bad child actor, monster bad, and at 15 I went into the music business. I was packing parcels, me and Reg Dwight, who became Elton John. We started together in the business and off it went from there.

'I switched to football by accident, in a strange way, really. It involved Terry Venables. I've known Terry since I was 16. He was a young kid at Chelsea. One of my bosses was very friendly with the Chelsea players and after training they used to come down to his offices in Tin Pan Alley, Denmark Street, which in those days was a bubbly street. Everybody was down there – Cliff Richard, loads of 'em.

'I was involved with Marc Bolan of T-Rex the last couple of years of his life. [*Name-droppers, try to beat that little lot in a few lines.*] I'd known him many years before that but I was actually working with him at the end of his life. After he was killed in a car crash I had to go to Granada TV studios in Manchester for a tribute show. I came back to London that night, still very depressed and down, and went to a club in Berkeley Square, met Terry, and he shot me off to a place in Epping, a country club, for some function. I didn't want to go but Terry persuaded me to.

'Anyway, I met this guy at the bar there, called Steve. I told him what I did, and he said, "How about being an agent in football?" I said, "Are you mad? I don't understand football." He said, "You don't have to to do what I'm talking about." Turned out I was talking to Steve Perryman. He was then captain of Tottenham. I don't believe in luck – you create your own luck – but Steve Perryman had known me two minutes and wants to know if I'll be his agent.

'I really wasn't that interested, so I gave him a tester. I gave him my number but didn't take his. If you want somebody you get him, don't you? So I thought if he's really keen – after all, we'd had a few beers – he'll call. He did call me and we met in the West End. There seemed to be more pluses than minuses and I became his agent. And that was it. All of a sudden I was a football agent.

'I've now got 30 to 40 players, a lot of big names from the Premier League but also people in the lower divisions. You get them because you never stop grafting. More come to me now than they did four or five years ago, yes, of course. I'm not being flash. I get phone calls. A player rings: "Can you get me a club?" But I still chase players. If I fancy someone, I will go out and chase them. I won't say I am the best agent – I *am* the best agent, but I ain't going to say that . . .'

But you just did.

'I know, it's the old showbiz trick – don't say it but still say it,' Hall returns, a triumphal grin spreading across his face. 'But I am the most famous agent, that's a fact.'

And the most controversial?

'Well, I don't think I am. People say I'm controversial. They say I'm flamboyant and controversial, but I can't see that. I wear bright jackets and normally I wear bright ties. This one's not too bright.'

How about the parasite, even a cancer?

'Tell you a story about that. I did the players' pool for Wimbledon when they played Liverpool in the FA Cup final, 1988, and Sam the Man [*Sam Hammam, Wimbledon's owner*] – to be fair, I love him, we're monster mates – he never really knew about agents then. This club from non-League is suddenly a First Division club – before the Premier, of course, this – and they were new to all this, and are now in the Cup final. At Wembley! Anyway, I represented John Fashanu and he asked me to look after the players' pool, on behalf of all the lads, you know, doing the business. Great for me, to look after the whole lot. It's a shame, really, for some poor agent who works all year on a player, suddenly it comes to the big Cup final day and he's blown out, that Eric Hall steps in.

'So, Sam says he doesn't want me doing the players' pool. He said he'd do it. I said, "Sam, you can't do it, you're the chairman, the owner, you can't work on behalf of the players." He says, "Baby, baby, I will do it, there won't be a conflict." I then explain to him he really can't do it, that there are other things he's got to do for himself and for the club.

'He was actually very frightened about it and he said in the papers he didn't want this Eric Hall, that he knew my reputation and didn't want me getting hold of the players, I was like a cancer and he didn't want it spreading through his club. But then three or four weeks later he apologised. He realised he shouldn't have said that. He realised I did a hell of a lot of hard work for the players.

'By the time the Cup final was over, as well as Fash I had Andy Thorn, Dave Beasant and Dennis Wise.'

Bobby Gould, then the Wimbledon manager, was dismayed by Hall's influence on Wise, who resorted to a campaign of mischievous pranks, including setting off fireworks from the team's hotel, in his attempts to be released by the club. That incident was referred to in a television programme about agents and featuring, in particular, one Eric Hall. Gould reached the conclusion that Hall should have stayed in music.

Hall replies: 'To be fair, it was the first time I heard that story. I phoned Dennis after the show and asked him what this fireworks business was about. He said, "I never told you, Monster" – he calls me Monster – "I just had a bit of fun at the hotel." But I swear to you, I never knew about that. I knew he was up to one or two little tricks, trying to get sent home and get Gould to say, "You can go, we don't want you at this club." But it never worked initially. It worked eventually because he got away to Chelsea.'

In the programme, another agent posed the question: Is Hall good for the game? Hall says: 'I think I am good for footballers and, yeah, I believe I am good for the game. It's relative. But I am certainly good for footballers, yeah. I can't really believe in the old saying, "Any publicity", but my concern is not what the public or journalists or even chairmen, up to a point, think about Eric Hall. It's the players. Eric Hall is good at his job, for the players.'

And how much do they pay for his services? 'I take 20 per cent commercially, and on transfers, or contract negotiations – put it that way, forget the word transfer – I will say, "If you get this, I want that." It's never near 20 per cent. That's a fact, hand on heart. Everybody thinks I'm monster rich. I make a living, I can afford to smoke cigars, big monster ones, and I can afford to go out and have a big night. I certainly can't see myself retiring on the money I'm earning for at least another 30 years.'

Agents, as we have heard, must now be licensed, yet as we speak, less than a month from the date the new regulations are to take effect, Hall insists he has had no official notification of the requirement. 'Nobody's told me and nobody's told other agents I've spoken to. Obviously we have to be informed personally. How do I know I've got to go to the FA if they don't tell me? I get a letter once a year telling me my TV licence has got to be renewed and I send in my money. I'm quite a high-profile agent. They do know I exist. There's probably hundreds of agents around, what I hear, but six or seven whose names they should know. I ain't being flash, but I'm definitely one of them.

'I've not been covered by any rules, I've not been under the jurisdiction of anybody. I've made my money but I pay taxes, I pay my VAT. If a club wants to work with me and they're not supposed to, they are breaking the rules, not me.

'Clubs come to me. They say they want to move a player but won't put him on the transfer list, so they come to me. If I want to get a player a new club I'll use the papers, I admit that. It's like selling records. If you want a new release plugged you go to the radio stations, don't you? I'm honest. Ask me a question and I answer. I don't mind saying I will use the media to let everyone know if my player is available.'

Another accusation levelled at Hall is that he does not necessarily get his players the right moves to enhance their football careers, that he is more interested in the fast buck. 'That's a load of rubbish,' he says, unequivocally. 'Give you a for instance. I have this kid, Nick Forster. He played for Gillingham, scored buckets of goals, sensational kid. He could have gone to Blackburn, he could have gone to West Ham. In my little knowledge of the game I felt, because I took advice from pros I know, that the best move for him, at that age, was not to go to a Premier club, where he might be in the reserves for a couple of years, but to Brentford. He went there and obviously got less money. So I can't be accused of that.

'Here's how it is with players moving, hand on heart. If a player's got a problem, I will say to him, "Go and discuss it with your manager or your chairman." If there is no solution I would say it is in the best interests of everybody that the player leaves the club. If you're at Safeways, supposed to be serving on the bacon counter but instead you're sitting around twiddling your thumbs, you're better off going and getting a job at Woolworths.

'I look after my players. Going back to that Cup final and Sam the Man. It was unbelievable. Wimbledon winning the Cup, beating Liverpool! Dennis Wise was probably getting about £300 a week then. I could understand. They got crowds of 3,000 or 4,000 for a League match. But the players had become stars overnight and at the press conference on the Saturday night, Sam says, "I know, baby, my players are not on big wages like the big clubs, but any of them can come and knock on my door and if they are not happy with their deal, I'll let 'em leave." My players asked me what they should do, so I got them to knock on his door. He did it himself.'

Hall makes no pretence at being a football aficionado. 'I enjoy football, I don't understand it,' he says. 'I know when somebody gets a penalty and when a goal's scored. But I'm terribly short-sighted. I'm vain, too, so I don't wear glasses. So far this season I've been to three matches – Brentford-Birmingham to see young Nicky, then QPR-Liverpool, and last Saturday Sam the Man invited me to Wimbledon-Blackburn. I said to somebody, "Who scored that?" He said, "Are you sure? It was Mark Atkins – you're his agent." I can't see, I can't see. Terry's wife bought me these opera glasses for my birthday!

'With players, if I don't like 'em I don't have 'em. I believe I'm the best and I don't have a contract with anybody. I don't need contracts . . .'

We are interrupted by a telephone call. Tim Sherwood is on the line, distraught because his girlfriend has called off their engagement after a magazine article alleged he had close encounters with Britt Ekland at Hall's birthday party. Hall assures the Blackburn captain he is on the case, demanding an apology: 'That's what we want, not money,' he stresses.

One distinguished client consoled, we turn to another: Dennis Wise. 'He's a star. We're very close, as I am with all my clients. He's got older and wiser, which happens. I've got to give credit to Glenn Hoddle. He gave Dennis the captaincy. Dennis loved it. He said, "I'm captain, Monster. Can't believe it. Made me captain." He's been a Chelsea supporter all his life. So I think that helped him. His ability to play had been great. I said before, I'll never interfere on the football side. I'd never say to a player."You should play on the left side, not the right" or, "You should be playing up front, not centre-half".

'Off the field is different. Like that video with Vinny Jones. I've been involved with people, ideas for me to do things for Dennis, and I've turned them down. I don't even let Dennis know about them. If somebody phones me and says, "You handle Vinny, I've got this hard man video about how you can break people's legs without the referee seeing", I'd say, "You are mad. On your bike." It wouldn't have gone any further.

'With Dennis, like this week, Christmas time, it's the old showbiz thing: if you're not working Christmas time, you should go become a bus driver. If you can't make a few bob at Christmas, when can you, like? Like today, we're doing a picture thing, Dennis the Menace, for the *Sunday People*, dress him up and everything. It might sound a silly thing to do but that's his image. He's doing a thing for *Today* newspaper, with his nieces and nephews, something for the *Sun* newspaper, and *Question of Sport* on Sunday.

'It's taken him ten years to become a star overnight. His football has got him there, but he's got a tremendous little cheeky face and, being from the showbiz world, I look for something as well as the football side. I check them out. They may have a great image, a great whatever, and be a schmuck and never get in the side, so you don't really want them. But I do look for that image situation. When I first got Dennis I knew then he was a star. I didn't know if he could play football or not but people I spoke to said he could. He's made it: Chelsea captain, playing for England . . .'

Just one thing, Eric, he's lost the Chelsea captaincy over the incident with a taxi driver which resulted in a court case.

'He'll probably have it back by the time this book comes out!'

The Game of Their Lives (Mainstream, 1995)

DOWN THE BOOKIE'S

Colin Cameron

It's 10 a.m. on Saturday on the International Desk at William Hill's Finsbury Park offices and it's the start of business. Over the next few hours, transactions will flood in to here from all over the world as William Hill's overseas clients, restricted by their own domestic laws, transfer funds by banker's draft to wager on Premiership action, much of which is shown live on television in their own countries.

Around 1,000 Germans and more than 4,000 Italians have accounts with William Hill. They bet, under English law, on Premiership and Endsleigh League action, as well as Coca-Cola and FA Cup games, and the domestic programmes in Germany, Italy and Spain.

There are also around 50 Far East-based clients who wager with Hill's. This exclusive half-century of high rollers generate a turnover that equates to the total European handle. (Little wonder, then, that Asia was the first region to come under suspicion when it was alleged that there was some 'fixing' going on in British football.) Asian clients usually enjoy a live televised game which kicks off at around 10 p.m. local time – on a recent February weekend, the north-east derby game between Middlesbrough and Newcastle, being screened that evening, prompted early calls from Malaysia from people anxious for team news: William Hill happily faxes details from the day's papers – it's good for business.

The weather in Germany this particular weekend is less helpful: four of the Bundesliga's games had already been postponed by the Friday. But a full Italian Sunday programme offers other opportunities. On the Saturday, Manchester United at home to Blackburn presents the many overseas followers of the Old Trafford club a partisan leg of a Premiership treble to supplement the Italian fare. The following day, QPR versus Liverpool, live on Sky, means a chance to wager 'win only', as does the Coca-Cola Cup semi-final first leg, Birmingham versus Leeds, being screened live on ITV.

By midday the phones are busy. The popular treble is Newcastle (away win), Aston Villa (away against Bolton) and Sheffield Wednesday (home to Wimbledon) with money for Liverpool on Sunday reflecting the club's popularity abroad – and the illegal Malaysian handicap odds. With coupons distributed to British betting shops early in the week, the odds available are relatively fixed (Newcastle evens, Villa 10–11 and Wednesday 10–11) but the 50 or so Eastern clients, one of whom wagers £10,000 to win around £50,000, often find their size of bet requires some negotiation with the William Hill price fine-tuners. The Sky game, in 24 hours, looks set to attract its usual six-figure sum from the region, although the Far East's involvement this time round seems unlikely to shift the market's prices.

Business builds up towards 3 p.m., kick-off time. The five telephone operators slip easily from Italian to German, then into slow, well enunciated English, to counter the quick-speak oriental chatter, complete with satellite delay, flooding down the line.

None of the five claim any great love of the game although Rosanna, a Swiss-born Italian, admits to an allegiance to AC Milan (as consistent short-priced winners, they are not popular with her employers). Tamara, a Croatian, remembers the World Cup in America, but more for the demands it made on the desk than for the excellence of some of the football. Alessandra, the chief settler, is under the greatest pressure. Even slow days are demanding as she must receive clearance from the boss for all bets above £250. She'd rather be skiing.

At the other end of the front desk, near screens relaying the best of British horse and greyhound racing, sits Eleonora, another Italian. Quiet, weather-affected football days have meant she's developed a passing interest in the dogs.

The customers can be difficult. As kick-off time approaches, tempers shorten. The Italians save their worst tantrums for Sunday wagers on the domestic Serie A. German punters usually (adhering to national stereotype) conclude business efficiently on Friday ready for the weekend: if not, they still remain Teutonically calm over the weekend. Eleonora's experience working in airport customer services training is useful in diffusing the most anxious Asian inquiry. You must, she confides, keep calm and 'not push the wrong button'.

Telephone technology means the origin of the incoming call flashes up on the screen so the operator can greet the inquirer in his native tongue – helpful in reassuring even the most frantic.

Familiar names – Newcastle United, Manchester United – crop up among continental vowels, with football jargon swapped easily for the betting vernacular of doubles, trebles, tax-paid and straight wins.

A bet from Italy for £400 requires approval from the day's floor manager, Mike Quigley. He nods a 'yes' if the company can shoulder the risk and waits for the required fax confirmation, which he in turn initials.

After 3 p.m. a few more calls. If they're chasing the day's prices, they are about to be disappointed. All bets are now off, Sunday is the same. Kick-off signals the end of business.

On Monday it is time to tally up and consider the continental divide. Quigley remarks that the popular Newcastle, Villa, Wednesday treble came up leaving Hill's around £50,000 short for starters. Faustino Asprilla's decisive intervention at the Riverside, helping his new colleagues to recover from a goal down, has taken its toll reinforcing Colombia's reputation in the betting world. 'It was,' says Quigley of Asprilla's (untimely) contribution, 'not too clever.'

Generally speaking it has not been a disastrous weekend. Liverpool were only a pretty short price for their 2–1 defeat of Queen's Park Rangers at Loftus Road. And the Far East was up over two days of frenetic betting. But for William Hill's international operation there will be better days. And there will be more good than bad: like every time Manchester United lose at a very short price at home, to start with.

Euro '96 is set to be comfortably the biggest football betting bonanza in bookmaking history. International football really gets the phones buzzing. The World Cups in Italy and America have been warm orders; Euro '96 will, by comparison, be absolutely white hot. As Euro '96 approaches the fax machines on international desks at William Hill's and elsewhere will be busy sending team news around the world. 'We are happy to do it,' says Quigley.

Quite a phone bill but it's well worth it to tap into the enormous overseas potential: for foreign football gamblers Britain is a betting haven. It's legal, there's plenty of action and, once creditworthiness has been assured, questions are never asked.

Since the 1960s betting has been above board in the UK. Off-course shops, the like of which Stan Bowles is said to have constantly struggled to pass, today number 9,000, down from a peak of 15,000 but still a hefty number.

Credit offices offer clients the chance to play a higher-stakes game. And with the home market taken care of, bookmakers looked further afield and found a lucrative secondary market overseas – the law in many foreign parts prohibits betting on sport: it is illegal throughout Italy, through most of the Far East, and in many German states whose nearest bookmakers work out of neighbouring Austria.

Looking back through history there's ample justification for this reluctance to allow betting. As recently as 1994, Penang banned four of their own players for taking bribes to ensure the club failed to reach the Malaysian Cup quarter-finals. A dozen goals conceded in two games did the job but it also aroused considerable suspicion.

Two years earlier in Germany, eight men were arrested amid allegations of match fixing and 30 referees were accused of accepting expensive gifts. And in Italy, persistent rumours surround the Mafia's involvement in illegal football betting (Ancona, Roma and Lazio were all embroiled in betting allegations, also in 1992). Compared with these, football in Britain smells of roses, current investigations notwithstanding.

But it is Asian illegal betting which has had the biggest impact on both the English game and English bookmakers. It is estimated that underground betting in the Far East on English football tops US $500 million a year with hustler-style names (like the infamous 'Short Man' in the recent allegations, and 'The Bankers' who command a bit more credibility on the Peninsula) dominating the whispers down mobile phones on street corners.

A William Hill client from Asia would be unlikely to wager a stake much below £500. With illegal handicap betting (where one team has from half-a-goal to a two-goal start) the centre of attention is on their domestic front. Asia-based players get the chance to hedge their losses abroad.

British bookmakers defer in acknowledging that they legally facilitate such a balancing act but it's not business that they're likely to turn down. After all they need to cover themselves for the next Newcastle United, Aston Villa, Sheffield Wednesday treble . . .

FourFourTwo, May 1996

RESCUING GILLINGHAM

Tom Watt

Second in the league and into the third round of the Cup. Enough to keep any Third Division club happy and they're happy at the Priestfield Stadium all right. It's been Christmas since August for Gillingham fans: the best defensive record in the country, a centre-forward who knows what it's like to score a hat-trick at Old Trafford and kick-offs delayed because the turnstiles can't cope with the crowds.

They're pinching themselves down in Kent. This time last year, down among the dead men, the Gills were losing games as fast as they were losing money. Unable to buy new players or even pay the ones they'd got, it seemed the only option was to knock it on the head. In January 1995, Gillingham FC called in the receivers. Relegation or financial ruin, either way the Gills' best chance looked like a decent burial.

But a world away from the cut-throat money-printing machine that is the Premiership, goodwill is a currency that, at the least, can buy you time. The results went Gillingham's way and the club hung on long enough for the cavalry to arrive in the unlikely person of a lifelong Millwall fan with time – and money – on his hands. What's happened at Priestfield since Paul Scally rode into town has a touch of *Boys' Own* adventure about it: good blokes, thrills and spills, and every chance of a happy ending.

The story of how Gillingham went to the wall in the first place, though, is a salutary tale. A lot's changed in football in the last 20 years, not least that clubs have become businesses, a transition that's made performance up in the boardroom as important for survival as how the team is doing out on the pitch. On both counts the Gills lost the plot completely in the mid-1980s and nearly paid the ultimate price.

In their 100-plus years, Gillingham have never been high achievers. Plodding along in the lower divisions with a gate receipt safety-net provided by the club's location – in an area of high population, 30 miles away from another League ground. Towards the end of the 1970s they were going nowhere but were reasonably comfortable under the unambitious, careful stewardship of chairman Dr Grossmark. The club was in credit and owned the freehold to Priestfield Stadium – not to mention 13 valuable club houses. While the team, by way of tradition, would lose more games than it won, the Gills seemed more than capable of keeping their heads above water indefinitely.

In fact the situation was considerably more fragile than it seemed. Some sleight of hand on a very successful lottery scheme led to financial deficits and criminal proceedings. Dr Grossmark – an honourable man by every account – found out and took it hard: he died a week later, on the way to Walsall for a game.

The succession of directors who took his place over the next five years presided over economic collapse. By 1988 all the club houses had been sold and Gillingham were £1.3 million in debt.

Like most Gills fans, Tony Smith had begun to worry about the club's future. A local man and lifelong supporter, Smith had money – if not experience – to commit to his team, thanks to the highly profitable sale of a chartered surveyors' partnership, and in September 1988 Smith decided to take the plunge. 'I was a regular season-ticket holder. My accountant phoned me up and told me the club had appointed Keith Burkinshaw as manager – we were bottom of the old Third Division at the time. I'd seen the accounts and I knew that football clubs were a very quick way to lose money, but we decided to get involved.'

The accountant went in as finance director to try and stop the rot behind the scenes while Smith himself made £150,000 available for players. That was soon swallowed up to pay interest on the club's debt as it became clear that the bank was getting ready to pull the plug on Gillingham.

By April the following year, Smith knew that a longer-term decision had to be made: 'I met with the local authority and with the bank. I'd been happy to fund the club as a fan, without becoming involved, but by now I could see that I either had to walk away and let the club die, or really go for it. My wife said I needed some stress in my life and – it was madness – I decided to go in as a director and draw up a five-year business plan to which I committed £1 million.'

Smith is the first to admit that he got it all wrong. In the five years that followed, £600,000 of his money disappeared on bank interest charges alone and with his wish to remain a behind-the-scenes benefactor, Smith's lack of day-to-day involvement meant that the club's affairs continued to drift downhill. 'If I'd started by paying off the whole debt it might have concentrated my mind. Instead all I was doing was drip-feeding the shortfall. I acted as a fan not as a director of a company. We controlled our cashflow but were always fighting the debt. And, of course, we needed success on the pitch.'

That success never arrived and the Gills found themselves propping up the bottom division. Come December 1994 the business was trading unlawfully. As one supporter put it: 'Tony had come in and given the club a blood transfusion. What it needed was a triple bypass.' Smith was left with little alternative and, early in the New Year, he put the club into receivership.

No one ever doubted Smith's intentions. Indeed, when he announced his decision to a packed public meeting, the response was a standing ovation from 600 supporters who recognised Smith as one of their own. Without that kind of goodwill, the events of the next 12 months wouldn't have been possible, practical or worth while.

After 20 years as a landlady looking after young Gillingham pros, Gwen Poynter had joined the club as a member of the office staff at Priestfield. She and her colleagues feared the worst when the receivers arrived expecting, no doubt, to be gunned down in a hail of P45s. Poynter, however, survived to tell the tale. 'The receivers had two full-time staff here and really came in and took over. The general manager was made redundant and so was the manager, Mike Flanagan. At first the receivers were very cautious about the staff here and took responsibility away from us. But as time went on it became easier. They cut back drastically on overheads like complimentary tickets which meant more money was coming in. We all had to take on a bit more responsibility but at least we had the basic things – like stationery! – which had been a problem before. We expected the receivers would be ogres but it didn't turn out like that at all.'

Short term, at least, the club began to pay its way and, under caretaker manager Neil Smillie, the team's results also began slowly picking up. But one well-publicised consortium, allegedly backed by the likes of Rod Stewart and *London's Burning* star Glenn Murphy, failed to materialise and Gillingham remained a struggling Third Division club, looking for a buyer.

Paul Scally, a Millwall fan for some 30 years, had had huge success with an office equipment business, among others, and – like Tony Smith – had sold up and moved on. Scally had lost a young son after a freak accident at his own offices, a tragedy that made him take a look at his life and priorities in a new light. As a result, a successful businessman became a full-time father and found out what a really demanding job was all about. But by the spring of 1995, perfect timing for Gillingham, Scally was starting to feel ready for something new to keep him up at night.

In March of last year, with his two boys in bed, Scally was half dozing in an armchair when he caught a piece about Gillingham on TV. Although he had plenty of money in the bank which he would gladly have put into the Lions, the New Den box-holder had never been asked to get involved with Millwall at boardroom level. He had, though, been close enough to the club and its relocation to have decided for himself how a football club could best be run. Scally decided that the Gills, two divisions down and 40 miles along the A2, were worth a second look.

'I phoned the receivers the next day, talked to them and then, the following Saturday, went down to meet Tony Smith in the morning and to watch a game that afternoon. Gillingham beat Exeter 3–0, as it happened, but that had no bearing on my decision. I sat on my own at the back of the stand and I remember being next to an old lady and her son – really nice people, I was really taken with them.

'After a lifetime of being with Millwall supporters, these people seemed just as enthusiastic about their club but without the hostility. I'd always loved Millwall's supporters' wit and sense of humour, and their passion, but it seemed to me that the atmosphere at the New Den had become more and more abusive. I didn't want to take my parents or my children there. Here I was at Gillingham and the club felt like the old Millwall – an old ground with a solid crowd despite where they were in the League.'

Scally went away and did his sums. The fact that attendances were holding up just below the division's 3,500 average, despite the club's problems, suggested that Gillingham had potential which, on the commercial front, wasn't being exploited. It was a viable proposition. Furthermore, those same people with whom Scally felt at home represented a challenge which made him sure he wanted to be involved.

'At one game I stood behind the goal at the Gillingham end, against Bury I think it was, and I remember getting into an argument with a group of supporters who started laughing when Gillingham went 1–0 down. It was as if they didn't believe their team was going to win. They accepted defeat. I suppose they'd got used to it but I couldn't get it into my head, this acceptance of mediocrity, this apathy. They were really nice people – you couldn't get angry with them about it – but I wanted to change all that, the acceptance of a lack of success. That apathy ran right through the club, you see: the offices, the coaching, the supporters and the team.'

Scally and Smith liked and trusted each other from the off. Left to their own devices, new money and a new administration would have been in place before the season was out. Instead, after Scally's first offer, on 15 April, crisis followed crisis. The bank, understandably, remained cautious. The League's bureaucracy, inevitably, proved inflexible. More surprisingly, the receivers dragged their feet over putting matters in hand – Scally suspects they'd enjoyed running the club and didn't really want to leave Priestfield come the summer.

As deadlines passed, the stakes – Gillingham's League future and bonds posted by Scally to ensure it – got higher. It took a gambler's last throw, a four-line letter to the receivers withdrawing from all negotiations, for Scally to bring matters to a head before the League cancelled Gillingham's membership or the bank foreclosed on the outstanding debt. With 87 per cent of the shares, Scally duly took control of the club on 1 July 1995.

Scally didn't take – didn't have – any time to congratulate himself. When he'd first set foot in the stadium he'd found a 'miserable' atmosphere behind the scenes ('everything was painted brown with bits of carpet on the floor, no bits the same, and the boardroom had old net curtains over a window that didn't even look out on to the ground') and he'd promised himself he'd start by giving the ground a facelift. Cupboards were emptied of a decade's accumulated debris. Out went the old furniture. Everything at Priestfield – with the help of a small army of Gills supporters – got a lick of paint.

The club's commercial activities got a similar going over. Scally makes no secret of the fact he went in with a big stick, intent on shaking people and their ambitions out of the 'comfort zones' that a decade of complacency had established. And he's the first to point out how positively people like Gwen Poynter, elevated to club secretary and asked to take on new responsibilities each day, have responded.

The new chairman had arrived at Priestfield more than confident of his own ability to run the business. But the most important decision was still to be taken: the appointment of a man to organise the football team, a star turn to head up Scally's supporting cast. And Tony Smith, of all people, was responsible for putting the new manager's name in the hat.

Tony Pulis had spent time as a player at Priestfield (most of it on the injured list!) and had stayed close friends with the Gills' former owner. His first job in management at Bournemouth had ended in tears – halving the club's £3.4 million debt had been achieved only by selling the club's most promising players as soon as the price was right, and when the Dean Court fans, understandably, grew restless, it was inevitable that the manager would be the sacrificial lamb. But by then Pulis had learnt his trade as both a coach and a boss and Tony Smith was quick to recommend him to his own successor.

Scally first met Pulis before he bought the club to ask his advice on the potential of the playing staff at Priestfield – Pulis had been brought in to assess the team for the receivers. The two found they had a lot in common, particularly their views about the relationship between chairman and manager. When Scally offered Pulis the Gillingham job it was on the basis that, as manager, he would have time to organise the side and lay foundations for the club's future.

When he'd assessed the team back in January, Pulis has said that few of the squad had much to offer Gillingham or anybody else. Come the summer his opinion hadn't changed, but his situation had. He had about a month to put a new team together in time for the first game of 1995–96.

'There were young players here who'd made 100 or 120 League appearances but had never really been taught how to play the game. The team had relied on them and they hadn't had the senior pros around to help them so it hadn't worked.

'I knew I had to break the team up. I've been lucky really. After I'd left Bournemouth I'd had the chance to watch a lot of games. When the list came through last summer with the names of players available on free transfers, I brought half a dozen of them here. The luck has been that they've gelled.'

Pulis points out that most of those 'frees' were established pros with a point to prove. He also went into non-League for two players hungry for a fresh start: Kevin Rattray and, bought with £5,000 raised by the Gills supporters club, Leo Fortune-West.

The one relatively hefty fee, £50,000, was spent on proven quality. Dennis Bailey had been Gerry Francis's first signing at QPR. But after a blistering start which included a hat-trick in a 4–1 win away at Manchester United, injury and a change of manager combined to deprive Bailey of significant first-team opportunities. Now aged 30, he sees Gillingham, and working with a manager he respects, as a great chance to relaunch his career. 'I came to the end of my contract at QPR and they offered me another year. At my age first-team football is vital so I'd made my mind up to move on. I came down to meet Tony after a pre-season game against Charlton. He was straight and very honest about the club and how he wanted me to be part of it.

'I knew about Tony from a friend. Derry Quigley, the youth development officer at Fulham, who said that he was a great coach and that I'd really enjoy playing for him. Despite the last four or five years' history here, that was enough for me to want to give it a go. I've signed for two years which is long enough to see Gillingham into the First Division!'

Bailey and Fortune-West, a classic 'little man–big man' combination, have been scoring goals for fun in front of the domestic game's meanest defence this season. Their goals saw off Second Division Wycombe in the first round of the FA Cup and have helped keep the Gills in the top three since August. Home gates have pushed up towards 8,000 making the club's plans for upgrading two sides of Priestfield Stadium a matter of some urgency.

Scally, though, isn't surprised how well the team has done and thinks he understands why the fans have responded so quickly: 'We've built a situation – Tony Pulis has built a side – where it's obvious that this isn't a club now that's going to lay down and get beaten easily. Most Gillingham supporters have never seen a side like that. Older people come up and say that this is already the best team they can ever recall playing here, after 30 or 40 years supporting the club. Well, I don't think we've even started. I know that, behind the scenes, my work's just beginning to happen. I'm just catching up with events.

'At first I was having to work out on Saturday morning what there was that needed doing that afternoon. Now I'm able to worry from Sunday onwards about the following week's game. We've got to turn a very old-fashioned football club into a modern-day business here.'

Of course Scally understands that aiming at the First Division and a stadium relocation need to be short-term goals if complacency and apathy aren't to make a return to Priestfield. But the new owner, already sure that he'll spend the rest of his working life at the club, has more than enough sense to take the longer-term view in looking to Gillingham's future. And that's an attitude which extends to the man in charge of things out on the park.

'How can you build something if you keep sacking the manager? If you appoint a manager you should give him at least five years and say: "Right, let's plan things from top to bottom." Crewe are a great example. I think, of sticking with a man, of saying, "Get on with the job of building something here". Dario Gradi's had the chance to build the club from the bottom up, often in spite of poor results and relegation. Fifteen years ago, Crewe were a joke. They're not a joke any more.'

After just six months with the new leaders, no one's now laughing at Gillingham's expense either. But the spectacular opening to the new season, a fresh start in every respect, comes with its own potential pitfalls. A little success, like a little knowledge, can be a dangerous thing. Around Priestfield apathy has been replaced with a weight of expectation. A year ago survival was the limit of most fans' and the club's ambitions. In the new year anything less than promotion will be a crushing disappointment.

Over the years the Gillingham crowd has been patient to a fault. Paul Scally and Tony Pulis, together with foot soldiers like Gwen Poynter, could be the team that brings the success that the long wait has been for.

FourFourTwo, February 1996

ARCHITECTURAL AWARDS

Pete Davies

Beyond the tall brick chimneys and the gasworks, beyond the car dealerships and the old industrial plant and the new B&Q, beneath leaden skies scattering snow over the trees on Kilner Bank, Huddersfield's Alfred McAlpine Stadium seems unreal. Arcs of white steel, swooping blue canopies, floodlight towers: it's more sculpture than structure. But why on earth here? Cologne, Verona, Montpellier, yes. But Huddersfield? Still, there's one thing very Yorkshire about it. They built this thing . . . and the fans went and christened it 'the Alf'.

When the Royal Institute of British Architects awarded the stadium their Building of the Year award for 1995 (and it was only three-quarters finished) the BBC local news show *Look North* asked club captain Lee Sinnott to comment. Now he smiles: 'You don't ask footballers to talk about architecture, do you? But still you've got hills all around, you look down and see it – it's like a spaceship, it's like it just landed here, it's magnificent. It's got to be a puller, hasn't it?'

A spaceship might find landing in Huddersfield a sight easier than it was to get this place built. After the Taylor Report some 60 clubs considered relocating. Only seven have managed it and only Huddersfield Town have managed it with such reckless panache – but no one will try and kid you it was fun. When they left dilapidated Leeds Road in spring 1994 (tears on the terraces as the curtain came down on a sun-drenched afternoon) they had nowhere to go.

That summer the club's backroom staff worked from a two-up, two-down terraced house. They got into the new stadium five days before the first home game that autumn with the place still being painted. It was officially handed over two hours before Saturday's kick-off.

In the away dressing-room, Wycombe's Martin O'Neill was climbing the walls – gremlins meant he was getting incessant piped music and, in August, the central heating on full blast. O'Neill thought Town were winding him up. But 100ft away in the other dressing-room, home manager Neil Warnock was climbing the walls for the same reason. The music was only shut off half an hour before kick-off by which time both managers were threatening to smash the speakers. Wycombe then won 1–0, as everyone in Huddersfield (including Warnock) expected. Mick Green, editor of Town fanzine *Hanging on the Telephone*, remembers the crowd that day gawping at the wild daring of their new home, barely watching the match . . . and he reckons the home players were all doing the same.

Looking back, club secretary Alan Sykes says: 'I don't think anyone understands what we achieved that first season – not building the place, but just learning to cope with it. From an administrative point of view, a quiet level of mediocrity would have been nice.' Instead, of course, Huddersfield won promotion to the First Division. Looking around him now Sykes says, with not unreasonable satisfaction: 'I don't think that's an accident either.'

The prime movers and shakers were John Harman, Graham Leslie and Paul Fletcher. Harman became leader of Kirklees Council ten years ago aged only 35 – 'I feel a lot older now'. Without him, says Sykes, the stadium would never have happened.

It was Harman who, against sometimes vociferous opposition, got the council to put up the initial £2 million of seedcorn capital. In cash terms it's not cost them a penny since. Two sell-out REM concerts last summer are reckoned to have put £3 million back into the local economy, jobs were created on the old site, and the stadium now hosts a steady stream of conferences and sports events. It looks like money well spent.

But for Harman it isn't, and never was, just a matter of money: 'We wanted to make a statement. Outside Yorkshire, people still think we're all cloth caps and ferrets and factory chimneys, so the design of it, and just the fact that we've done it, says more than you could ever put in print. I've had people say that this place, it's like going to Wembley every week anyway. But then,' he laughed, 'Wembley's a crap stadium, isn't it?'

Harman himself gives credit to the club's then chairman Graham Leslie: 'This happened because people like him were prepared to give up some of their jealously guarded independence. A football club board is a very closed world but they were prepared to take some difficult decisions, and ask not just what was good for them, but what was good for the town. It sounds corny, and it's so often untrue, but this was a real partnership.'

Given Harman's Labour majority for eight of the past ten years, I asked if the stadium stood as a 'New Labour' kind of project. He said: 'We talk about partnership, don't we? We're not afraid of the private sector, we're businesslike, we want to build things, in the widest sense. It's a reasonable example of that.' Then he smiled and said, with a mild curl of the lip, that because £1 million of the funding came from a government programme for urban regeneration, 'they've started to quote this as an example of what they call the Private Finance Initiative. It's nothing of the sort, of course. It's actually the commonsense initiative. But,' he added wryly, 'they've got a plaque up. Everyone who contributed has got due recognition.'

So far, the stadium has cost £18 million. The Football Trust put in £2.75 million and another £1 million came from the Foundation for Sport and the Arts, because – not standing on dignity – Town were willing to share the stadium with Huddersfield's then-bankrupt Rugby League club. A further £5.2 million came from the redevelopment of Leeds Road and nearly £4 million more was raised in sponsorship (hence the stadium being named after the company that built it). Commercial loans make up the rest. 'It's easy,' says Paul Fletcher with a shrug, 'to borrow money if there's a revenue stream.'

This statement, from the man who's now chief executive of the club, is deceptively casual. Stadium pundit Simon Inglis, author of *Football Grounds of Britain*, says: 'Behind every great stadium there's at least one absolutely indefatigable man, someone who's slaved to sell it. Anyone who hasn't sat in on the meetings with local politicians and football club people has no idea of the sheer persistence it takes.'

Now 44, Fletcher played with Bolton, Burnley and Blackpool over a 16-year period. After football he became marketing manager at Preston-based Miniprints; he wanted, he says, 'to learn about VAT returns and board meetings, all the things you don't learn when you're playing'. But he remembered what he'd learnt as a player too. How, as an apprentice, he'd swept paper rubbish under the wooden stands. And how Burnley plummeted from the First Division to the Fourth when they sold the team to build new stands.

When he got involved at Huddersfield the key thing was, he says, 'that it hadn't to cost the club a single penny. And so far it hasn't. So you share with the Rugby League and the town and suddenly the stadium's not a ball and chain any more. It's common sense. But I go up and down the country talking to stupid councillors and stupid club directors, and they've been doing business the same way for 90 years – they're not going to talk to each other, and you get this loggerhead situation. And football directors think too much about next Saturday's game – they can't see further ahead. We had it here, at board meeting after board meeting, where item number one on the agenda was always the Cowshed roof. It was leaking, it was a safety hazard, so do you spend £40,000 on the roof, or do you buy a player? They'd always buy the player because they'd want to win the next game – that's why our stadium fell into such disrepair.'

There's the old Gary Player quip that the harder you work, the luckier you get, but in one crucial respect, Huddersfield *were* lucky – with the land. There was, within a wind-assisted goal-kick of Leeds Road, an eyesore of a site crying out to be salvaged. The 51 acres on which the stadium now stands was a derelict site. Pollution from a coking plant and a chemical works (which during the First World War produced some gunk that apparently turned the workers yellow) had reduced Kilner Bank to a barren cliff. In recent years it had been replanted but it still took the best part of £1 million to clean up before building began. But better that and have the stadium stay in town where it belongs.

But why not just build a 'tin box' on the site? Fletcher gets impassioned (he has what Simon Inglis calls 'stadiumitis'): 'We weren't prepared to relegate Huddersfield Town to the Second and Third Divisions for eternity. If you build for 10,000 you are relegated for ever. There's no point getting in the Premier then, is there? And sooner or later we will.'

For Harman the building has psychological import; it's a talisman, a symbol for the town. But he knows that promotion would mean more column inches than any building award. Like Fletcher, he stresses that this wasn't design for design's sake. The McAlpine was designed for things to be won *in* it.

Of the first 33 league games played in the Alf the Terriers won 21 and lost only six. So Harman has the stats behind him when he says: 'We didn't want a Northampton or a Scunthorpe. If Huddersfield are way off the Premier just yet, we still wanted something which wouldn't limit their ambitions.'

For architect Derek Wilson of the Lobb Partnership the stadium was the best job he'd ever had. He says: 'I cried my eyes out after Hillsborough – people shouldn't have to die in a football ground – so for an architect who's a football fan, to build this is a dream come true. It'll sound like they're paying me to say this, but this club are so enthusiastic, they want the best they can get, and I find it amazing. In the building industry you have so many battles, but if there were more clients like these lot, you'd get a lot more decent buildings.'

It's hard to find a negative word about the Alf. Mick Green says when the plan was first mooted he was, like many, instinctively opposed, but even on that last, sad day at Leeds Road, there was the consolation of the new place taking exotic shape next door. Now, he says: 'I'm a total convert.' His editorial for issue 25 of the fanzine reads: 'An internationally acclaimed stadium. A Wembley promotion-winning team. A high-profile manager who likes to see his sides play football. A chairman who answers my letters. It's all too much. I need a lie-down.'

Green says he's heard of one man who refuses point blank to go in the new ground. But only one. And Sykes tells of another man who did go to the Alf, but then refused to sit down. The stewards would ask what to do with him: the board shrugged, and said to leave him. August turned into September and still this guy was lonesomely upright. Finally, in December, he sat down . . . and it was well worth seeing the look on his face when he did.

By then an average Leeds Road crowd of 6,000 had nearly doubled, to 11,000. This season it's up to 13,000. But like the movie said, if you build it they will come – and if you build it nice, they'll treat it nice too. There's no vandalism and no graffiti. And in 18 months there's been just one incident, a few morons from a visiting club having a go at some of the toilets. Fletcher admits that they do have a problem with the waste bins: the problem is that everybody's using them so they have to be emptied twice before the game's even started.

But he insists he's not blasé about the place: 'No one comes here to look at the stadium – not after the first time, anyway. They come to watch the team.' And there, of course, is the rub. Is that team any good? They've a Premier League facility (when the fourth stand's finished – they aim to start it this spring – the Alf will take 25,000) but can they compete in it with Manchester United? Or, more realistically, with Coventry and QPR?

The phrase 'sleeping giant' occurs here. A few others have woken up, so why not Huddersfield? It's a Blackburn-sized town and under Herbert Chapman in the 1920s it was, after all, the first club to win three championships in a row. Of the prospect of returning to the top, Sykes says: 'I think anyone with any degree of honesty would say we've a lot of work to do yet. But go back three years and look at where we were then, with the first sod not cut and the project in the balance, and if you'd said then that in three years' time we'd be in Division One averaging 13,000 in the Building of the Year people would have said you were talking a load of bollocks. So why should it be unrealistic now to say that some day soon we can find a way to compete at the top?'

Lee Sinnott, now 30 and an FA Cup finalist with Watford in 1984, says: 'They'd have to spend. I could probably talk myself out of a job here but we can all have a fairytale, we can all say we could go up and survive. Okay, wanting it bad enough can carry you so far but after that you need ability, and this club would have to come up with big money. And they'll know that.'

Brian Horton is the man who'll spend the money should it become available. Dumped by Manchester City, Horton came to Huddersfield after Neil Warnock left for Plymouth last June. Warnock, whose record in the lower divisions is one of the best around, took Town into the First with an all-action long-ball charge but probably felt he wasn't appreciated; certainly, there were fans vocally disgruntled that the ball spent more time in orbit than it ever did in the Alf. But he also had disputes over his unsigned contract, and personality clashes with the board. 'Neil,' says one observer more or less fondly, 'is one of the last great characters.'

Under Horton, Town are now mixing it up a bit. He says there's nothing wrong with a long ball if it's a good one: 'Glenn Hoddle used to hit 60-yarders for fun. But I do like footballers.' So, having recovered from the shock of having the stadium, fans are now watching agape because their team are starting to pass the ball around in it.

In pursuit of a return to the top flight, Horton has brought Lee Makel, a deft, inventive midfielder with bags of promise, from Blackburn's reserves for £300,000. When an all-star Endsleigh League side managed by Horton drew 1–1 with a Serie B XI at the Alf in November, Makel was widely thought the Man of the Match. Horton has also bought zippy wide man Steve Jenkins from Swansea for £275,000. The £2 million-rated England Under-21 and local boy Andy Booth is upfront. And then there's Kevin Gray, a £30,000 buy from Mansfield, of whom Horton says: 'I tell you, I couldn't buy a player like that for £250,000.'

Horton says that, in total, he's now spent £700,000. At the same time, he knows that in the Premiership that doesn't get you a carpark attendant: 'I'm a realist. Our target this year was just to stay in the First Division. But, of course, you look to the future, and everything's here to do that – if we went up we could get 20,000 in here and your finance starts to roll then, doesn't it? But money never, ever, guarantees you success. It helps, okay, and sometimes it hinders. Joe Royle said recently the more money you've got, the more mistakes you make . . .'

FourFourTwo, March 1996

McCANN OF THE CELTIC

Patrick Barclay

A chip on the shoulder is so much part of Celtic's tradition that you almost expect it to be incorporated in the club crest. 'Even when we were winning nine championships in a row,' the former captain and manager Billy McNeill once confessed, 'we went into Old Firm matches feeling like underdogs.'

They have, on the face of things, a rather more convincing claim to inferiority now that Rangers are after, and not too far short of, the record Celtic set in Jock Stein's time; five points ahead with as many matches to play, the Ibrox team seem certain to take their eighth consecutive Scottish title. But today, when football's most raucous rivalry occupies Hampden Park for a Scottish Cup semi-final Celtic must win to retain plausible hope of a trophy, we may be shown how the gap has been narrowed by Parkhead's odd couple.

Fergus McCann, chairman and managing director for the past two years, is a wee man who thinks big. Tommy Burns is a bespectacled manager of vision. Together – just about, for Burns nearly quit after the Cup triumph last season that put silver on the club's sideboard for the first time in six years – they have transformed the Parkhead atmosphere. You can see it in a stadium that has suddenly, even in the process of construction, become Britain's most impressive. And the only reason you did not hear it, if you were listening to *Radio 5 Live* last Monday night, is that the roar acclaiming a goal by the Portuguese débutant Jorge Cadete managed to smash the BBC's sound equipment.

This rounded off a 5–0 victory over Aberdeen that was Celtic's most emphatic in the league since October 1991. It contained not only all the stylishness, the elegance of construction reminiscent of Burns's own career in green and white, that has marked their progress but also a ruthlessness the significance of which can be judged by a glance at the table; while Celtic have been beaten just once (by Rangers, who also knocked them out of the League Cup), their ten draws explain why Gazza and company are still on top. But all the time there is diminishing justification for the old inferiority complex. The new Parkhead is a powerful statement.

McCann made it. When he ousted the three families whose narrow interpretation of *noblesse oblige* had brought Celtic to the verge of insolvency, he insisted the club was a business proposition; he would invest time and money (£10 million, about two thirds of a fortune made in North America through golf holidays and other enterprises), take a reasonable profit and retire after five years to his home in Bermuda. The fans do not wholly believe him. They think he is one of them. He certainly used to be. Before emigrating at 22 he held office in the supporters' club branch of a mining village.

His devotion was whenever possible cost-effective, as befitted a trainee accountant. Anxious to follow Celtic to a Cup-Winners' Cup match in Basle 33 years ago, when reporters seldom travelled, he asked *The Glasgow Herald* to engage him to cover it. After trying him out on Queen's Park v Dumbarton, they agreed. Armed with his new status as a commissioned writer, he secured an order from *The Scotsman* too. The combined fee of £20, augmented by expenses paid for a job interview that took him as far as London, made it a relatively inexpensive trip. Celtic won 5–1 into the bargain. A Special Correspondent began his *Herald* account: 'In a match that provided good entertainment for some 15,000 spectators . . .' The rest is history. McCann left Scotland and Hugh McIlvanney emerged from his shadow to become the country's outstanding contribution to sports journalism.

The impact of McCann's return on Celtic's football has been remarkable, and timely, because one-horse races were no more good for Rangers than the clubs left trailing. Celtic were especially frustrated also-rans. Boycotts testified to profound discontent with the boardroom régime. There was a massive problem in that Parkhead, with Britain's greatest acreage of terracing, had been declared obsolete by the Taylor Report. Yet McCann made light of it, harnessing the loyalty of the support.

The club was founded 108 years ago as a charitable institution for the benefit of Irish immigrants. Now their descendants dug deep as 10,000 fans raised £9.4 million by purchasing shares. Nowhere else, not even at Manchester United, has that happened. And no British club will have a home as grand as Parkhead when next season it accommodates 48,000, let alone if demand eventually permits its full projected sweep to envelop 60,000. Celtic, unlike United and Rangers, have avoided the expensive mistake of building too small.

It is Burns's task to keep pace, to field a team worthy of their surroundings, and at the end of last season the tension of his relationship with McCann went close to proving terminal. Celtic had finished fourth and Burns felt his efforts to reshape the side were suffering through interference. 'I'd come back from being player-manager of Kilmarnock,' he recalled last week, 'to a place where I dearly wanted to get things done as quickly as possible. Maybe Fergus, with the stadium and so many other things on his mind, wanted to do them a bit slower. But I felt my job was being taken out of my hands and was prepared to fight for it.'

Even as the Cup final approached, he dug in his heels and insisted that a player, Mike Galloway, should be sold for £200,000, half McCann's valuation. 'I told him we hadn't a hope in hell of getting £400,000. I told him to take my word for it. And after the Cup final I got what I wanted. In essence I got my job back. Fergus and I understand each other now. We let each other get on with it.' Not that McCann can resist the odd jibe. He keeps pointing out to Burns that his three most expensive signings (Phil O'Donnell, Pierre Van Hooijdonk, Andreas Thom) are not playing for their countries (Scotland, Holland, Germany). Burns might offer the riposte that his budget hardly caters for front-line stars such as Paul Gascoigne and Brian Laudrup who might be found on the other side of Glasgow. In general he has bought moderately and developed players, none to more startling effect than the left-back Tosh McKinlay, who had been around Scottish football for a decade without ever remotely suggesting that he could grace the national side as he has this season.

Burns's idea of helpful intervention is the divine. A devout Roman Catholic, he describes Christianity as 'without doubt the most important thing in my life, the source of my strength, my confidence and my hope'. And his success in the game? 'I think that every day. I can remember many times at Celtic when we won against all the odds. And afterwards, at Kilmarnock, when we brought them from the Second Division to the First in five months, then to the Premier in one season when, to be honest, our form never merited it. The team we were chasing, Dunfermline, lost about six games out of eight in the run-in – all at home. So many different things have gone my way and I like to believe that is coming from a higher power.'

Several Parkhead players shared this simple faith, he said, among them Paul McStay and Peter Grant. The latter's tackling has seldom brought to mind the bit about the meek inheriting the earth. 'That's part of the competitive side of the game. I'd never take that away from them.' He has undoubtedly added to the cerebral side by making Celtic more patient and appreciative of the need to vary their tempo. A visit to Ajax influenced him deeply: less a conversion than a confirmation. 'We have fallen so far behind in Scotland. Even our best players still tend just to perform without really thinking about why they've succeeded or failed. If we are ever to be able to hold our heads high in Europe consistently – I don't mean just the odd daft run – intelligence is the key. We can buy it to an extent, but part of my dream is that we should bring through our own young players, teach them for ten years, and for that we need a bigger training ground. Ajax are surrounded by a sea of football pitches.'

A recognition of inferiority may be essential if Celtic are to fulfil themselves in the European context that their stadium and support demand. Today, however, traditional aspirations hold sway and just 90 minutes as top dogs in Glasgow would be the answer to a prayer.

Sunday Telegraph, 7 April 1994

THE BOXING MAN

Chris Fewtrell

It was an early lesson for Hearn that in football, just as in boxing, hype and glory do not always go hand in hand. However, the Matchroom boss was far from downhearted by what he had seen at Brisbane Road that evening. Just as important as the 2–3 scoreline was another statistic – a gate of 10,830, by far the largest attendance of the season. For Hearn's pre-match optimism was not born of the blind faith of the fanatical supporter, but the shrewd judgement of the most successful sports promoter Britain has produced.

It is his unique skills as businessman-cum-salesman-cum-showman which fans hope will spark a long overdue upturn in the club's fortunes. Prior to Hearn's arrival, Leyton Orient had probably reached their lowest ebb. As if poor performances on the pitch were not bad enough, the club was left reeling by events thousands of miles away in Rwanda. The civil war crippled chairman Tony Wood's coffee bean business and fans suffered the ignominy of seeing the club put on the market for the princely sum of five pounds. The butt of every Cockney comedian's jibes, it was Hearn who eventually moved to spare the supporters' blushes.

Though Matchroom's rescue package ran to considerably more than the reputed fiver, Hearn insists his company's investment did not reflect any long-term strategy to diversify into football. 'I wasn't particularly looking to move into football,' he admits. 'I think Leyton Orient are probably the only club I'd have gone for, because when I was a kid I used to do what 25,000 other people did and bang down the ground of a Saturday afternoon.'

That said, Hearn's return to his roots is not simply a sentimental journey – he is not the sort of man to become misty-eyed where money is concerned. 'Obviously, as a sports promoter, the move made sense.

Football's a popular sport and the takeover represented a good opportunity for us to expand.'

Moreover, the Romford-based millionare has made it abundantly clear that Leyton Orient will not be a rich man's plaything and, as part of the Matchroom portfolio, must be made to earn its keep. However, he has a few concerns on this score, as he attributes many of the club's recent problems to misjudgements by the previous régime rather than intrinsic factors. 'When we arrived, the club couldn't pay the milk bill! It was in debt to the PFA and was barred from making any signings. To be frank, it was run by a lot of nice people who didn't really know how to run a business. But rest assured, if there's one thing me and my team are very good at, it's running a business.'

Yet, for all Matchroom's undoubted acumen, they arrived too late to prevent Orient's slide into Division Three at the end of last season. Again, though disappointed, Hearn was not overly concerned by relegation. 'Really, our first aim was financial stability, and with the help of a few hundred thousand pounds we've achieved that quite quickly,' he explains.

With the vultures no longer circling Brisbane Road, Hearn has quickly activated his plans to remodel the club, starting with the commercial and administrative structure. 'We haven't got the money the Premiership sides have got, but we've got a Premiership attitude,' he argues. 'We look to do things properly. We've rebuilt the commercial department from scratch and we've now got a set-up worthy of a Premiership outfit.'

On this bedrock, Hearn hopes to achieve twin targets of a spanking new stadium and a place in the First Division, both by the turn of the century. Ambitious plans indeed, but Hearn is confident Matchroom's experience and expertise in other sports can help them realise these aims. 'We've come to football in the same spirit we brought to snooker and boxing,' he says. 'We've tried to look at the game from a new angle.'

However, underlying this pioneering approach lurks the age-old dictum of 'bums on seats', as Hearn readily admits. 'First of all, we saw we had a 17,000-capacity stadium and asked, 'Why aren't we filling it?' So we immediately set about looking at ways to bring people in.'

The result has been some interesting season-ticket initiatives. Most eyecatching is the introduction of a £10 season ticket for juniors, a scheme particularly close to the chairman's heart. 'Kids are the future of the game, especially at community clubs like Leyton Orient.' Community is a word Hearn uses a great deal, and not with the contempt one might expect from a man who epitomises the Thatcher ideal.

'We also looked at other groups: OAPs, students and women,' he adds. 'I was amazed to discover that out of all our season-ticket holders last year, only a dozen were women. If we were going to attract families that had to change.' Consequently, a £50 season ticket has been introduced for women, along with concessions for pensioners and students. An opening-day gate of over 8,000 was the reward, though Hearn is realistic enough to realise that only success could sustain such attendances. 'Obviously, I was delighted with the biggest crowd in the division, but we couldn't expect that every week,' he admits. 'What the game did offer is a glimpse of what Leyton Orient is going to be all about – families watching football together. We're a community club, it's our greatest natural resource. We don't have a great big chequebook, so we have to reach out to local people and bring them into Leyton Orient.'

While his recurrent references to cash restraints make it obvious that Hearn will be no Jack Walker, for the moment his commitment to the club appears genuine enough. He has a clear vision of a lean, efficient, profit-making enterprise which is nonetheless regarded with proprietary affection by the community around it. But what about the football side?

For all the talk of community values, Hearn showed he would not baulk at ruthless decisions when popular co-managers John Sitton and Chris Turner paid the price of failure last year. In their place has arrived former West Ham favourite Pat Holland, a man picked to meet Hearn's very specific requirements. 'When I looked for a manager, I wasn't after an established, high-profile figure who'd done it all already – they'd be spoiled by the system,' Hearn explains. 'I wanted someone who had the same energy and raw enthusiams as ourselves, as well as the technical ability. Holland fitted the bill perfectly.'

As a former coach at Orient, QPR and Tottenham Hotspur, there is no doubting Holland's pedigree, and the chairman is delighted with the progress of his managerial prodigy. 'Both he and I are still learning the ropes, and no doubt we've made a few mistakes, but overall I'm happy with what Patsy and his assistant Tony Cunningham have done since they arrived.'

In terms of transfer activity, Holland has not exhibited the reforming zeal of his chairman, choosing to retain most of the squad he inherited. But the manager is adamant this reluctance to make major changes has nothing to do with a lack of funds. 'Both myself and the chairman have agreed there will be money to spend – but, to be honest, I'm not prepared to lash out £80,000–£100,000 unless I'm sure a player can add something to the existing team,' Holland says candidly. 'I don't know enough about the League yet, and I'm not going to spend for the sake of it.'

He firmly believes the current side is good enough to mount a promotion challenge, and that his financial prudence will allow for strengthening when the crunch comes at the end of the season. 'Realistically, we've got to be aiming for a play-off spot this year, even though this is my first season and Barry is in the process of rebuilding the club. It wouldn't be fair on the supporters if we weren't looking to get straight back up.

'The chairman's been very good to me so far,' he adds, realising that expectations will be at their highest in the boardroom. 'My biggest problem with him is whatever's he's touched has turned to gold. He only knows success and expects it at Leyton Orient. I only hope he gives me the time to deliver that success.'

Hearn himself has few doubts that the club will prosper, saying: 'Our attitude is summed up by a sign above the dressing-room door, it just says "Why Not?". When people say you can't do this and you can't do that, we say, "Why Not?" You can do virtually anything if you take a positive attitude to it. After all, football boils down to 11 men against 11 men, doesn't it?'

With such an upbeat, aggressive outlook, it will be interesting to see how long Hearn is willing to wait for a return on his investment. Should Leyton Orient establish themselves as contenders then there is no better man to maximise their potential. As a boxing promoter, Hearn knows all about selling the *Rocky* dream. However, if the club fails to live up to his ambitions, then East End supporters may well find comparisons with *On the Waterfront* rather more apt.

Matchday, October 1995

TRANSFER DEADLINE

Mark Robison

Chris Hull's eyes are fixed on Ceefax. Rumours around the Fylde coast suggest his beloved Blackpool are looking to recruit David Rocastle from Chelsea. Ten minutes later, he's visualising Rocky laying on a promotion winning goal for Tony Ellis. Given another hour, Blackpool could well be in the Champions League.

Today is transfer deadline day, and Chris is on the Football League frontline, manning the phones and fielding the fax at their Lytham St Annes HQ. 'The romance of deadline day is still there,' says Chris, 'but the situation has changed. These days, clubs are spending more money on improving their grounds and so are more cautious of how to utilise their funds. There's also the small matter of Bosman. This is our first deadline day since then and we're curious as to what effect it might have.'

The deadline is 17.00 hours sharp. Ninety minutes and counting . . .

15.30 hrs. The calm before the storm. Sheila Andrew, head of registrations, reveals: 'A few loans have gone through, but not many permanents. Bosman might have some effect later on, though. This is the last day for clubs looking to sign up players whose contracts are up at the end of the season. If they don't, they could go on free transfers in the summer.

'We only deal with transfers between Endsleigh clubs or transfers from the Premiership to the Endsleigh. Although if a player moves from the Endsleigh to the Premiership his registration has to be cancelled with us. The interesting thing is to see how one transfer can spark off other moves. A lot of people think it's new money coming into football, but most of the time it's just the same money going round.'

15.45 hrs. The flow of faxes increases steadily. 'We need up to five documents to complete a transfer,' explains Sheila. 'A simple transfer form signed by the selling club, the buying club and the player; a copy of the contract and any bonus schedules; a financial agreement between both clubs; and a medical report. Sometimes we wait for the medical report until the following day because some players won't sign until the deadline. After that, we fax confirmation of the transfer.

'Nowadays most of it's done by fax. Gone are the days when clubs shook hands on a deal in a service station carpark or Brian Clough turned up here with all the forms in hand. We used to use our boardroom here for clubs to discuss terms with players. Chairmen would be pacing up and down waiting for the player to arrive.'

The documents are keyed into a computer database which stores information on every registered player, including all their appearances and contract details. Once that's done, the transfer is complete and the press can be officially informed.

When a fax comes in, Sheila and her team know exactly what to look for: 'We make sure the documents have all been signed and that the finance details add up. The lower league clubs are more inventive than the top clubs. They'll spread the costs of both the transfer and the player's contract to give them more time to pay. For example, you'll often find a portion of the fee will only be paid after the player's made a certain number of appearances, or that the player will get relocation expenses instead of a big signing-on fee.'

Sheila's secretary, Debbie, adds: 'Tomorrow we'll receive bank transfers from the buying club. The accounts department will notify us and once we've allocated it to the correct transfer, we'll then authorise the money to be passed to the selling club.'

And if they don't? 'The transfer doesn't go through.'

16.15 hrs. The phones start ringing as soon as they are put down, with clubs eager to know if their transfers have been both received and completed. With the £1 million sale of Gary Croft to Blackburn, Grimsby boss Brian Laws is looking for a left-back. A deal is struck with Carlisle for Tony Gallimore. His registration details are checked, the clubs have signed the forms, the finance is fine. Five minutes later, Gallimore is a Grimsby player.

Debbie phones Hull City to confirm another deal. 'I'm sorry, I must have the wrong club,' she says, hanging up. Oops, she's rung Doncaster Rovers by mistake.

Sheila's phone rings. 'Is this a wind-up?' she enquires. 'Well, I think somebody's having you on, then,' she informs a caller from Leyton Orient who's heard that the deadline's been put back 24 hours.

16.45 hrs. The registration team make a list of transfers signed but not yet received. 'We know they're having trouble getting them through, so we'll take down details and wait for the fax,' says Sheila. 'You've got to remember that we can have up to 72 clubs trying to get through to just three machines, so it can get congested.'

After 15 years in the job, Sheila can recognise anybody trying to clinch a deal after five o'clock. 'Their voice can often give it away, although I won't say how in case it happens in the future.'

Last season, Phil Whelan's transfer from Ipswich to Middlesbrough went through so late the defender couldn't play until the following season.

17.00 hrs. Faxes stream in. It won't be until six o'clock, when the lines are free, that everybody will have been notified that their deal's gone through. In the last half-hour, Gerry Creaney has moved to Oldham until the end of the season; Lee Chapman has solved Jan Molby's Swansea striker dilemma and Paul Peschisolido has rejoined Birmingham.

There are no big surprises on the final list. 'One thing I have noticed, though, is that the number of goalkeepers moving has dropped,' says Sheila. 'This is probably down to the fact that, because clubs have a substitute keeper on the bench now, they've already got sufficient cover until the end of the season.'

Meanwhile, Chris Hull is launching a one-man vendetta against Ceefax. After all the speculation, he won't see David Rocastle in a tangerine shirt. Not this season, anyway. But they've got until next March to do a deal.

Goal, June 1996

WHERE DRUGS RULE
FOOTBALL

Jeff King

To the armchair sports fan, Colombian football means four people: 'That crazy goalie' (René Higuita), 'That geezer with the weird hair' (Carlos Valderrama), Newcastle new boy Faustino Asprilla, and 'That bloke who got shot after scoring an own goal at the 1994 World Cup' (Andrés Escobar). Colombia the country means only one thing – drugs. Cliché or not, in Colombia cocaine is still king and the aforementioned quartet really do represent its football; mad, bad and dangerous to know.

Despite producing 95 per cent of the planet's emeralds and the world's second-biggest coffee crop, the American continent's fourth-biggest country cannot shake off the stigma of its narcotics trade, which has permeated every level of society and produces 30,000 murders a year. Throw in the fact that, in their heyday, the drug barons loved to boost their profiles with an investment portfolio in football, and it's clear that the sudden death of Andrés Escobar and Asprilla's lurid lifestyle are not exactly distant relations. Live fast (play fast) and die young in the land of the drugs cartels.

Colombia in 1996 is trying to clean up its act, but it's a tortuous process. Corruption cuts deep. Last month, a special committee of the Colombian Chamber of Deputies began the investigation into the 'narco-financing' of the 1995 electoral campaign of Ernesto Samper, the current President, no less. Samper is accused of receiving 10,000 million pesos (£7 million) in campaign funds from the notorious Cali drugs cartel, However, the murder of the key witness just 72 hours before proceedings got under way, and the resignation of several committee members because of death threats to their families, suggests justice is unlikely to be done.

With the whole country awash in a sea of corruption, it would be a miracle if football had stayed in the hands of the good guys. In reality, however, Colombian football and scandal have always been fellow-travellers. The country's first professional league dates back to the 1920s, but it wasn't until a brief period of notoriety in the early '50s that Colombian football made waves beyond its frontiers. In that decade, Colombia was banned from FIFA and clubs, like the aptly-named Millonarios of Bogotá, capitalised by headhunting top international talent. If you're suspended by FIFA anyway, why bother paying transfer fees? Extravagant wages and juicy signing-on fees attracted a whole legion of South American mercenaries (most notably Argentinian demi-god Alfredo Di Stefano) and even the late England defender, Neil Franklin.

For three decades they remained also-rans, but the 1980s saw Colombian club sides at last making their presence felt in the only competition that really matters in Latin America, the Copa Libertadores (the equivalent of the Champions' League). Unfortunately, that international coming-of-age coincided with the rise of the now infamous drugs cartels of Cali and Medellín.

The infiltration of the drug barons into football began in earnest with the economic crash of 1975, a slump that left the major clubs filing for bankruptcy. With raging inflation eroding the value of gate money (and with no sponsorship or TV pickings, and little income from transfers abroad), the clubs were hardly in a position to say no to sugar daddies, whatever their source of income. In turn, football offered the mafia capos both social status and the perfect outlet for the laundering of narco-money.

Until his spectacular roof-top shooting at the hands of the Colombian police in December 1993, the leader of the Medellín cartel, Pablo Escobar, was a perfect example of the Good Samaritan-cum-wheeler-dealer. On the one hand, he was fêted by clubs in Medellín's poor barrios that depended on his largesse to survive. On the other, his 'ownership' of Atlético Nacional of Medellín (common knowledge in Colombia, though his name never appeared on the books) provided a perfect forum for money-laundering and career opportunities for his cronies.

América of Cali, Millonarios of Bogotá, Independiente Santa Fe, Unión Magdalena and Deportes Tolima (i.e. the rest of Colombia's major clubs) also fell into the hands of the cartel during the 1980s. It was the 'sponsorship' of the Cali overlords, Gilberto Rodríguez Orejuela, aka 'The Chess Player', and his brother Miguel, that converted América from poor relations to Colombian top-dogs in the '80s (the club had never won the Championship before 1979, subsequently they have piled up eight), a contribution glowingly acknowledged by the club's official history books. According to the American Drugs Enforcement Agency (DEA), the Cali cartel were at one stage responsible for distributing 80 per cent of the cocaine exported to the US, so clearly the brothers could afford to invest in their team. In the meantime, Millonarios players had their salaries paid by Gonzalo Rodríguez Gacha, 'The Mexican', the most feared *sicario* (hitman) of the Medellín cartel, whilst Unión Magdalena of Santa Marta were controlled by the Dávila brothers, heads of the dominant marijuana cartel.

The financial clout of the cartels produced swift dividends. Overnight, Colombian clubs could afford to pay top wages, both to keep homegrown stars and to attract overseas talent. For a while not even the top Brazilian and Argentinian clubs could seriously compete with the Colombian narco-dollar.

Buying overseas players was also an effective way of money-laundering. This was done by registering transfers at higher prices than were actually paid, with the balance staying in foreign bank accounts. In the mid-to-late-'80s, América (i.e. the Cali cartel) were so keen to filter cash abroad that they resorted to buying surplus foreigners and loaning them out to smaller Colombian clubs; at one stage there were six América-owned foreigners at 'offshoot' clubs.

Money was also used to buy favours. As early as 1978, Miguel Orejuela sent $550,000 in cash to the Peruvian team in the World Cup as inducement to throw their game against the hosts Argentina (a favour for his pals in the junta). Unfortunately, the loot was misdirected by the Colombian airline and arrived, not in Buenos Aires, but New York and the hands of the law.

The combination of perks and pressure led to unprecedented success. First, Deportivo (in 1978) and then América (three years running in the mid-'80s) were losing finalists in the Libertadores and, in 1989, Nacional finally brought the coveted trophy to Colombia. Nacional's victory was blemished by subsequent revelations that the Argentinian referee, Juan Carlos Loustau, had been offered $100,000 at his breakfast table on the morning of the second leg of the final. He turned the money down but, luckily (for him), Nacional beat Olimpia of Paraguay 2–0 before grabbing the title in the penalty shoot-out. After the game, Loustau was bundled into a car and taken for a 45-minute 'joy-ride'. Before being released he was told, 'Now you know we can do whatever we want to you. Make sure you remember that for the next time.' If the team from Medellín had lost, it's odds-on the reluctant passenger would never have made the return journey.

The very next year, Colombian clubs were banned from staging home games in the competition, after holders Nacional were accused of bribing officials. Before a quarter-final game against Brazil's Vasco Da Gama in Medellín, the Uruguayan referee was paid a visit in his changing-room by six armed hoods who first advised him to control the game properly and then offered him $20,000 for his troubles. And on the eve of the semi-final against Danubio of Montevideo, the refereeing trio from Argentina were roughed up in their hotel room.

The bribing of referees in domestic football was also rife. At one stage, the Colombian FA was forced to import referees from other South

American countries but to little avail. Being Chilean, Puerto Rican or Argentinian didn't make you immune to death threats and kidnapping. These on-the-record incidents alone cast a very long shadow over the sudden emergence of winning teams from the drugs mecca.

In 1989 there were no champions in Colombia. That was the year the government and footballing authorities made a show of tackling the climate of perpetual scandal. Proceedings were suspended in October after a spate of violence produced 20 football-related deaths in a couple of weeks. The machine-gunning of three players in Medellín and Cali, and the murder of referee Alvaro Ortega, was followed by the immediate retirement of Colombia's two World Cup-bound referees. The country's top official, Jesús Diaz, admitted in his resignation letter to FIFA mandarin, Joao Havelange, that, 'My wife and children have begged me to give up refereeing. When it's a matter of life and death you have to consider the feelings of others. I can't keep on tormenting my family.'

In fact, no one involved in the game was safe. In 1984, the Colombian Minister of Justice, Lara Bonilla, had become the first political victim of the footballing wars after denouncing the 'proliferation of dirty money in the game' and accusing clubs of 'paying players with money laundered from the drugs business'. The narco-gangs that controlled the massive legal and illegal betting that went on around the game dealt out 'justice' at a whim; players like Millonarios' Eduardo Pimentel and Uriel de Jesús (shot in 1982 by a rival fan *as he was about to score*), bureaucrats like Copa America organiser Carlos Arturo Mejía, and sports journalists such as leading Millonarios chronicler Jaime Ortiz Alvear, were other notable victims of the malaise that enveloped the game.

'The law of the bullet is killing our sport. We can't allow a competition to continue that is dominated by psychological coercion and physical threats,' pronounced the Colombian FA in 1989, a statement of intent that could have been made any time during the previous decade. 'No more deaths, no more massacres, and no more blood.' On the surface things improved for a while. Then the other Escobar scored for the USA.

Despite making their international début as long ago as 1938, Colombia has always been invisible in international football. Colombia's 1–1 draw at Wembley in 1988 was their first ever game in Europe. The side managed by Pacho Maturana at the Copa America in 1991 and 1993 has often been described as the best side never to have won that competition, and Colombia's 5–0 World Cup qualifying win against Argentina in Buenos Aires in September 1993 was quite simply the most astonishing result in South American football history.

As Maturano's plea for justice before the 1990 World Cup suggested, the most talented wave of Colombian footballers would always be tainted by association with the drug barons. 'Is it the Italian team's fault that they come from the home of the mafia? Are American players to blame that they represent the nation that has the highest number of AIDS victims? No. It's not my team's fault that Colombia has problems with narco-trafficking.' If you ignore on-the-field embarrassment when Higuita's walkabout made Roger Milla a star, Colombia's Italian job was untouched by disaster. Unfortunately, four years later in America, things would take a far more sinister turn.

After the 1993 smash-and-grab in Argentina, an inconsolable Diego Maradona had predicted that 'Colombia [would] do nothing in the World Cup. And if Maturano doesn't like that, he can go and fuck himself.' Despite that curse from the hand of God, Valderrama, Asprilla, Rincón and co arrived at the 1994 World Cup as highly fancied outsiders. Maturano had resigned as Colombia boss in June 1990, but he was back in charge for USA '94, claiming: 'We aim to play the most beautiful football possible. It's a great opportunity to change the image of Colombia in the world; an image so damaged by drugs.' So much for the American dream.

Maturano had to leave Gabriel 'Barabbas' Gómez out of his side to play the hosts after the defender's mistakes in the 3–1 defeat against Romania produced a volley of death threats: for the player himself, for Maturano (who received his warning by fax!) and for second-in-command Hernán Dario Gómez (who had stepped down from the top job in 1992 after a previous 'warning'). 'Barabbas' turned out to be the lucky one. Andrés Escobar – Colombia's elegant sweeper – played instead, scored at the wrong end (his second international goal, the first was at Wembley in 1988) and, on his return home to Medellín, was hit with 12 bullets in a restaurant carpark by a laughing assassin.

Like Gómez, his 'crime' was to mess up heavy wagers on Colombia by the narco-syndicates. Within days, two petty gangsters, Humberto Munoz Castro and Santiago Gallón Henao, were arrested and eventually convicted of murder, but few believed the government's claim that the murder was not linked to the narcos.

Not surprisingly, Maturano decided to take a post-US sabbatical far from home: 'I don't know if I'll manage Atlético Madrid next season because I don't know if I'll still be alive,' was his response to questions from journalists on his Spanish ambitions. Luckily, there were no more fatalities though, back in Colombia, midfielders Lozano and Alvarez were attacked and hospitalised.

Not that all the players were in danger. It was simply a case of what clan you were in collusion with (and who they were betting on). According to the DEA, several Colombian players were on the phone to Cali godfather Miguel Rodríguez Orejuela within hours of arriving home. After a grilling on the team's performances, Orejuela bade farewell to his chicos with a promise of a cash bonus to enjoy a well-deserved holiday.

Not surprisingly, disputes between rival club bosses (i.e. cartel front-men) often went beyond verbal exchanges. In the late '80s/early '90s,

Deportivo de Medellín president Pablo Correa, Deportivo Pereira president Javier Alsono Piedrahita, and Millonarios president Germán Gómez García, were all victims of the drugs-cum-football crossfire. Maturano best summed it all up with his response to the Andrés Escobar murder: 'Colombia is a permanent madhouse.'

Many players come from the same ghettos that spawn the cartels, so it's no surprise that some are married to the mob. René 'The Scorpion' Higuita (his team-mates actually call him 'The Frog') missed the 1994 World Cup after a spell in jail. The Medellín-born Higuita admits he was pals with Pedro Escobar, but denies involvement in drug dealing and kidnap. 'I helped negotiate the release of a little girl and was paid for it,' he claims. 'Maybe it was against the law, but $50,000 appeared in my bank account without my knowing.'

As for sampling the pleasures of the white lines, 'personal consumption' has long been a fact of football life in Colombia, but few major players have ever tested positive. In reality, with dope testing so lax (only Argentina and Brazil possess testing equipment that meets world standards), there is little chance of detection.

Regular drug testing was introduced in 1995 but so far América's international defender Wilson Cabrea is the only big name to have tested cocaine-positive. Not surprisingly, most of the players adopt a see-no-evil, hear-no-evil approach to anything concerning drugs.

'It's important for me to change the concept people have of my country,' says Faustino Asprilla. 'We're not all slaves to the drugs trade in Colombia. I played for Nacional in Medellín for three years. People say the club is run by drugs barons but, if so, I never saw them.'

At least trouble on the terrace is rare. Football grounds in Colombia are pretty safe places to be, and there are no organised ultra gangs like the infamous Barras Bravas in Argentina. In 1981, 18 fans were killed after a wall collapsed due to fighting at a game between Deportes Tolima and Deportivo Cali, and in 1982, drunken fans urinating from a top tier provoked a stampede at Cali's Pascual Guerrero Stadium that left 22 dead and 100 injured.

But these were relatively isolated incidents. In fact, Colombians are in most danger when their team wins. Medellín's citizens no doubt breathed a sigh of relief when Nacional lost last year's Libertadores final against Brazil's Gremio; the hysteria provoked by the club's 1989 triumph left 20 revellers dead. And the slightly over-the-top celebrations following that 5–0 rout of Argentina left a sad balance of 28 deceased.

The persecution of the most visible heads of the drugs cartels in the last couple of years has had concomitant cleansing effects on Colombian football. Escobar and Gacha are both dead, and the Orejuela and Davila brothers are locked up in top-security prisons in Bogotá. No one would claim that the cartel's tentacles have been severed completely, but the tenacious efforts of the Minister for Sport, Maria Emma Mejia, have arguably left football's house cleaner than society at large (all clubs are now obliged to provide the government with copies of every financial transaction, names of all shareholders and copies of accounts).

However, it's clear that until Colombian society as a whole puts its house in order football has no chance of being totally free of the narcos. Despite the high-profile detention the accumulated fortunes of the cartel (estimated at anything as high as $60,000 million, equivalent to Colombia's GNP) remain largely untouched. The most notorious cartel may be dead, imprisoned or on the run, but in 1995 detention of surviving members of the Cali cartel proved that their influence lives on. When police captured the Cali number three José Santacruz Londoño, his phone book contained the home numbers of practically every leading football administrator. The ensuing scandal forced the resignation of the president of the national federation.

América and Nacional have continued to dominate Colombian football in the 1990s. Then three-quarters of the way through the present championship, the top three sides were Deportivo, Nacional and América. The cartel may ostensibly be on the run, but the clubs of Cali and Medellín still enjoy a continuing football monopoly of questionable origins.

Total Sport, April 1996

The Media

7

JOURNALISTS
IN CHARGE

Ken Jones

A curious thing is that any number of people in every walk of life imagine themselves successful in football management. Some take the fantasy as far as to apply seriously for vacant situations.

On first being acquainted with this, the chairman of a club prominent in the old First Division expressed astonishment. 'You'd be amazed by the sort of people who've written in,' he said. It was loose thinking on his part, because despite serious gaps in football education, many think themselves capable. Typically, you may think, this includes one or two journalists.

All will be encouraged by the news that one of Brazil's most famous clubs, Flamengo, have replaced the former international Edinho as coach with an obese 59-year-old radio commentator, Washington Rodrigues, who is considered to be so underqualified that he would find difficulty in coaching kittens to play with balls of wool.

According to a respected Brazilian broadcaster, Jose Werneck, the appointment can be regarded as temporary, but no matter. As Rodrigues is a friend and former radio colleague of the club's president, Kleber Leite, this is the equivalent of Des Lynam gaining control at Tottenham and putting Barry Davies in charge of the team.

Holding opinions about the game and putting them into practice are entirely different things. This applies equally to identifying faults and bringing about improvement. However, as the former England and West Ham manager Ron Greenwood once said, expertise is assumed automatically on retirement from the game, even if that amounted to no more than a kick-about in the school playground.

Oddly, Rodrigues's appointment is not entirely without precedent in Brazilian football. It was as a result of his fierce criticisms in a newspaper column and on radio that João Saldanha was invited to manage the national team following a disaster in the 1966 World Cup.

A big difference was that Saldanha played the game professionally and had taken a Botafogo team that included Didi and Garrincha to the Rio championship. Having brought together the most brilliant assembly of players in Brazil's history, Saldanha fell out with the authorities and was replaced by Mario Zagallo shortly before the 1970 World Cup finals.

Seven years later, Brazil turned to an army captain and former volleyball international, Claudio Coutinho, whose only previous connection with football had been as the man responsible for ensuring the national team's privacy and the safety of their wallets. 'I am reading many books about coaching,' he said in Rio before a match against England.

As the list included one by a British journalist whose experience did not run beyond Sunday football, it was decided immediately to abandon the idea of betting on Brazil, an eminently sensible decision considering their futile attempt to impersonate Europeans and that the encounter passed without a goal. Not long afterwards, Coutinho drowned while scuba-diving.

A book Rodrigues should read is the autobiography of George Allison, who was persuaded to manage Arsenal on Herbert Chapman's death in 1934. He had spent more than 20 years as London correspondent of William Randolph Hearst's chain of American newspapers, and was the BBC's first football commentator. Inheriting a team that included the great Scottish schemer Alex James and eight England internationals, Allison, who gave up playing when still a teenager and who had never managed, put his name to three league championships and an FA Cup. Apparently Allison did not know much about football, but an awful lot about publicity.

Tottenham Hotspur also put their trust, albeit temporarily, in a man who had no qualifications as a coach or a player. While grooming Bill Nicholson for the job, they handed it to a member of the administrative staff, Jimmy Anderson. What Anderson knew about football would not have covered a microchip. He once suggested to Danny Blanchflower that the best way of playing against the famed Sunderland trickster, Len Shackleton, was to demoralise him. 'If he catches the ball on his shoulder, then you catch it on the back of your head,' he said.

Came the day when pressure proved too much for Anderson. 'They're at it again,' his wife called from the foot of the stairs after scanning the Sunday sports pages. Groaning, Anderson handed over to Nicholson shortly afterwards.

The Independent, 14 September 1995

MOTSON IS BACK

Stan Hey

With respect to Les Ferdinand, the most prominent comeback on the English football scene this week will be John Motson's return behind a BBC microphone for the highlights of England's friendly game in Norway on Wednesday. For Motson, the eternal schoolboy of football commentating, who turned 50 last July, has not been heard on the airwaves since 11 June. *Match of the Day*, already nine programmes into the new season, has been a Motty-free zone, prompting anxious viewers to wonder whether 'The Voice of Football' had been kidnapped by aliens or, at least, taken up with Sky.

The truth is rather more mundane – Motson says simply that 'after doing *Match of the Day* for 25 years, and facing a long season with the European Championship finals next summer, the BBC amicably agreed to let me start in October, so that my nine-month span would take in the tournament'.

The rumours that his replacement by Barry Davies for the 1994 World Cup final, and subsequently for the 1995 FA Cup final, was a yellow card from his bosses at BBC Sport, do not hold up in the light of their renewed, long-term commitment to a man who has defined the style of football commentary in the modern television age – bubbling enthusiasm, mixed with bags of match facts.

Brian Barwick, editor of *Match of the Day*, says: 'When Barry got the Cup final, some of the press put two and two together and made five. Barry covering the final and John's extended break were both discussed a year previously, so there was no mystery. And when I watch the series of *Match of the Day* in the 1970s, it brought home just how long John has been at it, and how he'd earned a break.'

Barwick also knocks down any notion that there is a dispute about

Number One status between the two commentators. 'We have never thought in those terms. They are both excellent, experienced front-line reporters, who share the load between them. From January to June next year we'll have football on Saturday and Wednesday nights almost every week, including the European Championship and its build-up.'

So how has John spent his time during what he calls 'my sabbatical'? Well, watching football, of course. 'I've seen quite a few Premiership games, but I've also been to Wycombe, Fulham, Barnet and Peterborough, watching just as a fan,' he enthused. 'It was a pleasure being able to spectate without having to prepare notes. I must say, I didn't find myself twitching to pick up a microphone!'

Those who fear that Motson suffers a 'Statto-like' addiction to football will be relieved that he also found time for a holiday, a luxury cruise down the River Nile. And the Motty verdict on the monuments produced by 3,000 years of Egyptian civilisation? 'Quite an eye-opener, actually!'

I wondered if this brush with history, and a period of calm, had provoked any reflections about his style of commentary. 'Well, I'm aware that some people find me a bit crash-bang-wallop,' he said, 'so I'd like to try to be a bit more rational and restrained. I don't know if I'll make it, because it's very difficult for me not to get excited. There's an exuberance in me, but it's genuine.'

Norway, the home of the 'Maggie Thatcher, Lady Diana, Winston Churchill, your boys took one hell of a beating tonight!' rant, should be an appropriate venue for the return of the commentator who etched 'Look at that, look at that!' on the soundtrack of our football-watching lives. 'I just hope there isn't a riot on Wednesday,' Motson adds edgily. England fans, spoiling Motty's big night? Now that would be a real talking point, Trevor.

Independent on Sunday, 8 October 1995

THE RADIO MAN

Derick Allsop

Younger fans may be astonished to learn there was a time, not so very long ago, when regular football coverage on television was limited to recorded highlights on BBC's *Match of the Day* and ITV's *Big Match*. The only live action came from FA Cup finals and big internationals. The sole medium for League football, as it happened, was BBC radio, and even then all you got was the second half. The chosen match was identified, in melodramatic ritual, after kick-off time. You imagined stampedes to grounds up and down the land at five past three as supporters realised there was no cheap and easy way of following their team that day.

It was generally supposed, of course, that any live commentary would discourage punters from paying at the gate and that over-exposure would seriously affect attendances. How things have changed. The onslaught by television, especially by Sky, has delivered us live league, Cup, representative and any number of other variations in the game, packaged as marathon spectaculars. The BBC and ITV, feeling their backsides suitably kicked, have responded as best they can. Now we have live football three or four days a week. Flick around the channels on a Sunday and the chances are you'll find an Italian match on Four, an Endsleigh League game on ITV and then Premiership fare on Sky. The game succumbed to the multi-million-pound offers – again, especially from Sky – and rearranged fixture lists to suit the schedules. And what happened to the gates? They went up.

Football, the culture, has taken on a new dimension and broadcasting has been an integral part of that process. Local radio and club-call services proliferated. At the forefront, however, remained BBC radio, national radio and, under its modern guise, Radio Five, it was able to bring coverage to homes and cars anything up to five days or nights a week. And

302

the most distinctive voice on Radio Five commentaries is that of Alan Green, partly because he is an Ulsterman and partly because he tends to speak his mind rather more than anyone else. His frank assessments have raised eyebrows at Broadcasting House, caused tut-tutting among his peers and incurred the wrath of at least one high-profile manager. Green is unrepentant. He refuses to 'talk-up' a dismal match and has no respect for those who do.

It is midwinter and mid-season, and Green is particularly busy. Apart from his commentary commitments he is currently hosting the Friday evening *Sportstalk* programme. But then talking comes easily to this chubby-faced enthusiast, and of course he can spare an hour to tell me about himself, his work and his game.

Green was born in Belfast, in 1952, and took a degree in modern history at the city's Queens University. From an early age he had an interest in journalism and earlier still a passion for football.

'My father was a complete lunatic,' he says. 'He supported a team called Linfield and was determined I should do the same. He took me to my first game, he assures me, when I was 18 months old. Linfield were playing Bangor, away, and seemingly I started crying so he took me outside the ground. He will tell anyone – and I've no reason to disbelieve it – that he walked me up and down saying, "Don't you realise the Blues are losing?"

'I remember football earlier than anything else, standing on packed terraces. This was when Linfield would regularly get 25,000–30,000. It sounds ridiculous for an Irish League game, but they did. I remember Newcastle United playing there in the 1950s when they first had floodlights at Windsor Park. My regular haunt when Linfield were at home was the Spion Kop, but I went everywhere. In the early 1960s they won every trophy, seven of them. I think they beat Glentoran in the County Antrim Shield and I remember crying my eyes out because my father wouldn't let me go on the pitch. He did, thousands of them did.

'England to me then meant Chelsea Football Club. I think it was just Osgood, all that era. I'm a great one for the crying, the passion, and I hope that comes through in the commentary. I remember Chelsea losing to Spurs in the '67 Cup final and I was in a terrible state. The English might find it really odd that people in Northern Ireland can be so passionate towards England.

'I remember the day of the '66 World Cup final, when the equaliser went in, you know, just seconds to go, and we came out of our little council house in Newtownabbey, which is north of Belfast, and we walked in a circle, my father and myself, around the front garden, heads down, thinking, "We'll never do it now." We were devastated. People were all out in their gardens, shouting, "We're going to lose it now."

'When I first came to England I didn't know how to get to Anfield or

Old Trafford, those places were overwhelming to me. They were images I saw on TV or heard of on radio, not something I could actually touch. I feel like a privileged punter now. I'd like to think I'm someone who's feeling the same emotions about the game as the guy who has had to pay his money. The difference is I've got a microphone which, through experience, doesn't intimidate me. It's like a friend and I can just voice what I'm thinking and what he might be thinking and transmit that to those who can't be there.'

Green began his journalistic career in a less privileged role, working as a copy boy at the *Belfast Telegraph* during school holidays. 'My sole ambition was to be a news reporter on the *Belfast Telegraph*. There was no journalistic connection in the family. My father was an overlooker in a mill. It was my careers officer at university who suggested I apply for the BBC news training scheme.'

It was the first of many unscheduled turns in Green's career. 'I really thought this was way beyond me, but I was offered it so I started with the BBC, 20 years ago. They take a certain number of graduates a year to train as broadcasting journalists, who are unsullied by newspaper techniques. I felt completely overwhelmed. This was Broadcasting House, in London, and every day on the way to the news training office you pass the *World at One* offices, to the left the *World This Weekend*. It was just mind-blowing. And all the others on the course – there were seven of us – were Oxbridge graduates and I felt completely inadequate. But things worked out all right.

'At that time I had only one interest and that was to be editor of the *Nine O'Clock News*. I wanted to run it, not present it, and I still feel more strongly, I'm still more critical, about how television news is presented than anything that happens in sports journalism. I feel I'm a journalist first and a sports journalist second. I did a series of attachments around the BBC, local radio, regional television newsrooms, that kind of thing, and I diverted into sport.

'I was a television news reporter in Belfast, didn't like the atmosphere, and got a job on a weekly sports magazine programme. Then they pushed me into commentary because they had nobody else. I did the Irish Cup final for television and found it pretty pathetic. Didn't sleep the night before, certainly didn't sleep the night after, thinking how bad it was. There weren't that many commentaries to do, maybe eight or nine a year, European Cup matches involving Irish League teams or Northern Ireland games. But you get to know a little bit about it and I improved.

'I reached the stage in Belfast where I thought that was it, that I couldn't really go much further and I'd be doing this for the next 30 years. There were jobs in radio sport in London and I applied for them. They'd basically already been allocated but I was offered a job in Manchester. I said no because if I was going to make the break and bring my wife anywhere it would be to London because logically that's where I'd like to end up.

'Anyway, I was talked into Manchester. I started essentially as the reporter/feature-maker for Northern football and again commentary wasn't even on the horizon. Except that just before I made the move to Manchester the Head of Sport in Northern Ireland said to me: "By the way, your first commentary is on 28 February, England against Northern Ireland at Wembley." I said, "What are you talking about?" and he said they wanted me to do some radio commentary. I said I couldn't do radio commentary, but it had been sorted and I had to do it.

'Robson scored after less than a minute and I was sweating. There I was working with a legend, Peter Jones, and Ron Greenwood summarising. I felt so out of my depth. I barely recognised . . . well, I knew it was Robson and got it out, but I thought it was awful, and I cringed. I was treating it like a television commentary – "I'm not telling you what's happening here, you can see it for yourself." That first experience of radio commentary, 12 years ago, told me I couldn't do it. Other people persuaded me to carry on. This is very hard to take for the young boys who write to me because they automatically assume I had that ambition, but I didn't. It just happened.'

Green's promotion to senior status in the commentary team came in tragic circumstances. It followed the death of that broadcasting 'legend', Peter Jones. 'No one could touch Jonesy,' his apprentice says. 'He would do all the main commentaries – and remember we did relatively few games then. You're talking about Saturday games, Wednesday night games, internationals, that's it. Not this five or six days a week business that we go through now.

'So, when Jonesy was doing all these big games it left very few opportunities for the third and fourth strings, people like myself and Mike Ingham. We would get, if we were lucky, a League Cup replay that Jonesy didn't fancy. But there was no resentment at all, because Jonesy was the best and that was just the way of life. We would all do more as the commentaries increased, but we were still missing out on the big ones.

'When Jonesy died in 1990, on the day of the Boat Race, I was doing commentary at Wolves. They were playing Leeds and they'd just built their new stand. Martin Chivers was summarising. I was disturbed that day because we seemed to be so far from the pitch and I couldn't really make out the players, a nightmare to do a commentary. Peter was at the Boat Race and it was Martin who noticed it first. "I think there's something wrong with Peter," he said. Peter was an old friend of his and he said, "Peter doesn't sound great." Then Peter didn't pick up a link and we thought, "What is this?"

'We tried to buzz the studio with an electronic device we have but they said they were busy. Eventually they told us Jonesy had collapsed on the towpath but they didn't know what condition he was in. It was announced on television that night that he had collapsed. I think he died in the early hours of Sunday morning.

'That very day the Head of Sport rang me and said, "Look, unfortunately we've got to think business." That week or a couple of weeks later I was due to go over to the World Snooker, which I'd covered for eight or nine years straight, but they said they'd got to pull me off it, I'd got to go full-time football commentary, and that's how it was. It's terrible because it's "dead men's shoes".'

Green prepares for his work by simply soaking up the football flooding our lives. 'I can't afford to miss anything that's on, say, Sky. I don't actually like Sky's approach but I need that input. Because I see so much football and because so much of it happens to be at the top level, I shouldn't have to prepare that much to go and do, for example, Newcastle and Manchester City. If I don't know these teams I shouldn't be doing it. But on FA Cup third-round day I'll be doing Birmingham and Liverpool. Well, I don't need to know about Liverpool but I've never seen Birmingham play live, so I'm going to have to make sure I know that side.'

So what is it about Sky's approach he does not like?

'It isn't doing my career prospects any good but even if anybody in television sport or satellite television thought I was any good, they wouldn't take me on, because I'm not going to say things they want me to say. If a game is bad I'm just going to call it that way. That may seem unfair on commentators in television and on satellite I respect, but I think there are pressures on them. We're talking about contracts here.

'If, for example, commentator A, working for Channel A, has seen a lot of drivel in terms of the games he's watching, he's reflecting that, but he doesn't have to go too far because the viewers can see it for themselves. But if he's not trying to bluff the viewer then the sponsors, the people who allow Channel A to get the contract, are going to say, "Hold on a second, they're not selling our product the way we want them to sell it." So there are pressures there that I don't have to work under and I appreciate that.

'I certainly like to be provocative, that's true, but that's inbuilt. If you are a punter and you see an incident in the penalty area you are going to have a view on it. I see my role beyond just describing. It's not something that is generally liked, even within my own department. There are times when the head of department will say, "I thought you went a little bit over the top there." On the other hand, my current head of department is of a view that if he said to me, "I want you to commentate without attitude", or, "I want you to commentate without letting your feelings come across", he knows he would ruin me as a commentator. So, if he feels I've gone over the top he'll say so quietly and I'll take it on board.

'I don't get much reaction from players. I'm not sure how many of them listen to the radio. Or maybe they just don't get offended. Managers do sometimes. Alex Ferguson and I simply do not have a relationship. I don't think it was anything specific. I remember very well the day Alex got the job at Old Trafford. I'd known him at Aberdeen and I went to interview him and we were standing on the touchline looking at the floodlights. It wasn't quite the stadium it is now but it's always had something special. I said, "Do you realise what you are taking on here?" He was looking sort of starry-eyed and I felt a great empathy with him at the time. I'd come across the sea and it dazzled me too. Stadia like that still dazzle me. Alex was looking and saying, "Isn't this fantastic?"

'I thought at that stage we were going to get on well, but I did feel he came to England paranoid about Merseyside, absolutely paranoid. I think it was a paranoia born in his own feelings when he was manager of Aberdeen and he was looking at Rangers and Celtic when they were dominating everything. He was coming to a scene at Manchester where Ron Atkinson had basically got the sack because he couldn't match Liverpool and Everton. Fergie had to do that and I think he felt this was the big bugbear that he had to get rid of, so he had this inbuilt paranoia.

'Secondly, and like so many people, he misunderstood my enthusiasm for good football as support for a particular side. Over the years I've had letters claiming I supported X, Y and Z, but what it actually boils down to is that I praised X, Y and Z because they played good football. So, if you praise teams playing well and winning, you're supporting them. It's just not true. But since Liverpool were winning everything in sight, and I praised them, Fergie misinterpreted that and labelled me a Liverpool fan.

'There were a couple of scenes, one at Anfield, during the period when he had a row with Kenny Dalglish. He had a major scene with me that day, accusing me of being a Liverpool fan and saying he wouldn't talk to me, and I told him he was crazy. He's never got over that. I think he has an appalling attitude towards me. In a perverse way it's flattering because why should the manager of the biggest club in the country give two damns what I say? But he appears to care about it and to care to such a degree that he is forever slagging me off, publicly and privately, and it means, frankly, that from a situation where I quite liked the man I now have no time for him on a personal level.'

The Game of Their Lives (Mainstream, 1995)

MATCH OF THE DAY

Paul Simpson

'Four-Four-Two,' booms Alan Hansen. 'That's a formation I don't have a lot of time for.' He shakes hands anyway and wanders over to the producer Vivien Kent to put his £2 into the sweepstake on the scores for the games to be televised on today's programme.

I have already put in my £2 worth and stand to win an astonishing £18 if my predictions come true. Albert Frindall, the man who supplies the team with its statistics, wins most of the time although Hansen has scooped up the winnings for the last three weeks.

Hansen looks casual in jeans, baggy jumper and stubble but he's not as casual as Gary Lineker who is sitting back in his chair, his state of mind somewhere between relaxed and comatose. He winks. Des Lynam is sitting nearest the row of six TV monitors and in front of a plate of flying-saucer-shaped sweets. Lineker looks at the tray and turns over a packet of green crisps. 'Premier League crisps,' he says. 'Whatever next?'

We are sitting in a windowless office which bears a passing resemblance to the kind of bunker Hitler used in Berlin. The sign on the door says simply 'Production Office'. If the national institution that is *MOTD* can be said to have a nerve centre, this is it although, at 2.35 p.m., there's no sign of nerves or excitement. In fact, there's not much sign of any conversation about football. Alan and Gary are talking earnestly (and very technically) about golf swings.

In walks Brian Barwick the editor. Barwick, a man with a fearsome reputation at the Beeb for not suffering fools, drives the programme behind the scenes. His secretary Marianne Sparks keeps everybody constantly supplied with team sheets and coffee. 'We have so much caffeine some weeks we don't go off to sleep till Tuesday,' quips Barwick.

Today's main attraction is probably going to be Everton v Man U but Newcastle v Southampton and Coventry v Nottingham Forest are being filmed and commentated on by Clive Tyldsley and Jon Champion respectively. Barwick is the man who has the heinous responsibility of picking the games which are going to be broadcast. It's the one subject he gets most complaints about. 'Why are Man United on the telly again?' he says wearily. 'What they don't realise is that when Man United are on, the audience is that much bigger.'

From 3 p.m. onwards he is subjected to sporadic abuse from 'the boys' (Hansen, Lineker and Lynam) if the games he's selected are goalless. Matches are fed through the monitors along with whatever other sports the boys want to watch. (Usually golf, golf and golf.) While they study the screens quietly, upstairs the games are being transmitted and logged. If the games weren't accurately logged, *MOTD* would never come out, the games would never be edited down in time for that night's show.

Emma Josling, a video-tape producer, is logging the Newcastle-Southampton game. Every time something happens she makes a note of the time and marks on a miniature pitch where the incident took place. So, for instance, if nothing happens between two goal-kicks at the Southampton end, they can be cut into each other. The aim is to give the viewer a perfectly seamless edit.

Josling notes everything while being updated by Graham Wellham on the progress of her favourite team, Luton. Wellham, a Wolves fan, is known as Spike because at moments of extreme stress his hair tends to stand on end. When not talking to Josling he's watching a bank of monitors outside or popping into the editing suites where the other two games are being logged.

Robert Lee tries to lob Dave Beasant and as the keeper scrambles back to save, the screen flickers, goes blank for a second and springs back to life. 'Probably somebody stamping on the line,' says Josling but one of her colleagues goes off to investigate. The transmission is a free live feed from Sky and, when pressed, Sky's reply is: 'There are good outside broadcasts and bad ones.'

Tyldesley, Champion and Barry Davies are all commentating blind in the sense that they don't know which of their pearls of wisdom are going to end up on the editing-room floor or even which of the games is going to kick off the show. (It's just possible that if Everton and United battle out a 0–0 draw, Barwick will want to lead off with one of the other games.)

In another editing suite Ray Stubbs, sporting a new bushy haircut which may be designed to soften his image, is recording a trailer for the Liverpool v Vladikavkaz game on Tuesday. He sits patiently in the sound booth waiting for Asmi Ahmed to give him his cue. He starts but stops after a few seconds because he's mispronounced the Russian side as 'Vladikazkav'. He repeats it endlessly. 'Kav kaz, kav kaz. Trouble is I've got kaz kav in my head now.' Ahmed tries to encourage him. 'You got it right the other day,' she says.

In the production office Hansen is looking animated. 'Good shot!' he shouts, his voice thundering around the room as he sits up straight in his chair. If he'd been a knee-slapping kind of guy he'd have slapped his knee at this point. But he isn't. And the shot he's referring to isn't (as I'd naïvely assumed) an effort from Ryan Giggs but a drive onto the 15th fairway at some international golf tournament.

Barwick is looking relaxed because there are already plenty of goals in tonight's games. Lineker jerks forward when Amokachi gets a chance. He squanders it and Lineker sits back. I ask how Amo's doing. 'His finishing's terrible,' says His Garyness. 'It's like he panics when he gets a sight of goal.

Wimbledon are beating Liverpool 1–0, a score which gets a triumphant cheer from Lineker but is received more quietly by Hansen. 'He's biased,' says Lineker nodding in Hansen's direction. 'It's Liverpool, Liverpool.' Hansen looks across the office sternly: 'What's he saying?'

'That you're biased towards Liverpool.'

Hansen snorts derisively. 'Biased?' he says, faking rage. 'For Liverpool? Wimbledon more like.' He then launches into a brief speech on the importance of team spirit while Gary's eyebrows shoot up as if to say 'I'm sorry I've heard this one before'.

Speech over, Hansen returns to the golf. I ask whether he'd have liked to have presented a golf programme instead of a football programme. 'That's a good question,' he says. Could he have played golf professionally? 'Nah.' The head shakes emphatically. 'I was never good enough. Being a realist, as I am renowned for being [he looks up to make sure that I'm catching the note of self-parody], I knew that.'

So who does he fancy for the League? 'Liverpool have that extra edge with Collymore. The last few years they've always had to play their way through; now if the other side's defending deep they can knock it over the top. It's like Ferdinand at Newcastle. The way most British teams play you need that option in the air. The trouble with Newcastle is when they play away from home they can't defend, they have to go all out to attack and you can lose games that way. Which team do you support?'

'Nuneaton Borough.'

'We'll have trouble mentioning them on the programme,' he says before furrowing his brow. 'Have they had any League players?'

'Trevor Peake.'

'Oh, good player. Coventry City 1987 FA Cup final.'

At this point Gary interjects: 'Do I detect a note of irony there?'

'No, no, Peake was a good player.' Hansen has this way of looking you straight in the eye, giving you his best Troy Tempest look and daring you to doubt him. It's a very smart tactic and all further discussion of Trevor Peake's merits is cancelled.

He now swivels back towards the monitors and espies a golfer on a green. 'Bet he misses it.'

'How much?' says Gary.

'A pound,' says Hansen cautiously.

'All right and it will be a pleasure to lose to you,' says Gary. Which is just as well because he does lose.

Gary Wolstenholme is now on the green and Hansen says: 'Bet he misses it too.'

Lineker laughs and digs into his pocket to fish out another pound coin: 'Okay: double or quits. He's the son of a BBC commentator . . .' the sentence trails off into laughter.

'Exactly,' says Hansen. 'He'll bottle it.' Whether he bottled it or not is a moot point, but he definitely missed.

The results are coming in. 'Six points out of six for Brighton,' chirps Des Lynam. They have five minutes to decide who they want to grab for post-match interviews. Requests are shouted from Barwick and Lynam. 'Kinnear, Vinnie, Bryan Roy.'

Kent writes them all out. There are already rumours about whether the referee meant to send off Vinnie Jones or someone else. The beaming faces of Big Ron, Fergie, Joe Royle and Frank Clark fill the screens. Lineker appears to be distinctly depressed about his bit of analysis. 'Maybe I'll do something on the young United players,' he says doubtfully.

One of the chasers comes back in and says: 'I'll read this out as it's written.' Everybody turns to look. He reads from the piece of paper in a triumphant voice: 'Get me an interview with Roy Kinnear and Vinnie Jones.' There is the briefest of silences before everyone collapses into prolonged, uproarious laughter. But the story isn't over. 'And Ralph Dellor came back and said: "I can get you Kinnear but you'll never get Vinnie Jones."' Lineker is now hooting with laughter as is everybody else in the room and Barwick appears to be trying to flick a tear out of his eye.

Hansen has won the sweepstake not because he is remarkably prescient but because, unlike the rest of us, he has managed to predict at least one score correctly. He insists on reading my predictions (which, over the three games are only 11 goals out) out loud. 'And you call yourself a football magazine editor!' he tuts before collecting the money.

Lynam and Barwick nod at each other and retire to the room next door to write the script. Lynam actually writes it; Barwick is mainly there to run though the order of the show. Barwick has a running sheet for the show with every item logged right down to the second. For instance, the first bout of 'live' analysis is scheduled to last exactly two and a half minutes.

'Rosendundgrozeenblaatt!' This is Barry Davies as you've never heard him before. Played backwards on a piece of BBC video tape. In one of the editing suites the Everton v Man United game is being cut down to 22.5

minutes (including interviews). This means Barry Davies's finely honed prose is going into the mangler. Stuart Cabb is the man responsible for overseeing this gargantuan task. His problem is to condense five goals, eight bookings, one controversial injury and several near misses into 20 minutes of free-flowing television.

And it's the pictures that drive the process, not the commentator's words. For example Davies's fine line about the Kanchelskis tackle ('And injury is added to insult as far as the Kanchelskis transfer is concerned') disappears because as he says it you can hear a whistle blowing in the background.

'The trouble is if they hear the whistle they'll be expecting the free-kick,' says Cabb. The Kanchelskis incident is already taking up too much time and they have goals galore to come. At the same time, they also cover for Davies who, innocently enough, observes that Kanchelskis's shoulder looks a little better. That line is cut too.

Barwick rushes in to check everything's okay. It is. Just. Outside, Wellham and his mates are wondering what the video of the Vinnie Jones sending-off is going to show. Hansen has just finished highlighting where he wants his white circles to be drawn showing exactly where (and why) the Forest defenders have completely lost the plot. He, Lineker and Lynam have all left now to wind down for a few hours while the backroom staff make sure that everything is going to be ready.

Barwick is chasing the Vinnie tape. Stubbs is watching it with some of the staff. They're pursing their lips and replaying it. Over and over. 'You have to watch it very carefully,' says Stubbs, finding a convenient fence to sit on.

One of the bank of phones rings. Stubbs picks it up: 'Hello *Match of the Day*. Oh, hello, Sam.' It immediately becomes apparent that at 9 p.m. Wimbledon's Sam Hammam has phoned to protest the innocence of his boy Vinnie. 'He swears he didn't do anything,' says Stubbs, repeating Hammam's words and keeping his voice in neutral. 'It's very hard to tell from the video. You can see he did rush over but it's hard to make out if he made any contact.'

Hammam tells Stubbs that if Vinnie swears he didn't do it, he didn't do it. Stubbs says they're going to look at the video again and try to talk to the referee, Keith Birch. Hammam hangs up and then Stubbs rings the referee who, his wife says, will probably be back home at around 10.20 p.m., the very moment the show is due to go on air.

Lineker waltzes back in wearing a tie and jacket but still in jeans (which will, when he's sitting around the table, be completely invisible to the watching millions). He offers mints around and wanders over to look at his bit of film. He and Barwick discuss what they'll talk about.

Le Tissier? Lineker looks as though he'd rather be tied to a bed with Graham Taylor than go through all that again. 'Well, he's made the decision hasn't he?' he says. 'If I was the manager I'd give him a few games' run, but I'm not.' The very tone of his voice says 'End of story'.

He says finally: 'He's lazy and great players are never lazy.' As the one flaw in Gary's sainthood as a player was his alleged laziness, this must be a private joke.

He reviews the tape of David Beckham before being dragged in front of another screen to have a look at the Vinnie incident. Lineker thinks it's a booking at most. 'What time are we on?' he asks Barwick. 'An hour from now,' comes the reply. 'That's 10.20 p.m.,' says Lineker. 'Gee, I worked that out all by myself.'

He has a moment to try and define his relationship with his sparring partner: 'Al's more negative than I am. When he sees a goal, he's looking for a defender to blame, but being a forward I always want to praise the striker.'

Barwick wants to know where Hansen is. Minutes later Jocky, as Lineker calls him, appears stubbleless in suit and tie. 'How did Nuneaton Borough get on?' he asks.

'You can't get the result on Teletext,' is my excuse. I had actually considered ringing the Club Call from the studio but thought that would be taking the mickey.

Now it's Hansen's turn to be drawn into the Jones affair. He and Lineker watch the film once. 'You have to say, what is he doing rushing over there?' says Hansen, exasperated. 'He's making it easy for the referee to make a mistake.'

Now they have to decide the Goal of the Month. I'd looked forward to seeing what criteria they used to decide this. How do they balance team goals against a great solo strike? What makes a Goal of the Month? Or the season?

Lineker and Hansen watch the goals and then Hansen turns to me and says: 'Come on then, what's your top three?'

Surprised, I stutter: 'Yeboah . . . Barnes . . . Platt.' Hansen looks at me as if I have just conclusively proved that I know nothing about football. 'Not even close,' he says. 'Not one in the top three.'

Lineker breaks up at this point until Hansen relents. The real order is Yeboah, Barnes, Yeboah. 'It doesn't matter if Liverpool concede the goal,' Hansen says as if he's dishing out some fatherly advice. 'As long as they're in there somewhere.'

It's almost time. Hansen and Lineker wander down to the studio where Lynam is already ensconced and preoccupied by the result of the Eubank fight. 'Did Collins win?' The patented sparkly-eyed Des Lynam look, not much in evidence earlier on in the day, suddenly appears.

Hansen confesses that he does get nervous: 'It's a different kind of nerves to playing. When you're playing, you're nervous in the dressing-room but when you come out of this tunnel there's just a massive release. Here, the last five minutes are the worst.' Lineker affects to find the whole idea of Hansen being nervous as somehow deeply comic.

I am escorted to a seat in the gallery where I can see Lynam and hear the producers talking back. The show is now 65-minutes long as Barwick asked for an extra minute. It has to be bang on because BBC Scotland come back onto the BBC1 programming after it ends and if it overruns they'll get the last few minutes of Des, Gary and Alan.

The BBC sports globe spins. The credits roll. Barwick comes up into the gallery. He can't bear to watch the opening of the show from the studio floor. Lynam gets the boxing result (Collins has won). The externally avuncular host stares pensively at the camera and after 47 seconds, camera one focuses on him and he says: 'Good evening. No doubt about football's main topic of conversation this week . . .'

It's all written down on the pink sheet of paper in front of him but it's part of his peculiar gift that he delivers the words (especially the jokes) as if they've just come into his head. But he has to be able to react swiftly. After the Coventry-Forest game he asks Hansen if Forest could win the League. The Scot says flatly: 'No.' Even for Hansen this is dismissive and Des chuckles: 'Well, there's no point in them playing then.'

The Jones affair, after all the agonising, seems a tad tame. Joe Kinnear's summary of the incident is funny but Lineker and Hansen agree that the referee and Vinnie were both wrong. What more can be said?

Barwick comes up into the gallery again to watch. The show is on time. Goal of the Month rolls and lasts for its scheduled four minutes. There's precious little to go wrong now. Des does his closing bit. 'Sixty-five minutes and two seconds,' says Barwick proudly.

The biggest feeling as they come out of the studio is relief. 'It was okay,' says Lineker coyly. Lynam strolls back into the empty production office, gathers his papers into his briefcase, gives one of his knowing smiles and says: 'So what did you make of all that rubbish?'

FourFourTwo, November 1995

ANOTHER BOOKING FROM SPORTSPAGES

Frank Keating

Sportspages Bookshop next week celebrates a tenth birthday at its alcove shrine off London's Charing Cross Road. Doubtless the fizz will be popped too at its three-year-old Manchester branch.

The hoorays are heartfelt. In 1985, Sportspages brought us buyers and book browsers, high and low, tumbling out of the closet and gaily into our addicts' den. It has become a worldwide club. Even Yanks take vacations to pore in front of its baseball shelves.

Remember when the high-street bookshops stocked only half a dozen crummy titles under 'Sports'? It doesn't matter any more that W.H. Smith still does, and that the dimwit assistant looks at you as bonkers if you inquire about a title other than those six. The editor of *Wisden* asked in there the other day about his bible: 'Do you stock *Wisden*?' Smith's poor girl stared at him blankly: 'Norman Wisdom, is that?'

Few gave John Gaustad much hope when he bravely opened his treasured trove on the morning of 6 September 1985. Not till 3.20 that afternoon did a customer approach the counter. He bought a copy of *Concise Light on Yoga*. Gaustad was up and, well, hobbling gamely. But it wasn't till a year later when David Massey, acquisitions librarian for Walsall borough council, came in and tucked £1,250 worth of various gems under his arms for his lucky Walsall readers that the still broke and insecure Gaustad was convinced of his own daring.

For the past six years Sportspages, with William Hill, has sponsored the sports book of the year. For the birthday it will announce the book of the decade. Presumably that will be Nick Hornby's seminal, sensational classic *Fever Pitch*. As Greg Williams writes in his new Penguin anthology, 'Hornby's book struck a chord [and] demonstrated that it's possible to write on sport in a way that is personal yet universal'.

In a way, just as *Fever Pitch* was waiting to be written, so with Sportspages for us nuts. When Gaustad tremulously opened his doors ten Septembers ago he was tapping into a new culture that had begun to blossom colourfully here after being sown and nurtured in the United States from the 1960s.

From the mid-1970s in Britain a spontaneous and fecund stream of good sporting books began to be delivered. At that time, and on the cusp of the new decade, books on team games and written by players still playing – such as Eamon Dunphy, Mike Brearley and Peter Roebuck – suddenly set new and glistening standards.

Simultaneously, the first academic history students whoopingly determined to change their syllabus and theses from dry-as-dust medievalism after coming across such definitive and resplendent research by the likes of Tony Mason and his *Association Football & English Society*, or the voluptuous story of Welsh rugby, *Fields of Praise*, by David Smith and Gareth Williams.

Also in those daisy-fresh days for our gaping sports shelves there was the wonderment of Gordon Forbes's tennis tales in *A Handful of Summers*; or David Foot on Harold Gimblett's paranoia and end; Peter Heller's glorious *In This Corner*, which presaged Robson Books' knockout boxing list; even Peter Tinniswood's invention of his Brigadier. Most of a certain generation will remember the leaping *oomph* of a convulsion in the soul when those books were discovered, then devoured.

But it does not take an accidental discovery any more. It is no unmapped trek to Sportspages. You can get the lot now, on anything and from everywhere: videos, fanzines and books, books, books. In the shop's ten years, apart from the six so far infallibly chosen annual prize-winners, the handful of titles I've best enjoyed have been Bob Wilson's stupendous and critically ignored history of goalkeeping; Pete Davies's crackling chronicle of the 1990 World Cup; Michael Marshall's valuable and unputdownable social text on cricket, *Gents & Players*; Pat Pocock's perspicacious Oval memoirs, whose line, length and laughter make it easily 22 yards ahead of anything else of its type; and probably the most irreproachably perfect sports book ever published, Simon Inglis's *Football Grounds of Great Britain*. Which came out in paperback the very autumn Gaustad first cried 'Shop!' – and waited nearly five and a half hours for his yoga book sale, and destiny.

The Guardian, 31 August 1995

PROGRAMME EDITOR

Tom Watt

Cliff Butler has been watching Manchester United since he was eight. Indeed, he hasn't missed a first team, youth or reserve team game at Old Trafford since 1965. Butler's enthusiasm for the history and detail of the club and the game has led him, almost inevitably, to do the job of editor of the United Review. *He took up the position in 1989 after three years as assistant, only the programme's fifth editor since the war.*

Like it was my dad initiated me. He was always a football supporter, although, before the war, he was more of a Manchester City fan, I think. He was a PoW in the Far East for three and a half years and he came back with a rather jaundiced view of the world. I don't think he took very kindly to City signing a German goalkeeper, Bert Trautman. Otherwise, I might have turned out to be a City fan. As it was, he pushed me towards United, kept telling me that they were the team and that he'd take me down to see them one day.

The first game I can vividly remember was Boxing Day 1958. We played Aston Villa. We were right at the back of the Stretford End paddock and I was only a kid, so it was a question of peering between people's shoulders. But I can remember the sense of occasion. It was a really big adventure for me, coming all the way over from east Manchester where we lived. Straightaway the whole thing had an effect on me: the crowd, the noise, the atmosphere. From then on, I was hooked. Almost instantly, it was an obsession. And it was a serious thing with me. I started keeping statistics. It was part of history, not just a football match. I started collecting books, programmes, press cuttings. When I left school I wanted to be a joiner, but I got in a factory that made lapping boards – things you wind lengths of fabric around in the clothing trade. It was a disappointment but, at the same time, I knew I didn't want a job that would take over and interfere with watching United. The important thing was to have the money to finance the obsession.

I ended up moving from job to job until I worked for ten years as a crane and fork-lift driver in the Port of Manchester. Of course, that brought me close to the ground. I'd started doing stuff for the Supporters' Club and, by now, I was coming into the ground at lunchtimes, answering letters from people wanting information, writing up the records. It was great. Here I was, an ordinary supporter, welcomed into Old Trafford. But I wasn't a nuisance. I didn't go running after the players or anything. Football was more serious for me than that. I've had my idols – Denis Law still is an idol – but I was more attached to the club than to any individuals.

I started doing articles for the programme. When they offered to pay me, I said I didn't want that but I'd like the title of club statistician. I think my first historical piece for the *United Review* was 20 years ago. After I was made redundant from the Port, I spent more and more time here and ended up with a part-time job in the ticket office, although most of my time was spent helping to put the programme together.

About three years later, in the mid-'80s, it was decided the club should have a museum, and I was taken on full time to set that up. That was my first full-time job at United: curator of the museum. I'd still be doing that, only I kept taking on more and more – at one point I was curator of the museum, programme editor and club photographer – and you can't carry on like that without the job suffering, not at a huge club like this, anyway. I wouldn't shed any of the jobs but, eventually, they were shed for me and I was left as programme editor. I wasn't happy at the time but, after all, if you'd sat me down as a kid and asked me what my ultimate ambition would be, I'd have said to be editor of the *United Review*. It would have been beyond my wildest dreams.

The first programme of the season is the most difficult. You want it to look fresh. I mean, we're lucky in that the cover isn't a problem. It's instantly recognisable, more or less the same as we've had since 1946. It's an identity, something that belongs to United. It takes about two and a half days non-stop to collect the material together. Then it needs proofing and so on. I decide what goes in unless something big breaks and we get the word down from 'upstairs'. Most of the time I'm left to my own devices!

I don't know where I go from here. Just carry on and try to make it better. I've done a couple of books and I'd like to do more of that. I'm a historian, really, and perhaps because of that I tend to dwell in the past too much. I can still remember coming down Warwick Road with my dad and tens of thousands of people just like us, in flat caps and red-and-white scarves, devoted to United. Those were the people this club was built on when football was a working-class game. I mean, there have always been the haves and have-nots at football but I feel the balance may have gone the other way. Lots of our fans can't get into the ground. I know we've got to generate money and income but I feel that football may be losing its heart along the way. And perhaps that's football just reflecting society as a whole. I think back to those huge crowds, the atmosphere of the '50s and '60s. United are actually more successful now than they were then, but somehow it doesn't feel the same. Maybe that's just me, of course. You know, my interest, my obsession, has become my job – the mystique and the sense of release on Saturday can't be the same. I sometimes wonder what I might have done with all that energy and time if it hadn't gone on United.

A Passion for the Game (Mainstream, 1995)

Euro '96

PATRICK'S NIGHT

David Lacey

Patrick's Night it might have been at Anfield but Holland, not the Republic of Ireland, will be joining the other 15 finalists in Sunday's draw for the 1996 European Championship. If Jack Charlton is now going to call it a day, after ten years as Ireland's manager, at least his last match was decided by someone with the right sort of name.

Two goals from Patrick Kluivert, the gifted 19-year-old who won the Champions' Cup for Ajax last May, took Holland back to the finals of the tournament they had won so memorably in 1988 and blown in 1992. This was a modest reflection of Dutch superiority. Kluivert also headed against the bar and early on Dennis Bergkamp saw a shot hit a post.

For the Irish, determination on the pitch and passionate support from the stands were not enough. Superior Dutch technique, along with the precocity which had enabled Ajax, who supplied eight of last night's team, to overcome Milan in the Champions' Cup final, always threatened to take the contest way beyond Ireland's reach.

Only a strange period of passivity during the second half, when Bergkamp, who had been out of the Arsenal side with a calf injury, was replaced by De Kock, who became an extra defender, promised to hand the initiative to the opposition. By the end, however, it took some brave goalkeeping by Alan Kelly to keep the score down.

The principal frustration for Ireland was that they quickly recognised Holland's defensive weaknesses in the air, especially at the far post, but could not exploit them. Intelligently though Cascarino played, the suspended Quinn was sorely missed.

For a time in the first half the regularity with which Phelan and Kenna were getting behind the Dutch on the flanks promised the Irish a goal against the earlier run of play. But chances were either missed or not recognised and Ireland's best opportunity proved to be the moment on the hour when Cascarino flung himself full length to meet McAteer's hard, flat centre from the right only to miss the ball by a whisker.

McAteer had replaced Townsend, who was not fully fit at the start, shortly after half-time. With Keane also absent, the Irish were short of the qualities which in the past had enabled them to overcome, or at least run close, the sort of odds they were up against last night. The talismanic Ray Houghton stayed on the bench.

The Irish had little answer to the intuitive passing, movement and interchanges of position that De Boer, Davids, Bergkamp and Kluivert brought to the match. Holland are going to be a handful next summer but they are suspect at the back.

Again Ireland's supporters were marvellous. If an era was about to end last night nobody had passed on the information to them. Faith had moved mountains before and why not again? So Aldridge was nearly twice the age of Kluivert; that merely made it men against boys. In the event the boy knew more than most of the men.

At the start the lurking Bergkamp promised to dominate the evening, setting up chances for Kluivert and Davids before turning on a square pass from Kluivert to drive in a low shot that ricocheted off the foot of a post.

On the half-hour Holland's initial surge appeared to be ebbing. But then Seedorf opened up the left flank for Davids, whose pass inside found Kluivert moving on to the ball with the defence helpless to stop him. Kluivert's left foot did the rest, Kelly being beaten by a shot which swerved sharply into the right-hand corner of the net.

Had Bergkamp not pulled his shot wide eight minutes later, the contest might have been all but over by half-time. Yet the Irish should have levelled in the 38th minute. After a garryowen from Gary Kelly was scrambled for a corner, Irwin's cross to the near post came out to McGrath, striding towards the penalty arc. A straight, firm shot and Ireland were level but, while McGrath found the power, he missed the glory – and the net.

Clearly the cross now represented Ireland's best chance of salvation, which made Charlton's decision to pull off Aldridge and bring on Kernaghan as a third centre-back, presumably with the idea of pushing the full-backs forward, seem perverse.

As Holland's attack reasserted itself, Kelly deflected a shot from Kluivert over the bar, kept out another from Overmars and saved one from Davids feet first. But Kluivert was not done. In the 64th minute he had risen alone to head a centre from Bogarde against the bar. Now, with two minutes left, he sidled on to a cunning through pass from De Boer to draw the goalkeeper and end the hopes of Ireland, and their big English fisherman, with a gentle chip.

The Guardian, 14 December 1995

A SLOW START

Paul Hayward

For two and a half years the English waited listlessly to see their country play a competitive international. When it came, the team finished about as strongly as most of our Derby bets. If football had the equivalent of a racing form book it would read under England: 'Quickly away, no headway after halfway, soon tailed off.'

Only the most parochial observer would argue that England's 1–1 draw with Switzerland wrecked an enthralling weekend of sport. A win for the family Piggott at Epsom, the start of the biggest event here since the 1966 World Cup, and English cricket's continuing revival at Edgbaston (not forgetting a sublime century from Sachin Tendulkar) guaranteed the country's claim to have supplied a festival of sporting drama. But in England's disconcerting draw with a nation of seven million souls, severe doubt was cast on the notion that Terry Venables and his squad have spent the last 30 months preparing to take over the world.

The bubbling expectations that attended England's opening match have been lowered to the extent that the home nation is now perched fretfully on the edge of its sofa to see how Holland, Scotland and Switzerland – England's rivals in Group A – perform this week before the English meet the Scots at Wembley on Saturday.

As England began to look increasingly weary and uninspired against a fitter and more passionate Swiss side, it was possible to imagine the rattling of bludgeons and broadswords in the Scottish headquarters near Stratford. Shakespeare's Stratford, for heaven's sake.

In the minds of English supporters the mathematical juggling has already begun. Asked, late on Saturday, what his hope was for today's match between Holland and Scotland at Villa Park, David Seaman, the England goalkeeper, said: 'A draw, or Scotland to win.' In that short reply

England's predicament became clear. After 90 minutes and before any other teams had played, their fate was already partially in the hands of others. It is legitimate to wonder whether England will progress beyond their group.

In a 45-minute opening ceremony, a gaudy pageant of English heritage was laid before the watching people of Europe. We got Merrie England (not so merry by 5 o'clock), St George and the Dragon, medieval knights, a Middle Ages free-for-all (strangely reminiscent of a Wimbledon match), an England Hall of Fame, the Red Devils and Simply Red. For England's second-half performance that should have read Simply Dead. 'We never came out after half-time,' said Venables, who was let down by some of his players for the second or third time in a fortnight.

It could be argued that English heritage was also worryingly evident on the pitch. In passing and technique, the England players were mostly inferior to the Swiss, who are probably among the four or five least likely winners of the tournament, and in the waning of England's energy levels there was a disturbing implication that some aspect of their preparation has not been right. The public is bound to wonder why England's stamina level was so poor, and how they can possibly compete with the best when their primary creative force, Paul Gascoigne, is spent 60 minutes into a game. Against Aberdeen or Raith Rovers, Gascoigne resembles something like the puppy-faced star of Italia '90. Against well-organised and fit continental opponents like Switzerland, he is a flash of light which fizzles and fades within the hour. Only his peroxide hair kept him visible before he was substituted a quarter of an hour before the end. In the second half Paul Ince, Darren Anderton and Teddy Sheringham also played as if they had come straight from an American dance marathon.

From the faces of the players on Saturday evening, you could tell that Venables had not been in the mood for karaoke as he closed the door of the changing-room. 'He's very disappointed with the way we played, especially in the second half,' said Stuart Pearce, whose handball allowed Switzerland a deserved equaliser. 'Maybe when we came out with the goal in the bag, we felt we had the game won. The game was built up as a one-sided match and people assumed Switzerland had no chance.'

If that was so, nobody mentioned it to the Swiss, who had been in poor form coming into this championship. Artur Jorge, their coach, said in the same dark tunnel: 'I think the England players were a little afraid of us. A draw is not a good result for us. When we look at the tape, I think we'll feel we could have won.' Jorge was embarrassed that the Swiss supporters had celebrated the draw as if it were a victory.

For now, coolness of judgement is required to avoid the easy mistake of abandoning England's attempt to seize their first trophy since that honey-coloured '60s day when Bobby Moore held the World Cup aloft on the steps of the same Royal Box. It would also be a sin to become so embroiled in England's labours that we ignored the other innumerable attractions of the world's second-biggest football tournament taking place in our own shires.

Despite all the pessimistic grumbling, it appears that the event has been well planned and organised. Thousands of people are working round the clock to ensure that Britain is regarded as a viable host for such events. We may not be able to build a high-speed rail link to the Channel Tunnel but we seem, so far at least, to be capable of staging a major sporting event, even if the ticketing process has been chaotic, and the presence of Swiss supporters among clumps of England fans suggests that segregation is far from perfect.

As the crowd dispersed on Saturday night, a fleet of chauffeur-driven cars assembled beneath the Twin Towers. They were taking the England players to their homes for a brief rest before the training process begins again today. There can be no excuse for tiredness so early into such an important tournament. The faces of the players' families and friends will have told them as much when those black cars pulled up at houses across England.

Daily Telegraph, 10 June 1996

THE SPIRIT
OF CULLODEN

Nick Harris

Unbowed by defeat, they danced to the tune of a lone piper. Twenty minutes earlier, the Tartan Army of the Chieftain pub, Inverness, had gone completely berserk when Scotland were awarded a penalty. It was as if they had won the championship with a last-second goal.

A minute later, after that Seaman save and that Gascoigne goal, the mood was more sombre. 'There's no bigger occasion than this,' Roddy McLeod, the pub's football-team manager, said before the game. 'It doesn't matter who wins, as long as England lose. And that's a fact of life.'

More than a hundred Scots (red-wigged, kilted and thirsty) had piled into the pub to find a space in front of the big screen. In their midst was a solitary pony-tailed England fan, going only by the name of Doj. Was he comfortable in here before such a big game? 'Yeah, I've lived here six years. Anyway, I like being here for a sure win.'

His Scottish companion grinned. 'He's a bloody masochist, more like.'

In April 1746, three miles down the road on the windswept moorland of Culloden, Bonnie Prince Charlie was defeated by the English. On a Saturday in June, 250 years on, the battlefield was being trampled only by a group of middle-aged Americans on a Scottish country-dancing tour, indifferent to the day's significance. One man, sporting the name-tag 'Bob' pinned to his blue-checked shirt, said: 'I'm sorry. We're from Pennsylvania. I really don't know anything about the soccer match.'

At the Chieftain, there had been talk of little else for weeks. 'As soon as the draw was made, the European Championship was nothing,' said David, an amiable local. 'This game is everything. Just beating the English. In fact it doesn't matter if we don't beat them. Just score against them.'

Bruce, a PE teacher at a nearby school, had been experiencing some rivalry problems of his own, when dividing his classes for football practice.

'They all want to be Scotland,' he said. 'If I tell them: "You're England," they just shake their heads at me and say: "Never".'

The first half was buoyant. Armloads of beer passed across heads and, when arms weren't sufficient, trays and large cardboard boxes did the job. The piper struck up intermittently, leading yet another chorus of 'Flower of Scotland'.

Every camera shot of Terry Venables was heralded with an eruption of booing, and every Gascoigne touch elicited a chant of 'You fat bastard' or 'Su-mo, Su-mo'. (Never mind the fact that he will be an Ibrox hero again come the first game of the season.)

When Gordon Durie went down in the 35th minute, blood pouring from his face, someone said: 'It's just a wee head wound. Probably needs stitches, but it's nae bother.' The spirits were riding high.

Half-time came and went with more enthused trips to the bar. Then Shearer scored and the place fell silent. Thirty seconds later, the chants began again, and carried on until the end. Every shot, every pass, every tackle. Even every throw-in. Everything. Except the Gascoigne goal.

The history books tell us that Culloden was won on tactics. Bonnie Prince Charlie: 'The English hit us early on, Des. Them cannons were a right shocker.' McLynam: 'Yes, you never quite got back into the game after that, did you, Chuck?'

It was hardly the same on Saturday. The 1746 fixture took just 40 minutes from start to finish. The 1996 equivalent, in the Chieftain at least, started about noon and went on all day.

'Up here we live in hope, not expectation,' said one fan. 'And that's what makes us different from the English. When you live in hope, everything has more passion.' On Saturday, that much at least was obvious.

The Independent, 17 June 1996

UNEXPECTED AND UNFORGETTABLE

Richard Williams

By the end of last night's tumultuous match at Wembley, Stuart Pearce was coolly playing a clearance off his right kneecap to Steve McManaman 20 yards away while a man called Cruyff was failing to control the ball when clear in front of goal. Who on earth could have imagined that?

England were, in a word, amazing. Against the best side they have so far met in this competition, they made those of us who have scorned their chances bend the knee to a performance in which they looked thoroughly credible contenders for the Henri Delaunay Trophy. And even if they stumble at the next hurdle, or the one after that, at least Terry Venables and his team have given us a night we never expected, and will never forget.

Actually, we can be very precise about how good England were against Holland. The first half contained the best football the team have played since 28 April 1993, when they were 2–0 up after 45 minutes against the same country in a World Cup qualifying match. But this time fate had arranged a different and much more satisfactory outcome.

This time there was no Jan Wouters to break Paul Gascoigne's cheek-bone, nor a Marc Overmars to destroy the career of Des Walker, the most gifted English defender of his generation. And no trenchcoated Graham Taylor slinking away into the night.

The difference this time was that England saved their second goal until after half-time, and then sustained the quality of their performance virtually to the end, taking handsome revenge on opponents who had cost them a place in USA '94.

As compensation, Euro '96 will do just fine. In the process of handing the Dutch a beating that will stay on their minds for years to come, a team appeared to discover itself. When Teddy Sheringham slid the fourth goal past Van der Sar, the sound of pure joy was heard all around Wembley.

England's fans had found 11 players whose deeds matched their dreams. And you can bet that in the Spanish tent, not to mention those of the Germans, the Italians and the French, new plans were being designed. The England of last week would not have unduly occupied the strategists of the teams who considered themselves favourites. The England of last night will be considered formidable opponents.

From carthorses to thoroughbreds in the space of a few days? Perhaps the confused state of mind in which the Dutch approached this match had something to do with the confidence with which England began it, but the men in orange shirts were undone by Venables's planning, and by the diligence with which his players stuck to their tasks.

For supporting Gascoigne through thick and thin, Venables deserves admiration of his fellow professionals and a nation's thanks. Last night Gascoigne was in his pomp, a marvellous and majestic sight. In the first half he dedicated himself to the team's cause, running and passing with tactical acumen, immense vigour and never a hint of self-indulgence. After half-time he was able to open his bag of tricks in the knowledge that he had earned the right to express himself.

His and Shearer's goals against the Scots must have raised the whole team's morale. Last night they expanded those cameos into an entire 90-minute show overflowing with creative thinking and fine touches. When Gascoigne gave Aron Winter the slip on the edge of the area and cut the ball back to Sheringham, who angled his boot to redirect it square to Shearer, the Blackburn striker found himself in a position to score a goal which was not an isolated moment of beauty but an expression of the whole. In fact it was the best goal England had scored since, oh, last Saturday.

And what was so nice about it was that each of the three players contributed something characteristic: a Gascoigne shimmy, a selfless Sheringham lay-off, a piece of Shearer smash-and-grab. The whole team was like that all night, each giving the best of himself.

All right, it was only a group match, not a knock-out round (except for the poor Scots, who will be cursing Venables's decision to take off Ince, which loosened the stays of the England defence and let Kluivert in for the goal that allowed the Dutch to remain in the competition). But so much worked well for England that it is hard to envisage their performances sliding back into the old mediocrity.

Any suspicions that this match was going to be a carve-up between the two sides to ensure their continued participation did not survive the first quarter of an hour, which included the clattering late tackles by Richard Witschge on McManaman and by Winston Bogarde on Gascoigne. Subsequently Danny Blind's trip on Paul Ince and Ince's own foolish challenge on Jordi Cruyff confirmed the level of commitment to winning the match which ran through both sides.

But Venables's defence held, on a day which proved the continued relevance of the flat back four to England – and to France, for that matter. Faced with only one striker, Dennis Bergkamp for Holland and Stoichkov for Bulgaria, both teams held fast to the supposedly obsolete formation that has served them well in the past, and found that they lost nothing as a result. But then a lot of received wisdom suddenly came up for reassessment at Wembley last night.

The Guardian, 19 June 1996

A SLICE OF LUCK

Ken Jones

Shortly before Euro '96 got under way, Alex Ferguson put forward a case for the team England defeated on Saturday. 'Spain are my dark horses,' the United manager stated television. When Terry Venables heard this, he felt that Ferguson could have made even more of Spain's chances. 'I don't know why people are holding back on them,' he said, 'because to my mind they are among the favourites. They have extremely skilful players and are now much better prepared for the demands of a championship.'

The respect Venables held out for Spain and their coach, his old Barcelona rival Javier Clemente, was borne out in the first half of a gripping encounter. As the interval approached you could imagine Venables thinking that it would take a great deal of grit and passion to overcome Spain's technical superiority. In his efforts to modernise England's national team, Venables has come up against problems that arise from the intensity of play in the Premier-ship. Keeping the ball figures prominently in his teaching, along with patience and concentration.

Watching first from above to get a clear view of shape and tactical deployment, England's coach must have been alarmed by proceedings. One or two openings had been made but Spain looked the better team, playing with a relaxed fluency that even the most fervent English patriots found impressive. By then you could sense bemusement in the audience. High on the chauvinism aroused by downmarket tabloids, dolled up in give-away hats and favours, it was as though they could not understand why England had not taken a commanding lead inside 20 minutes.

Perhaps they will now understand that this is not a great England team but simply one that is responding to intelligent tuition and powers of motivation.

As England went off at half-time, a reasonable analogy was that of a boxer returning to his corner in the middle of a fight in which he is being visibly embarrassed by a more adept opponent. He is still in the fight but needs his seconds to come up with suggestions. When interviewed before the match Venables emphasised the importance of an alternative strategy. 'I'm sure it will be different from the game against Holland and depending on how it goes we may have to change a few things,' he said.

When England came out again it was with a renewed sense of purpose, especially in midfield, which had belonged mostly to the Spaniards. Press earlier on the ball would have been one of the things he called for. Picking up the pace, England immediately looked more threatening and got more out of Steve McManaman.

Most important, however, was the spirit for which British football is famous. As only a few thousand Spaniards were present in the crowd, England had overwhelming support and they made the most of it.

What must be said, too, is that England had good fortune going for them. Tony Adams was outstanding in a stout defence but had Spain possessed a quick-footed finisher they would surely have reached the semi-finals, and in any case are entitled to feel hard done by. Television replays showed that an offside decision against Salinas cost them a perfectly good goal and Alfonso, who was ludicrously booked for diving, had in fact been tripped by Gascoigne in the penalty area. These incidents may have strengthened England's sense of destiny but that much rub of the green amounts to a commercial for liniment.

When the teams drew breath before engaging in what turned out to be a maximum period of extended activity, one thing struck me as being historically interesting. I know these comparisons keep cropping up but before extra-time in the 1966 World Cup final Alf Ramsey ordered his players to remain on their feet to establish a psychological advantage over the Germans who were sprawled on the turf. Something similar happened on Saturday. England stood up. The Spaniards lay down to have their legs massaged. No metaphorical significance should be read into this because Spain went on to cause England considerable anxiety.

The idea that penalty shoot-outs are an ordeal for goalkeepers is nonsense. No blame is attached to them and there are opportunities to achieve lasting celebration. All the pressure is on the takers.

When Hierro strode up for the first penalty on Saturday the whistling was enough to have drowned out the noise made by Concorde at take-off. I guess it would have been matched everywhere else in football but so much for the ideal of fair play UEFA keeps going on about. Having rarely put a foot wrong in the match, poor Hierro lost his nerve and shot against the crossbar. David Seaman's save from Nadal finally put paid to Spain, but Hierro's miss was the moment of truth for them.

The Independent, 24 June 1996

A PLACE OF HONOUR

Matthew Engel

The great resurgence of English football, which had lasted all of 11 days, ended at Wembley last night when the history England did not want repeated itself and they were knocked out of the European Championship by Germany in a penalty shoot-out.

Gareth Southgate will have to live with the mantle worn for the past six years by Stuart Pearce. After ten kicks from both sides had gone in, he hit the 11th only just right of goalkeeper Köpke and it was comfortably saved.

He returned to join his team-mates in despair: Andreas Möller, the German captain, calmly took the kick that gave his team victory. And, after a brief eruption from the German contingent, the mass of the crowd left the ground in near-silence.

Germany, as ever, will now be hot favourites to win the tournament on Sunday night. They meet the Czech Republic, who beat France at Old Trafford in the other semi-final – also on penalties.

That was a terrible match. In contrast, the game at Wembley was a night of heroes. Alan Shearer scored for England after only 132 seconds, leading to chants of 'What a Load of Rubbish'; Nemesis came after Hubris and Germany equalised after 15 minutes. The game itself produced no more goals, but it was a night of terrific, skilful and unexpectedly attacking and fluent football.

The most heroic performance, however, probably came after the game when Southgate gamely faced the media and admitted: 'I feel I've let everyone down. I just have to live with that.' His team-mates had all tried to tell him otherwise. But Southgate, regarded as a nice and intelligent man, understands how the public mind works.

The match ends a manic period, which began only with Paul Gascoigne's amazing goal against Scotland two Saturdays ago. It is hard to remember but, before that, the England players were regarded as drunken louts. They will be remembered now among the gloriously vanquished which, in a nation which traditionally distrusts success, can still be an honoured position.

The population of England, most of whom were believed to be watching on television last night, can now resume the normal summer-time business of watching Wimbledon and washing their cars. The result was especially disastrous for anyone with a ticket for the final and thoughts of selling it; they will be difficult to give away now.

The long-term consequences of this adventure cannot be immediately assessed. It may be assumed that English sport as a whole will return to normal after its brief flourish and the cricketers and tennis players will start losing again. However, the excitement created may lead to a lasting upsurge in interest in routine football. If that happens the winner – even more predictable than Germany – will be Rupert Murdoch, whose satellite company holds the television rights to the Premiership. That seems a more probable outcome than a continuing boom in St George's flags and patriotic anthems.

The sun will probably still rise this morning and the birds will carry on singing. But the fervent English jingoism, most of it not unhealthy, that came from England's three previous victories will have gone – at least until the 1998 World Cup in France or the sudden discovery of a small, just, distant, winnable and uncomplicated war.

The result will confirm the pessimism of those who said England should have played in the red in which they won the World Cup and not the dreary grey used last night.

The atmosphere was far tenser than at the fiesta of the Spain match last Saturday, as though people sensed that this was the real final. And England did dominate long periods and were desperately unlucky not to win. England may have to wait another 30 years to get their revenge over Germany on an occasion as impassioned and important as this one.

By then we may all be partners in a Federal Europe. If so, it can be taken for granted that the inter-provincial sporting rivalries will be torrid on the field and redolent with the ghosts of history off it at least throughout the next millennium.

And if they ever produce a game as glittering as this one, it would be great to be there.

The Guardian, 27 June 1996

THE FANS' GAMES

Matt Tench

Strolling up Wembley Way an hour before England's third match of Euro '96 it was clear that only one set of fans felt at home. The Dutch. Luxuriously decked out in their team's colours, they marched on the Twin Towers with the nonchalance of those who belonged. They even managed to make lurid orange wigs appear the epitome of European chic. The English, by contrast, were like teenagers at their first disco. Wide-eyed and gauche, they displayed none of the sang-froid of the visitors.

Two hours later these memories made England's victory all the sweeter. As the Dutch watched in disbelief, the home following exploded in raucous, unthreatening celebration, and a remarkable transformation was nearing completion. The England fans were finding a new identity.

Where once their collective image was one of tattooed machismo and white-knuckle hatred, at this tournament it had become flag-waving and endless choruses of 'Football's Coming Home'. For nearly three weeks the nation has become increasingly overtaken by the feel-good factor, one that found its cradle at Wembley. On the pitch, certainly, where England's players have competed with the best and shown themselves to be the most enterprising side in Europe. But also in the stands. Here too England's fans have demonstrated that stereotypes need alteration. I know. I was there.

Such an upbeat conclusion may attract derision this morning after the wearyingly familiar images of violence that have returned to our screens in the last few days. Certainly they are a depressing reminder that football, particularly when allied to alcohol, has not lost its capacity to inspire viciousness. But what has happened needs to be put in context. These were sporadic incidents, very few of which involved either sets of supporters at Wembley on Wednesday night.

In assessing the behaviour of the England fans over the duration of the tournament, it is worth pointing out that before it began organised hooliganism was widely expected, particularly from the home following. It simply did not happen. So that while it would be foolish to be too positive – the real test will come abroad – it is difficult to avoid the conclusion that England's fans emerge from Euro '96 with as much credit as their team.

This has not always seemed very likely. On the tube to the Switzerland game, we were quickly joined by a small but vocal group whose deafening cries of 'In-Ger-Land' demonstrated all the consideration for their fellow-travellers for which football fans are so widely known.

On the platform at Baker Street the Ingerlanders spotted four middle-aged Swiss, faces painted, attempting with no success to fade into the background. A stout 30-something who barely fitted into his England shirt and casual shorts, made straight for them, and with the tournament still a couple of hours from its kick-off the first outbreak of mindless violence seemed imminent. 'How are you? How long are you here for?' the stout one asked, as he offered his hand and a smile. The Swiss responded with bewildered reserve, but the stout one was not to be denied. 'Are you having a good time? What do you think your chances are?'

It was a happy moment, but the rest of the journey did little to alleviate a sense of foreboding. True, it soon became clear that most English fans regarded the Swiss as, well, neutral, but that was only because they were reserving their real spite for the Scots.

The songs were a strange mix. To hear 'We are Ron's Twenty-Two', the 1982 World Cup song, was bizarre; to then get the national anthem was warming and chilling at the same time; but 'No Surrender to the IRA' was just chilling.

The latter proved the favourite and sitting on the tube on that first day, cocooned among a mob of Chelsea fans, it was easy to be depressed. 'It's like the last five years in the Premiership didn't exist,' my brother said, and looking around all you could see were white males, mostly between the ages of 16 and 30. In fact this sample proved completely misleading, and over the five games there was a broader spectrum supporting England than at the average Premiership game, and certainly a lot more women.

Once inside Wembley the fans passed the first test by managing not to boo the Swiss national anthem. The atmosphere was supportive if hardly rapturous. An early goal helped but as England lost the plot, so did the support. 'Come on, England, you're just like watching City,' a blue-shirted onlooker in a nearby row screamed.

'They're not that bad,' his mate replied.

In the second half, as collective torpor engulfed team and fans, the two Mancunians tried in vain to exhort their neighbours into a more animated support. 'It's true what they say,' the first concluded. 'Shit stadium, no fans.'

As we trooped away that baking summer evening, Venables's men were not the only ones to have made an uncertain start. Consolation was found in focusing on the next match, and the virulence of the chanting suggested a bloodbath, particularly as it was difficult to envisage the Scots backing out of the challenge that was being promised.

As things turned out the game proved a turning point, on and off the field. There was precariously little policing outside, but there did not need to be. The atmosphere was robust but good-humoured. Plenty of baiting, but little battling.

Once inside, the Scottish fans were brilliant. Outnumbered, they were never outshouted and maintained a stupendous level of support even after the cause had been lost. They exuded a marvellous sense of communal lunacy, suitably demonstrated by their rendition of 'Rocking All Over the World' at half-time, which remains one of the highlights of the tournament.

It was difficult not to envy their sense of nationality. A disparate bunch, they were united by one common notion: that to be Scottish is to be better than anything else in the world, a belief that their passionate endorsement for a toothless football team only served to enhance.

In watching the Scots that day I think the English drew inspiration. A realisation, perhaps, that letting your hair down was not only permitted on these occasions, but made them more enjoyable. Certainly the atmosphere at the Scotland game surpassed that of the Swiss, and the Dutch game was better still.

By now 'Three Lions' had established itself as the national football anthem, each airing attracting more support than the last. Strange song, this. Unaided by the public address system it proved impossible to link the 'Coming home, football's coming home' segment to the verse, 'Three lions on the shirt'. As a result the fans simply stuck with 'Coming home, football's coming home', a refreshingly non-partisan sentiment that was in keeping with the growing atmosphere of exuberant celebration.

The joyous rendition of the song at the end of the Spain game was the best moment of a tense and slightly deflating afternoon. As we finished it for the second time the middle-aged woman in the row behind me could hold herself back no longer and began crying uncontrollably.

And so to the semi-final, and the apparently inevitable clash with the Germans. Once again fears were expressed about how the two sets of fans would react, but walking back along Wembley Way the theme seemed to be one of irony. The vast majority of the crowd were English, but an outbreak of booing signalled a pocket of Germans. Closer inspection revealed that it was the Germans booing their hosts. Seconds later a group of identically clad teenage girls strode the other way, all sporting Coca-Cola T-shirts, with the smallest screaming at her puzzled onlookers, 'Get your tits out, get your tits out . . .' Presumably it was irony.

The match itself was as enthralling and passionate as any club game I have been to, Cup finals included, the support as committed and intense. It seemed a wonderful night until the end, and I hope when it crystallises in the memory it is the many positive aspects that will prevail. Like the chanting of 'One Gareth Southgate' that echoed within seconds of the finale.

Likewise the competition itself. There were negative images, not least of Wembley stadium which remains a decaying and dated edifice whose prime rationale appears to be to rip off its most loyal customers. And not all my memories of fans are good ones. There was the unnecessary heckling of a good-natured Spanish trio before that game, and a few nutters searching (in vain, I think) for Germans after the semi.

But most of them are, and most of all there was a feeling that English supporters might, just might, have found a middle way between the self-conscious passivity with which they began Euro '96 and the mindless boorishness for which they are famed. That like the Scots, the Dutch, and even, for goodness sake, the Swiss, they have found a way to express their nationalism without becoming a national embarrassment.

If so, whatever happened on Wednesday night, the tournament can be declared a success.

The Independent, 29 June 1996

I HAVE SEEN
THE FUTURE

Richard Williams

It's a humid Sunday night in the summer of 1998. We're in Saint-Denis, the unlovely Paris suburb just north of the *périphérique*, now home of the magnificent new French national football stadium. The concourse around the Grande Stade is awash with red, white and blue: the tricolour of France, the St George's flag of England. Helicopters clatter overhead, carrying television news cameras and VIPs.

This is the day of the 16th World Cup final. Aimé Jacquet's France, the hosts, after beating Germany on penalties in the semi-final, are meeting Glenn Hoddle's England, who eliminated the possibility of an entirely Francophone final by accounting for George Weah's Liberia, a young team exhausted by their historic conquest of Brazil.

The 1998 France side is a settled line-up consisting entirely of players who were in the squad that reached the semi-final of the Euro Championship in England two years earlier: in goal, Barthez; in defence, Thuram, Desailly, Blanc and Lizarazu; in midfield, Karembeu, Martins and the captain, Deschamps; as playmakers, Zidane and Djorkaeff; in attack, Dugarry.

All except the goalkeeper have spent the last two years playing in Italy and France. They are a seasoned group, approaching this match after a two-year unbeaten run. The oldest is 32, the youngest 26; their average age is 28 years and one month. Their average number of caps is 53. If Jacquet's plans have been well founded, this is the day his consistency of vision and their experience and maturity will reap a due reward.

As for Hoddle, his team offer a more unpredictable prospect. Of the squad that came close to making home advantage pay off in Euro '96 he has retained a handful of names. One received his first cap under Graham Taylor; others were blooded in the last months of Terry Venables's reign. But several are relative newcomers, protégés of the current manager.

This is the team: in goal, David James of Liverpool; in defence, Gary Neville of Man United, Gareth Southgate of Real Madrid, Rio Ferdinand of West Ham and Michael Dubarry of Chelsea; in midfield, David Beckham of Man United, Chris Bart-Williams of Nottingham Forest, Darren Anderton of Parma and Nigel Quashie of QPR; in attack, Alan Shearer of Barcelona and Emile Heskey of Leicester City. Their average age is 24 years and four months, average number of caps 16. Gazza, the veteran of the squad at 31, is on the bench, alongside McManaman, Barmby, Stone, Redknapp, Walker, Sol Campbell and Phil Neville.

On Monday, five days after England's elimination from Euro '96, Glenn Hoddle becomes their coach, the eighth man to take charge since the war. He has exactly two months to contemplate his task before selecting his squad to meet Moldova in the first match of the 1998 World Cup qualifying campaign, before going on to meet the other opponents in European Group Two: Italy, Poland and Georgia. There will be 14 qualifiers from nine groups: the winners of the groups, the best runner-up, and the four winners of play-off matches between the eight other runners-up. Against the talent of Italy and the perennially troublesome challenge of Poland, Hoddle's task even to surmount this first hurdle will be extremely difficult.

What kind of a leader will he prove to be? On the basis of his known character and his brief management career to date (two seasons at Swindon Town and three at Chelsea), we can guess that he will be imaginative and, when necessary, pragmatic; he will follow Venables in his desire to update the way the team plays the game, in line with trends outside Britain; he will enforce standards of behaviour; and, given his experience in the battle of Stamford Bridge between Ken Bates and Matthew Harding, he will not easily be deflected from the task by childish posturings on the periphery. What we don't know is whether he will also be lucky.

Perhaps the only true beneficiary of Wednesday night's result outside the frontiers of Germany was Hoddle. If Venables had gone out holding aloft the Henri Delaunay Trophy, the pressure on his successor would have been compounded. A lot of nonsense is talked about pressure in sport, as if being subjected to it were an unnatural or undesirable condition. But still Hoddle's task going into the 1998 World Cup at the head of the European champions, would have raised English expectations to an unendurable level.

As things stand, he is taking charge of a squad who did pretty well, but not (by world standards) brilliantly. Their performances over the past fortnight have raised their stock, but not unrealistically. What Venables has achieved, despite all the nonsense in nightclubs from Hong Kong to Essex, is to lift the players' self-respect. After putting four goals past Holland and taking Germany all the way, the present bunch can at least feel secure in the belief that they have the right to share a stage with the world's best players. There have been times over the past decade – such as the moment when San Marino scored a goal against them inside ten seconds, or the entire campaign at the 1992 European finals in Sweden – when even that basic assumption has been open to question.

Venables concentrated on modernising the squad by getting the individuals to be more flexible. You can't do that with a Tony Adams or an Alan Shearer, and it may be that those two represent the last of their respective lines. It's hard to imagine that a big, blunt, stopper centre-half will figure in anybody's future blueprint, although there will probably always be a place for the specialist centre-forward with a cannonball shot in each foot and a lethal forehead, so long as (like Shearer) he has a brain.

But the future, as we have known since the Dutch started demonstrating it 25 years ago, is multi-functional and belongs to players like Southgate, the Neville brothers, Anderton and Duberry.

There is plenty of young talent around, and it can only benefit from exposure to the standards of the foreign players being imported into the Premiership. Duberry has the power, technique and initiative to become the English Desailly, which would make him a priceless commodity. QPR's Quashie and Leicester's Heskey, a former youth international, are bright prospects whose tremendous potential deserves careful nurture. And Bart-Williams, who spent last season learning how to link Nottingham Forest's defence with the midfield, shielding one while servicing the other, will be a mere 24 by 1998.

And Rio Ferdinand. When England's first open training session for Euro '96 took place at Bisham Abbey three weeks ago, a handful of promising young players had been drafted in to make up the numbers for full-scale practice matches. The game that journalists were allowed to watch was essentially unserious, although Venables stood thoughtfully in the centre circle and Bryan Robson ran around shouting encouragement. Yet one figure stood out: a tall, slim, black defender, playing alongside Adams. Within minutes his control and relaxation was the object of a lot of touchline interest. That's Rio Ferdinand, someone said. Les's cousin. He's 19. West Ham put him in the first team for a few games at the end of the season and their Youth Cup final side.

There is a danger in catching a glimpse of talent at that stage and getting carried away. But sometimes you can't miss it, and Rio Ferdinand looks like the real thing. If he is a fixture in the senior international squad by 1998, it will say something positive about Hoddle's tenure.

And if Hoddle does prove to be a success, he may look back to these weeks in June 1996, which began in such turmoil and ended in such rich emotion, as the time when the England team rediscovered their place in the world.

The Guardian, 28 June 1996

FOOTBALL'S COMING HOME

Ian Ridley

From Cathay to catharsis. In four weeks, English football seems to have been transformed from a laughing stock to serious players in the world game. It was never quite as bad as it appeared, nor may it be quite as good away from Wembley, but let us enjoy for a while at least the measure of redemption and rehabilitation.

It did not take just one month for England to return themselves to the top rank of European nations. In fact, it took 29 months, and the place in the last four was so nearly a perfect final curtain, testament to Terry Venables's best 'My Way' theory and practice.

Players win and lose matches but a coach makes a difference, as Graham Taylor and Venables have shown. Their records may not differ immensely but the mood that each has engendered does. Now, after the pride of the Three Lions has been restored, there is the bonus of respect that has been extended towards the game's mother country.

As Venables himself says: 'Not long ago we were saying "we don't want to play them, they'll kick us". Now we are saying "bring them on".' And bringing them on has been a crucial part of a measured business plan he could at times have done with applying to his commercial life.

On taking over, he worked with the attack, to make sure they absorbed the new lessons of deep-lying strikers, and he tried to achieve a few morale-boosting results. The more experienced players were given their chance. Then came the midfield as Venables emphasised the need to match up numbers with modern teams who moved men more smoothly around the field. Gradually the younger players were introduced.

Finally, the defence became accustomed to the idea of operating with just three men at opportune times, so that one player could be used more beneficially further forward. When there were doubts, Venables ate them up and spat them out.

It all came to fruition last Wednesday against Germany in a match that transcended nationalism. This was an event that confirmed why this game is worthy of so much attention, one that improved with each intensely absorbing minute as had the World Cup encounter between the two nations in Turin six years ago. It brimmed with quality and heroism and celebrated the human spirit in its shared experience and sportsmanship.

One moment typified it. Paul Gascoigne played a wall pass with Darren Anderton and seemed to be through on goal. Then, from nowhere, Thomas Helmer stretched every sinew of his right leg to flick the ball away for a corner. Gascoigne, frustrated, returned to the prostrate Helmer with a smile on his face and patted the colossus of a defender on the head.

More followed. David Seaman and Andreas Köpke came together to exchange best wishes before the penalty shoot-out; the injured Jürgen Klinsmann hobbled on to commiserate with the hapless Gareth Southgate at the deflating conclusion. Then Southgate, a tear never more than a word away, stood tall to face the press. His reward was an ovation.

Here was redemption all around for the English. The collective response of dignified sympathy for Southgate showed the nation at its best; the collective responsibility of the players was an example to the young of what a team sport can instil. Venables's team had a brave, true and honest soul. Their easy, efficient displays of flexibility were recognised as the very stuff we need and should nurture.

Heartening, too, was the reaction to the pre-game jingoism trained on the Germans. Those seeking cheap laughs or looking to score easy, distasteful points were quickly shown to have misjudged the mood and they quickly withdrew in shame.

So did the hooligans who finally crept out under cover of that night's darkness. The real fans had been inside Wembley turning it into a museum of the moving image. Football may not truly have come home but something more important has. The class has turned on the disruptive bullies spoiling it for everyone else. England has moved on – as Venables's team and the genuine supporter have shown.

The coach's aim was always to marry the fabled English heart to a new tactical thoughtfulness. If Germany confirmed the former, the breath-taking hour against Holland revealed the latter for the most satisfying moment of his tenure.

'We'll always have Paris,' Bergman said to Bogart at the end of *Casablanca*. Venables will always have the Dutch. The day before the match he spent 90 minutes dissecting their game and suggesting an antidote. Impressed by the information, his players emerged from the meeting feeling like world-beaters.

Regrets? He's probably had a few, but too few for him to mention.

Certainly England would have relished a final against the Czech Republic. Anderton's lack of match sharpness was probably one regret and the period of nervousness after Alan Shearer's early goal against the Germans another.

It did point out a shortcoming of Venables's England teams. Always hard to beat, they only looked like finishing off the opposition against Holland, and too often left themselves open to the draw that was to prove their undoing. As many matches were drawn – 11 – as were won under him.

His legacy is evident beyond results. He was initially uncomfortable when asked about it, but did consider the improvements. 'We have shown that if it's physical we can handle that and if it's a football match, we can deal with that too,' he said. 'We have men for all seasons. Intelligent players who can adapt a lot quicker than we thought they may have been able to.'

Now young minds are open to the sophistication that international football demands and the Premiership often feels forced to abandon in the scramble for points. Now there is a base of belief after the abasement of club competition in Europe last season.

It is a hard act for Glenn Hoddle to follow, but an easier task than it would have been two years and five months ago. 'I think Terry and myself are quite similar in our philosophies on football and as people as well,' he said on Friday at Bisham Abbey's media centre some 19 hours after Venables's departure.

'You have to cocoon yourself. He has that gift and I can do that myself. I have never lost any sleep over a game of football [unlike Graham Taylor and his soaking pyjamas] and I won't do in the future. I have got other things in my life to fulfil it.'

He hoped his experiences abroad, he added, would be used to as good effect as Venables's. 'Perhaps if Graham, Bobby Robson and Ron Greenwood had been abroad they might have approached the job a little differently,' he said in what may have been a minor barb aimed at the latter two, who were largely indifferent to his talents as a player.

The fallacy about Hoddle is that he will let loose an entertainers' XI. In fact he will be as pragmatic as Venables. 'It would be lovely to put in eight offensive players but we have to learn from Brazil. The nation was clamouring for the most skilful players but the manager had a nice balance. In world football you have got to win the ball back. Players with immense talent can't do anything without the ball.'

Naturally enough, Matthew Le Tissier's name cropped up. 'I'm not thinking about one player,' he said. 'There are probably 20 players outside the squad I have thought about.' He would, he added, be foolish to change the make-up drastically for the World Cup qualifying match in Moldova on 1 September. None was ruled in, none ruled out. It does seem certain, however, that he will play with wing-backs and a three-man central defence that might include a sweeper or libero.

It seemed somehow irreverent that Hoddle had his feet under the table so quickly – he wanted to put the reporters doorstepping him out of their misery – and that he should be talking of heroes no longer being guaranteed a place. There is, though, an opportunity to be seized, a wave to ride. Venables would want, and deserves, as much.

Independent on Sunday, 30 June 1996

GETTING HIGH
ON DECENT STUFF

Hugh McIlvanney

If many more fantasies are peddled about the wonders of the Euro '96 experience, football may have to be designated a hallucinogenic drug. Happiness should never be disdained, whatever its source, and it is good to know that so many people across the country have been joyously uplifted by the tournament and England's honourable contribution to it. But now that the party is over for the hosts, and they find themselves sitting out the last dance, off in a corner among the empties, perhaps a few facts should be allowed to intrude on the mass delirium that has been gripping the nation. The first and most obvious is that, however enthralling and memorable Wednesday night's semi-final between England and Germany may have been, this European championship thus far must be seen as no more that a moderate advertisement for the most popular game in the world. It has produced no team with any entertainable claim to greatness and its few matches of exceptional quality have been isolated in a preponderance of ordinariness and sterility. Of the six matches so far completed in the knockout phase of the competition, four have been settled by a penalty shoot-out. Four quarter-finals and two semi-finals delivered just six goals from 11 hours of football, an average of one every 110 minutes. It was enough to make resorting to penalties look like an attempt to impose sudden-death after rigor mortis had set in.

England supporters will insist that their team rose above such criticisms, providing drama and exhilaration on the way to the excruciating moment in midweek that saw them removed by one young player's sad aberration. Fairness, rather than the fear of lynching, persuades me to go some of the way with that partisan assessment. The English team responded admirably to the intimidating responsibilities that accompanied the huge advantage of playing all their games at Wembley. They found the commitment and team spirit to create benefits from an intensity of expectation that might have broken a less determined or united squad. And, healthily influenced by the mixture of intelligence, inventiveness and practicality that Terry Venables brings to his coaching, they performed with increasing conviction on the field. Even when put under pressure by the superior technique of opponents, they maintained more shape and coherence, more resistance to panic and dishevelment, than English teams of the recent past could have mustered.

Compliments must, however, stop far short of the unjustifiable eulogies that have been pouring over England for nearly a fortnight. What they achieved as a football power in Euro '96 was a restoration of respectability. Those who believe they witnessed something more triumphant are victims of self-hypnosis engendered by a desire for success too feverish to accommodate objective indicators of the team's limitations. The hysterical acclaim can, clearly, be traced to the occasion 12 days ago when they slaughtered Holland 4–1. This was undoubtedly an exciting and stylish demolition but it was invested with an outrageous significance that took no account of the blatant shortcomings of the Dutch, who, like the French, spent their time in the tournament demonstrating how inflated their reputation had been. In any skill-for-skill comparison with the outstanding Dutch squads of the 1970s and 1980s, the latest group emerged as distinctly inferior and when it came to morale, the fighter's mentality, they simply could not be mentioned in the same breath. For most of the hour and a half against England, they displayed a collective will of purest marshmallow and, if anything, they were flattered by the scoreline. Flattery for the English took the form of a grotesquely over-the-top reaction to their victory, a spate of tributes within which calling them world-beaters almost qualified as faint praise.

Suddenly it was close to treason to recall their struggles against Switzerland and Scotland. The favoured argument was that the hosts, after a faltering start, had hit their true stride and were about to become unstoppable. Unfortunately, no one had explained that script to the Spanish. During much of the 90 minutes of regular time in the Wembley quarter-final, they enjoyed a technical superiority bordering on the embarrassing. That English nerve and sinew held out into extra-time to keep the two hours of open-play goalless and gain victory in a penalty shoot-out was definitely cause for rejoicing. Whether it was just cause is another matter. Leaving aside the referee's questionable rejection of Spain's strong demands for two penalties in the second half of normal time, the ruling that the goal scored by Julio Salinas 33 minutes into the first half should be disallowed as offside was shown to be thoroughly and cruelly wrong by the testimony of the camera. All who have blithely dismissed that episode as a rub of the green should try to imagine the uproar that would have erupted if England had been denied such a totally legal goal and gone out of the competition as a consequence. The reverberations would still be shaking sports departments and commentary boxes now. In the midst of all the celebration (and it has been nothing less than that) of the heroic exit on Wednesday, it is surely incumbent on us to admit that nothing of the kind could have happened but for the injustice inflicted on Spain. For the Spanish, the pain must have been deepened by the knowledge that they, along with the Italian squad who were doomed by the egotistical extravagances of their coach, were probably more comprehensively equipped than any other challengers to bring the pleasures of creative attacking to the climactic stages of Euro '96. Of course, the public's pursuit of what is defined, in one of the more boring clichés of the day, as the 'feelgood factor', is entirely understandable and only the foolish or mean-spirited would reproach them for it. Yet it must be said that the loss of perspective – the eagerness to recognise the performances that carried England to the semi-final, and the one they produced in that match, as more than they were – was too severe and widespread to be healthy. There is no doubt that the xenophobia flaunted, in the guise of humour, by certain tabloid editors is disowned by the majority of the population as honestly as is the havoc visited on central London and other parts of the country by hooligans in the aftermath of defeat. But it is equally plain that a mood of unreality had infected English minds, from those of sports-page ranters to those of intellectuals who found themselves taking an unlikely interest in the pastimes of the masses. The net result was a reminder that football, like any other sport, is diminished when people try to make it more than it is.

One of the practical manifestations of the distortion was a failure to give full and proper recognition to the scale of Germany's achievement in the semi-final. They arrived at Wembley with a grossly weakened team. Having lost a vital defender, Jürgen Kohler, because of injury early in the competition, they were then deprived of Fredi Bobic from the limited ranks of their forwards and suffered more dramatically when a calf strain removed the brilliant and inspirational Jürgen Klinsmann, forcing them to rely at the front on Stefan Kuntz, who had not scored in an international for two years. Had England been without Tony Adams and Alan Shearer, the implications would not have been more ominous. In facing their problems, the Germans could take heart from the awareness that they were seeking to secure a place in the final of a major championship for the eleventh time, whereas England's successful appearance in the World Cup final of 1966 was the single occasion on which they made it to the last stage of either that competition or the European championship. Further examination of the statistics emphasised the yawning gulf that separates the records, showing that Germany have won the World Cup three times and the European title twice. In addition, the Germans had beaten England three times (and not lost) in major championship meetings since 1966. If England had established such superiority, *The Mirror* and *The Sun* might have suggested that beating Germany again would mean having to put them on the national mantelpiece. Obviously it was natural that, when the opposition won, the English media should concentrate on the narrowness of a defeat which, if assessed on the balance of play and the number of chances made, was undeserved. Human nature guaranteed that few would be concerned with giving due credit to the winners for all the nerve, resilience, organisation and skill they had shown. But perhaps we should spare a moment to reflect on how we would have reacted to an England victory if it had been accomplished by a depleted team in a German stadium resounding with hostility.

Deciding whether England and Germany provided a genuine epic last week is best left to others, since it was my own fate to be at Old Trafford, where France and the Czech Republic ground through a seemingly endless exercise in negativity calculated to make the sparse audience crave the thrills of watching car bumpers rust. However, even a television viewer had the right to hail the Wembley semi-final as a marvellous flowering of positive endeavour amid much conservatism. The Germans, for whom Matthias Sammer and Dieter Eilts nourish faith in Europe's capacity to go on breeding players comparable with the best of any era, are inevitably favourites. But the Czech Republic, with their resolute and disciplined application of their ability to absorb pressure and then launch sporadic, penetrative counter-attacks, are far from negligible. They have a high degree of technical competence and are backed by a depth of football tradition already represented by their winning of the European title in 1976 and their loss to Brazil in the World Cup final of 1962. Their price soared to 200–1 after they were defeated by Germany in their first match of this tournament. They are now 9–4 to win the trophy. Odds against a free-flowing final may be somewhat longer.

Sunday Times, 30 June 1996

VOGTS' TRIUMPH OVER ADVERSITY

Ken Jones

At last a 'golden goal', Oliver Bierhoff's strike in the fifth minute of extra-time bringing Germany yet another triumph. First, confusion as the German squad streaming on to the field in celebration were brought to a halt by the delay caused when a linesman's flag seemed to rule out the winning effort.

Then joy for Berti Vogts and his team, who had struggled manfully through the tournament, overcoming injuries to key players that made their defeat of England last Wednesday a monumental achievement in their history.

Anybody who supposed that Germany's 11th appearance at a final of a major football championship was guaranteed to enhance their reputation as the pre-eminent force in European football ignored the technical expertise, collective and individual, that helped inspire the Czech Republic to a place in the ultimate match of Euro '96. European champions in 1976 when they defeated the Germans on penalties, and World Cup finalists in 1962, the Czechs lived dangerously through this tournament, but their technical proficiency and teamwork was always enough to suggest that they would give the favourites all they could handle.

A personal point of view is that the Germans were not given nearly enough credit for the efficiency and resilience that enabled them to overcome the loss of such notable performers as Jürgen Kohler and Jürgen Klinsmann when defeating England in the semi-final after a penalty shoot-out that had pulled the plug on national expectations and euphoria.

That disappointment ensured that the Czechs would have the backing of most neutrals in the crowded Wembley last night even though the Germans were able to again include Klinsmann, who achieved great popularity when turning out at Tottenham Hotspur two years ago and was voted the 1995 Footballer of the Year in England.

Whatever remedies have been applied to Klinsmann's damaged right calf, an obvious impairment in mobility suggested that the Germans were looking more to his talismanic effect rather than expecting any dramatic contribution. In any case, it was soon apparent that a glowing encounter against England had drained more from the Germans than the Czechs had expended when defeating France at Old Trafford at the same stage in similar circumstances.

Of course, it was ridiculous to suppose that the Czechs would be inferior in their understanding of practical strategy, a point they proved when putting a strain on the discipline and method that had quickly established Germany as a team to beat throughout the championship.

In denying Matthias Sammer the space he cleverly exploits when breaking out in support of attacks, the Czechs reduced the effectiveness of Germany's sorties from midfield, and if they were less threatening generally than England were last week, plenty of anxiety was caused to German defence. A patched-up German team showed signs of weariness, and winger Karel Poborsky was always willing to exploit an instinctive talent for running the ball at defenders and seeking imaginative routes to goal. The Germans were frequently at full stretch.

However, neither goal had been threatened seriously until the Czechs were awarded a penalty in the 59th minute when Sammer was judged to have brought down Poborsky in a race for the German goal-line.

As with so many decisions in this championship, it was dubious and television replays showed the Italian referee, Pierluigi Pairetto, had blundered. Not only did Sammer play the ball, but contact was made outside the penalty area. The possible irony then was that one of the championship's best players would be involved in a moment that cost his team a great victory.

Patrik Berger drove the ball past Andreas Köpke, and here was another opportunity for the Germans to display the fighting spirit that stood them in such stead against England. Bierhoff was not reckoned to be good enough for a place in the starting line-up but a crisis brought him into the game, and almost with the first touch of the ball he brought the Germans level in the 73rd minute.

His winner in extra-time, a shot that sneaked just inside the far post and Petr Kouba's fingers, brought Germany their seventh major championship and left England and their supporters wondering what might have been.

The Independent, 1 July 1996